ir
p
y

OPERATION LENA AND HITLER'S PLOTS TO BLOW UP BRITAIN

OPERATION LENA AND HITLER'S PLOTS TO BLOW UP BRITAIN

Bernard O'Connor

AMBERLEY

First published 2017

Amberley Publishing
The Hill, Stroud
Gloucestershire, GL5 4EP

www.amberley-books.com

British Library Cataloguing in Publication Data.
A catalogue record for this book is available from the British Library.

ISBN 978 1 4456 6963 2 (hardback)
ISBN 978 1 4456 6964 9 (ebook)

Typesetting and Origination by Amberley Publishing.
Printed in the UK.

Contents

Prologue   7

1 The 'S-Plan': the IRA's Nazi-backed plan to sabotage
  England – January 1939–March 1940   10

2 The British Intelligence Services' response: Bletchley Park,
  Aston House, Brickendonbury Manor and the Sabotage Section   17

3 The Royal Victoria Patriotic Schools, Camp 020,
  the Twenty (XX) Committee and double agents   24

4 Arthur Owens, Gwilym Williams and the
  Welsh Nationalist Party (Part 1) – 1937–August 1940   47

5 The Nazis' pre-invasion saboteurs in Eire – 1940   62

6 Operations MAINAU and SEAGULL: Dr Hermann Görtz
  and Helmut Clissman – May–August 1940   68

7 Operations SEALION, GREEN, LOBSTER, SEAGULL and
  WHALE I and II – July 1940   73

8 Operations DOVE/PIGEON and SEA EAGLE (DOVE II)
  – August 1940–Summer 1941   82

9 Operations OSPREY (FISCHADLER), PASTORIUS and
  SEAGULL II – January–May 1942   87

10 Operation LENA: Infiltrating pre-invasion Nazi agents into
   England, September 1940 – The 'Brussels Four'   106

11 Mrs O'Grady, sentenced to death for sabotage –
   August 1940–February 1941   133

12 Arthur Owens, Gwilym Williams and the Welsh Nationalist Party
    (Part 2): October 1940–June 1942   139

13 Three Cuban saboteurs land in Fishguard, Pembrokeshire,
    South Wales – November 1940   172

14 MUTT and JEFF: Plan GUY FAWKES –
    April 1941–August 1942   176

15 Plan BROCK: August–October 1942   198

16 Plan BUNBURY and Operations HAGGIS and
    PORRIDGE – September 1942–June 1945   202

17 Agent ZIGZAG and Operation THOMAS –
    December 1942–March 1943   226

18 Agent PRINS, Potential Dutch saboteur – December 1942   251

19 More potential saboteurs – Agents
    September 1941–September 1943   261

20 ZIGZAG's return and Sabotage before D-Day – 1944   271

    Conclusion   278

    Appendix: Diary of Mainland Attacks   287

    Notes   294

    Bibliography   308

    Index   316

Prologue

Most people have no idea that in the 1930s and early-1940s there was what has been called a 'spy-psychosis' or 'Fifth Column neurosis' in Britain. Many of the most popular films were spy thrillers. *The Thirty-Nine Steps* (1935), *The Lady Vanishes* (1938), *Foreign Correspondent* (1940) and *Night Train to Munich* (1940) were all box-office hits.

Films released in 1939 included *Spy for a Day*, *The Spy in Black*, *Spies of the Air* and *Traitor Spy*. Beloved familiar characters of the time such as Inspector Hornleigh got in on the act by capturing spies on an express train in *Inspector Hornleigh Goes to It* (1940). *Cottage to Let* (1941) included fifth columnists and secret inventions. In low-budget comedies, Arthur Askey and George Formby would foil the plots of swarms of German spies as well as unmask quislings and traitors, and everything would turn out nice again. All these films reinforced the Government-endorsed message that not only did careless talk cost lives; anyone could be a spy and a traitor.[1]

There were rumours of Nazi agents disguised as nuns operating from a disused London Underground station. The population was encouraged to report any suspicious activity, especially by foreigners, to the police. Lt General Robert Baden-Powell, the founder of the Boy Scouts and the Girl Guides, claimed to be able to identify German agents from the way they walked, but only from behind. General Sir Walter Kirke, Head of the Home Forces, claimed that 'the gentlemen who are the best behaved and the most sleek are the stinkers who are doing the work and we cannot be too sure of anybody.'[2] There was a fear that enemy agents were using carrier pigeons to send their messages.

In January 1939, the Irish Republican Army (IRA) issued an ultimatum to the British government to withdraw all their troops from Ireland or they would launch a sabotage campaign against Britain. When their ultimatum was ignored, the IRA started attacking targets in London and other major British cities.

What was not realised at the time was that the Nazis were providing financial and technical support to the IRA, promising them independence for Ireland in return for helping their plans for a British invasion. German saboteurs were involved in the campaign with their bomb attacks being attributed to the IRA. These attacks continued throughout 1939 and after war broke out in September, the Security Forces started finding evidence of Nazi involvement.

The British Government began to be seriously worried that the Nazis were supporting the IRA and planning to sabotage important military, industrial and communication targets before invading Britain.

The Government initiated a widespread counter-sabotage programme. You may well have read books or watched films about the sabotage attacks undertaken by British or British-trained agents in enemy-occupied Europe; how they destroyed aeroplanes, trucks and trains with plastic explosives; how they blew up canal lock gates, railway lines, electricity power stations, bridges, viaducts, aqueducts and tunnels; how they sank ships with limpet bombs and halted production at mines, engineering works and factories; how they brought down pylons, telegraph poles and cut cables with strategically placed and often cleverly camouflaged explosive devices. But where are the stories of the IRA's sabotage attacks? Where are the stories of the German-trained agents infiltrated into Britain to attack important targets? Where are the documentaries? Where are the films?

I researched Station 17, Brickendonbury Manor, the requisitioned country house outside Hertford, Hertfordshire, where overseas 'students' were trained as secret agents for my book *Churchill's School for Saboteurs*. Later the house was used to provide agents with specialist courses in industrial sabotage before being infiltrated to undertake attacks on targets across Europe. Before researching sabotage in Poland and Italy, I got waylaid by writing an account of the women involved in deception schemes during the war.

I spent several years poring over and transcribing secret agents' personnel files and mission papers from the National Archives in Kew, downloading files from the Central Intelligence Agency (CIA)'s website, trawling the Internet for details, reading biographies, autobiographies, newspapers, history books and journals, and writing numerous accounts of top-secret sabotage operations during the Second World War. I discovered that the IRA and the Nazis made numerous attempts to sabotage targets in Britain and that the British Intelligence Services made concerted efforts to stop them. This book provides a detailed account of their successes and failures.

I have to acknowledge the research done by Rupert Allason, Mary Berbier, John Bowyer-Bell, Giles Colchester, Terry Crowdy, T. Ryle Dwyer, Bryce Evans, Lalislas Farago, Thomas Hennessey, Mark Hull, John Humphries, Tommy Jonason, David Johnson, Ben Macintyre, John Masterman, David O'Donoghue, Eunan O'Haplin, Simon Olsson, Terence O'Reilly, Adrian O'Sullivan, Frank Owen, Günther Peis, Lee Richards, Mike Scoble, Adrian Searle, Claire Thomas, Des Turner and Charles Wighton.

The staff at the National Archives in Kew and the CIA online archives need especial thanks for generating a searchable catalogue and allowing many of the documents I found to be downloaded. The staff of the Lancashire Archives also helped provide access to their files. Steven Kippax, Phil Tomaselli, Stephen Tyas and fellow members of the Special Operations Executive Yahoo user group have been particularly helpful in providing files and answering my many queries.

Martin Briscoe kindly provided photographs of the Fort Willliam hydroelectric power station, Mal Durbin the photograph of Cray Reservoir and David

Howard the photograph of 35 Crespigny Road. I acknowledge with gratitude a number of websites on which I found other illustrations.

Trying to provide a detailed account of what were considered at the time to be top secret activities over a six-year period has been a challenge, based as it is on often redacted transcripts of interviews, memoranda and correspondence. There may be gaps; there may be errors, but this book is more the work of an archaeologist than a historian. It is an attempt to piece together bits of information so that they tell a human story, one which I hope will not only give you fascinating details about little-known aspects of British wartime history but also an insight into the mind-set of the people involved in the British and German Intelligence Services, the saboteurs and the counter-saboteurs.

Bernard O'Connor

1

The 'S-Plan': the IRA's Nazi-backed plan to sabotage England – January 1939–March 1940

Before the Second World War, the British people were well aware of sabotage. Newspaper articles, radio reports and television newsreels covered sabotage attacks against English targets by the IRA. There had been many hundreds of years of conflict between Ireland and England and sabotage was one of the IRA's weapons in their attempt to win independence.

Seán Russell, the IRA's Director of Munitions after the Easter Rising of 1916 and its quartermaster in the 1920s and 1930s, visited both the Union of Soviet Socialist Republics and the United States to win political and financial support for Irish independence. In 1936, while in Philadelphia with Joseph McGarrity, a prominent Irish-American businessman who helped finance the IRA, they devised a plan to force the British to withdraw their troops from Ireland.

Although court-martialled in 1937 for misappropriation of funds, Russell was reinstated the following year and appointed IRA's Chief of Staff. He contacted Seamus 'Jim' O'Donovan, a chemistry graduate from University College, Dublin, and Michael Collins' 'Director of Chemicals' (explosives) during the War of Independence, intending to start a sabotage campaign on the mainland.

In the 1920s, O'Donovan had lost two fingers from his right hand when one of his home-made bombs exploded unexpectedly. Having worked for the Irish Free State's Electricity Supply Board on their rural electrification programme, his engineering background helped him write papers on how to disable engines and destroy bridges without the use of explosive material. Also known as the IRA's chief weapons expert, he drew up a plan of sabotage against installations and public utilities in England. It ran to 17 typed pages and became known as the 'S-Plan'. Prioritisng electricity supply, its aim was to destabilise Britain's economic infrastructure. It was hoped that plunging British cities into darkness would embarrass and inconvenience the Government without causing civilian deaths and force them to negotiate. To ensure it was implemented, stockpiles of explosive materials were built up in Liverpool, which had a large Irish immigrant community.

O'Donovan and Russell taught sabotage skills to volunteers in Killiney Castle, in an affluent Dublin suburb, who were then sent to English cities to prepare the attacks and await orders.

In his unpublished memoirs, O'Donovan boasted that while Russell

...became responsible for personnel, organisation and finance [...] I evolved the whole details of the sabotage campaign [the S-plan] ... conducted the entire training of cadre units, was responsible for all but locally-derived intelligence, carried out small pieces of research and, in general, controlled the whole explosives and munitions end.[1]

At that time, the IRA and *Cumann Na mBan*, the Irish women's provisional army, had an estimated 15,000 members but how many of them were trained as saboteurs and operated in England is unknown.

In March 1938, what was reported as malicious damage prompted Thomas Barker, the General Manager of Fairey Aviation Company's works in Heaton Chapel, Stockport, to issue the following memo to his employees. One imagines similar warnings were issued in other industries involved in the Government's Re-armament Programme.

<u>PRIVATE AND PERSONAL</u> 24.8.38
<u>TO ALL EMPLOYEES OF THE FAIREY AVIATION COMPANY,</u>
<u>STOCKPORT.</u>

In connection with the recent cases of malicious damage to aircraft in this factory, the Management with to draw your personal attention to the effect of criminal acts of this nature.

The security of this country and its inhabitants depends on the success of the present Re-armament Programme especially as regards aircraft. Any action, therefore, which prejudices or delays such work affects the safety of each individual.

It must be remembered that, if such damage is not detected, our pilots and men employed in testing the aircraft run the risk of being killed or seriously injured.

I earnestly appeal for the co-operation of all to detect and to prevent repetition of these acts.

Thomas Barker, General Manager[2]

In November 1938, attacks started on Northern Ireland border control posts, during which three saboteurs were killed when the bombs exploded prematurely. Research by Bryce Evans into the S-Plan on Merseyside revealed that,

During Christmas 1938, a twelve-man team of IRA operatives travelled to five major British cities to scope targets and contacts. Of this crack team of twelve, three volunteers were dispatched to Liverpool, headed by Joe Deegan, a seasoned republican from South Armagh [...] Deegan and his men soon procured large amounts of potassium chloride, sulphuric acid and iron oxide. The Liverpool IRA moved within the local Irish community. Known republican sympathisers were relied upon to secretly store these materials; others knew nothing of the 'S' Plan or exactly what substances were contained in the briefcase they were looking after for a friend of a friend.[3]

On 12 January 1939, claiming to be the 'Government of the Irish Republic', the IRA sent a letter to Lord Halifax, the British Foreign Secretary, with an ultimatum to the Government, which

> ...gave them four days to withdraw all British armed forces stationed in Ireland and declare that they would renounce all claims to interfere in Irish domestic policy. If they received no response, they said they would be compelled to intervene actively in the military and commercial life of Great Britain. Four days passed with no reply so a campaign known as the 'S-Plan' was launched against Britain.[4]

In David O'Donoghue's *The Devil's Deal*, he argued that forcing a British withdrawal from Ireland was the secondary aim of the S-Plan. Attracting Germany's attention was the primary reason. Russell, he claimed, 'saw Hitler as the only European leader capable of destroying Britain. His logic was that with England on its knees, nothing could prevent a German-backed reunification of Ireland.'

One of the IRA's first acts of war was in Liverpool. The *Liverpool Echo* for January 1939 reported:

> At 5.48am, in the early morning of 16 January 1939, residents in the Crosby and Waterloo areas, suburbs in the north of the city, were woken by the noise of a large explosion and the shaking of houses. Startled, many fumbling around in the darkness, people entered the street in their pyjamas asking one another what was going on. Some thought they had heard gun fire; others thought the noise must have been caused by a large domestic boiler exploding.
>
> Later that day it was speculated that the disturbance was connected to two explosions which had occurred around ten minutes later in London and Manchester. One man, a young fish porter on his way to work, was killed when a device exploded in a main in Manchester's Stevenson Square at 6am. In London, the control rooms of the South-Eastern Electricity Board had been targeted at the same time. Yet confusion still remained over the Liverpool explosion because there was no visible damage to any property in the area.
>
> The following day the local press excitedly reported that the mystery of what had caused the Crosby explosion had been 'solved' by two fifteen year old schoolboys. Playing in a field near the Leeds-Liverpool canal, they discovered the remains of bombs near a large electrical pylon. One of the legs of the pylon had been blown off and the others damaged by a blast that had created a hole six feet deep. Beside the pylon, the boys found a charred attaché case with a small blue alarm clock in it. They reported the find to workmen nearby and as the press descended on the field the two were snapped by photographers, their proud schoolboy smiles appearing in newspapers the next day.
>
> Although the metal structure had survived, the IRA cell had chosen their target carefully: the pylon carried the main transmission line between Liverpool, Warrington and Manchester on the one side and that of Liverpool, Preston and Scotland on the other. It was by now obvious that the attack was

part of a bigger campaign. In the north of the city it was reported that posters of the 1916 proclamation had been stuck to walls, signed underneath by both the original signatories and the current IRA leadership.

Reaction in Liverpool was swift. It was feared that moisture caused by a thick fog would prevent fingerprints being taken from the scene of the pylon explosion, but reports of seven arrests in Manchester were soon accompanied by news that police were searching all Irish lodging houses, apartments, pubs and clubs in Liverpool, as well as poring over reports of attacks on the Liverpool docks carried out by the IRA during the Irish War of Independence in 1920. Boats arriving from Ireland were being 'closely watched for suspicious characters' by plain clothes detectives and Clarence Dock and Lister Drive power stations were placed under heavy police guard.

In an atmosphere of fear and terror mingled with swirling foggy weather, several panicked incidents occurred in the following days. Several witnesses saw a lorry and six men unloading boxes near Wallasey Golf Links, although these men had vanished by the time the police arrived. On the Ormskirk to Liverpool train two windows mysteriously smashed as the train passed Maghull. This could only have been caused by bullets, it was claimed by shaken passengers, although none were discovered. In Bootle, a dark green 1934 Morris containing four men was seen parked by an electricity substation at 2 am in the morning. Approached by a policeman, gun fire was said to have sounded; the policeman took cover before requisitioning a passer-by's car and giving chase unsuccessfully. In the light of day, the policeman admitted that the gun shots could have in fact been the noise of the car backfiring.[5]

Arrests in Liverpool led to a search of 32-year-old Thomas Kelly's tobacconists' shop at 425 Edge Lane. When four kegs of potassium chlorate were found in the basement, the police alleged he masterminded the Liverpool bombings.[6]

Documents seized at Kelly's shop led the police to the Hannan family, who lived on Great Howard Street. From the Hannans', they travelled to Wavertree to quiz another suspect, Jim Murphy. As a result of these enquiries the police came to discover one of the main arsenals of the Liverpool IRA. In a lock-up in nearby Lilley Road large amounts of potassium chlorate, iron oxide, sulphuric acid, gelignite, detonators and ammunition were found. The owners of the Lilley Road garage, a suburban married couple named the Thistlethwaites, were shocked that their garage had become an arms dump. They claimed an unidentified man had paid them one week's rent but was never seen again.

The discovery of the Wavertree arms dump was a coup for the local authorities. On 20 February Kelly, the Hannans, Dowley and Murphy again stood trial at Liverpool Police Court. The prosecution called 70 witnesses. The showpiece scale of the case echoed the mass trial of IRA suspects that had taken place a week previously at Bow Street. There, to accommodate all 18 suspects (including the two Liverpool lodgers initially arrested on Great Nelson Street, who had been sent down to London for sentencing) the dock was removed and replaced with a boxing ring.

The main defendant in the Liverpool case was the tobacconist, Kelly. It was alleged that Kelly had knowingly received the potassium chlorate delivery from London IRA man Jack Healy, who had originally bought the chemicals in the capital in September 1938 (and would receive ten years for his trouble). Kelly himself had not received the goods; when the kegs were delivered a shop girl had signed for them in his absence.[7]

On 3 May, a week after five attacks on commercial properties in Liverpool, there were tear gas attacks on the crowded Trocadero and Paramount cinemas in the city, which caused widespread panic. Witnesses described a mysterious young woman taking no notice of the film, looking around then knocking something off her knee and leaving the cinema in a hurry. Both times black smoke rose from where she had been sitting and then an explosion like a firework. The suspect was descibed as tall, about 23, with long dark hair, a good figure and wearing a smart reddish-brown two-piece suit.[8]

Another tear gas attack on 30 May, thought to have been carried out by the same woman, put twenty people in the Liverpol Infirmary, caused widespread revulsion at the IRA's tactics and further intensified anti-Irish feeling. The same day, a soldier of the King's Liverpool Regiment prevented a serious explosion at his barracks in Seaforth when a man on a bicycle threw 20 sticks of dynamite tied to a fuse over the wall. The soldier managed to pick it up and drop it into a bucker of water.[9] Public demand for the police to respond to these and similar attacks in other cities hastened government action.

> Across Britain … the authorities' crackdown was impressively thorough. Reports detailed the typically defiant, eloquent and unapologetic declarations of IRA men sentenced to five or ten year sentences, responding to their sentences with cries of 'Up the Republic' or lengthy historical correctives. Such defiance was met with uncompromising legislation. […] the British government secured powers for the compulsory expulsion of people considered a threat to public security. By 24 July, the Home Secretary, Samuel Hoare, informed the Commons that in response to 127 separate incidents 66 IRA men had been convicted, and 1500 sticks of gelignite seized. Many hundreds more would now be forcibly removed from Britain, he promised, under the Prevention of Violence Act. This act further impacted the wider Irish community by binding Irish citizens to register with the police.[10]

The response of the IRA in Liverpool was swift. The *Liverpool Echo* reported on 27 July that a few hours after a series of bomb explosions at London railway station which killed one and injured 22, IRA volunteers blew up a pillar box on Ranelagh Street, a canal bridge and Mount Pleasant Post Office. A courting couple narrowly missed death crossing the bridge and two electricity workers found 78 sticks of dynamite tied to a leg of a nearby pylon. The alarm clock fastened to the explosive was successfully removed two hours before it was due to go off.

On 30 July 1939, The *Sunday Express* ran an article identifying Seán Russell as the man responsible for the wave of bombings. Despite an exodus of Irish immigrants who were thought to include the mysterious young woman and Deegan, the leader of the Liverpool IRA, in mid-August there were bomb attacks on hotels in Fleetwood and Southport.

In Tim Coogan's book on the IRA he argues that they ought to have made more use of women as they were less likely to be arrested by the police. 'Pretty young English girls' were reported to have been duped by the IRA to hide packages for them. Two young women in Manchester were arrested and tried for being involved in attacks and two of writer Brendan Behan's aunts and his grandmother in Birmingham were arrested and given between two and five years imprisonment for carrying sticks of dynamite, despite them claiming that they thought they were sticks of rock.[11]

The worst incident during the IRA's campaign was on 25 August 1939 when a bomb carried on the back of a bicycle which was reported to have been intended to blow up an electricity sub-station, exploded in Broadgate, a busy Coventry shopping street, killing five people and injuring 72. The same day, bombs exploded at two branches of Lloyd's Bank in Liverpool and a further six went off over the following four days.[12] Police action led to the arrest of four young men and a woman, which marked the end of the IRA activities in Liverpool.[13]

Behan claimed that as a 16-year-old living in Everton, Liverpool, he was thwarted in September 1939 in an attempt to reactivate the sabotage campaign.[14] The opening lines of his autobiography *Borstal Boy* read:

> Friday, in the evening, the landlady shouted up the stairs: 'Oh my God, oh Jesus, oh Sacred Heart, Boy, there's two gentlemen to see you.'
>
> I knew by the screeches of her that these gentlemen were not calling to enquire about my health, or to know if I'd had a good trip. I grabbed my suitcase, containing Pot. Chlorate, Sulph Ac, gelignite, detonators, electrical and ignition, and the rest of my Sinn Feacutein conjurer's outfit, and carried it to the window. Then the gentlemen arrived.
>
> A young one, with a blonde, Herrenvolk head and a BBC accent shouted, 'I say, greb him, the bestud.'[15]

Taken to court, he claimed that the potassium chlorate was for an ear infection. Who provided him with the sabotage equipment is unknown but on 7 February 1940 he was sent to Borstal for three years for possessing materials which he was going to use to blow up ships in Liverpool docks.[16]

The media reported threats to blow up war factories, munition dumps, police stations, the Natural History Museum, Buckingham Palace and the Houses of Parliament. Tom Barnes, another Liverpool bomber, admitted that he had planned to blow up the *Queen Mary*. Although most of the attacks were in London and Liverpool, there were others in Bristol, Manchester, Coventry and Birmingham.[17]

Enno Stephan's research for his *Spies in Ireland* revealed that between 16 January 1939 and March 1940, there were 290 reported attacks on English electricity generating stations, pylons and electricity transmission lines, gas and water mains, a telephone exchange and telephone boxes, bridges, a gaol, a ship, aqueducts, mainline and underground railway stations, post offices and post boxes, mail trains, department stores, cinemas, hotels, food markets, council buildings, banks and a newspaper office. Although the plan was not meant to target civilians, over the course of the campaign seven were killed and 96 injured. Further details can be found in the appendix.[18]

Jupp Hoven, a German intelligence officer working for Joachim von Ribbentrop, the German Foreign Minister, had regularly visited Ireland, both North and South, and been in contact with the IRA from as early as 1929.[19] Guy Liddell, an officer working for MI5, Britain's Home Security Section, since 1931, reported that in the spring or summer of 1939, Hoven had taken Tom Barry, the IRA's then Chief of Staff, to Germany. 'He had a quarrel with Seán Russell, and when he returned, he found Russell in charge of the IRA and that he had been turned out. It is understood that the object of Barry's visit to Germany was to discuss the further action of the IRA in the event of a European war.'[20]

Although there were rumours that the Germans had funded the IRA's sabotage campaign, it was some time before MI5 obtained hard evidence. An MI5 officer, signing himself as B, reported in March 1939 that he had discussed the 'recent Irish outrages' with Mr Howe of Scotland Yard and

...Threw a fly over him to find out whether they were financed by German money. Mr Howe said they had found nothing over this side to indicate this and with one exception the arrested men had very little cash on them.

This is interesting in view of the fact that half an hour before, Sir Robert Vansittart had told me that he was convinced that the Germans were financing the IRA outrages. Later in the evening I got information from a casual informant in Ireland taking the same line that Sir Robert did, but it appeared to me pure surmise.[21]

2

The British Intelligence Services' response: Bletchley Park, Aston House, Brickendonbury Manor and the Sabotage Section

The British government has had a long history of employing people to collect military, political and economic intelligence and undertake clandestine work. In 1907 a Home Section was created, headed by Captain, later Major, Vernon Kell, who was given the responsibility of investigating espionage, sabotage and subversion within Britain and overseas.

Two years later, the Committee of Imperial Defence established the Security Service Bureau, which was known to those involved as the 'Secret Service', the 'SS Bureau' or even 'SS'. A separate section, known as the Foreign Service (Military Intelligence 6 or MI6) and headed by Mansfield Smith-Cumming, was responsible for overseas security while the Security Service (MI5) dealt with issues within the United Kingdom.

MI5 officers collected intelligence, often clandestinely, getting the Home Secretary's permission to open mail, listen into people's telephone conversations and even break into people's property and photograph or take objects or documents. Microphones were hidden in suspects' property, and a team of listeners would tape and then transcribe their conversations. Where appropriate, local people might be paid to supply intelligence or undertake secret operations like infiltrating what were considered to be criminal or subversive organisations.

Following the outbreak of the First World War, there was a need for closer liaison between the War Office and the various military intelligence organisations. The Foreign Service had to work with the Military Intelligence Directorate, known as MI1(c). Smith-Cumming managed to separate the Foreign Service from Military Intelligence and his organisation became known as the 'Foreign Intelligence Service', the 'Secret Service', the 'Special Intelligence Service' or just 'C'. From 1920, it was more widely known as the Secret Intelligence Service or SIS. Headed by Admiral Hugh 'Quex' Sinclair, its headquarters were at 54 Broadway, opposite St James's Park and close to St James' Underground Station, Westminster. It had additional offices in St Ermin's Hotel, opposite New Scotland Yard, London where 'D' Section was based. This group was employed to undertake undercover operations, dirty tricks and sabotage as explaied below.

In the 1930s, top secret messages sent from the German High Command to their Army, Navy and Air Force were encoded using what was called an Enigma machine and transmitted in Morse. Although these messages were detected by staff employed at listening stations in British Embassies around the world and at 'Wireless Intercept' stations at Knockholt and Denmark Hill, known as 'Y' stations, the Germans were confident that their code was unbreakable.

With the prospect of war becoming increasingly likely, in March 1938 Sinclair asked Major Laurence Grand of the Royal Engineers to create a secret section within SIS, known as D Section, the D standing for destruction. Its aim was to plan, prepare and, when necessary, carry out sabotage and other clandestine operations, as opposed to the gathering of intelligence. As well as planning attacks on Germany's electricity industry, phone communications, railways, food supplies and agriculture, Grand wrote a report on how to defend Britain against sabotage – including the protection of power stations and communications. Up-to-date knowledge of explosives was essential, and a safe, isolated location was needed for research and development.[1]

Conscious that London would be a target for German bombers should there be another war, in May 1938 Sinclair bought a mansion and 58 acres of Bletchley Park, Buckinghamshire, about 55 miles north-west of London. As the government did not have a budget for secret operations at that time, he paid £6,000 of his own money to have the property as a D Section training school and base for SIS.[2]

Before being used for codebreaking, Bletchley Park was used by D Section to develop sabotage material, particularly plastic explosives and incendiaries. One of its early boffins was Colin Meek, who graduated in Physics from Manchester University in 1931 and worked for the Imperial Chemical Industries at their Frodsham works in Cheshire. In 1938, when he was 29, he got a job as a scientific officer at Woolwich Arsenal working for the War Office on the development of plastic explosive.

Meek and his boss, Dr Drane, were seconded to D Section and moved to Bletchley Park. Des Turner's research revealed:

> It was coded D/X Section: D for Destruction, X for Explosives. Dr Drane (D/X) and Meek (D/X1) began work there on 15 June 1939 and were joined by Capt. C.R. Bailey (D/X2), Capt. L.J.C. Wood (D/D1) and another. Mr E. Norman acted in a part-time capacity. Mr G. Doe and B.S.M. Stalton were laboratory assistants.
>
> They occupied an office in the house, a workshop in the stables and a small magazine for explosives and incendiaries where full-scale experiments with weapons could begin.
>
> Before the war, little was known about the principles, methods and weapons required to wage a successful sabotage campaign. Here they initiated a study on the time pencil fuse, pocket incendiaries and explosives. The work involved testing explosives in various parts of the Bletchley Park estate.

When the war began, some MI6 staff moved in and complained about the bangs. And when the code-breakers arrived they said they lost concentration with each explosion. So, Meek and his colleagues had to depart. In November 1939, they moved to Aston House [near Stevenage, Hertfordshire]. Here, not only was there a large house and country estate where nobody complained about the bangs, but a chalk pit quarry as well, known to the locals as 'The Dell Hole' where, until then, children often played.[3]

With the outbreak of war, the British Government allocated more funds to SIS, which increased its staff and requisitioned many stately homes and other large secluded houses in the countryside where important military and other organisations were relocated. There was also the belief that the Luftwaffe would be given orders not to destroy these fine properties as, should the Germans ever conquer Britain, they would want them for themselves.

Aston House, an isolated country house in Hertfordshire, just over 30 miles north of London, was allocated to D Section. Sinclair gave its Commandant, Lieutenant Colonel John Langley, Royal Navy, the following terms of reference:

> To study how sabotage might be carried out.
> To make experiments on carrying out sabotage.
> To produce special sabotage ammunition.
> To train saboteurs.
> To study methods of countering sabotage.[4]

As well as making the estate out of bounds to the local population, the house was given the cover-name 'Signals Development Branch No. 4, War Department.' The time pencils were code-named 'Signals Relays', incendiary bombs 'Signal Flares' and demolition charges 'Sound Signals'.[5]

Given Langley's naval background, his initial mission was to study the ways in which Hitler's forces might sabotage British shipping but with the IRA's 'S' plan they also had the opportunity to learn about attacks on military, industrial and transportation targets. Langley:

> By mid-1939 we had accumulated a good general grounding in sabotage methods and possible modern sabotage weapons. If I, with my meagre resources, working in a generally hostile environment, had been able to dream up better weapons than the Germans had twenty years ago, there was every reason to suppose that the Nazis would have done equally well if not better when working with enthusiastic official backing. We found out later that they hadn't. That was probably because they had not worried about what to them would have appeared an utterly insignificant phase of warfare. You do not waste time on feather dusters when you are busy making sledgehammers capable of crushing entire nations in one blow. [Poland was crushed in eighteen days. A year later, France was crushed in a month.]
>
> Anyway [by August 1939], with the help of my immediate chief [Grand], we had amassed enough information about sabotage to enable me to describe suitable counter measures. A handbook containing these counter-measures

was drafted. It would be issued to 'naval boarding officers' if war came. One of the duties of these officers would be to board all merchant ships just before they entered British ports, search out any sabotage devices and neutralise them. Prototypes of our 'pencil time fuses' were made secretly so that boarding officers could recognise the sort of device they might be looking for. Making these wasn't difficult. All you needed, except for a little ampoule of corrosive liquid, could be bought in the local ironmongers or hardware store. Any chemist capable of doing a little glass blowing could produce an ampoule.[6]

Copies of Langley's handbooks have yet to come to light. Whether subsequent handbooks containing counter-sabotage advice for military installations and factories were prepared and developed at Aston House is unknown.

In June 1938, the Polish Intelligence Service informed Menzies that a Polish mathematician who had worked in the Berlin factory manufacturing the Enigma machines was offering his knowledge to the British in exchange for £10,000, a British passport and residency in France. Stewart Menzies of SIS sent two boffins from the Government's Code and Cypher School to Paris to ascertain the veracity of his claim. In an apartment on the Left Bank, Richard Lewinski, his new identity, suitably impressed the boffins with the replica he built, which could crack the Wehrmacht code.

When war broke out in September 1939, the school at Bletchley Park was transferred to Brickendonbury Manor, near Hertford, and the Government's Code and Cypher School moved in. Known as Station X, the London Signals Intelligence Centre or Government Communications Headquarters, the people who worked there knew it as B.P. By early January 1940, their boffins had constructed a Bombe machine which was capable of deciphering the Wehrmacht's messages.[7] Consequently, the War Office had advance knowledge of virtually all Germany's military plans. In theory, MI6 and MI5 knew the code-names and details of the arrival of all Abwehr and Sicherheitsdienst agents.

The Abwehr was the German Military Intelligence organisation whilst the Sicherheitsdienst was the Schutzstaffel (SS)'s security service in the occupied countries, largely an intelligence agency. The Gestapo, the Nazi Party's secret police, were not directly involved in sabotage operations against Britain. The Allies' difficulty, however, was taking advantage of what were called 'Most Secret Sources' without letting their enemies know that their codes had been broken.

In a lecture about counter-intelligence given by Dick White, an MI5 officer, he referred to these sources as ISOS, the key to the Security Section learning beforehand the details of German agents and their arrival in Britain.

This word was derived from the fact that Oliver Strachey was head of all services which dealt with it. The question of controlling of sources is a very important matter and rests with M.I.6. When an agent moves from point A to point B, his movements show up clearly and a good deal of administrative work has to be done. The German Intelligence Machine is so very centralised that their agents constantly have to refer back to H.Q. The reference back is by wireless and in this way our knowledge about agents is considerable. We learn when they are on the move. It is not until an agent is actually on the move that he tackles a problem which could not be tackled before. Usually, we know where he is intending to go. I should say that we have caught a large percentage of our spies on this material although of course if you take the messages by themselves, further enquiries have to be made on them by S.I.S. or ourselves. Quite complicated machinery has to take place before the rather abstract figure becomes concrete. When you are in the field it is not until you have seen the scope of this important source that you will realise that the questions have to be asked from a centralised position.[8]

Following the outbreak of war, British diplomats were evacuated from Czechoslovakia and Poland, dramatically reducing the British government's intelligence capabilities in Eastern Europe. Over the following months, as other countries were occupied by the Germans, other British embassies and consulates were vacated. Many of SIS's local agents were left without financial support or a base to forward their intelligence to. Although neutral countries like the American or the Swiss embassies acted on Britain's behalf, SIS faced an intelligence quandary.

Guy Burgess, a Cambridge University graduate and D Section officer who was later found to be a Soviet agent, suggested that a special school be established to train agents to be infiltrated behind enemy lines to support those left behind, gather intelligence and encourage resistance. His idea was acted upon and in late 1939, the British government requisitioned Brickendonbury Manor, a large country house with 1,000 acres of parkland outside Hertford, about 25 miles north of London. His idea that it should be called the 'Guy Fawkes School' was rejected. Instead, it was called the 'D' School. Its commanding officer was Frederic Peters, RN, with Burgess as his second-in-command. The man responsible for its syllabus was Kim Philby, another SIS officer who had been Burgess's friend at Cambridge University and who was also a Soviet agent.

As well as physical training, weapons training and espionage skills, sabotage was included in the syllabus. One of Brickendonbury's first sabotage instructors was George Hill, who had worked for the SIS during the First World War and the Russian Revolution and had written a number of books on his sabotage activities. Maybe he told his students Lenin's saw, 'An ounce of resistance is worth a pound of hope.' The course included what had been learned about the tight-knit communist cell structure and the guerrilla tactics being used by the Irish Republican Army.

When war broke out, MI5 had a staff of about 50 with two part-time officers devoted to collecting intelligence on German political and national groups. By 1942, as a result of additional funding for the Intelligence Services, its numbers had risen to 1,500.[9]

As early as December 1939, MI5 had appointed Captain Godfrey of B.1 (b), their counter-subversion unit, to coordinate all reports on sabotage. D Section was instructed to pass on detailed reports of any sabotage or suspected sabotage to him, and a request was made that the Navy appoint a local Security Officer 'whose duty would be to study where and how acts of sabotage could be done, and to take the necessary precautions. It may be desirable for action to be taken by Military and R.A.F. Authorities.'[10]

By March 1940, B.18 had been formed to assist D.S.S. (Section D's Security Section) and John Curry, an MI5 officer, commented:

> The general functions and responsibilities of the D.S.S. include action to counter the activities of enemy agents, as directed by the enemy Intelligence Services. In the light of present information, it must be assumed that the activities of the German Intelligence Service may be supplemented by those of the Russian. Both of these organisations must be expected to contemplate the employment of saboteurs, who may be recruited by them either among enemy aliens and other aliens, or those elements of the British people who have been influenced by subversive activities, either of the extreme Right or the extreme Left.
>
> After six months of war, no large-scale sabotage has been directed by the enemy, all our information regarding German military theory leads us to suppose that they would be likely to reserve such action so as to make it synchronise with the general requirements of their military strategy. They would aim at the combined effect of a military campaign and sabotage behind their enemies' lines, as they did in Poland. We must therefore anticipate the necessity of taking action against intensive sabotage at a time which would be critical in connection with the general military situation.
>
> We have to consider at this point what should be the responsibilities of B.18 in accordance with their duty of assisting D.S.S. to discharge his functions and responsibility. The latter includes those of B. and D. Divisions of this Office, D being responsible for Security and B. for Investigation.
>
> The functions of B.18, therefore, come under the following headings:
>
> 1. The collection, collation, dissemination and utilisation, by all practical means, of all information relating to sabotage, from whatever source, whether within the U.K., the Dominions and Colonies, or other foreign countries (through S.I.S.).
> 2. As the investigation of cases of sabotage is the duty in the first place of the police forces concerned, it is for B.18 to render assistance in such investigations by making available to the police all the pertinent expert knowledge and information regarding enemy organisations, intelligence services and methods, which may be in the possession of the Security Service as a whole.
> 3. For the proper discharge of (2), it is necessary for B.18 to be informed of the general activities of other Sections of this Office, and to establish satisfactory liaison with them, both in B. and D. Divisions.
> 4. It is also for B.18 to establish satisfactory liaison with other departments concerned, especially the Service departments, through D. division, and particularly D.1, 2 and 3, in regard to munition and armament factories; the Government Establishments of the three Services; Railways; electric supply and distribution and other public utilities – in short everything

covered by the term 'Home Front', which offers a target to the saboteur, in particular such places as are the concern of the Director of the Key Point Industries Branch of the Home Office. In addition to this is the liaison with the Ministry of Shipping with regard to sabotage of the Mercantile Marine and neutral vessels in British charter. (This also involves liaison with the authorities of the Dominions and Colonies and with S.I.S.).

5. The collation of advice from experts (scientific and engineering) in regard to possible methods of chemical, bacteriological and technical sabotage (the question as to the utilisation of such advice is a matter for collaboration with D.1, 2 and 3, in regard, for instance, to firms with which they are concerned. D.1 2 and 3 are themselves in a position to obtain and, in fact, do obtain from their contacts, valuable information of this kind).

As some responsibility for sabotage is inescapable, it appears that the functions and the responsibilities of B.18 must be defined as above. We are so satisfied that sabotage of a wide scale is inevitable, that we think it is vitally important that the foundations of this Section should be well and truly laid beforehand.[11]

3

The Royal Victoria Patriotic Schools, Camp 020, the Twenty (XX) Committee and double agents

Throughout the 1930s, MI5's counter-espionage section had become aware not just of IRA activists but also fanatical anti-British Welsh and Scottish nationalists, communists and fascists of British and foreign origin, even individuals who officially were working for their governments in Britain but who were unofficially engaged in intelligence gathering or other clandestine activities.

In autumn 1940, SIS requisitioned three adjoining luxury mansions in a gated community next to the Russian Embassy in Kensington Palace Gardens. Known as the 'London Cage', this top secret establishment could accommodate up to 60 captured German prisoners-of-war who had refused to 'talk' in other camps. The commander Lt Col Alexander Scotland and his staff subjected them to 'special intelligence treatment', which included torture and the use of drugs.[1] With the dramatic increase in refugees arriving in Britain following Hitler's invasion of much of Western Europe, in June 1941 what became known as the London Reception Centre was established. MI5 gave it the code-name B.1.d. Most foreigners arriving in this country were sent there to be interrogated. It was located in the Royal Victorian Patriotic School in Wandsworth, which by the end of 1942 was processing about 1,000 people a month. Over the course of the war, it was estimated to have processed some 33,000 refugees. Under the direction of Colonel Pinto, many of its staff were returned employees from evacuated British Embassies and Consulates across Europe.[2]

Dick White, an MI5 officer, described its function as to separate the sheep from the goats. Its officers were keen to determine whether the newcomers were bona fide refugees and not German, Austrian, Italian or Japanese spies. MI6 officers wanted to learn more about what conditions were like in the countries they had just come from and collect any relevant economic, political or military intelligence. MI9, the section responsible for assisting escape organisations to get downed RAF pilots and crews, escaped prisoners-of-war, Allied agents and members of the Resistance back to Britain, wanted to know the details of how they reached this country, the individuals and the groups that helped them. The

RAF wanted to know details of the enemy's planes, aerodromes and airfields. The Royal Navy wanted to know about the enemy's shipping, particularly its U-boats, and the Army wanted information about the enemy's armed forces. This latter job was also part of SOE's remit as they also wanted to know about the resistance groups operating overseas.

ROYAL VICTORIA PATRIOTIC SCHOOLS

The Sabotage Section has a representative permanently at the R.V.P.S. under the M.I.5 head of this establishment. Although this representative takes photos of people passing through the Patriotic Schools, the reason for his being there is to X-ray all property of suspects passing through the Schools with a view to discovering whether secret equipment of any type is hidden within it. This examination is entirely done by X-ray, and the examiner is provided with innocuous samples of the things that persons normally carry about with them for purposes of comparison. In the event of the examiner being dissatisfied with any object after X-ray examination, photographs and any report that is necessary are sent to the Sabotage Section who make a further examination, and if the section is unable to reach a finite conclusion or requires more information, the suspected object is sent to Dr J.A.T. DAWSON, Radiological Branch, Research Department, Royal Arsenal, Woolwich. This second examination may be necessary because metal objects need a highly specialised X-ray technique.

Exact details of the suspected bomb must be available before an officer takes the object to pieces (to avoid booby traps).

All D.S.O. [Defence Security Officers]'s links abroad and S.C.Os. [Security Control Officers] are familiar with the camouflages used by the German Secret Service for bringing bombs into this country, and in the case of S.C.Os., instructions have been given for suspected objects to be sent to Head Office, from where they will be sent to the Patriotic Schools for X-ray examination.

General
When the sabotage consists of foreign matter or abrasives being placed in lubricating oil, a sample of the polluted oil, together with a sample of the pure, unaffected oil, should be sent to Head Office, if it is considered necessary that an analysis should be made to determine the nature of the foreign matter.

In cases where a mechanical or clockwork device or some form of infernal machine is employed, the article should be forwarded to Head Office for expert examination after it has been rendered safe. A circular has already been issued describing the measures to be taken when infernal machines and bombs are found.

In any form of technical damage to machinery or equipment, the damaged part should be forwarded if it is possible. Failing this, a photograph or sketch should be submitted. This action should be taken whenever any characteristic or unusual object is used for sabotage.

When sabotage occurs, and it is thought that one of the firm's employees may have been responsible, lists of employees who are suspect should be forwarded to the Sabotage Section, so that they can be looked up in the General Registry records.

If these suspects are thought to be aliens, S.I.S. are tele-printed for a look-up.

When suspects are found to have either Fascist or Communist tendencies their names are passed to the section concerned, and they co-operate with B.1.C [Sabotage Section] in further investigations.

It should be emphasised that all cases of suspected sabotage should be reported as soon as possible in order that investigations can be made without delay. R.S.L.Os. should in all cases where urgent action is required, report by telephone to B.1.C.[3]

Usually, the interrogation process took several days, but those men and women MI5 were still suspicious of were not released. Instead, they were escorted, sometimes in handcuffs, to London Oratory School, code-named Camp 001 for interrogation and medical checks. They were then transferred to Latchmere House, code-named Camp 020, a secure internment camp and interrogation centre on Ham Common, near Richmond. It was opened in July 1940 and from December it was commanded by Lieutenant Colonel Robert Stephens. Known to his colleagues as 'Tin Eye' Stephens, he was never seen without his monocle.[4] Research by Ian Cobain revealed that throughout the war, 480 individuals passed through the gates of Camp 020. Some prisoners were held in brightly lit cells 24 hours a day, others in total darkness. Several were subjected to mock executions and beaten by the guards. Some were reported to have been left naked for months. Luminol, a mind-altering drug, was reported to have been used.

Harold Dearden, the resident medical officer, was a psychiatrist who worked out regimes of starvation and sleep and sensory deprivation intended to break the inmates' will. His experiments left few marks, methods that the torturers could deny and which government ministers and civil servants could claim did not happen.[5]

Whilst some enemy agents tried to enter Britain officially and bluff their way through customs and immigration controls, a small number tried to enter illegally, either being dropped by a fishing boat, speed boat or submarine with a rowing boat or rubber dinghy which they had to row ashore or being dropped by parachute into some remote part of the country. The IRA's sabotage attacks had heightened security across the country with a propaganda campaign encouraging people to report any unusual or suspicious behaviour.

About 115 agents trained by the Abwehr or Sicherheitsdienst were reported to have passed through Camp 020. One used his potassium cyanide pill to commit suicide rather than be caught. Some enemy agents, despite having courage and optimism, were reported to have been caught after making elementary mistakes with their English language or inappropriate customs or behaviour. The police were also surprised by a significant number who voluntarily handed themselves in shortly after their arrival, claiming that they had agreed to work for the Germans to reach Britain. Some admitted that they were trained saboteurs, whose details can be found later.[6] These men, and some women, were given a much more intense interrogation. They were reported to have been well looked after; 'Tin Eye' Stephen's aim was to persuade his 'guests' to change sides and work for the Allies.

When the first captured enemy agents who refused to collaborate were tried in the courts under the Treason Act, found guilty and executed at the Tower of London and later at Pentonville prison, the media gave their cases huge publicity. This less than subtle persuasion explains in part why 39 captured enemy agents agreed to be 'turned' and become double agents. While some who refused to cooperate were interned for the duration of the war, the double agents were paid by the British and provided with decent food, accommodation and entertainment. In exchange they had to live in a 'safe house' with an armed guard who ensured that they complied with their instructions and an MI5 'minder', referred to as an agent handler or case officer. They ensured that the content of the messages they sent, either transmitted by a wireless set or written in secret ink to 'dead letter-boxes' in neutral countries like Spain, Portugal, Switzerland or Sweden, contained everyday conversations about conditions in Britain as well as specially worded intelligence aimed at deceiving the enemy.

This necessitated the establishment in June 1941 of a committee known as the Wireless or W Board. Without the knowledge of the Chiefs of Staff, it comprised the directors of army, navy and air force intelligence, Sir Findlater Stewart for the civilian authorities, Guy Liddell for MI5, and Colonel Menzies, who had taken over MI6 following Sinclair's death in November 1939. It only met when one of them requested a meeting and its aim was to generate information that appeared genuine but which could mislead.[7] In the case of agents infiltrated as wireless operators, someone would take a gramophone recording of their transmissions so that another wireless operator could master their 'fist', their individual style of tapping out the Morse code messages. They would then take over the set should it ever become necessary, and the enemy would continue to believe that it was being operated by their agent.

Those who had been given sabotage training and infiltrated to collect intelligence on specific industrial, military or communication targets and then arrange their destruction had to be dealt with in a different way. This account tells the stories of their successes and failures.

The deliberate deception of the enemy, sending disinformation or misinformation, was very carefully planned. It was the work of a special team of MI5's counter-espionage officers, headed by Major John Masterman, a history professor at Oxford University who had used some of his students to infiltrate the Trades Union movement during the 1930s and help MI5 break the General Strike. When war broke out, he was drafted into the Intelligence Corps and then MI5, chairing what was called the Twenty Committee, a pun on the Roman numerals XX meaning twenty but also double-cross.

Masterman and other members of what was known as BI(a) section, set in place a counter-espionage and long-term deception scheme using double agents. It was run by Lieutenant Colonel Thomas Argyll Robertson, known by his initials 'TAR', with Major William Luke, known as 'Billy' as his deputy. Over the course of the war, they and their team of intelligence officers successfully double-crossed the Germans, transmitting British-inspired messages and receiving messages from the Abwehr for their agents, information which identified the date and time of arrival of many of the new agents and their landing sites. It also helped Britain defend itself against the threat of German-inspired sabotage. Their major claim to fame was convincing the Germans that the Allied invasion of France was going to take place at Pas de Calais, not the Normandy beaches, thus diverting enemy troops to allow them to create a bridgehead.[8] In Masterman's book, *The Double-Cross System*, he listed the objectives of the Twenty Committee.

1. To control the enemy system, or as much of it as we could get our hands on.
2. To catch fresh spies when they appeared.
3. To gain knowledge of the personalities and methods of the German Secret Service.
4. To obtain information about the code and cypher work of the German Service.
5. To get evidence of enemy plans and intentions from the questions asked by them.
6. To influence enemy plans by the answers sent to the enemy.
7. To deceive the enemy about our plans and intentions.[9]

The expansion of MI6 and MI5's activities was not the only reason why the S-Plan failed. MI5 had liaised with the *Gardai*, the Irish police, and by February 1940, 119 Irish had been deported back to Ireland and an unknown number were detained in British or Irish jails or internment camps. The IRA's links with the Abwehr were brought to light and given media coverage, intensifying the general British public's antipathy. It was claimed that O'Donovan purchased explosives used in the London bombings during one of the three visits he made to Berlin and Hamburg between February and August 1939. This could have been deliberate disinformation as although German arms, ammunition and explosive were promised in exchange for bombings and destruction, O'Donoghue claimed they did not arrive. A safe address in London for IRA visitors was provided, along with contact details of an IRA/Abwehr courier in Brussels.[10]

MI5 had evidence that in July 1939, two U-boats were sent to Reykjavik with secret instructions and two agents to assist Gestapo agents already in Iceland to distribute funds and explosives by sea to Ireland. A German naval officer admitted that his submarine 'had landed explosives from Hamburg and a large sum of money in £10 notes sometime in the first week of July on the south side of Belfast Bay, 10 miles from Belfast, with the aid of Irish fishermen'. They also reported Nazi agents providing explosives training to IRA members:

We now have to expect, not only a continuation of the outrages, but their development on a more extensive scale, with the further possibility looming behind such merely local occurrences that the Germans may have so far miscalculated political realities in Ireland as to imagine that the IRA constitutes a party worthy of support on a wider political basis. if this is the case it would only be another example of their technique of indirect aggression.[11]

Counter-sabotage measures introduced in early 1939 improved security at government buildings, power stations, gas works, telephone exchanges, railway stations, docks and airports. It was generally additional police officers but, when war broke out in September, night-time curfews were introduced which allowed the stopping and questioning of people after dark. Air raid wardens and fire watchers became increasingly vigilant. Ships and ferries were searched, especially those crossing the Irish Sea, and the population was much more conscious about potential threats from enemy agents, IRA, German or otherwise.

In June 1940, following Kell's forced retirement, Guy Liddell was transferred to head the counter-espionage section of B Division. A large-scale propaganda programme swung into gear to raise public awareness and encourage the population to inform the police of anybody behaving suspiciously.

Joan Miller, an MI5 secretary, reported that over 20,000 reported cases had to be dealt with, which led to arrests, interrogations and in some cases imprisonment or internment.[12] While some reports were petty, Liddell mentioned that 16,000 Communists and Fascists were being vetted on 19 September 1939, but there were no checks on the IRA. He commented that they were 'by far the most dangerous from a security point of view'.[13] In his diary entry at the end of September, he commented that an SIS report on Eire was 'somewhat alarmist as regards the internal situation. An attempt at revolution by the IRA does not appear to be out of the question.'[14]

While there was an increased police presence on the streets, especially at night, there were also undercover operations to identify and arrest those responsible for the attacks. Investigations were made on purchasers of large quantities of charcoal, potassium chlorate, iron oxide, powdered aluminium and sulphuric acid. Increased security was introduced at explosives stores of dynamite and gelignite, detonators and fuses at mines and quarries.

The reaction of the British people to the explosions was one of alarm and outrage, but the government's response was that the IRA did not exist. They did not want them getting what has subsequently been termed 'the oxygen of publicity'. The German view was different, however. In David Johnson's *Germany's Spies and Saboteurs*, he quoted an editorial in the *Volkischer Beobachter*: 'The bomb attacks ... demonstrate that the Irish Republicans are in earnest, for all their fantasy.'[15]

In August 1940, against its wishes, MI5 was forced to take on half a dozen officers from the Metropolitan Police's Criminal Investigation Department (CID), complete with their warrants with the power of arrest. These officers were led by Len Burt, subsequently Head of Special Branch, who later escorted Lord Haw Haw, William Joyce, a member of Oswald Mosley's British Union of Fascists (BUF) and Nazi broadcaster, to Camp 020. While his staff worked mainly on alleged sabotage cases, they also did some work against the supposed Fifth Column, conducted security reviews at public utilities and did a lot of work for SOE regarding indiscretions by some of their agents, and in some cases these resulted in convictions by Courts Martial.[16]

In the early years of the war, MI5 identified Admiral Wilhelm Canaris as the Chief of *Heeresnachtrichtdienst* (German Foreign Intelligence), known as N.D., under the command of Field Marshal Wilhelm Keitel of *Oberkommando der Wehrmacht* (OKD). Its headquarters was in the Reichskriegsministerium, 72–76 Tirpitzufer, Berlin. Canaris had responsibility for the *Abwehrabteilung*, the German military intelligence and espionage service, whose headquarters, known to its officers as the 'Fox's Lair', were in 76–78 Tirpitzufer.

Abwehr II, its sabotage section, was headed by Lieutenant-Colonel Erwin von Lahousen, whose offices were on the third floor of 78 Tirpitzufer with the legend 'II N/W' on the door. Their activities against Britain, the United States and other Western countries were initially based in the Hamburg Abwehrstelle (or Ast) on Sophienstrasse. Following the German occupation of Western Europe, they set up offices in the major European cities, as well as in neutral Spain and Portugal.[17]

Herbert Wichmann, an Abwehr officer captured at the end of the war, claimed that before the war started Canaris was disappointed with the Abwehr's attempts to spy on England, and that in spite of all their efforts the Germans had achieved nothing. They had no success in recruiting crews of British steamers visiting the port city of Hamburg; but by studying adverts in *The Times* and German newspapers, they succeeded in identifying British companies with trading links with Germany. Adverts were placed asking for people with a German connection to contact addresses in Hamburg. Firms were set up to answer these advertisements, often a single room with a doorplate, where an Abwehr officer posing as a German businessman might recruit agents. Developing links with the IRA was another potential solution.

In an MI5 file on pre-war IRA/German links, Dr Carl Petersen, the Press Attaché at the German Legation in Dublin, was identified as having connections with the German Intelligence Service and was thought by MI5 to have 'given a written guarantee to the IRA Army Council that if the Council renders assistance to the Germans in an emergency, the Council will be handed over the Government of the country when victory has been achieved'.

Dr Jupp Hoven, who had been studying folklore in Ireland, was reported to be a close friend of Helmut Clissman, a Nazi Party leader. Frank Ashton-Gwatkin of the Foreign Office told Special Branch that a German informer told him Franz Fromme, who had recently visited Ireland, acted on Intelligence Chief Heinrich Himmler's behalf as a go-between for the IRA and was the channel through which funds were transferred to Ireland from Germany.

On 4 March 1939, Lieutenant-Colonel Noel Mason-MacFarlane of the Berlin Embassy wrote: 'From information which I have received, and which goes back in one case to HEYDRICH who is Himmler's No. 2, and in another to a man in the Gestapo, it appears that the whole business (IRA outrages) has been instigated by Himmler's organisation in this country.' MI5 thought Mason-MacFarlane had been told by Colvin of the *News Chronicle* who 'had information on the connection between the Gestapo and the IRA.'[18]

As regards to German organisations in Ireland, the report admitted:

We have no evidence that an ad hoc organisation exists to exploit IRA terrorist activities. There is, of course, in Eire an Ortsgruppe of the Auslands Organisation of the NSDAP [Nazi Party]. This, with its subsidiary organisations, is doubtless a valuable means of collecting and collating information about the state of opinion in Ireland and also of fostering anti-British propaganda.

In addition it has been reported to us, with considerable reserve, that an organisation exists for underground activities against this country, headed by a member of the *Propagandaministerium* in Berlin, a certain Major STASSFURTER. This organisation is said to have the co-operation of the German Consulates in Southampton, Portsmouth, Liverpool, Hill and Harwich, and also of certain of the officials in the Nazi Party, the *Handelskammer* and the *Kraft durch Freude* organisation. The unreliable nature of the source of this information, precludes us from taking it very seriously.[19]

At the time the report was written, 1939, MI5 had no evidence that German agents had been primarily responsible for the recent outburst of IRA terrorist activities and concluded that it was 'inclined to regard the danger of Germany organising sabotage with the help of IRA terrorists as a very serious one.'[20]

A note in the file, dated July 1939, reported that conferences took place in Berlin on 24 and 25 June between Canaris, a representative of the German War Office and 'a responsible member of the Irish Terrorist organisation'.

At these conferences the Irish representative (whose name source has not been able to establish and has little hope of finding out) made a report on the tactics which his organisation had adopted in Great Britain.

As a result of this report, Admiral CANARIS undertook to supply him with arms and funds. The latter were provided by all the AST (Abwehrstellen – Military Intelligence centres), who were advised telegraphically to surrender to the Chief Paymaster (Obersellmeister) all their stock of sterling. These stocks were replenished about a week later.

As regards the supply of arms, source is not certain whether these have been already sent or not, but he does know <u>for certain</u> that Admiral Canaris has ordered a stock to be earmarked for this purpose, if and when required.[21]

Two days later, a letter was sent to Gladwyn Jebb, Assistant Under-Secretary of the Ministry of Economic Warfare (MEW) informing him of the above decision.

As you are no doubt aware we have been endeavouring since its beginning, to ascertain whether there has been German initiative or encouragement behind the IRA campaign; and hitherto have not had any definite or reliable evidence to this effect. The funds seized in this country from the possession of arrested IRA terrorists have not led further afield than Dublin, while the materials used have either been purchased locally in the UK or have been found to be the results of thefts from stores of explosives in this country. There has, of course, been a very general suspicion, both in Ireland and elsewhere, of German complicity in the matter, but the only reports we have to this effect have been of such a nature and from such sources that we have not considered them worth the notice of the Foreign Office.

The present report is in quite a different category. If, indeed, the first serious contact between the Germans and the IRA took place towards the end of June, this would account for the negative results of the previous enquiries, and we may now have to expect not only a continuation of the outrages, but their development on a more extensive scale. We are bringing this information to the notice of the Special Branch and MI5.[22]

Subsequent evidence confirms that the Abwehr provided the IRA with not just financial and logistical support but also personnel. Twenty-six-year-old Dr Kurt Haller, an expert in economic warfare, was in charge of Abwehr II's section dealing with the British 'minorities'. From September 1939, he was one of the key men in charge of Irish affairs, first in Abw II's 'Nest' in Rennes, Brittany, and from autumn 1940 onwards as personal assistant to Colonel Dr Edmund Veesenmayer, the SS head of Irish Affairs at the German Foreign Office. Haller also had responsibility for infiltrating agents into Africa, the United States and Britain.[23]

In Haller's post-war interrogation report, he detailed how O'Donovan and his wife visited Hamburg in August 1939 where he was introduced to *'Pfalzgraf'*, the code-name of Hauptmann Friedrich Marwede. Also known as Neumeister and Messerschmidt, Marwede worked for Abwehr II as head of the section dealing with political subversion in the West.[24]

When O'Donovan requested German help in the occupation of Northern Ireland, Marwede asked him for the IRA's help in attacking military targets in England. O'Donovan agreed and asked for weapons, ammunition and explosives, particularly bullets for Colt revolvers. Although the exact quantity was not agreed, it was intended to land a cargo on the South or North Irish coast and an unspecified quantity of potassium chlorate, disguised as flour, was to be smuggled into a bakery or flour mill in Limerick from Hamburg. Although these were promised, Haller claimed they were not delivered; but O'Donovan took 30,000 RM in £5 notes.[25]

In Ladislas Farago's *The Game of the Foxes*, he mentions Dr Jupp Hoven and Helmut 'Howard' Clissman, German intellectuals who were living in Dublin in the late-1930s, as being impressed with the IRA's plans. Clissman, alias Harvey Goff, was a member of the Nazi Party and ran the German academic exchange service at Trinity College.[26] When they were forced to return to Germany in late-1939, they joined the Abwehr and met Lahousen at 78 Tirpitzufer. As Lahousen was responsible for sabotage and insurrection operations and liaison with potential Fifth Columnists, Nazi sympathisers and anti-Allied governments overseas, Hoven and Clissman recommended

…that he plug the Abwehr II into this live socket and tap the 15,000- member IRA for a large-scale sabotage campaign in England.

Although the English were wont to pooh-pooh these boisterous unforgiving Irish terrorists as 'men of no account' (*The Times* of London editorialised at the time of their campaign in January that the IRA was dead), the Germans took them very seriously. Their bombings ingratiated them to von Lahousen who agreed that the IRA was very much alive and could do for Germany what they were doing on their behalf.

He created a special Irish desk in Abwehr II and named a man called 'Dr Pfalzgraf' to establish contact with the 'Terrorists.' 'Pfalzgraf' was Captain

Friedrich Karl Marwede, a beefy, rather pompous career intelligence officer specialising in 'dirty tricks' with the help of a civilian expert named Dr Kurt Haller. They approached the IRA leaders Hoven and Clissman had solicited and found that they already had an elaborate 'S-Plan' which had as its object 'the paralysis of all official activity in England and the greatest possible destruction of British defence installations'.

The Irish responded avidly but on a rather mercenary ground. They regarded the Germans' interest in them as manna from heaven and proceeded to shake them down. In the end, they bilked the Abwehr out of very substantial endowments, in exchange for which they delivered only relatively few genuine outrages, while shrewdly claiming credit for all sorts of industrial, marine, and railroad accidents with which they had nothing to do. [27]

The British media coverage intensified the anti-IRA feeling amongst the population, as did reports that its leaders held meetings with Nazi agents and that the Abwehr supported the S-Plan. It was also reported that German agents were involved in some of the sabotage attacks and that explosives, fuses and detonators were supplied by the Germans. While this may have been the case, Haller denied it. He claimed that had the IRA consulted the Abwehr, 'they would most certainly have deprecated the idea since the military results were nil and it only served prematurely to weaken the IRA forces.' [28]

The Special Branch of the Metropolitan Police had its own intelligence section and undertook investigations into subversion, terrorism and other extremist activity. It was reported to have already known of the 'S' Plan from its network of paid informers but chose not to act on the information as it would give the IRA an indication that their organisation had been infiltrated.

Instead, in response to the early attacks, on 8 February 1939, the British Government introduced two Acts of Parliament, the Treason Act, which imposed the death penalty on perpetrators of acts of sabotage, and the Offences against the State Act, which gave the police greater powers of search, arrest and detention without trial. On 28 July, the Prevention of Violence Bill was passed giving the government powers to prevent the immigration of foreigners, for their deportation and extending the requirement for Irish people to be registered with the British police.

The leaders of IRA groups in each English district who had been identified by informers were arrested and interned. The response was that other IRA members were sent to make attacks in neighbouring districts to hopefully avoid being identified. Having lost significant numbers, the IRA then sent replacements from Eire, who were followed by the police to identify their contacts and more arrests followed.

Following the outbreak of war, the Special Powers Act in Ireland allowed the government to make precautionary arrests of 46 IRA members. Guy Liddell, an MI5 officer since 1931, was transferred to head the counter-espionage section of B Division and wrote in his diary entry for 30 September that an SIS report on Eire was 'somewhat alarmist as regards the internal situation. An attempt at revolution by the IRA does not appear to be out of the question.' [29]

What helped to reduce the chances of open revolution was the press coverage given to the trial which opened on 11 December in Birmingham of 29-year-old labourer Joseph Hewitt, 29-year-old labourer James Richards, 22-year-old Mary Hewitt, 49-year-old Brigid O'Hara and 32-year-old clerk Peter Barnes. They were all accused of murder as a result of the Coventry bombing. The Hewitts were a married couple, and Bridgid O'Hara was Mrs Hewitt's mother. As the prosecution had limited the charge to one victim, all pleaded not guilty to the charge of murdering 21-year-old Elsie Ansell. Three days later, the verdict of guilty was returned, and James Richards and Peter Barnes were sentenced to death. Despite protests, they were hanged in February 1940. The British media largely supported the verdict.

The Emergency Powers Act introduced on 3 January 1940 provided the police with even greater powers of search, arrest and detention for seditious acts and permitted trial by military tribunals, which could order executions. It also gave the Secretary of State for Labour unprecedented control over the labour force. He could dictate where all citizens should work, where they should live, and could command them to allow others to live in their homes if it was necessary for the war effort. He could, and did, order whole villages and towns to be evacuated if the land on which they stood was required by the military. In the south and east of England, most of the beaches were prohibited areas under the Emergency Powers Act. They were being defended against invasion. All directional road signs were dismantled to make it difficult for an invading army to navigate and if anyone wanted to buy a road map, they had to take a British birth or naturalisation certificate to a police station to get a permit. The 'Keep Calm and Carry On' poster was prepared should an invasion be imminent but was never distributed whereas the 'Careless talk costs lives' and 'Freedom is in Peril: Defend it with all your might' posters were seen across the country. The code-name the British used for the suspected invasion was 'Cromwell'.[30]

In John Bulloch's history of MI5 he claimed that intercepted messages and scraps of information gathered from workmen suggested that the Royal Gunpowder Mills at Waltham Abbey, Essex, 15 miles north-north-east of London was one of the IRA's targets. Chief Inspector William Salisbury, the former head of Scotland Yard's murder squad who had been seconded to MI5, was sent to investigate. A week later, on 18 January 1940, there were three violent explosions within seconds of each other at various parts of the factory. The nitro-glycerine plant was almost completely wrecked killing five people and seriously injuring 30. Three of the dead were thought to have been vaporised in the explosion, and the surrounding neighbourhood was badly damaged by the blast. The explosion was reported in *The Daily Telegraph* the following day:

SABOTAGE SUSPECTED IN ARMS EXPLOSION
WORKS VISITED THIS WEEK BY DETECTIVES
SCOTLAND YARD WARNED OF NAZI PLOT
5 DEAD, 30 HURT: MIXING SHED BLOWN TO FRAGMENTS
The possibility that sabotage was responsible for three explosions yesterday at the Royal Gunpowder Factory, Waltham Abbey, Essex, was discussed last

night at a conference between Scotland Yard officers, local police and factory officials.

Information of a suspected plot by Nazi agents to cause explosions at factories had been received some time ago.

Detectives, it was also disclosed last night, had spent a week investigating a suspected sabotage conspiracy at Waltham Abbey factory, where three previous attempts had been made to cause damage.

Five men were killed and 30 injured by yesterday's explosion, the first of which occurred at 10.45 a.m. in a mixing shed.

The shock was felt 25 miles away. Houses in the district were rocked, doors were torn off their hinges and thousands of panes of glass were shattered.[31]

According to Farago, MI5 described it as an industrial accident. Although the news reports blamed Nazi saboteurs, the Government denied that it was enemy action. From the IRA's point of view, it was a great success, an attack on a military target and a message to the British people that the government's counter-espionage measures were not working. The Abwehr diary described it as the work of 'a group of Irish patriots with whom we are in contact.'[32]

However, Bulloch's investigations showed that efficiently made time bombs had been strategically placed to detonate the masses of explosives stored in different parts of the works.

It was months before it could resume production of the material so urgently needed for armaments. Again, all the security branches were called in. Every workman at the factory was interrogated, every visitor who had called there was exhaustively screened. Nothing was ever found to show who was responsible.[33]

Recent research by Richard Thomas into explosions at the works revealed two more occurred on 22 February and 8 April 1940, but his investigation of the evidence indicated they were all caused by human error.[34] At the time though, this intelligence failure led Neville Chamberlain, the British Prime Minister, to demand Kell's resignation and rush through amendments to the Defence of the Realm Act giving the authorities powers to arrest and detain people without charging them with an offence.

Kell's replacement as head of MI5 was Brigadier Oswald 'Jasper' Harker, who was himself replaced by Sir David Petrie in April 1941. Two months earlier, Petrie reported that the Security Service's rapid and poorly planned wartime expansion had led to organisational breakdown and confusion. B Division, for example, had 135 officers distributed among 29 sections, which were sub-divided into about 80 sub-sections. The major reforms he introduced significantly improved MI5's morale and their success in dealing with the threat of sabotage.[35]

John 'Jack' Curry, who worked in counter-intelligence before the war, described MI5 as being in a state of confusion that almost amounted to chaos.

In 1939 we had no adequate knowledge of the German organisations which it was the function of the Security Service (MI5) to guard against either in this wider field of 'Fifth Column' or in the narrower one of military espionage and purely material sabotage. We had in fact no definite knowledge whether there was any organised connection between the German Secret Service and Nazi sympathisers in this country, whether British or alien nationality.[36]

In early February 1940, there were demonstrations and renewed protests against the executions of the Coventry bombers all over Ireland. Eamon de Valera, the president of Eire and previously an IRA member, appealed for a reprieve. *The New York Times* analysis was that 'opinion here is either that two innocent men will hang, or that it is the partition of Ireland by the British who forced these young Irishmen to perpetrate such outrages. Anglo-Irish relations could markedly deteriorate through the hanging of these men.'[37]

Three days later, two mailbags exploded in Euston Station, London, killing four people, and another exploded in the General Post Office on Hill Street, Birmingham. *The Times* regarded both attacks as an Irish reprisal for the Government's failure to reprieve Barnes and Richards. Ignoring the protests, the British government ordered their execution at Birmingham Prison, an action which sparked many protests. Simon Donnelly, former IRA leader, made a speech in Dublin in which he proclaimed, to the crowd's jubilation:

We know very well what outcome we want to this war. We want the enemy, who has kept our people in bondage for 700 years and who continues to pour insults on us, to be pitilessly vanquished. Until such time as the Irish Republic is established, Ireland's youth will continue to sacrifice itself. If the government does not bring foreign overlordship to an end, others must be entrusted with the task.[38]

Who the others entrusted with the task were was not mentioned, but there must have been an expectation that further IRA action would take place. On 21 February *The Times* reported that, since being enacted, the Temporary Provisions legislation had led to the expulsion of 119 people from Britain. The same day two explosions occurred in the West End of London, injuring 13 people. The devices had been placed in rubbish bins.

There was then a lull until 18 March when a bomb exploded on a rubbish dump in London. Liddell reported suspicions in MI5 that the decline in IRA sabotage had been ordered by the Germans and that they had been instructed to lie low until the German invasion.[39]

According to Paul McMahon in his *British Spies and Irish Rebels*, local police forces and the Special Branch were sure that the IRA in Britain had been broken by government action and that they posed little threat. MI5, however, thought the police were complacent and viewed the IRA solely as a sabotage organisation. Liddell commented that, 'provided pillar boxes are not catching fire, and so on, they do not feel that they are called upon to investigate matters too closely. They ignore the possibility of the I.R.A. being used as an espionage organisation.'[40]

Liddell's wartime diary provided another explanation for the failure of the IRA's S-Plan in that the Postal Censorship Office had been given instructions regarding any material obtained which related to IRA activities:

(i)   In cases where suspicious activity is disclosed, and it is not clear whether the activity refers to IRA, the original letter and in the case of telephone conversations a copy of the report on the conversations should be sent to MI5. If the matter is of interest to the police MI5 will send a copy to SB [Special Branch].

(ii) All letters of purely IRA interest are to go in original to HO [Home Office] who after consulting SB will retain or send on the letter in question.

(iii) Telephone conversations of a purely IRA interest are to be sent directly to Sir Norman Kendall [Assistant Commissioner (Crime) Metropolitan Police]. Where they relate to serving members of the armed forces, a copy should be sent to MI5[41]

George Rheam, the new head of Brickendonbury Manor, produced a sabotage training handbook for SOE instructors which summarised what had been learned from the IRA's activities.

NOTE ON 'S' PLAN OF I.R.A.
The Plan pointed out that action was not to be taken when war or a major crisis existed (public opinion too much inflamed), but when major trouble was anticipated (to exploit potential panic) and, if possible, at the beginning of winter (darkness helpful to subversive activities).
The Plan was divided into two Sections – Propaganda and Action – and the latter into two main branches – Direct and Political – but no attempt was made to divide Direct Action into tactical or strategical considerations.

Under Direct Action it was noted that: -

1. Aeroplane and munition factories and stores so well guarded as to provide very inaccessible targets.
2. Public Services are justifiable targets.
3. Key industries to be attacked if possible.
4. Commerce, banking, shipping, ordinary industries constitute important targets, but political implications might render such action inexpedient.

1. PUBLIC SERVICES.

(i)   Public Service lends itself to a wide range of destructive activity through pillar boxes and similar Post Offices.
(a) Dropping incendiary material into post boxes.
(b) Despatch of incendiary packages.
(c) Major operation might be possible, e.g. blockage of G.P.O. tunnel.

(ii) & (iii) <u>Telephone</u> and <u>Telegraph</u> action at a later stage. Tapping, destruction of instruments; disconnection of Police Boxes and other important clearly defined lines; cutting wires and cables.

(iv) <u>Radio</u> and <u>Broadcasting</u> provide doubtful type of operation. Interference; sending conflicting, disturbing news; destruction of instruments or stations; demolition of aerials.

(v) <u>Cables</u> usually well marked and in isolated places. Delay action mine might be involved.

(vi) <u>Water</u> essential to life and pollution etc., rigorously ruled out. Scarcity and rationing, however, a warrantable dislocation. Delay action mines against exposed viaduct pipe-lines in isolated districts, flooding being caused as well as shortage.

(vii) <u>Drainage</u> in large towns object of early stage attack. Method suggested is dumping backs of quick-setting cement in manholes.

(viii) <u>Fire Brigade</u> does not provide major operation for humanitarian reasons. Methods adopted by Black and Tans {former soldiers appointed by British government as temporary constables in Royal Ulster Constabulary to quell IRA activity} for cutting fire-hoses. At last stage of operation of diffused type, false alarms could be raised.

(ix) <u>Electricity</u> (Detailed figures given to show importance and vulnerability of this service). Study of 'Grid' maps should indicate towns which could be isolated by simultaneous attack on two or more alternative feeds. Stations and sub-stations in towns open to attack, but lines in open country are easiest target. Delay action land-mine attention indicated, but must be practically first action before defensive methods and patrolling are adopted. Even if no action carried out, inducement to initiate defensive methods and patrolling would be successful achievement. London eliminated as underground cables inaccessible. Birmingham centre recommended as first point of attack. Liverpool, Manchester, Leeds area as second.

(x) <u>Gas</u> ruled out as damage could not be inflicted without loss of life and ever-present danger of fire ensures that maximum precautions are taken. (Latter consideration applies to petrol stores, explosive factories, etc.)

(xi) <u>Government Offices</u> are a legitimate target. (Sympathetic Government employees can deposit incendiary in cupboard, etc., on Saturday afternoon.
    Older buildings offer more favourable targets. Admiralty, W.O. [War Office], F.O. [Foreign Office], etc. constitute early jobs; and P.O.s. Customs and Excise Offices, Coastguards Stations, etc. immediate or late jobs.

(xii) <u>Transport</u> provides more important target as its serious dislocation would have paralysing effect on industrial and commercial life, and would dissipate energy by necessitating policy of protection and watchfulness.

SECTION I(b)

(a) <u>Sea</u>. Incendiaries in sheds and cargoes. Embargo on interference with navigational lights, etc.

(b) <u>Air</u>. Military aviation a legitimate target. No action during flight in civil aviation, only delaying action on ground.

(c) <u>Rail</u>. Steam and electric, latter including tubes. Action at sidings, junctions, locosheds, involving no personal injury. Electric signal cabins would be target as nerve centres. Railway cloakrooms, luggage stores, sheds constitute first-class objective for incendiaries.

(d) <u>Trams, Trolley-Buses and Buses</u> can all be tackled in garages. Incendiaries may be dropped in petrol tanks. At late stage sugar or molasses or golden syrup (in suitable capsules) could be added to petrol.

(e) <u>Private or Commercial transport</u> open to attack at intermediate or late stage.

2. KEY INDUSTRIES.

These constitute a very important target, especially armament or aeroplane factories. Well-organised or timid attack on particular key industry might have crippling effect on re-armament programmes. Magneto factories offer best examples. General location of particular key industries, chemical, coal, cotton, etc. indicated.

3. COMMERCE, SHIPPING, BANKING, OTHER INDUSTRIES.

Too wide in scope to commit in detail.

4. PRESS, NEWSPAPERS.

Recommended to devise some type of sand or spanner work which will ensure gradually increasing gumming up or disintegration of machines.

5. MORAL SABOTAGE – AUXILLIARY ARM.

(a) Secure from every possible source clean stock of stationery (letter-heads, official envelopes, rubber stamps, etc.) from Government and other Departments. Instructions and documents of all kinds could then be counterfeited. With use of imagination, these could be used to co-operate with direct attack on certain objectives. Use of some safe and express method of delivery as the District Messenger Service recommended.

(b) Desirable for I.R.A. members to join civil defence units, e.g. A.R.P. [Air Raid Precaution]. Would give insight into precautions being taken; would make them respectable; would serve as a cloak; badge, pass, etc. would prove useful in case of suspicion in tight corner.

(c) Destruction of National Register records.

ADDENDUM TO DIRECT ACTION SECTION.

GENERAL PRINCIPLES (N.B. These are given in full).

1. For every man we have, the enemy has ten thousand men. Operation must therefore be so fool-proof and so certain in action as to afford a 10,000:1 margin of safety – i.e. freedom from detection or capture.

2. Included in the very first series of operations should be those major operations at centres where the favourable population available is very small and where at a later date such major operations would be difficult. This would incidentally put off the scent those whose duty it would be to try to locate the headquarters of the organisers of the campaign.

3. The most major and 'centralised' operations should come first. This, because at the first spot of bother, all precautionary measures, special patrolling corps, watch guards, etc. will be put on a war-time basis. These will probably be sufficient to render operations of this type impossible or much more chancy at a subsequent date.

4. The discovery of one dud incendiary or delay action mine would give away the focal points of action, the probable scope of activities, and still more vital, the materials on which the weapons were based. The procuring of even the most innocent of these materials at a subsequent date might conceivably arouse dangerous suspicions. Supplies (adequate to the campaign) of all materials down to the last item, must, therefore, be laid in and suitably divided into at least three dumps in each area so that capture of one would inflict only a 33⅓% blow at that area's organisation.

5. Since the avoidance of the discovery of a dud is important, two units should be incorporated in every case where feasible instead of only one.[42]

Over 330,000 Allied troops were evacuated from Dunkirk at the end of May 1940. On 10 June, Mussolini sided with the Nazis and declared war on Britain and France. The British intelligence community had to come to terms with their diplomatic staff returning home after being forced to leave embassies and consulates as well as losing their contacts in occupied countries. The British government found itself in a quandary.

On 18 June, General Charles de Gaulle, the leader of the Free French forces who had escaped to England, made a speech on the BBC French Service telling the people of France that they had lost the battle but not the war. To assist not just the French but people in other German-occupied countries, Hugh Dalton, the Minister of Economic Warfare, suggested the establishment of another secret intelligence organisation. With the agreement of Sir Stewart Menzies, the new head of SIS, Sir Alexander Cadogan, the Head of the Foreign Office, and the Heads of the Armed Forces, the Special Operations Executive (SOE) was formed on 22 July 1940. Major Joe Holland of the Royal Engineers, who had written about irregular warfare, persuaded Winston Churchill, the British Prime Minister, that groups of five to twenty men operating in secret could do more damage than hundreds of trained soldiers. Churchill agreed and was reported to have ordered Dalton 'to set Europe ablaze by sabotage'. Churchill instructed the SOE 'to rot the buggers from within'.

Headed by Sir Frank Nelson, SOE was divided into three branches: SO1 for underground propaganda, SO2 for unacknowledgeable operations, supporting the resistance groups in enemy-occupied countries and sabotage, and SO3 for planning. D Section became part of SO2. The SIS's training schools were moved to Beaulieu in the New Forest. Aston House became SOE's weapons and explosive research centre, and Brickendonbury Manor became their specialist industrial sabotage training school.

On 11 September 1940, the role of counter-sabotage research and development was given to Victor, Baron Rothschild, a millionaire scientist and Labour Party Peer, who headed B.1.C, MI5's wartime explosives and sabotage section. Their headquarters was in Wormwood Scrubs, the specially requisitioned prison in Hammersmith, London. Following a bomb attack in October 1940, the administration staff moved to Blenheim Palace near Woodstock, Oxfordshire, and the officers moved to an office in St James's Street where other MI5 sections were based. To disguise its real purpose, what was called the 'town office' by its staff had a sign saying 'To Let' outside. Blenheim Palace was known as the 'country house'.[43]

While studying at Trinity College, Cambridge, Rothschild had been a friend of Guy Burgess and Anthony Blunt, who joined Liddell in the counter-espionage section on 7 June 1940, and shared a flat in London with them during the war. His was also listed as one of B.18's experts on the Colorado Beetle – and his dissection skills helped him dismantle enemy explosive devices.[44]

With a staff of four, Police Inspector Donald Fish, a marine engineer, Theresa Clay, and another secretary, Rothschild's role was primarily counter-sabotage. His job was to identify vulnerable British military, industrial, commercial and communication targets and ensure they were suitably protected as well as collecting examples of the various sabotage equipment being used by the enemy.[45] One of his jobs was ensuring that Winston Churchill's cigars were not booby-trapped while others included defusing German bombs and explosives hidden in coat hangers, Thermos flasks, petrol cans and horse droppings. Another job was producing and disseminating counter-sabotage handbooks, arranging factory inspections and providing advice and guidance when asked.[46]

While both the British Fascist and British Communist parties had been successfully infiltrated by MI5 agents before the war, MI5 found them 'insufficiently proactive'. They had concerns that employees of Siemens Schukert, a German electro-plating company operating in Landore, South Wales, were engaged in supplying intelligence to the enemy and providing cover for German spies and potential saboteurs.

Marita Perigoe, a violently anti-British woman of Swedish/German origin, whose husband had been interned as a BUF member, had made it clear that she was willing to do everything in her power to aid the German cause. Rothschild, assisted by Clay, set up an operation to penetrate and control her and her supporters. The 35-year-old Eric Roberts, who had already been infiltrated into the BUF, posed as a Gestapo stay-behind agent. Provided with a fake identity as Jack King, an office on Edgware Road, North London, he identified a number of individuals who passed him intelligence about WINDOW, the anti-radar 'smokescreen' then under development to protect RAF bombers from German radar, the Mosquito fighter-bomber under secret development at de Havilland's factory in Hatfield, research into jet propulsion, Handley Page's airplane factory, secret trials of an amphibious tank and the location of fuel dumps.[47]

Instructed not to encourage direct action against British targets, there was no indication that BUF was contemplating sabotage as a means to achieve their political aims. However, one BUF member Roberts identified as a threat was Ronald 'Noah' Creasey, a Suffolk farmer living in Cranley House, near Eye. He had been temporarily detained in 1940 under Regulation 18B of the amended Defence of the Realm Act but, by his own admittance, lied to secure his release. MI5 monitored his and his wife's movements and correspondence; Mrs Creasey was Women's District Leader for the Eye Division of BUF.

On one occasion, Creasey was reported expressing disappointment that the Germans had not dropped any bombs on the East Anglian aerodromes. On another, he and some friends were apprehended by the control tower of a nearby airfield after a donkey derby. They also had a German friend who had a smallholding in the fens who was reported to be preparing a potential landing strip when he began clearing ground of trees.[48]

Creasey was reported to be passing on information to a contact in London, which MI5 thought could then have been forwarded to the Germans. He reported 75 Flying Fortresses returning to the twin airfields of Thorp Abbot and Horham from the raid on Cologne and on another occasion that 150 American bombers had left to bomb the continent. There was also a report that he had offered to help the German cause by offering accommodation to any of their agents or parachutists. He suggested a possible target for sabotage, which is referred to later.

> The CREASEYS have discussed the possibility of committing acts of sabotage, and of engaging in espionage, against our armed forces, and on more than one occasion they have actually passed on pieces of military information believing that they would be transmitted to the enemy, they really seem to think that anything is justified which would cause Great Britain to lose the war.[49]

Under MI5 pressure, the Home Office, no doubt aware that D-Day was approaching, agreed that Mr and Mrs Creasey be placed under a Restriction Order under Regulation 18A of the Defence Regulations Act of 1939.[50]

Infiltration of the British Communist Party had helped MI5 learn that there was little threat of sabotage from the extreme left. Churchill's agreement to support Stalin in the USSR's fight against Germany had intensified the communists' anti-Nazi stance.

A dedicated Sabotage Section, known as B.1.C. and headed by Rothschild, drew up a list of names and contact details of 36 technical experts on subjects ranging from bacteria and viruses to X-ray, as well as a distribution list for those who needed to be informed of suspected sabotage and how often. This enabled him to tackle the problem of presumed enemy sabotage, for example, bacteriological warfare, time-bomb mechanisms and secret writing. His section generated two reports on general sabotage and sabotage on ships. The former can be seen below, and the latter can be found in the appendix.

SABOTAGE (OTHER THAN ON SHIPS)

All cases of suspected sabotage occurring in the U.K. are reported to the Sabotage Section (B.1.C) in London.

It is the function of B.1.C. to collect all information regarding sabotage from every possible source, whether in the U.K., the Dominions and Colonies or foreign countries and to investigate this information so that all available knowledge of enemy organisations and intelligence services methods may be obtained.

FACILITIES FOR THE INVESTIGATION OF SABOTAGE

POLICE. The investigation of sabotage is primarily the duty of the local police, and a copy of the police report in every case of suspected sabotage is forwarded to B.1.C. via the R.S.L.O. [Regional Security Liaison Officer] of the Region. Every assistance is given to the police to enable them to make their enquiries, and all expert knowledge and information which may be in the possession of the Security Service as a whole is made available.

SPECIAL INVESTIGATIONS. There is available at the London Office a staff of special investigators (B.5), whose services are utilised in certain cases, and practically always in co-operation with the police. The following are types of cases in which a B.5 officer would make personal investigation at the site of the incident: -

(a) Where it is doubtful whether the occurrence is sabotage, or due to an accident, inefficiency or technical default.
(b) Where it appears that great skill was used in carrying out the sabotage.
(c) Where it appears that specialised technical skill is required.
(d) In cases of great gravity evidencing hostile sabotage.
(e) Where there is a possibility of a subversive element among the personnel.
(f) At Service stations, at the special request of the Service concerned.
(g) Where the local police are inexperienced in this form of enquiry.
(h) Where local police ask for assistance.

SCIENTIFIC RESEARCH. B.1.C. has facilities for obtaining the knowledge and advice of many eminent scientists and authorities in almost every branch of research. Laboratory tests, chemical and bacteriological investigations can be obtained.

TECHNICAL AND INDUSTRIAL etc. experts. Expert guidance is available on a wide variety of subjects.

MINISTRIES AND GOVERNMENT DEPARTMENTS. Arrangements have been made whereby information is readily available from the authorities of the Post Office, National Registration Office, Food Office, Labour Exchange, etc.

GENERAL REGISTRY RECORDS. These contain all available information regarding the activities of subversive organisations, agents, saboteurs and suspected persons, etc. an index of actual and suspected saboteurs is also kept in the Sabotage Section.

SOURCES OF INFORMATION REGARDING SABOTAGE

Information regarding cases of suspected sabotage are received from the following sources: -

(a) Police. Copies of police reports are sent to the R.S.L.O. who forwards them on to B.1.C. in urgent cases the information is telephoned.
(b) Special Branch.
(c) Firms employed on work for the Admiralty, War Office or Air Ministry. In these cases the firms report direct to D.1, D.2 or D.3 who in turn notify B.1.C.
(d) Ministry of Supply.
(e) Ministry of Aircraft Production.
(f) Provost Marshal, Air Ministry, via D.3, with regard to cases at an Air Force establishment.
(g) Home Office.
(h) N.I.D. [Naval Intelligence Division] in the case of suspected sabotage at a Naval establishment.
(i) Press.
(j) Ministry of Home Security – Daily Damage Summaries.
(k) Censorship – intercepted letters, telegrams or telephone conversations. Security Service representative abroad.
(l) S.I.S.
(m) Colonial Office.
(n) Foreign Office.
(o) D.S.C. [Defence Security Coordination] New York, through Security Executive.

PROCEDURE

The general practice, when a case of suspected sabotage is reported to B.1.C, is that the local police are informed through the R.S.L.O. and asked to investigate. All possible assistance is given to the police from the resources of the Sabotage Section. Should a prosecution follow, it is undertaken by the police. A copy of the police report is forwarded to B.1.C. through the R.S.L.O. and the information stored in it passed to the Service Department of Ministry interested. The names of the culprits or suspects are included in the General Registry and Sabotage Section indices.

In cases where it is considered advisable for an officer from the Sabotage Section to investigate at the scene of the incident, the R.L.S.O. is informed of the fact. The officer, on arrival, contacts the Chief Police Officer in the district, and in almost every case acts in collaboration with the local police. Before departing, he again sees the Chief Police Officer and gives him the result of his enquiries and conclusions. At the end of the case, the officer submits a report which is dealt with in a similar way to the police reports, except that a copy is sent through the R.S.L.O. to the Chief Constable, if required.

Cases of sabotage occurring in the London area (Metropolitan Police District) are investigated by the Metropolitan Police, and the reports are passed direct between the Deputy Assistant Commissioner, Special Branch, New Scotland Yard and B.1.C.

In the Northern Ireland District, enquiries are made by the Royal Ulster Constabulary, and the reports submitted direct between the Royal Ulster Constabulary Office at Belfast, and the Sabotage Section.

Where cases of sabotage occur at an R.A.F. Station and only R.A.F. personnel are concerned, the case is not necessarily reported to the police and the investigation may be made by officers of the R.A.F.

CASES OF SABOTAGE ABROAD

When cases of sabotage occur on one of our Dominions or Colonies, investigations are made by our representative abroad, with whom we are in direct communication.

When sabotage which affects British interests occurs in the U.S.A. or South America, information is sought through S.I.S.

Should a report or any information be required from one of H.M. Consuls abroad, application is made to the Foreign Office.[51]

Rothschild's section was involved in producing booklets which gave advice to industries regarding protection themselves from sabotage attacks, particularly those supplying the War Office with military equipment. The security of these factories was initially under D Section's remit but, when the SOE took over, by SO2 Section.

In Nigel West and Oleg Tsarev's *Crown Jewels*, they quote Anthony Blunt:

D1, D2 and D3 are the sections which cover the security of certain factories which have secret contracts. As far as I can understand, they are run in a very mechanical manner. The principle is that in each factory a security officer is appointed, and he receives a booklet of instructions from MI5. These booklets give general instructions about anti-sabotage precautions, fencing, guards, etc. in addition the MI5 officers make visits to the various factories and discuss problems with the security officers on the spot. But there are so few in number that they can only visit any one factory about once a year, and there is little doubt that the actual security regulations are not generally applied with any efficiency. Rothschild, whose job is primarily interested in counter-sabotage precautions, has tried to make them more active, but without success. As a result, he is himself organising a scheme for testing out the security of factories by having Field Security men trained to try and get into factories which are supposed to be securely enclosed. He has also tried to make the D officers concentrate on the factories which really matter, i.e. those which are bottle-necks or which are peculiarly liable to sabotage, but without success. D Division also refuses to have anything to do with utility undertakings as not being their business, so Rothschild is now organising schemes for their security. In fact, he is now doing a great deal of the work which they should be doing themselves.[52]

Liddell's wartime diary shed valuable light on MI5's role in counter-sabotage, for example, on 6 March 1940, over dinner with Rothschild and John Maude, a fellow MI5 officer, they discussed sabotage and afterwards he commented in his diary that Rothschild

> ... is quite ruthless where Germans are concerned, and would exterminate them by any and every means. He outlined our [anti-sabotage] problem as we saw it [need to concentrate defences against chemical sabotage weapons] ... Rothschild mentioned the existence of a rocket bomb known as the UP bomb [Unrotated Projectile]. I gather this is a somewhat epoch making invention but whether it has reached the production stage or not is not clear. ... We shall probably find that it is being made in a small tin shack in the corner of a field and that anyone can get inside with the aid of a tin opener.[53]

The following week, Liddell detailed a French report that the Germans were using a chemical labelled 'Purgen' as a secret ink and Cutex liquid, a nail polish remover, as a re-agent. It stated that if the two substances were found in a man's kit, it was conclusive proof that he was a German agent. He also mentioned having found documents hidden in hollowed-out cigars.[54]

A fortnight later, he reported Rothschild going to France to discuss with his French counterparts questions relating to bacteriological warfare. 'He wanted to know whether he should take the opportunity of finding out what the French are doing generally about sabotage.' When Rothschild returned, he reported to a committee about the French counter-sabotage plans.[55]

4

Arthur Owens, Gwilym Williams and the Welsh Nationalist Party (Part 1) – 1937–August 1940

With the IRA's sabotage plan not achieving its objective and their potential for assisting the Germans in an invasion of England much reduced, the Abwehr's attention turned to the more extreme fringes of the Welsh Nationalist Party (WNP) and Plaid Cymru. They were calling for a more active struggle to achieve independence. Reinhard Heydrich, the then head of Heinrich Himmler's intelligence service, had some undercover agents in Wales during the 1930s. These included Heinrich Kuenemann, the managing director of a German engineering firm with a branch in Cardiff; Professor Friedrich Schoberth, a visiting professor at Cardiff University; Franz Richter, the manager of an enamel company at Barry; and a nurse in Pembrokeshire. The German consul in Liverpool, Dr Walter Reinhard, concentrated on the Welsh extremists in North Wales and was expelled from Britain for spying in 1939. The others managed to escape before they were interned.[1] One has to imagine that part of their work included identifying potential German sympathisers and anti-British Welsh nationalists and passing their names to Heydrich.

Although the WNP had organised political demonstrations during the 1930s, their most significant direct action was an incendiary attack on 8 September 1936. After the British government decided to develop an RAF bombing school in Wales, three WNP members – dramatist and lecturer Saunders Lewis, poet and preacher Lewis Valentine and novelist D. J. Williams – set fire to the school at the Penyberth training camp and aerodrome on the Llyn Peninsula in Gwynedd. They then walked to the police station, admitted the offence and spent the evening discussing poetry in a police cell. Convicted at the Old Bailey in London, they spent nine months imprisoned at Wormwood Scrubs. When they were released, they were greeted by a crowd of 15,000 Welsh Nationalists at a pavilion in Caernarvon.

While there was some anti-British feeling in sections of the Welsh population, there was little, if any, enthusiasm for sabotage. Anti-terrorist legislation and media coverage of the IRA's sabotage campaign meant that known Irish activists were arrested. Suspected activists were reported to the police or stopped and searched when they arrived or left Holyhead, Fishguard and other ferry ports for Ireland. In an attempt to avoid the controls, an Irish couple who regularly visited Wales were stopped at Goodrich in Pembrokeshire and explosives, detonators and fuses were found stuffed inside their briefcase.[2]

Following the outbreak of war, most of the 156 people from Wales who were interned as potentially dangerous foreign nationals were Germans, Austrians and Italians and their families.[3] However, one of them, 40-year-old Arthur Owens, a Welsh manufacturer of battery accumulators living in London, was arrested as a German agent.

While Owen's biography is covered in Charles Wighton and Günther Peis's *Hitler's Spies and Saboteurs* and in other books, this account is largely focussed on the documents in Owen's personnel file which shed light on his involvement in sabotage operations.

Owens grew up in Cardiff but lived most of his life as an electrical engineer in Canada where he became naturalised. In 1933, when he was 34, he returned to England and settled in Morden, South London, and set up the Expanded Metal Company manufacturing ship batteries for the Royal Navy and the Kriegsmarine, the German Navy. As this involved regular visits to German ports, in 1936 he agreed to a request from SIS to report to the Admiralty on technical and military observations seen on a trip to Kiel and other German shipyards. His SIS contact was Lieutenant Colonel William Hinchley-Cooke, known as 'Cookie'. What financial arrangements were made to recompense him for his intelligence work are unknown. In 1937 he was living in Hampstead and was a member of a German club in Bayswater, known as a centre of German spying activity. According to Wighton and Peis, it was there that he obtained the address of an Abwehr agent he contacted in spring 1937 at the Metropole Hotel in Brussels, offering the Germans his services in exchange for money.

In the summer of 1938, Owens was approached in Hamburg by Dr Rantzau, the cover-name of Major Nikolaus Ritter, the head of the Abwehr's counter-espionage section with oversight of sabotage activities against Britain, including infiltrating agents. He had visited the United States as a Luftwaffe officer the previous year and recruited some Nazi agents.[4] Ritter had learned that Owens was an ardent Welsh Nationalist with little loyalty to Britain, claiming that the British government had swindled him and his father out of hundreds of thousands of pounds over one of their inventions. As he had a perfect cover for visiting German ports and a keen interest in members of the opposite sex, it made it easy for Rantzau to bribe him with offers of large sums of money and attractive women. In return, Owens provided him with military, economic and political intelligence.

Farago, who interviewed Ritter after the war and had access to captured Abwehr files, claims Owens, known to the Germans as 'Johnny', already had four wireless sets and 35 sub-agents across Britain, including Welsh nationalists, who were supplying him with intelligence.[5]

How aware 'Cookie' was of Owens' dealings with the Germans is unknown, but he had given him the code-name SNOW, said to be a part anagram of his name. Special Branch was ordered to follow him and open his mail to and from Hamburg hoping to identify other German agents. In their reports, he was described as 5' 3" with a thin face, pale complexion, dark brown hair and often wearing a pin-stripe suit and tie.[6]

By 11 August 1939, Owens had left his wife and taken Lily Funnell, his girlfriend, and Alexander Myner, a business associate, on a trip to Hamburg. While he was away, his wife reported him to the police as head of a group of German agents who had been trying to recruit her, their son and other family members. She told them that she had been with him on a trip to Germany and had met Rantzau (Ritter) and other German Secret Service officers. He had stolen RAF codes, was operating a wireless set and had hidden coded messages wrapped in tin foil in his mouth and cigarette lighter when he passed through Immigration controls.

By the time the three returned to London, Britain had declared war on Germany and German residents were being arrested and interned. A railway worker warned SNOW that the police were searching all passengers returning from Germany so he threw his incriminating documents out of the train window. He was not arrested straight away but, perhaps to frighten him, Lily and Myner were taken to Kingston Police Station for questioning. He rang 'Cookie', his MI5 contact, and arranged to meet him at Waterloo Station where he was promptly arrested and interned in Wandsworth Prison under the Defence Regulation 18B.

Using Lily and a 'Mr X's statements, TAR questioned SNOW over the next few days, and he willingly provided details of his dealings with the Germans. It was undocumented, but one imagines that he would have been told that he would be executed for treason if he refused to comply. He told TAR of the wireless training he had been given by Herr 'Thieler', the head of the Abwehr's wireless section, and that a new wireless set was to be delivered to the left luggage office at Victoria Station. He also told him the time he was to transmit, 04.00 hours, the frequency he had to use, 60 MHz, and the cyphers Lily had been given for coding and decoding messages.

These cyphers were sent to boffins in MI8(c), the Signals Intelligence Service's German section, who, by early-1940, had successfully broken them allowing them to decode and read all the captured agents' in-coming and out-going messages. Along with the breaking of the Germans' Enigma code, the British knew the agents' cover-names and when they were due to arrive.[7]

On 4 September, SNOW agreed to become TAR's first double agent and transmit messages to the Germans to assure to them that he was safe and still working for them. TAR's aim was to develop someone who the Germans trusted well enough to send him details of the arrival of other espionage and sabotage agents. He also wanted them to send explosives, arms, ammunition, wireless sets and money as well as to identify their targets so that counter-sabotage measures could be put in place and security increased. Over the next two years, TAR used SNOW to convince the Germans that, like the IRA, there were some Welsh nationalists who would also be prepared to undertake sabotage operations. He later recalled that his golden rule for the officers running double agents was that his personality needed to be stamped on every message he transmitted.[8]

This was the beginning of a series of elaborate deception schemes which MI5 played against the Abwehr throughout the war. Apparently, five B1a case officers supervised nearly 120 double agents, over 25 each. Six were German but the rest were from 35 different countries, including Britain. Amongst the 11 turned at Camp 020 were some of the most successful double agents of the war.[9]

While Owens' family and friends believed him to be imprisoned, they did not know that TAR had arranged for the wireless set to be picked up and taken to the prison. It needed repairing by Lieutenant Colonel Yule as SIS had dismantled it to see if it contained anything and had failed to reassemble it properly. Yule then made a gramophone recording of Owens' 'fist' when he transmitted his first British-inspired messages to the Abwehr. This allowed MI5 to send messages pretending to be SNOW.[10]

Arrangements were made with the Secretary of State to have SNOW's detention order lifted and on 11 September, TAR transferred him to a top-floor flat in Kingston-upon-Thames where, having broken up with his wife, he lived under supervision with Lily. MI5 even paid for it to be furnished. TAR reported that

> Having fixed up the set, we transmitted a message to Germany at 11.30. 'Must meet you Holland at once. Bring weather code radio town and hotel. Wales ready.' This message was allowed to go after SNOW had explained that in accordance with the instructions he had received from RANTZAU, he was to meet him in Holland as soon as possible in order to pick up the weather codes which would enable SNOW to give the Germans information regarding the state of the weather over certain places in England, which they intended to bomb. The reference to Wales is explained by the fact that RANTZAU is anxious to get hold of a Welshman, who is a permanent member of the Welsh Nationalist Party. Apparently, RANTZAU wishes to use this organisation to create disturbances in Wales. Once he has established this link, he proposes to supply them with arms, which will be brought up the Bristol Channel.[11]

Although there was no response to this message, TAR arranged SNOW's passport and papers for a trip to Holland, trusting him to return. Before he left, he contacted an MI5 agent, a fanatical Welsh nationalist who worked as an immigration officer in Swansea docks. Referred to only as 'WW', he was asked if he would be willing to be trained by the Germans as a saboteur.

SNOW went to Swansea to meet WW before going to Rotterdam on 16 September. On his return, he reported to TAR that he had told Rantzau he had set up the wireless set in a new flat and given him WW's details: 'I had made three trips to Wales to organise the Welsh Nationalist Bombing Scheme. I had contacted a gentleman there (in South Wales) – just an ordinary sort of man, not very flush with money – who was in touch with the head of the Welsh Nationalist Organisation, who I understood was working in North Wales.'[12] He also reported that the Abwehr

> ...proposed to make their first attempt, provided that the Bristol Channel was not considered too dangerous, to land somewhere between Penmaen in Oxwich Bay and Rhossili Bay, which is North of Worms Head, their object being to make an effort to sabotage what they believe to be ammunition dumps and steel works at Briton Ferry near Port Talbot.

If this attempt failed or if they considered the Bristol Channel too dangerous, they were to try and land near Linney Head with the object of sabotaging the military positions and supplies around Pembroke Dock and the Milford Haven seaplane base (I believe very considerable supplies of petrol are stored there).[13]

When he was asked to arrange a meeting between WW and Rantzau in Brussels in mid-October, SNOW replied that 'there were certain other things to be arranged first and that I could not just pick up a man and send him without knowing anything about him, though so far as I know, he is perfectly reliable.'[14]

For some unspecified reason, possibly not being very good at German, WW declined the offer of being trained as a German saboteur and recommended his friend, 52-year-old Gwilym Williams, to go in his place. When SNOW was informed, he told MI5 that WW's replacement 'should look, speak and act like a Welshman and have enough knowledge of German to be able to understand what was being said when Rantzau and his colleagues were not speaking English.'

Born in 1887, Williams lived with his second wife at 42 Mount Pleasant Hill, Swansea. After 29 years in the South Wales Constabulary, in January 1939 he started his own private enquiry agency investigating divorce cases and knew WW through his work as a court interpreter. GW was described as an imposing figure of 6' 2", a Welsh Nationalist and claimed to be a linguist proficient in 17 languages or dialects. He was also an explosives expert who had learned his skills in the artillery during the First World War. Rantzau was told that he was ready to go to Belgium to be trained in sabotage and would start work attacking English targets as soon as the necessary supplies could be delivered.

While it was an opportunity for TAR to infiltrate another agent into the Abwehr, there was no mention of GW being paid by MI5. SNOW received payment per piece of information, £20 for some, £100 for others. One imagines that he would have received a commission for finding a useful agent, and that Williams would be paid a retainer fee and a bonus for results. It was mentioned later in SNOW's file that he had been given £20,000 in US dollars and told that if he could persuade a Spitfire pilot to fly his plane to Germany, he would be given £50,000 and a job for life.[15]

The change of plan entailed further negotiations with Rantzau, who eventually agreed to the first meeting between the Abwehr and GW in the Savoy Hotel in Brussels with the Welsh representative having to arrive before SNOW and carrying an identification coin.

Before that, SNOW was instructed to investigate the best location in South Wales for a U-boat to deliver explosives, rifles and ammunition, to supply nightly weather reports and to collect intelligence on RAF Squadrons between London and South Wales, particularly in the areas around Guildford and Bristol. He was also asked to find the exact location of all the reservoirs in the country, especially those around London and advised to get a gas mask and leave Kingston for a few days.

Rantzau told him that, although it would be the last weapon they would use if all else failed, they were going to start a concentrated bacteriological warfare against Britain. A far as SNOW could gather, 'their main objective would be the reservoirs, into which they would endeavour to drop bombs charged with bacteria.'[16] When SNOW went to meet Williams and WW in Swansea, he hired a car and drove along the south coast of Wales to Haverford West discussing the best places where submarines could safely drop supplies. They decided that the ideal location was Oxwich Bay, on the Gower Peninsula, about 10 miles west of Swansea.

While in a pub in Pontardawe, SNOW reported overhearing two men discussing the cost of living in Belgium and the exchange rate, which convinced him that one must have been a German agent attempting to recruit a member of the WNP.[17] The Abwehr's foreign outpost in Belgium was AST Brussels, headed by *Obersturmführer* Servaes. It mission was to organise many of the projects against England, whereby agents were parachuted from planes or landed by fishing boats or submarines.[18]

On his return to London, SNOW related the result of the meeting to TAR, telling him that he found Williams quite suitable. He then reported to the Germans that WW's replacement was an ardent Welsh Nationalist, who travelled around Wales as an enquiry agent investigating road accidents.

Invited to London for discussions, SNOW warned GW that he might be questioned about sites of ammunition factories, oil refineries and steelworks in Wales and activities in various Welsh ports. Consequently, MI5 supplied him with a crib sheet which he was to learn off by heart.[19]

MI5 allocated Williams the code-name GW and two days before their departure, he and SNOW met Lord Cottenham (Mark Pepys), who had been a racing driver before the war and was then the head of MI5's transport section, at the Bonnington Hotel in Bloomsbury. Cottenham's heavily redacted account of the interview revealed that:

> SNOW told [redacted but obviously Williams] that, when in Holland, he would be introduced to a doctor who is in charge of the Secret Service organisation of the Western area, i.e. England and as far as America. [Redacted] must play up the fact that in his capacity as an inquiry agent investigating road accidents, he gets about Wales a good deal and sees working conditions of the people and how they are pressed and exploited by measures decided upon in a Parliament largely composed of Englishmen. He must dwell on his intensely pro-Welsh convictions, and also indicate that he has pro-German sympathies.
>
> SNOW warned [redacted] that he would probably be questioned about sites of ammunition factories, oil refineries and steelworks, and also about activities at various ports. [Redacted] asked for instructions at this point.
>
> I said he could certainly tell about any factory, oil refinery or steelworks of which the existence is a matter of local knowledge, e.g. I.C.I. Works at Landore, and the new munitions factory going up in Bridgend, near NEATH.
>
> SNOW reverted to the U-boat project. He said that perhaps anything up to two or three submarines would come over to land explosives for the blowing up of factory sites etc. No rifles were mentioned. SNOW said that [redacted] will be expected to point out, on an ordnance map, the most suitable place

for landing this stuff. I said that, after due consideration, we should appear to approve this project and express gratitude for anything that could be sent to his confreres in the way of arms, explosives and money to support a rising.

I then drew a map of Oxwich Bay, indicating the two coves towards the eastward end of the bay as being most suitable for the purpose. I did not leave with [redacted] as he had a good memory. [...] He said he would attribute his information to what he had heard all his life from fishermen along the coast.[20]

On 19 October, Lord Cottenham checked to ensure SNOW and GW had all the correct documents for their trip, and when Williams asked him what he was to say if he was asked who had sent him, Cottenham reminded him,

No one in the Welsh Nationalist Movement was supposed to know of his visit to Brussels except [redacted] who had asked him to go in his place. He should say that, when told of this whole project, it seemed almost too good to be true – and here he might make a smiling apology to SNOW – but he had arranged to come over and find out all he could about it because, if true, it is the kind of chance that his Welsh Nationalist friends have been waiting for for years.

I then put him through a catechism of names of prominent members of the Welsh Nationalist Party which I had instructed him to learn by heart.[21]

On their return from Belgium, they were both interrogated at length about their visit and told to write down a detailed account of each day's activities. In GW's report, he admitted that they had been taken to Antwerp by taxi and visited a large block of offices opposite the Canadian Pacific Railway wharf. Here they were introduced initially to three 'doctors', one of their wives, and finally to the 'Commander', Dr Rantzau.

Farago identified the other men as Major Brasser, Abwehr Chief of Air Intelligence, and *Kapitanleutenant* Lohar Witzke, the head of the Hamburg Abwehr's Section II, its sabotage section, with specific responsibility for attacks in Britain.[22] After a lunch of bottles of beer and sandwiches, they discussed the need for him to receive training in wireless telegraphy so that communication could be established between them. However, for the rest of the trip, he was given sabotage training, specifically in how to make and use explosives.[23]

When he told Rantzau that under no circumstance would he purchase any containers, explosive chemicals or fuses, Witzke told him not to worry on that score. 'We have a band of Belgian smugglers who operate from Ostende across the English Channel and know how to elude the British coastal patrols. We'll send whatever your friends need via them, carefully camouflaged as their usual contraband, like canned goods, cartons of cigarettes, tins of coffee and other such things.'[24] Photographs of these sabotaged items were in the counter-sabotage file.

Whether Liddell was involved in Williams's interrogation is unknown, but he knew enough about their case to comment that, 'the idea is that they should both be employed in blowing up factories and works of importance in this country, for which ample funds are to be available. There is a suggestion that explosives should be sent by submarine and landed somewhere on the Welsh coast.'[25]

SNOW brought back microphotographed documents which included the names of two British nationals already working for the Germans in England. He also reported that GW told Rantzau that he had about thirty men in South Wales he could rely upon to do sabotage work, and further the aims of the Third Reich. According to Hennessey and Thomas,

> They discussed arrangements for the moving of some of these Welshmen to factories in England for sabotage purposes. The German also wanted some advice on the landing of explosives, and it was decided that Oxwich Bay was the best spot on the South Wales coast, where the submarine could be brought fairly close into the shore. The Germans had previously suggested to SNOW, 'who had jibbed', that they should drop explosives by parachute from an aeroplane. They also suggested that they should drop pamphlets in Welsh for propaganda purposes. The Germans seemed to be very keen that the explosives should be brought by submarine. At this stage they mentioned that it was quite possible to get explosives into the United Kingdom by ship, especially through Liverpool. The explosives were to be brought in large quantities but packed in small cases and small bottles, so as to make the storing of them much easier.[26]

SNOW was given over £500 and offered £30,000 in American dollars to pay members of the Welsh Nationalist Party to commit acts of sabotage. He refused, arguing that it was far too dangerous and demanded payment in English currency. GW was given £50, which more than covered his expenses but during the conversation, Rantzau let slip a remark that the IRA were being run, or were going to be run, by the Germans. Apparently, this remark came out as a result of the Commander saying that 'they had made a mistake in paying their people here in dollar notes, instead of paying them in English currency.' They were also told that Flemish Nationalists were 'all organised and that as soon as the Germans advanced into Belgium, they would start sabotage and a revolution.'

SNOW and GW were asked when they returned to Wales to find two or three places where sabotage materials could be safely stored; to find the location of various explosive stores and ascertain if any means could be found by which they could be entered to steal explosives. They were also asked to suggest propaganda that would encourage Welsh people to want peace and think of ways of disseminating it; to ascertain whether Lloyd George could be persuaded to influence Welshmen against joining the forces and to suggest that Welsh troops taken as prisoners should send letters home demanding separate and preferential treatment. They were told about the wireless training they would receive and advised to start collecting stamps as a hobby as the Germans would be able to send micro-photographed messages on them, which could be read using any reasonable microscope. According to GW,

> The Commander on this occasion also dealt with various methods of sabotage, but for the time being, he stated that he would deal principally

with incendiarism. He gave a lecture on the method of preparing material for this purpose and stated that the following formula was the safest and most effective to work, viz.

Potassium Chlorate; 3 parts, Sugar; 1 part

Grind the two to a powder separately and thoroughly mix without friction in a large bottle or stone jar by rolling the bottle or jar and thoroughly mixing the two ingredients. Then obtain a small cork-stoppered bottle, boil the cork in paraffin wax so as to exclude all air from the cork, place a small quantity of undiluted sulphuric acid in the bottle, place the cork in the bottle after piercing the cork so as to enable the acid to filter through. Next cover the cork with a piece of paper of previously tested thickness, such paper being waxed except a small portion in the middle covering the hole in the cork, this would enable the acid to percolate through the paper in a given time. The mixture of potassium chlorate and sugar should be placed in a paper or other kind of bag, or a cardboard box and the corked end of the bottle inserted into the mixture at the scene of the act of sabotage. Experiments should be carried out with various thicknesses of paper so as to ascertain the time that the acid will take to percolate through. By these means, the margin of safety for getting away from the scene can be established. The various other means of committing acts of sabotage will be demonstrated to me at a laboratory when I visit Germany in about a month's time. The necessity of especial care in carrying out the work and of finding two or three places for storage of material has been emphasised by the blunders of the I.R.A. whose claims for self-government will also be considered at the proper time. [...] During this interview two wooden contrivances containing fuzes were given to my friend. They were well made.[27]

The targets they were given were not identified specifically but included the destruction of dockyards, ships, sheds used for the storage of stores and cotton, electricity generating stations, aerodromes, munition factories and munition dumps. It was suggested that such destruction should be carried out not only in Wales but also in places like Bristol, Manchester, Liverpool and Glasgow.

Two methods were agreed for the delivery of the sabotage equipment for their mission. It would be brought by submarine to within 10 miles of Oxwich Bay and transferred to a small fishing boat on the flashing of an agreed signal; or be dropped by parachute to a site on the top of the Black Mountains indicated by a fire. The time and date for the drops would be arranged by wireless message.

He estimated that he could count on the assistance of about 500 Welsh Nationalists, most from North Wales, and Rantzau recommended that they applied for jobs in Bristol, Manchester, Liverpool, and Glasgow and committed acts of sabotage 'when the opportunity offered itself. Such men were then to be bought jobs elsewhere as compensation for their services, the means to buy the jobs and all expenses in connection herewith to be obtained from my friend.'[28] SNOW reported Rantzau's opinions:

Germany wished to live in peace with England and France; that they did not desire to kill a single Englishman in this senseless war. They had sufficient work in Germany in connection with the National Socialist Movement to keep them occupied for the next hundred years and for this reason they did not want war. The talk about the Maginot Line being impregnable was all rot as the Germans could walk through it at any time they wished, but they did not want to kill their young men or the young men of England and France in doing so. They did not intend forcing matters at all, but were anxious for this silly senseless war to end, as they wanted nothing better than peace with England and France and for this purpose they would appreciate any acts of sabotage committed by the Welsh so as to bring to an end this unnecessary war, which serves no useful purpose either to Germany or England or France, and the way to bring this war to a quick conclusion is to cripple England internally so as to make her listen to sense and reason without slaughtering the youth of the various countries concerned in the conflict. He went on further to say that the sinking of an occasional ship would not expedite the termination of the war as England had such abundant means of transport at her disposal, but internal disruption by means of sabotage at places of vital importance from a National point of view would be of immense value in bringing those in England who are responsible for the conduct of the war to such a state of mind as would cause them to listen to reason. In the matter of Poland, it was Germany's intention at the proper time to give Russia 200,000 square miles of Polish territory, 80,000 to the Poles, 60,000 to the Jews, and retain 100,000 square miles for herself.[29]

In return for the Welsh saboteurs' assistance, SNOW was told that when the terms for peace were discussed, the Germans promised to include self-rule for Wales. However, there was one issue which worried him. He was told to expect women agents to meet him in Britain, but he claimed that working with women was dangerous. It later transpired that the Abwehr arranged for Mrs M. C. M. Krafft to post him packs of £5 and £10 notes at regular intervals as his payments and that when GW needed funds, he had to ask SNOW. MI5 already had Krafft, a British subject of German origin, under surveillance as a German agent.[30]

According to Farago, by the end of 1943, there were as many as a dozen female agents held at Camp 020 'including "Francine," a little Belgian, "Nelly," an aristocratic French lady, a simple girl from Brittany, and a Czech redhead'. A Mrs Maud, described as a sweet-voiced, kind lady with grey hair and twinkling eyes helped put these 'girls' at their ease.[31] Whether any of these women were involved in sabotage is unknown as none of their details have come to light.

Whilst in Brussels, SNOW was provided with some detonators for use in sabotage operations which he handed over to MI5. They were hidden inside a wooden block 4" by 3" and ½" thick which prompted an enquiry as to the possible import of such blocks hidden in the structure of suitcases.

Once back in Swansea, GW joined Plaid Cymru to make contact with what he called the 'Movement'. On 27 October 1939, his first communication from the Germans arrived, a letter from Mrs L. de Ridder of Antwerp enclosing a selection of Belgian stamps on which microphotographed instructions had been hidden. The agreement was that all the relevant detail would be included in the fifth paragraph of their letters.

At the beginning of December. Liddell reported the case of Mr Millbank, a BUF member, who reported to Special Branch that 'a Miss Dorie Knowles had asked him to communicate various information to Germany relating to explosives being manufactured by the firm in which she works. Both the girl and Millbank have been interviewed, and we are suggesting to Special Branch that her house should be searched. She is only seventeen, but nonetheless a sophisticated and a confirmed liar. Her mother, who is of German origin, is in a mental home.' As there was no further mention of Knowles, one imagines that MI5 thwarted her offer to sabotage the explosives.[32]

Nothing related to sabotage was mentioned in SNOW's file until just before Christmas when he arrived back from another trip to Antwerp. He reported to TAR about the weather reports he had to send, a new wireless procedure and German disappointment with the IRA. They had 'spent a lot of money on the IRA and have had no really satisfactory results. They are placing their bombs in the wrong places and are thoroughly unreliable. They suggested that if things do not go better they would have to put SNOW in touch with their leaders.' SNOW was asked

if he could get information about the source of the Manchester and Birmingham water supply and to find out if possible whether by blowing up the water mains leading from the reservoirs the water supply in Manchester and Birmingham would be cut off. He has also been asked to find out whether the reservoirs are guarded by troops as they are anxious to find out if it would be possible to put bacteria into the water. They intimated that during his next visit to Antwerp he would probably meet an expert in bacteriology from Berlin. It was also suggested that he might bring back samples of bacteria to this country. B.3.[33]

SNOW must have had brought back information for GW as, just after Christmas, he reported to TAR that he had visited London

...to receive additional instruction in receiving and transmitting Morse, and also in the mixing of components used for incendiarism and explosives. I appreciate that he may not be qualified to give the required instruction, but I am of opinion that it would be made possible for me to visit him occasionally for the supposed purpose of receiving such instruction as, if what I have been given to understand is correct, I would then probably be seen in his company and frequenting his house, these facts would strengthen what has been said to our 'special friends' concerning our activities.[34]

In early 1940, while SNOW was involved with other Abwehr agents, GW was concerned with collecting intelligence and in February he sent a further MI5-inspired report on 'Welsh Activity'.

Attention has been called in the publications of the Welsh Nationalists to the heart-breaking situation in the South Wales coalfield. Destitution and poverty and unrest are growing apace.

Referring to the 8,000 women and children from London's bombed slums that have been sent to the Rhondda Valley it is said that a capitalist war has thrown these refugees into homes exploited by that same capitalist power – English Capitalist Government. There is no end to the misery and devastation caused by English Government. On it rests the responsibility for the bare homes of the Rhondda and the Devil – London's homeless ones received by Rhondda's homeless. What a sum of human misery.

Wales has been told by every English Prime Minister from Ramsey MacDonald to Chamberlain; English Government will not lift a hand to help South Wales. Largesse in the shape of schemes of social service or Depressed Areas Acts it distributes with a certain calculated abandon. The real problem it deliberately evades by mass transfers of population, to which only the Assyrian and Babylonian Empires offer any parallels.

When Welsh Nationalists argue with South Wales socialists, we are told to remember that the class is more fundamental than the nation and that the Welshman's loyalty to his English fellow worker must take precedence over all other loyalties. Unfortunately, however, the traffic along this RUE INTERNATIONALE is only one way, from Wales to England, never in the other direction.

Now that most of the overseas markets for South Wales coal have been lost there is, under the present system, only one other market in which it can be sold, and that is the home market. An attempt has therefore been made to secure for South Wales coal an increased share of this market, which has hitherto been the preserve mainly of the Midland and Lancashire coalfield. Here was a splendid opportunity to demonstrate working class solidarity, and to rise to the heights of the international doctrine, by the sacrifice of part of the prosperity of the English coalfields to the salvaging of the South Wales miner. Alas for the international utopians of South Wales! The English miners have defended their monopoly as selfishly and stubbornly as any of the capitalists, they profess to despise.

South Wales is faced with ever rising prices and stationary wages plus an enormous unemployed population. We have no means of gauging the hardships of the European countries under German control. What we do know is that this winter will bring to our fellow countrymen in South Wales, under English control, hardships beyond even the bitter experiences of the last twenty years.

The only hope of the sorely tried people of South Wales is an early peace, bringing the restoration of at least a proportion of the lost European markets. England can, at a pinch, dispense with the Continent; for Wales, it is essential. If Mr Churchill means to extend the war into 1944 and 1945, then he will, among other things, complete the work he began in 1925. The Welsh Nationalist Party, on the contrary, will never cease to reiterate that peace as soon as possible is the supreme interest of Wales.[35]

He heard nothing from Germany until a second envelope of stamps from de Ridder arrived on 5 April 1940. It included the address of a dead letter box: Louis de Mercedes, 57 Rue Bosquet, Osborne residence, Bruxelles. A friendly letter was duly sent but, as the Germans invaded Belgium on 10 May, the Postal

Censorship Agency returned it, thus temporarily restricting Williams's link with his 'friends' to mentions in SNOW's traffic.

MI5 interpreted the Germans' requests to SNOW for regular weather reports not just to test the reliability of their agent but to assist the Luftwaffe in their plans for the invasion of Britain. Nothing came of these reports, and there was no mention of any sabotage activity until later in April when, according to an entry in the Abwehr II War Diary, a Reuter message reported a fire in aircraft works in Denham, Buckinghamshire, which was assumed to have been the work of Welsh Nationalists. Whether there was a fire, whether it was sabotage and whether it had been undertaken by Welsh Nationalists is unknown. A note alongside read 'Sheer guesswork again', suggesting that the Abwehr was claiming all reported fires in Britain as being the work of their agents in the hope of impressing German High Command.[36]

Also in late April, Rantzau asked SNOW to arrange a trip by trawler to meet him on the Dogger Bank in the North Sea and bring another British man who would be willing to be trained in espionage and sabotage and then be sent back to Britain to carry out attacks. MI5 recommended Sam McCarthy, one of their informants; Masterman described him as a reformed criminal after a long career of petty larceny, drug smuggling and a confidence trickster.[37]

Code-named BISCUIT, McCarthy was suitably briefed and introduced to SNOW. Both men were driven to Grimsby from where, with the agreement of the Fisheries Board, they set off in *Barbados*, a trawler, on 19 May. However, BISCUIT suspected that SNOW was being controlled by the Germans and SNOW was under the impression that BISCUIT was as well.[38] Attempting to convince him that he really was a German agent redoubled BISCUIT's conviction so that when a plane circled overhead two days later and flashed a recognition signal, BISCUIT ordered the captain to extinguish the trawler's lights and return to Grimsby, during which time he kept the drunken SNOW under armed guard. This was two days before the agreed rendezvous.

When SNOW was searched back at Grimsby, some unauthorised documents were found in his possession which he claimed he had been given by a friend in the hope that they could be sold to the Germans. To rescue the situation, Masterman sent a submarine with a naval crew to the rendezvous point with orders to sink the enemy U-boat or if it was a trawler, to board it, capture Rantzau and bring him back to Britain. There was no U-boat or trawler on 23 May. It was a particularly foggy night so the crew returned and SNOW sent a message to Rantzau apologising for failing to rendezvous using the fog as an excuse but added that he had recruited a volunteer.

Once the mutual misunderstandings were discussed, MI5 decided to accept SNOW's bona fides but had to make arrangements for BISCUIT to travel to Lisbon under cover as an importer of Portuguese wine and with MI5-inspired disinformation. Rantzau told him that he was beginning to question SNOW's form but that a German born in South African, known as Rose, was waiting in Belgium to be sent to England to act as his subagent and even told him where he was to be parachuted. There was no indication that this man was to co-ordinate sabotage activity or that BISCUIT received any sabotage training, but he was told to prepare for parachute drops of equipment after he got back.

Major Julius Boeckel, aliases Karl Bruhns, Beyer and Ernesto Werner, worked at Ast Hamburg, known as Ast X. Interrogated after the war, he admitted that he had been involved with the training and despatching of agents between September 1940 and February 1942. He reported that Rose had been recruited by Kapt. Lt Tornow of Ast Hamburg and trained in map reading and sabotage. Given SNOW's contact details, Tornow took Rose to France in July or August 1940 to superintend his departure via Eire but that contact with him was never established. Boeckel described him as aged about 21, slim, 1.65m tall with blue eyes.[39]

SNOW also provided details of Schmidt and Björnson, two Danes who had been trained in espionage and sabotage and the first Abwehr agents to be parachuted into England in late-August 1940. Their account is detailed later. He also gave the Germans a general report on conditions in England, but Rantzau was dissatisfied, claiming that he could read about them in British newspapers in Berlin. According to Wighton and Peis,

> At once he became almost pitiful, pleading and protesting that he had done his best. It was clear to Randzau [sic] that Owens was in a state of hysteria. Randzau decided things must be getting tough in Britain for German spies, but he was scarcely prepared when Owens, half-weeping continued:
> 'Is it not enough that I've brought you this RAF chap? He can tell you more than I can ever find out. Things are getting worse and worse. I can scarcely find out anything. You've no idea what it's like. From now on I'll have to concentrate on sabotage only. Getting information is too risky. My brother-in-law is Welsh and is foreman in a munitions factory outside London. If you can give me explosives, he will help me to start explosions.'[40]

Before they returned to England, SNOW was given another wireless set, probably for the new agent, another questionnaire to complete and $3,000. Dr Rudolfs, the head of the Abwehr's sabotage section in Lisbon, at Rantzau's request, gave SNOW a supply of fuses cleverly disguised as fountain pens in a presentation box.

Even before their return, Liddell was convinced that SNOW was in communication with the other side.

> They, first of all, wanted him to give them the name and address of a suitable individual in the North of England or Scotland who would be prepared to receive explosives. They subsequently cancelled this, and asked him to find out whether his friend in the Welsh Nationalist Movement would be prepared to act in this capacity. This may possibly indicate a change of [invasion] plan. Some time ago we heard that the points for the invasion were Anglesey, Scotland, and the SE and E coasts. The latest message to SNOW may mean that the Germans will go for Ireland first, and subsequently for Wales. On the other hand it seems to be an indication that an attack here is not likely to be impending. In fact, the indications from SS sources are confirmation of this view.[41]

SNOW took BISCUIT to South Wales to visit Williams who drove them to Oxwich Bay. While there, SNOW took photographs and, after visiting various inns, met the WNP representative at Ystalyfera, near Swansea. They were told that there were few local members, meetings were poorly attended, they had little funds and whilst there was sympathy for the Irish nationalists: 'their ideals were similar, but the methods adopted by certain sections of the Irish people did not meet with the entire approval of the Welsh Nationalists.'[42]

Their seeming lack of enthusiasm for direct action one imagines was reported back to the Germans, but they appeared ready to spark some action by infiltrating three agents, presumed by SNOW to be saboteurs.

In August, when Williams was told by SNOW to make arrangements for a safe house for them, he discussed it with Robertson who told him to liaise with Mr Ford, MI5's German-speaking MI5 officer in South Wales.

5

The Nazis' pre-invasion saboteurs in Eire – 1940

In Mallmann Showell's *U-Boats at War*, he states the Abwehr asked the German Naval Command in September 1939 whether agents could be landed in Ireland to organise resistance. Kapitan zur See and later Kommodore Karl Dönitz was unenthusiastic. His uncommitted but amenable fobbing off did not work, and just a few days later, powerful forces in the High Command were back, asking for the Abwehr's plans to be given highest priority. At this stage, several people started working on different parts of the same plot without knowing of each other's existence and therefore produced a rather vague and disjointed set of plans, which resulted in the most chaotic operational consequences later on.

The U-boat Command's Operations Department produced a set of blank orders because it was not yet known which boat would carry out which mission. The main instructions were:

1. Two agents are to be landed in Ireland, somewhere near a railway line with connections to Dublin.
2. The choice of the exact location is left to the U-boat commander.
3. This mission must not be discussed with anyone anywhere. The crew may not even talk about it while on board the boat. Anyone breaking this order will face the death sentence.
4. The agents are to be landed in a rubber dinghy of the type used by the Luftwaffe and this must be destroyed immediately after use.[1]

Research by Enno Stephan, John Bowyer-Bell and Mark Hull revealed that, following the German's success in occupying much of Western Europe in only a matter of months, the Abwehr had plans to develop their relationship with the IRA to recruit and train Irish agents to be infiltrated into Ireland, Wales, Scotland and England to create espionage and sabotage teams. The idea was that in return for independence from England, Irish, Welsh and Scottish nationalists would assist the Luftwaffe and Wehrmacht in their invasion of Britain.

An initial problem was that the wireless transmitter the IRA had been given by the Abwehr was not powerful enough to transmit clearly, and the operator was 'less than efficient'. The first successful transmission, a request for weapons and equipment, was on 22 October 1940, eight weeks after the start of the war. The Abwehr's War Diary complained that the message did not indicate which supply route was possible.

Lahousen was reported to have been less than impressed with the IRA's sabotage of left-luggage offices, letter-boxes and telephone coin boxes. He was expecting attacks on military and industrial targets.

Marwede was equally unimpressed and was reported as sending a letter urgently requesting the IRA to carry out its S-Plan and to be more effective against military as opposed to civilian targets.

The IRA were not pro-Nazi or even pro-German. They were anti-English and keen to avail themselves of money, weapons and ammunition in their struggle to drive the British out of Northern Ireland. However, animosity against the IRA had increased because innocent civilians had been killed during their sabotage campaign. There was also the non-aggression pact signed between Germany and Russia and the subsequent invasion of Catholic Poland that had turned many Irish people anti-Nazi; they accused the IRA leaders of making 'a pact with the Devil'.[2]

In July 1939, Jupp Hoven and his younger brother Viktor were trained in a military camp west of Berlin and then joined the Brandenburg Regiment. This was a specialist Commando unit set up on 25 October 1939 to train German expatriates, fluent in foreign languages, in physical exercise, small group tactics, parachuting, the manufacture of explosives and incendiaries using locally purchased materials, their use in demolitions, covert operations, use of vehicles, aircraft and enemy weapons. Infiltrated behind enemy lines, their missions were to destroy their command, communication and transport infrastructure.

The Abwehr's explosives training camp, known as Quentzgut, was on the banks of Quentz Lake, about ten kilometres southwest of Brandenburg and about 65 kilometres west of Berlin. Its cover-names were Quatsch and Quelle. Under the command initially of *Obstlt* Mauritius and later Major Poser, the buildings were used for instructional purposes in sabotage, handling of explosives, incendiaries, judo, etc. Its 'graduates' went off on sabotage missions to Britain and other countries across Western Europe, the Middle East and Africa.[3]

The lake and dense forest made it an ideal training camp for Brandenburger Commandos. Although the locals heard explosions and gunfire, the site was relatively quiet after its early graduates were sent to the Eastern Front. The two-storey house had been confiscated from a Jewish boot merchant. It had a large drawing room, twelve bedrooms and a cellar. A new building was constructed alongside with a garage on the ground floor and with classrooms and a laboratory upstairs. There was an explosives testing range in the grounds with lengths of railway track to practice. Security was paramount. Surrounded by War Office land, there was a high wall around the estate and armed guards to ensure privacy.[4]

Jupp Hoven had seen action in the French, Belgian and Dutch campaigns between May and June 1940 before serving in the Sonderstab Hollman, a unit formed in the autumn of 1940 for the invasion of the British Isles. By the end of 1940, the two brothers, known to the Irish prisoners-of-war they recruited as the Owen brothers, were working for the Abwehr in Paris.[5]

When Germany invaded the Channel Islands, they transferred prisoners they considered useful for their cause to France. As early as January 1941, Hoven was entrusted by Abteilung II to set up an Irish Brigade, men trained in bomb-making, sabotage and espionage missions in Eire and England. They were to cooperate with the IRA in the event of a German invasion of Eire.

With Clissman's assistance, he selected a group of fifty Irishmen to be sent to Friesack, a military camp, designated Stalag XX (301) in the village of Damm I, about 95 kilometres north-west of Berlin. They included John Codd, Frank Stringer, William Murphy from Enniscorthy, Patrick O'Brien from Nenagh and Andrew Walsh from Fethard, County Tipperary. Those unwilling to cooperate were sent to Sachsenhausen concentration camp.[6]

The Irish Brigade had been envisaged by Haller and his Irish Section in Abwehr II as being similar to the Irish Legion formed by Sir Roger Casement in the First World War. Their plan was for a body of highly trained men, similar to the Brandenburg Regiment, keen and reliable and who would fight with or without German troops in a National War for the Liberation of Ireland, or later, as defenders of Ireland against British aggression. However, when it became clear that there were only about 150 Irish prisoners and that their moral fibre and loyalty to both Ireland and Germany was suspect, the proposal never won the support of Abwehr II or Ausw Amt.

Canaris and Lahousen's policy of passive sabotage might also explain why the proposal was largely unsupported. Haller and Stringer's interrogation reports shed more light on the Brigade's organisation and personnel trained for sabotage and espionage operations.[7]

Throughout Lahousen's diary there were recurrent references to Allied shipping losses and explosions in the UK attributed to sabotage.

LAHOUSEN has contemptuously dismissed each reference as 'puffing'. He explained that enemy losses announced in the Allied press were frequently seized on by Abw II and claimed as the work of the IRA or Abw II agents. This looked well on paper, and never failed to impress the OKW [Oberkommando de Wehrmacht, the German Army's High Command], but in the absence of some sort of proof, such as a report from the agent responsible, they fooled no-one at Abw II. Similarly, when the British press announced unexplained explosions and the more hysterical papers darkly hinted at sabotage, this was taken by Referat WN to mean that the IRA had been at work. If any of the chronicled disasters should turn up to have been engineered by IRA saboteurs, this should be regarded as pure coincidence.[8]

In Lahousen's interrogation report there was a section on the German Embassy in Dublin:

From the War Diary, it is apparent that HEMPEL, the Ambassador in DUBLIN, was better informed on the IRA nexus than HALLER had previously suggested. There is still some doubt as to what extent he was put in the picture before the agent sent over had become the subject of official enquiries by the Irish government. Both WEBER-DROHL and GORTZ, contrary to instructions, appear to have approached the Embassy through Irish intermediaries, probably at a time when they were in danger, and lost their heads, since the IRA was obviously incapable of protecting them. KEITEL seems to have been opposed to Abw activity in EIRE, since this necessarily complicated diplomatic relations between GERMANY and EIRE. LAHOUSEN relates that HEMPEL visited him in June 39 – the last time HEMPEL was in GERMANY – and tactfully sounded LAHOUSEN about stories which had appeared in the Irish and British press that the German Secret Service was backing the IRA. LAHOUSEN blandly assured HEMPEL that there was no foundation in such rumours, and HEMPEL, greatly relieved, advised LAHOUSEN not to compromise Irish-German relations by any such action in the future.[9]

The MI5 comment proved that Hempel knew of Abwehr agents as he had been asked to pass on instructions to them. One entry in Lahousen's diary, dated 3 August 1940, caused huge embarrassment for the Irish government when the press reported that Veesenmayer had informed the Abwehr that Seán Russell would receive advance warning of the German invasion of England by a red flower pot being shown in the window of the German Embassy, 58 Merrion Square, Dublin.[10]

According to Wichmann, the Abwehr officer in Hamburg responsible for sending agents sent to Ireland, Britain, France and Switzerland was Lieutenant Hilmar Dierks, but he was killed in a motor accident in Hamburg in September 1941. Like SOE and SIS's agents, as well as giving agents codenames and cover names, Dierks allocated them numbers. Several Lufteinsaetze, air operations, were undertaken from Brussels to drop agents into England with wireless sets to report back to A/M Funkzug. Wichmann recalled three men supplied from the Sonderkommando in Hamburg, of whom two were reported killed or captured as soon as they landed as nothing was heard of them again. The other, referred to only as 3275, and who sent messages back throughout the war, is referred to later. He made no mention of agents being given a sabotage role.[11]

The secret Luftwaffe unit given responsibility for parachuting espionage agents and saboteurs into Britain and other countries was Gruppe Rowehl, a long-distance reconnaisance formation. Set up by Göring under the command of Colonel Theodor Rowehl, it was the German equivalent of the Special Duties Squadron, priding itself on accurate navigation by night in preferably cloudy conditions. Using the Heinkel III, two of its pilots, Gartenfeld and Knemeyer, reported dropping agents into Britain.[12]

Although not directly involved in sabotage, the first German agent destined for Ireland was 28-year-old Günther Schutz, sometimes written Schuetz, the son of a metal manufacturer in Schweidnitz who had trained as a soldier before being selected by Hauptmann Dr Friedrich Praetorius, the head of the Abwehr's economic warfare section in Hamburg. Schutz was trained as an agent in Hamburg and sent to London in early-1938 on an intelligence gathering mission. This was to report on the IRA's S-Plan which involved him travelling around England taking photographs of factories, using the cover as a representative of Remy & Co. He was assisted by a Portuguese man named Pierce who he attempted to recruit into the Abwehr. Although Pierce agreed, he informed MI5, who used him as a double agent, code-named RAINBOW, to send the Germans faulty reports on bomb damage, transport infrastructure and air defences until 1943.

Schutz returned to Hamburg in August 1939 and was prepared for another mission in Ireland, but this was cancelled in July 1940 and rescheduled for September. Before that, however, Ernst Weber-Drohl, a 61-year-old Austrian former wrestler and circus strongman, was trained for a mission to liaise with the IRA in Eire. He had performed a strong man act in fairs in Eire before the war and fathered two illegitimate children who he could claim to be visiting. Two days before the voyage, his wireless operator refused to accompany him, arguing that he could not cope with his harsh attitude. Determined to complete his mission, he arrived at Wilhelmshaven pretending to be a war correspondent with two heavy suitcases. On 9/10 February 1940, he was brought by U37 to Sligo Bay but the waves were too high for a dinghy so he was taken to Killala Bay. Once he and his suitcases were in the dinghy, the U-boat submerged but from his periscope the captain realised he would capsize. Against the rules, a crew member came to his rescue and managed to help him and his luggage into the wooden dinghy kept on board and rowed him to shore near Enniscrone. His Afu wireless set was ruined by the water and he claimed to have lost all his personal cash in the sea.

He made his way to see Stephen Hayes, the IRA chief, and then caught the bus to Shankill, Killiney, near Dublin, to meet Seamus 'Jim' O'Donovan, the IRA's chief weapons expert who the Abwehr referred to as 'Agent Hero'. Although the wireless set was useless, Weber-Drohl handed over new wireless transmission codes and $14,450 in cash for the IRA. It was thought he kept $650 but gave O'Donovan the following message:

'The Pfalzgraf Section very urgently requests its Irish friends and IRA members to be so good as to make considerably better efforts to carry out the S-plan, which they received some time last summer, and to be more effectual against military as opposed to civilian objectives.'[13]

As shall be seen, this request was largely ignored; the IRA's major interest being in the Abwehr's money.

Drohl's mission in Ireland lasted less than two months as he was arrested in Dublin on 24 April 1940 in violation of the Aliens Act. However, his cover story that he was shipwrecked coming from Belgium to be reunited with his two illegitimate sons was believed, and he was released, only to be re-arrested by Irish Intelligence two days later and charged under the Emergency Powers Legislation. The Irish Justice Department was lenient with him, and he was released. The German Embassy supported him with £15 a month, but he made more by performing an act as 'Atlas the Strong' at the Olympia Theatre, all the time under the surveillance of G2, the Irish Military Intelligence Service, and the *Gardai*.

During this time, he had a relationship with Rosalind Park, a married woman, who bore his third illegitimate child in May 1942. When she reported him to the police for harassing her and claiming that he had told her he had been landed by submarine, he was imprisoned again on 13 August 1942. He spent the rest of the war in gaol and was deported to Germany in 1947.[14] Whether it was Drohl or another German agent is uncertain but Eduard Franz, an Abwehr recruiter, trainer and despatcher, reported that an agent brought by submarine to Eire with a camera in a suitcase had been arrested at a railway station because he spoke with a slight accent.[15]

On 10 May 1940, the SIS showed an anonymous letter to Guy Liddell which was believed to have been written by a German and handed in to the Home Office.

> It speaks of a plan for the invasion by air and sabotage on the S.E. Coast on Saturday night. The alleged German said that he had landed here some two months ago, and he had been deputed to carry out certain acts at Lee-on-Solent. In view of this message we are recommending the internment of all enemy aliens in the East Coast area and the restriction of ordinary aliens who had entered these areas since the war.[16]

Three weeks later, Liddell noted that the author was a British crook and that no action was to be taken against him as it had encouraged the government to intern enemy aliens.[17]

Fears of a German invasion of Eire led Liddell to visit Liam Archer, the head of G2 in Droitwich, who told him that there was nothing to prevent the Germans from landing and that he could not envisage resistance being maintained for more than a week. However,

> ...he thought he could persuade his ministers to lock up the Fifth Column in Eire ... As regards organising for defence, some 30,000 men were called up in December last and half of them disbanded... the difficulty was that they had no equipment. Orders had been placed in this country as much as 18 months ago, but it had not been possible owing to pressure of work for the firms to fulfil them. He mentioned to me quite privately that in some quarters of the [Irish] Government it was thought that these arms were being intentionally withheld owing to doubts about the use to which they might be put ... I gather the principal requirements are Bren guns, ammunition, trawlers, coastal patrols and aeroplane parts ... We raised the questions with Archer as to the possibility of some sort of staff talks in preparation for a possible German landing in the interim. We told him that in our view it was a thing which might happen any day. He said that he was a soldier and that this was more of a matter for the politicians ... Archer seemed to think that if the Germans landed in Eire, there would be general resentment and a certain amount of resistance but he thought there might be quite a number of people who would say, 'Oh, well. They are here in force, we can't do anything about it,' and be quite prepared to accept the situation. He was quite emphatic that Eire would be thinking about her independence and that many people would not mind Great Britain getting a licking. On the other hand, somebody who had expressed this view to him concluded by saying, 'But what would happen to us if they did?'[18]

6

Operations MAINAU and SEAGULL: Dr Hermann Görtz and Helmut Clissman – May–August 1940

Despite the Abwehr's failures in Eire, Canaris gave his consent for Operation MAINAU, a plan to infiltrate another Abwehr agent to initiate sabotage against the British. On 5 May 1940, a month later than planned, a 50-year-old lawyer and Abwehr officer, Dr Hermann Görtz, was flown out of Fritzlar airfield and parachuted from the Heinkel at 5,000 feet, landing near Ballivor, County Meath, in full Luftwaffe uniform and with $165,000 for the IRA. Using the cover-name Heinz Kruse, he walked 80 miles to Laragh in the Wicklow Mountains, where he was picked up by O'Donovan. Having damaged his transmitter on landing, Görtz was unable to maintain wireless contact with Germany so used the secret ink he had brought with him to post letters to a dead letter box.[1]

Guy Vissault de Coetlogon, a Breton Nationalist who is referred to later, claimed when he was arrested towards the end of the war, that 'he had never heard of Dr Herman GOETZ, but he remembers the OWEN brothers [one was Jupp Hoven] mentioning the case of a German officer who landed by parachute in Ireland in about the Spring of 1940. This officer, according to DE COETLOGON, buried his uniform in order to escape arrest, but the uniform was later found, and he was taken into custody.'[2]

The British Intelligence Services already knew about Görtz as he had visited England in 1935 with a girlfriend on an espionage mission and, despite claiming he was collecting military sensitive intelligence for a book arguing for the enlargement of the RAF, he was convicted and spent four years in Maidstone Prison. Deported to Germany in 1939, he was prepared for a similar mission in Ireland. It is likely that MI6 were aware of the overseas dead letter boxes and had his mail opened and read. It is also probable that they informed the Irish Military Intelligence of Görtz's presence in Eire who arranged to have him followed, opened his mail and tapped his phone-calls to identify his IRA contacts.[3]

On 21 May, Görtz met Stephen Hayes, the IRA's chief of staff, who had sent details of Operation KATHLEEN, a plan for the invasion of Northern Ireland by German troops to Germany, the previous month. He asked Görtz, whose mission was to act as liaison officer with the IRA, for money and arms.

Although Görtz undertook to liaise with various Irish political and military figures to encourage a national revolt against the British, he quickly became disillusioned, deciding that the IRA was too unreliable.

Shortly after he arrived, his parachute, identity papers, his World War medals, $20,000 in cash, documents about Ireland's defence infrastructure, potential military targets including airfields and harbours and Operation KATHLEEN's plans were found following a police raid on the house of Michael Held, a supposed IRA safe house. Shown the document, Liddell commented in his diary that there was 'an elaborate questionnaire in Good English but in German handwriting, which shows that preparations are being made for a landing in the north and also at Dingle Bay and Ventry Bay.'[4] The discovery allowed the British and Irish military to accelerate their joint defences to a prospective invasion, known as Plan W.

Forced to move regularly to evade arrest, one property Görtz stayed in was 95 Seafield Road, Clontarf, in Dublin, where he set up his repaired wireless set. While there he got to know 33-year-old Joseph Andrews, a jeweller's assistant who lived in the house with his wife and daughter. Andrews was described in his heavily redacted file as a 'shrewd, forceful personality. Not averse to doubtful tactics to attain his object.' He got to know Görtz well, acted as his courier and, over time, acquired a copy of his codes. These he gave to his friend, Robert Campbell, an ex-bank robber who, after sixteen years in America, reappeared in Dublin in 1941 with instructions to try and sell the codes to an American consular official.

However, when Andrews was arrested in October 1941, he collaborated with the *Gardai* and gave details of Görtz's work before being released as a double agent. On 27 November, both men were arrested; while Andrews was released again, Görtz was charged and detained in Curragh Military Prison. While inside, he continued to communicate in code with his supporters, unaware that his messages were being intercepted and the code was broken. Pretending to be German Command, G2 successfully persuaded him to outline his activities and contacts since arriving in Eire.

Unknown to the *Gardai*, Andrews had agreed to continue Görtz's work and sent messages via a sailor friend to a dead letter box in Lisbon. MI6 was aware of this so had them intercepted, opened and transcribed before being left for the Abwehr. When Andrews' sailor friend was arrested, he sent some coded messages through the German Legation in Dublin offering to continue Görtz's work. In these he referred to Robert Campbell who then worked in the Supply Department of Short Brothers and Harlands, aircraft manufacturers in Belfast, who 'was very well placed to recruit others, to collect information or to organise sabotage or strikes'.[5]

No doubt Campbell was investigated, but no details were found in Andrews' file. He was arrested again on 19 August 1943 and interned for the rest of the war. Released in August 1946, he set up a charity for German children, but when he was told the following May that he was to be deported to Germany, he swallowed a poison pill and died.[6]

One of the documents in Görtz's file shed light on a planned sabotage operation that never happened.

Message No.64: Text – 'Time opportune for working occupied Ireland, men waiting. Notes up to fifty useful or as you have then do not disappoint.'

Explanation – He had made no approach to anyone to work for him. However, he knew quite a number of people in Northern Ireland who were more pro-Axis than otherwise, who would, he felt, be prepared to assist him if he was in a position to pay them. The phrase 'men waiting' was intended to be impressive as Goertz had advised him that when one is dealing with his people, he must 'talk big' or he would get no hearing. If he had succeeded in extracting big money, he would have pocketed the bulk of it, but he would have spent some of it to collect reports sufficiently good to extract further monies. He had not worked out precisely what he intended to do, but if he got money in sufficiently large quantities, he would have spent some of it in anti-British propaganda in the North and some of it on the collection of intelligence reports. He believed he would not have got enough money to make sabotage attempts a paying proposition. He had no idea as to what organisation would be required but felt that there were a number of disaffected people who would be willing to help if they were paid for it. Generally, he had not thought that far ahead, and might in fact never have developed the idea. His immediate preoccupation was money for himself. He had vaguely realised he was getting a bit out of his depth but resolved to hold on as long as there was a possibility of extracting money.

'Notes up to fifty useful' meant that he could change bank notes up to £50 denomination without arousing suspicion.

Besides message 64 the following relate to this subject:

No. 43: 'With money have men ready for sabotage etc. in occupied Ireland.'

No, 56: 'Men in occupied Ireland impatient for action.'

No. 58: 'Present IRA is a potent and reliable organisation in occupied Ireland, capable of useful work. Have established reliable contact,'

No. 78: 'IRA in occupied Ireland potent organisation hampered by lack of money. IRA in Eire unknown quantity for integrity since HAYES affair. Large number of people throughout country waiting for organisation to express their attitude against Britain. We have contact with these elements and want your full cooperation.'

Although it is realised that messages 49, 56 and 55 cannot be disclosed, they are of interest as showing the frequent reference made by ANDREWS to his contacts in Northern Ireland. They may all be covered by CAMPBELL and certainly there is no evidence to show that ANDREWS or his contacts in Northern Ireland had actually done anything or supplied any information.[7]

Liddell's investigation of the IRA's links with Germany led him to the conclusion that they obtained intelligence of military importance in Northern Ireland.

The most important instance of this is the case of Dr Hermann GOERTZ, who landed in Eire in May 1940 by parachute with a special mission from the Germans to examine the possibility of a proposal made to them by the IRA for an attack on Northern Ireland, and to establish through the IRA an intelligence service which would provide the information necessary for carrying out this attack.

It is, however, most important to distinguish between members of the 'Old IRA', who include most, if not all the members of the present Eire Government, and members of the 'New IRA', who, under the leadership of Seán RUSSELL, Stephen HAYES and other persons, are engaged in activities against this country and against the Eire Government themselves.[8]

In another Abwehr operation, two other German agents, Walter Simon aka Simonsen and Andersen, and Willy Preetz, were dropped by U-boat at Brandon Bay, south-west Kerry, on 12/13 June 1940. Their official mission was to report on weather conditions designed to help U-boat operations around Ireland. Simon was to contact Werner Unland, a German import/export agent living at Gresham House, Kingstown, and Preetz was to contact Welsh nationalists with a view to sabotage.

They split up on landing and Simon, disguised as a naturalised Australian named Karl Anderson, was caught getting off a train in Dublin the following day. The Irish government sentenced him to three years' imprisonment. Herbert Wichmann, the Abwehr intelligence officer who was to be in charge of the Abwehr stelle in London following the invasion, reported Dierks sending Simon on this mission but Ritter had sent him on an espionage mission to England in 1938, where he was imprisoned for six months for breaching the Aliens Order and then deported. It was likely that Irish Intelligence were aware that German agents were being infiltrated and were on the look-out.[9]

Preetz, who had married an Irish girl before the war and acquired a passport in the name of Paddy Mitchell, had been given large amounts of British and American currency. He travelled across Ireland by taxi and managed to survive three weeks in Dublin, successfully sending weather reports until he too was arrested in July. The censored Irish press reported on suspicious activities by foreigners which increased public awareness of potential agents operating in the country. One imagines rewards were offered for information leading to arrests.[10]

On 9 June, Liddell noted in his diary that, following a document being found on the railway lines near Manchester suggesting that the Germans and the IRA were planning an attack on the West Coast and that caravans might be used for wireless communication or for arms, he contacted the Home Office with a request that a general search of all caravans be undertaken across the whole country.[11] Just over a week later, he noted that 'We have prepared a memo on sabotage. A certain amount has been going on but it is in a way remarkable that there has not been far greater activity, particularly as regards ships. It is, of course, possible that an organisation is lying low, awaiting the moment of maximum embarrassment. Personally, I think the IRA are more likely to be concerned than any other body.'[12]

On the same day, confirming the public's heightened security awareness, Liddell commented:

The Air Force produced two very sinister photographs taken from the air. One had the appearance of an arrow, said to be pointing in the direction of an Ordnance factory. It led from a Church said to belong to the Under Order. Then some 20 miles away, was a bow in the middle of a plantation.

Everybody on the Swinton Committee became wildly excited. Investigations have been carried out with the following results. The Under Order turns out to be the Undenominational Church, and when it was built the local borough council insisted there must be a car park. This car park made the head of the arrow, which broadened out rather naturally at the tail, where the drive came up to the front of the church. There was a wireless receiving set in the church but it could not even pick up the national broadcasts ... The bow was in the middle of a pheasant covert on Lord Iliffe's estate. It had been there since 1923 and showed up white on account of the chalky ground. Its purpose was to provide food for the pheasants. At the moment it is planted with potatoes which had been put in in accordance with the 'Dig for Victory' campaign. It would have been completely covered with green in about another 10 days. The local Air Force unit took the law into its own hands, cut down the trees and laid them across the offending space.

[...] As regards sabotage, it would be wrong to take a complacent view. It may be that the Germans are holding their hands until the day of invasion, when we may see things going on, either through the agency of the IRA or possibly of certain elements of the BUF.[13]

While Germans, Austrians, Italians and Japanese civilians resident in Britain were interned, so too were 750 members of the BUF. Whether they had any plans to commit acts of sabotage on behalf of the Germans is not known; but this would have reduced the chances of such action.

In the early years of the war, the Nazis planned bizarre propaganda campaigns to undermine the morale of the British public, including telling them that they had to eat frogs for breakfast. A fake copy of London's *Evening Standard* in 1940 says: 'There are billions of frogs hopping merrily round the British Isles. Their vitality should be harnessed.' They reported that there were plans to kill the deer in the country's parks to make sausages and pies. Another piece of propaganda, said to have been issued by 50,000 Hitler supporters in Whitehall, branded British men 'abject cowards unwilling to leave your Mamas' and Wifey's Apron String'. Professor Charles Andrew, an MI5 historian, commented on the Nazi's propaganda that 'a lot of it looks like it was produced by Monty Python.'

On 18 July 1940, SNOW received a message that the Germans were proposing to drop someone in Ireland or England, and he was asked to provide information as to what documents and formalities were needed to get into England from Ireland. Liddell noted that 'It is very important that he [the new agent] should not fall into the hands of the military or the parashots [sic] either here or in Ireland until we have got his whole story and instructions.'[14]

An intercepted Abwehr cypher about ten days later referred to a man called Donaghue arriving in the next few days but no mention of a Donaghue appeared in SNOW's file.[15]

7

Operations SEALION, GREEN, LOBSTER, SEAGULL and WHALE I and II – July 1940

Canaris would probably have been aware that in Hitler's *Mein Kampf*, Britain was described as one of Germany's natural allies so when the German invasion of Norway, Denmark, Holland, Belgium and France had succeeded so quickly, he knew Hitler must have changed his mind when he was ordered to assist in the invasion of Britain. On 22 June 1940, the day France surrendered, Canaris told Colonel Hans Pieckenbrock, the head of Abwehr III, its espionage section, that Hitler's plan to invade Britain would need the rapid infiltration of spies and saboteurs. Five days later, he warned Lahousen to make urgent preparations.

Günther Peis, who interviewed Lahousen after the war and gained access to his war diary, liaised with journalist Charles Wighton to publish *Hitler's Spies and Saboteurs* in 1958. Without access to the British and American intelligence reports released following the Freedom of Information Acts in Britain and the United States, there were some chronological inaccuracies and names of individuals were changed to avoid them being arrested.

In his war diary, Lahousen mentioned a discussion he had with Canaris about the exceptional difficulties of a naval invasion in which he was told, 'But that does not matter to us in the Abwehr. Whether or not there is to be an invasion – and I must say, as a sailor all my life, some of these desk-bound field-marshal heroes have just no idea what an amphibious operation involves – we in the Abwehr have to get as many spies and saboteurs into England in the next few months as possible.'[1]

Lahousen had to plan combined espionage and sabotage missions and, as shall be seen, the immediacy of the situation led to many of these operations being undertaken in haste, being poorly planned and ending in disaster.

Haller devised Operation WHALE (WALFISCH), a plan to infiltrate an agent by seaplane onto one of the Irish lakes but Canaris specifically prohibited operations in Ireland so this operation was aborted in July 1940.

The German plan to launch an amphibious and airborne invasion of Britain, code-named Operation SEALION (Seelöwe) included Operation GREEN (GRUN), a diversionary plan to invade Ireland. According to the Oberkommando der Wehrmacht's planning directives, Abwehr I and Abwehr

II were tasked with collecting intelligence on Britain's defences, landing an invasion force in Ireland and investigating the possibility of creating or inserting a fifth column into Britain that would undertake sabotage and link up with the invading German ground troops. The planning and preparation were the work of Major Klug and his staff at their Berlin office, but all Abwehr operations in Ireland were the work of Dr Veesenmayer.[2]

Having defeated the French, Operation LOBSTER (HUMMER) I, the first stage for the invasion of Ireland, began on 7 July 1940. Christian Nissen, also known as Hein Mueck, piloted a motorised French trawler to the South Coast of Ireland and in the early hours of the morning three men were transferred to a rowing boat with a considerable quantity of explosives hidden in their luggage. They included two German South-west African saboteurs, 19-year-old Otto Dietergartner and 22-year-old Herbert Tributh, and Henry Obed, a British Indian, as their guide. Their mission was to travel from Eire to England and undertake sabotage that would help the planned German invasion.

However, their lives as secret agents in Eire lasted only two hours. After landing at Toe Head, about 5 miles south of Skibbereen, County Cork, they hitched a lift in a truck to the bus station at Drimoleague from where they bought tickets for Cork. It appeared that Obed had told the driver that they had just come off a boat at Baltimore and asked him if he knew any members of the IRA. It was probably the driver who reported them to the local *Gardai*, but one of their officers was reported as knowing immediately from looking at Obed that something did not appear right. When the Baltimore harbour authorities denied any knowledge of them, the authorities in Cork were instructed to arrest the three men when they got off the bus.

Taken to Mountjoy Prison in Phibsboro in the centre of Dublin, they were interrogated by Irish military intelligence officers. None of them carried any identification papers and they subsequently claimed that they were told by their superiors that these would not be needed as German troops would shortly be arriving in Eire. There was no mention of them rendezvousing with SNOW or GW and no mention of Wales, so whether they carefully avoided mentioning them, or were acting independently, is unknown.

When their luggage was searched, £850 and various camouflaged sabotage equipment was found. The first document in Dietergartner's file included the following details. Although his first name was Otto, the Irish police generally referred to him as Dieter Gartner.

Dieter Gartner
Amongst a number of personal effects which included some toilet requisites, the following were also found:-
1 Roll of insulting tape.
3 Detonators No. 8 enclosed in small wooden slab 2¼" x 3" x 7/16".
1 Cutting pliers.

Henry Obed
Amongst a number of personal effects including toilet requisites were found:-
1 Leather belt into which was sewn 3 lengths of safety fuse each 2'3" in length.

1 Cutting pliers.
1 Roll of insulating tape.
8 Incendiary grenades.
4 Tins labelled 'Prepared French Peas'.
3 Detonators No. 8 enclosed in small wooden slab 2¼" x 3" x 1/16".

Remarks:
With regard to the detonators No. 8, these were found inserted in wooden blocks which had been bored out to receive them and a slip of timber glued over to conceal their presence. The lengths of fuse sewn into the two leather belts were the ordinary safety fuse used for the ignition of detonators and blasting charges. It was in good condition.

The eight incendiary grenades were found to be of the thermite type but containing a high percentage of sulphur. The grenades function very effectively burning with an intense flame which, if brought into contact with inflammable material, would start a conflagration. Weight of each grenade = 8 ozs.

The four tins labelled 'French Peas' contain three small slabs of nitro-cellulose explosive also known as gun cotton. Each slab weighed 8½ ozs. so that in each tin there were 25½ ozs. of gun-cotton. The total of the four being 102 ozs.[3]

The details of their sabotage equipment were forwarded to Rothschild. It was later suggested that the explosives were 'travellers' samples to demonstrate to the IRA the simple ingredients and workmanship of the explosives to be used in assisting a German invasion of Ireland later in 1940.'[4]

According to Dietergartner's testimony, he claimed that he was born in Oritjiwo, Otjiworongo in German South-West Africa but arrived in Germany in 1937 to study medicine at Berlin University. He joined the Wehrmacht and later the Brandenburg Regiment.[5]

The notorious Lehr Regiment Brandenburg, Z.B.V.800 which was formed in the early part of the war, and was a special unit of the German Army largely under the control of the Abwehr and which acted as a pool from which personnel was drawn for specific espionage and sabotage operations. [...]

The unit is of a para-military nature, recruited largely from Auslanddeutsche, who have a knowledge of foreign languages and/or are familiar with the topography of foreign countries. The Regiment has been extensively used in connection with all German blitz invasions. It played an important part in Holland, where formations were dropped in civilian clothes to commit acts of sabotage, or to capture strategic points or guard installations. It was also used in Yugoslavia and Russia operating behind enemy lines and in other than an orthodox military manner. Several agents belonging to the Lehr Regiment Brandenburg have been captured, some of them in German Army uniform when attempting to indulge in legitimate military activities behind the British lines, others when acting as spies and saboteurs, wearing civilian dress.[6]

Tributh claimed that he was born in Grootfontein, South-West Africa, but he moved to Germany when he was 19 to study philology, history of English and German languages and philosophy, initially at Marburg and then at Kiel University where he qualified as a gymnastics teacher. When the war started, he volunteered for the German army and, after five months on the Polish campaign, was transferred first to Saarlauten and in April 1940 to the Brandenburg Regiment. After training, both men were promoted to sergeants for the mission to Ireland.[7]

Obed, a British Indian from Lucknow in India, sometimes known as Henry or Abid Hussein, had married a German woman and worked as a trader in zoo animals. He had been to Eire and England several times before the war, had engaged in smuggling small arms to India and attempted unsuccessfully to sabotage Royal Navy ships in Belgium. Although captured and imprisoned by the Belgians, he was released by the Germans when they invaded the country and given this mission. His role was to rendezvous with an Irish friend who had been a travelling tinker and then help the others make their way to England.

According to Tributh's testimony, he met Dietergartner at Brandenburg, probably Quentzgut, where they were trained in the use of sabotage, rifles, machine guns and pistols.

About the middle of June, he left Brandenburg in company with Dieter, was instructed to go to Berlin. Went to Berlin by train and reported there. At that time, he had made up his mind to get away to England as he did not want to remain in Brandenburg during the war. He volunteered to go to England and do damage there. Dieter also volunteered.

In Berlin, he met two engineers, whose names he would not give. With these two engineers, he made his plans to get to England. They supplied them with an Opel motor car and a driver. He left his uniform in Brandenburg and travelled in mufti to Berlin. The two engineers told them to go by car to Brussels, and they arranged to meet them there.

He and Dieter left Berlin in an Opel car about 17th June [1940]. They went by the main motor roads past Magdeburg, Cologne and Aachen. They crossed over the Belgian frontier near Aachen and went to Brussels. At Brussels, they met the two German engineers again. They remained in Brussels for three days and were given sufficient money (Belgian) to pay their hotel expenses there. They had a further discussion with the engineers as to whether they would leave from Le Havre, Cherbourg or Brest [important Channel and Atlantic ports in north-west Brittany]. They decided to go to Brest.[8]

The Abwehr's base in Brest was led by Korvettekapitan Erich Pfeiffer with Feldwebel von Meyenburg in charge of Gruppe II sabotage operations, and Major Schroeder in charge of Gruppe III espionage.[9]

The Abwehrstelle was housed in a large, detached building in the Place du Chateau and was closely linked with the Kommandtur and the Kriegsmarine. They also owned a villa outside the town [identified subsequently as Villa Jeannette, seven miles south-east of Brest on the road to Quimper] where agents were trained in sabotage The Breststelle was in close wireless contact with Paris, Brussels and Berlin. [...]

LEBEL, sabotage instructor at the villa outside Brest, assisted by LEO interpreter. [...] The Abwehr ran a branch Stelle at Le Touquet which was in close wireless contact with Brest. Crews were also lodged here, and agents who had finished their training in Brest were given additional instruction – rowing, for example – in Le Touquet. The Le Touquet Stelle was in the charge of Kapian KLAPS.

Generally speaking, Le Touquet was the setting-off point for missions to the United Kingdom and boats were mostly sent first from Brest to Le Touquet before setting out.[10]

Gottfried Treulein, an interpreter at Brest in 1940, was captured towards the end of the war and admitted working with Captain Schneierwind, Lt Witze, Lebelle, Leo, van Dam and Krag. His role was requisitioning fishing smacks and arranging supplies for German-trained agents sent to Ireland and England.

They reached Brest about 25th June. They stayed in the Hotel de Paris. They remained there until the two engineers arrived about 27th June. They stayed at a different hotel, the name of which he did not know. About the same time as the engineers arrived Dieter and he met an American seaman in a cafe. This meeting was arranged by the two engineers. They discussed with the American the possibility of getting a boat to England. He said that it was impossible to get a boat to go to England but that he could get one to go to Ireland. He agreed to take them to Ireland if they paid £50 each for the trip. They agreed to pay him that amount.

While they were in Brest, they were meeting the two engineers almost every day. They showed them some French explosives and explained to them how to use them. On 1st July, they handed them over eight incendiary bombs, four tins of explosives labelled French peas, two waist belts, fuse and two wooden slabs in which detonators were concealed. He took possession of one wooden slab and a waist belt and Dieter took possession of one of each. All the incendiary bombs and explosives were put in his case. Dieter had no suitcase, and most of his property was in Tributh's.

On the same day the two engineers handed them over a sum of money. He got £135, made up of English one pound notes and ten shilling notes. Dieter got about the same sum. Immediately before the money was handed over to them they were introduced by the two engineers to a man named Henry Obed. This introduction took place in a café. The two engineers told them that Obed was joining their party, that he was several times in England and knew how conditions were there. Obed was not present when Dieter and he got the explosives and money. He did not see Obed getting any money from the Engineers. The American was present also when they were introduced to Obed. It was agreed also that Obed should contribute the sum of fifty pounds (£50) to the American for the journey. It was further agreed that Obed, Dieter and he would meet the American at a small fishing village outside Brest on the same night after dark. The American was then to have the boat ready, and he was to be accompanied by a Frenchman as a second member of the crew. When these arrangements were completed, the American went back to the fishing village and got the boat ready. Obed, Dieter and he remained at the café until the American called back for them that night at about 9 p.m. The American then took the three of them to the village outside Brest and aboard the boat. The American had provided all the necessary provisions. He paid the American in instalments of £15 before leaving. They left the harbour of Brest at about 2 a.m. on the morning of 2nd July. They were towed by a tug boat to the mouth of the harbour. They then put up sails and sailed in a westerly direction for two days. They then changed the course to North and arrived off the Irish coast on Saturday night of 6th July at about 8 or 9 p.m. They saw a lighthouse and the American then knew their position. He gave them the name of the lighthouse, which, he thought, was the Fastnet. They then sailed in an Easterly direction and kept well off shore. There was little wind, and they moved slowly, and it was about 3 a.m. on Sunday morning when they prepared to get off the boat. They came to within three miles of the shore. They had a dinghy aboard, and they put their suitcases and props, three life belts and two oars into it. Obed, Dieter and he entered the dinghy, and he rowed the boat ashore. Just before they got off the boat Dieter's property was placed in Obed's suitcase. His money was put in Obed's case. He kept the waist belt containing the fuse round his waist and kept the wooden slab containing the detonators in his pocket.

When they got ashore, they joined a road leading inland. They met a boy on a bicycle, and they enquired from him the nearest railway station. He told them they could go along the same road and get to a bus stop. They continued along the road and reached a village but found that the bus was gone. They asked a lorry driver to take them to the nearest bus stop, and he agreed. They travelled in the lorry until they reached another village where there was a bus. They boarded that bus and travelled to Cork.[11]

Tributh only gave military installations as their intended targets but did not specify which. Whether he was asked for details is unknown but C. H. Mooy, a Dutch agent who was imprisoned with the three men in Mountjoy Prison, reported that their aim was to use the explosives to blow up Buckingham Palace. According to an unnamed MI5 officer's report,

...this was rather fantastic as the explosives in their possession were of the most primitive kind, and it is perhaps probable that all three were anxious to convey to the Eire authorities that their designs were against belligerent Britain and not against neutral Eire. At the same time, the explosives they had brought would not have been of much value in reinforcing the IRA's supplies. At the start, one of the Germans, probably TRIBUTH, appears to have alleged that the party was to proceed to England to do acts of sabotage there, and was to be followed by up to 28 others who might be travelling to England direct in fishing boats.

In MI5's opinion, de Valera was unofficially on friendly terms with Germany but officially denied that his country was being used as a base for sabotage operations against England. His concerns were more about what the IRA's plans were for his country.

The imminent arrival of 28 enemy agents led the Admiralty to issue a warning to all coastguards and coast watching authorities, the immigration and customs authorities, chief security officers at the ports and the police in coastal areas to be on the look-out for small boat landings.[12] Wardens were appointed in every community. The black-out, introduced two days before the war started, was strictly enforced and tighter security was introduced. Any glimmer of light visible in one's window led to a reprimand by the Air Raid Precautions' staff. Posters, advertisements, radio and television broadcasts encouraged the general public to report anyone behaving suspiciously to the police, especially if they had a foreign accent.

One of the prisoners with Obed claimed that he had told him that he had been in contact with Joseph McDermott, an IRA member before the war, and that 'the Germans were going to supply small arms and money to the IRA. They were to use them to commit acts of sabotage against British troops and municipal undertakings in Northern Ireland.' He also suggested that one of the Abwehr II officers who sent them was Witzke as he was known to have been in Brest at that time.

After analysing Tributh, Dietergartner and Obed's stories, Arnold Silver, an MI5 counter-intelligence officer, concluded that their case had been badly planned and that there had been a lack of liaison between the various departments in the Abwehr. If they had representatives in Eire, they had been of no assistance.

When Canaris learned that the operation had failed, on 18 July 1940 he ordered that Eire would no longer be used for sabotage operations against the United Kingdom.[13]

Adm[iral] Canaris had previously issued strict orders that no agents were to be sent to Eire without first notifying the Veesenmayer Bureau for Irish Affairs and receiving approval from it. However, a number of Asts [Abwehrstelle] repeatedly violated this order to win prestige for themselves. This seems to have been the case in the account described above [...], the Veesenmayer Bureau had no knowledge of the mission on which the three men were sent until word of their arrest was made public through the press. The failure of the dispatching agency to cooperate with the Veesenmayer Bureau may account for the hurried and insufficient briefing and preparations for the mission on which the men were sent.[14]

Other criticisms of their mission included Obed openly asking the first person he met if he knew anyone in the IRA. There was also a lack of accurate, up-to-date intelligence as the contact he claimed to have known when he was in Dublin in 1934 had moved to Liverpool.[15]

Helenus Milmo of MI5 doubted the veracity of their statements and suggested that if they could be induced to talk, a great deal of interesting intelligence could be obtained from them. It is worth noting that G2 refused to allow an MI5 officer interrogate the men. The reason was not stated, but it is possible there was rivalry between the two intelligence agencies. Also, as Eire was neutral at that time, they had no wish to antagonise Germany.

On 29 July 1940, Milmo informed Cecil Liddell, the then head of BI(h), the Irish Section of British counter-intelligence, that

> The tins containing the H.E. [High Explosive], were cylindrical, about 6" long by 3" diameter, similar to those normally used for tinned fish. In one end of each tin was partly cut a small circle. This could be pressed in with a pencil and the detonator and fuse inserted. Each tin apparently constituted a single bomb, and there is no delay mechanism.
>
> The incendiary bombs consisted of a cylindrical cardboard tube, four to five inches in length with a cap at each end held on by adhesive tape. A piece of copper wire attached to the friction strip protruded from one end. They look very crude.[16]

The Irish Military Intelligence, known as G2, determined that Tributh and Dietergartner were fanatical Nazis who would not hesitate to join a resistance movement if the opportunity was presented. They were all charged with possession of explosive material and sentenced to seven years' imprisonment, initially in Mountjoy Prison where they mixed with IRA prisoners and then in Athlone military prison in West Meath, alongside other captured German agents. In September 1946, the three men were paroled and operated a carpentry and handicrafts business in Dublin until they were deported to the American zone in Germany in July 1947.[17]

When news of Dietergartner, Tributh and Obed's fate reached Abwehr II, they made alternative invasion plans. In their diary for 18 July 1940 was the entry:

> Message received from Dr [Eduard] Hempel [head of the German Legation in Dublin] that agents landed in Operation Lobster I have been arrested. Equipment provided incriminating evidence. By director's decision further sabotage acts against England are not to be made via Ireland but direct against England.

There were, however, still British fears of a German invasion as Guy Liddell reported in late-August 1940 that he had received decoded intelligence that the Germans wanted to know the strength of British forces in Northern Ireland. He also reported that SNOW had been informed that another agent was to be dropped, this time in England, and he had been asked to find a house in an out-of-the-way place for him and future agents. MI5's concern was to pick them up before the Local Defence Volunteers apprehended them. The agents dropped in England, Wales and Scotland will be covered later.[18]

As Abwehr II had already planned a second mission to infiltrate agents into Ireland, they ignored Canaris's wishes and Operation SEAGULL (MOWE) I went ahead. Christian Nissen, the German captain of the boat that delivered LOBSTER 1, set off with Helmut Clissman, a non-commissioned Brandenburg officer, and Bruno Reiger, a trained Abwehr I wireless operator. Their mission, once they landed in Galway Bay, was to establish contact with the IRA, get their help in reaching England and prepare for a Brandenburger invasion near Dover. However, bad weather and sabotage thwarted their plans. For three days a force 10 gale buffeted their boat, the *Anni Braz-Bihen*. The bilge pump stopped working, thought to have been sabotaged by the French owners after the boat had been commandeered. As the Danish mechanic was too sick to be able to help, Nissen had no alternative but to abort the mission and return to Brest.

The above missions were planned to coincide with the German invasion but the RAF's success in thwarting the Luftwaffe during the Battle of Britain in the summer and autumn of 1940 led Hitler to abandon Operation SEALION.

8

Operations DOVE/PIGEON and SEA EAGLE (DOVE II) – August 1940–Summer 1941

Shortly after the S-Plan started, Russell, who saw Adolf Hitler as capable of destroying Britain and reunifying Ireland, met Oscar Pfaus, an American-German Abwehr II agent undercover as a reporter of the *Frankfurter Zeitung*. With his agreement and assistance from Hoven, O'Donovan made three trips to Germany in 1939. Initially, Hitler refused to provide the IRA with funds for fear of provoking conflict with Britain.[1]

According to an MI5 report, Russell was 'always very secretive and it is possible that he did not even inform his fellow members of the step that he was taking to secure German cooperation.'[2] Research by J. Bowyer-Bell and Tim Pat Coogan into the history of the IRA revealed that in April 1939, unable to secure financial support from the Germans, Russell went on a fund-raising mission to the United States. He was arrested in Detroit by the American Secret Service as a precautionary measure because King George and Queen Elizabeth were on a Royal Visit to Canada. McGarrity paid $5,000 bail to secure Russell's release, who was then expelled from the country. Unable to get back to Ireland on an American or British passenger ship, the Germans agreed to take him under a false name via Italy and Germany.[3]

When Russell arrived in Berlin on 5 May 1940, Hitler had changed his mind and gave Russell $15,000 for the IRA. He also agreed to send wireless sets and agents. At Veesenmayer's request, Russell then

...spent his time taking a refresher course in sabotage and investigating the latest German work in chemical explosives. As often was the case with IRA men, Russell was a man without personal vices. He led a disciplined, routine existence, attended Mass regularly and expressed little interest in the charms of Berlin beyond his explosives classes. He was a pure Irish nationalist who had dedicated his life to achieving Tone's Republic and had no time for even the most attractive diversions of flesh or spirit. The Germans were impressed. For months, the Abwehr tried to decide how to use Russell. Everyone, including Russell, assumed that he should be sent to Ireland, but when and how, with whom and for what purpose, was uncertain. The discussions dragged on while Russell bided his time and occupied himself in the chemical laboratory.[4]

His training in the latest German explosives and time-delays was at the Abwehr training laboratory in Tegel, about 5 miles (8 kilometres) north-west of Berlin, which specialised in manufacturing explosives and hiding them in household objects. Russell also observed trainee saboteurs and their instructors in the Brandenburg Regiment doing practical work in the field.[5]

In the middle of July, he was introduced to Frank Ryan, a Dublin journalist and former IRA activist, who had been caught fighting for the Communists with the Irish Brigade in the Spanish Civil War and sentenced to life imprisonment by General Franco's government. After eighteen months' concerted efforts by de Valera's Irish government to secure his release, Ryan was helped to 'escape' in a deal arranged by Canaris, the head of the Spanish secret police, Clissman and Hoven.

Bowyer-Bell described how, in a frail condition, gaunt, drawn, nearly deaf and quite confused, Ryan was taken to a country house outside Paris and 'found himself an honoured visitor to Nazi Germany, the fountainhead of the fascist menace he had gone to Spain to fight'.[6]

The Abwehr employed Ryan as head of their Irish Section, and it was in this capacity that he was introduced after Christmas 1940 to Guy Vissault and Olivier Mordrelle, Breton nationalists, at Quai Louis Berthou in Rennes. Both had been imprisoned by the French authorities for their involvement in an illegal arms shipment but released by the Germans following their occupation.

Russell had insisted that Ryan should return to Ireland with him. Ryan's political views were very much the opposite of Russell's. Veesenmayer introduced Ryan to von Ribbentrop, Canaris and Lahousen. What was discussed is unknown but despite the capture of the LOBSTER agents, arrangements were made for Russell and Ryan to be infiltrated back into Ireland with their sabotage and wireless equipment on Operation DOVE (TAUBE), sometimes referred to as Operation PIGEON.

Code-named Richard I and Richard II, they sailed from Wilhelmshaven on 8 August 1940 on board Commander von Stockhausen's U-boat. However, Russell became seriously ill with stomach cramps and severe pains during the journey. With no doctor on board, he was reported to have died from what was thought to have been a burst gastric ulcer and was buried at sea on 14 August, about 100 miles west of Galway Bay with full military honours. His body was reported to have been wrapped in a German flag. Some Germans suspected that his death was not an accident.

The writer Henry Francis Stuart, known as 'Australian Stuart', was reported to have been sent to Berlin in January 1940 as an IRA courier. In an MI5 interrogation report, he stated that Russell and Ryan's mission was to contact the IRA and prepare for a landing of a cargo of arms which Stuart was to take to Eire.[7] De Coetlogon claimed not to know Stuart, 'but recognised the man's photograph, saying that he thought he has seen him at an Irish meeting held in the Cite Universitaire, Paris, in 1939. The man he saw was wounded in one arm, but DE COETLOGON never learned where he received the wound.'[8]

With Russell's death, Operation DOVE was cancelled. Ryan returned to Germany on the submarine and never saw Ireland again. Although Veesenmayer wanted him to return on another mission, his health destroyed by his imprisonment, he had a stroke in January 1943 and died in a Dresden sanatorium on 10 June 1944.[9]

Günther Schutz, mentioned earlier, asked the Abwehr for contact details of IRA members before his mission, but they refused, telling him to keep away from them. Presumably, they had learned of their agents' early failures. On 5 March 1941, he was flown from Amsterdam in a Heinkel He 111 but bad weather prevented his parachute drop. Another attempt on 12 March dropped him near Taghmon, County Wicklow, 100 miles off target. Spotted on landing, he was questioned by the *Gardai* and found to be carrying a wireless transmitter, £1,000 and $3,200 in cash, a microscope for reading microdots and a bottle of German cognac in his suitcase.

The Irish Times ran an article: 'The Government Information Bureau states: "The Guards arrested today, at Taghmon, Co. Wexford, a stranger who stated that he had landed during the night by parachute from a German plane at a place near Ballycullane, in the same county"'.[10]

On his arrest, Schutz confessed that his mission was to collect and send weather data, observe convoy movements and collect economic intelligence on targets in Northern Ireland. Praetorius claimed that Schutz was to contact Unland in Dublin and act as his wireless operator.

Imprisoned in Mountjoy Prison, his first attempt to escape with Jan van Loon failed when their tunnel filled with water. Van Loon, a Dutch seaman with German sympathies, had jumped ship in Dublin and offered to work for the German legation on intelligence gathering. Thinking he was a British agent provocateur, his offer was refused, and he was then picked up by the Irish authorities and interned.

Schutz's second escape attempt on 15 February 1942 was more successful. With IRA assistance, he evaded arrest until April when the house in Rathmines where he was staying was raided by the Irish Special Branch, who were looking for someone else. He was identified, sent to Bridewell Gaol then Arbour Hill Prison in Dublin until the war ended, when he was due to be deported, but his marriage to an Irish woman allowed him to stay. He ran a desk lamp business until his death in 1991.[11]

Peter Schagen, another of the Abwehr II officers working in Paris, commented when he was captured that the Abwehr were 'chiefly concerned with investigating the possibilities of organising sabotage enterprises in foreign countries. Possibilities when existing were very limited, largely because the Germans possessed virtually no materials in foreign countries for sabotage. Also, Abwehr II was not very efficient and badly organised.'[12]

Although Operation WHALE (WALFISCH), the plan to land a seaplane on an Irish lake, had been aborted in July 1940, Haller devised another plan, Operation WHALE II. To avoid Canaris's order not to interfere with Irish affairs, his alternative was to send Clissmann to England to contact anti-British Welsh and Scottish nationalists to help in the planned invasion.[13] The plan was for Nissen to sail to England, anchor offshore and lower a boat to allow

Clissman to row to the beach, but this too was abandoned in April 1941 in favour of another attempt to land him in Eire.

After the failure of Operations WHALE and DOVE, the aim of Operation SEA EAGLE (SEEADLER), also referred to as Operation DOVE II, was to supply the IRA with a long-range wireless transmitter and operating funds to support Operation OSPREY (FISCHADLER), military action against the prospective arrival of American troops in Eire. The operation was organised by the German Foreign Ministry with the Abwehr being given only a technical role. Its aims were to provide the IRA with £40,000, reactivate the S-Plan in England, engage in acts of terrorism in Northern Ireland which would necessitate the deployment of British troops, the establishment of an Irish resistance movement in advance of British or American occupation and reporting intelligence to Germany.

The agents selected for the mission were Clissmann with Bruno Reiger as his wireless operator, but when the mission expanded to include direct liaison with the IRA, Frank Ryan, was added. It was hoped that Ryan would be able to reconcile de Valera with the IRA. The plan was for a Heinkel He 59 seaplane to land in the Brandon Bay area in County Kerry between 15 and 25 September 1941 and leave the three men in a rubber dinghy with folding bicycles.

To Veesenmayer's disappointment, Hitler refused to endorse the operation as he was convinced Operation BARBAROSSA, the invasion of the Soviet Union which started in June 1941, would be successful.[14]

On 18/19 July 1941, 35-year-old Joseph Lenihan, alias Leniham, parachuted into County Meath, near Dublin. Having hidden his parachute and suitcase radio in a hedge, he took the second suitcase containing his personal belongings and hitch-hiked to Dublin. From there he went by train to Athlone to see his brother about the division of his late father's estate, returned to Dublin and took a train to Belfast. En route, he asked to be put in touch with the British military authorities in Northern Ireland and on arrival handed himself in to the Royal Ulster Constabulary, offering to provide details of the German Intelligence Service.

Taken to Camp 020 for interrogation, he reported that his mission was to provide the Nazis with weather reports from the Sligo area and an assessment of the morale of the Irish population. There was no mention of contacting the IRA or involvement with sabotage activities. He admitted being a customs officer before the war and being charged with forging frontier passes to allow the IRA to smuggle guns. Offered a free pardon, a large sum of money and free passage to the United States if he would reveal details on the contraband and gun running organisation, he refused and was imprisoned for nine months. On his release, he joined up and fought against the Japanese in China and later found work picking potatoes on Jersey. Following the German occupation of the island, he stole a 22-foot boat and made a run for it; but in a strong south-westerly gale, water flooded the engine and he was blown ashore on the Contentin peninsula instead of England. Caught by German soldiers, he was interrogated at Carteret. Four days later, Abwehr officers from Paris, impressed by his anti-British convictions, persuaded him to agree to work for them on a mission in Ireland. According to Hoare,

He was driven to Paris and lodged in an apartment to which came a stream of German IS instructors in radio, meteorology, secret writing. He was a popular recruit and pupil; he met many Abwehr officers and NCOs from the notorious Hotel Lutetia and enjoyed the confidence of them all. He studied the men, their methods and their haunts with close attention; he had decided already that he would betray them all, with their bags of tricks, to the British.

His Irish contrariness got him into trouble only once in Paris. He was at Freddy's Bar at the Normandy Hotel one night and was overheard by the German soldiery speaking English. Some inspired officer decided he must be an English spy, and cried 'Englander'. Another pointed a gun at him. The insult and the menace were too much for [BASKET]. He slapped them down, and himself into gaol. His friends at the Lutetia secured his release the following day.

[BASKET] received further training at The Hague and also made a two-day visit to Brussels with one of his would-be masters. He learned more about the German Secret Service and its personnel and improved his radio transmission.

In January 1941, he was ready to be planted in Eire. GARTENFELD allowed him to choose his own preferred place of landing and he opted for the Curragh. The plane left Schiphol airport in the direction of Athlone, but after two and a half hours' flight, when they should have been nearing the Irish coast, the heating system broke down. They were flying at an altitude of some 30,000 feet at the time, and GARTENFELD decided that the weather conditions militated against a safe landing; he ordered the pilot to turn back. By the time they had landed again at Schiphol everyone save the pilot, who was wearing an electronically heated suit, had suffered severe frostbite.

The Luftwaffe personnel was dispatched to military hospitals at The Hague and to a hospital at Suresnes, where he remained for three months. 'WERNER, one of his most assiduous sponsors, called on him daily with expressions of German sympathy and fond hopes for the future.

[BASKET} left hospital in May and received fresh training and instructions both in Paris and at The Hague; in both places he learned much that would be of value to the British, for he was an exceptionally observant and intelligent type. By July he had been voted fit and ready to land in Eire. His despatch on this occasion suffered no hitch. It might have been more profitable to the Germans if it had, for [BASKET] as a source of accurate information on the G.S.S., was indeed heaven-sent to the British. The volume of intelligence which he yielded to them was only surpassed by its quality. And having spoken, he left Ham Common with a clear conscience, probably to continue in his home land the legitimate struggle against the English oppressor.[15]

Given the code-name BASKET, he initially cooperated with MI5 in sending disinformation to the Germans but constantly expressed his pro-Irish views. Eventually, he proved uncooperative. His MI5 handlers were reported to have been driven to distraction as he often refused to undertake simple instructions. Offered £50 if he would leave and refuse to divulge what he knew, he refused to accept the money and was interned until the end of the war under the Defence Regulation 18B.[16]

9

Operations OSPREY (FISCHADLER), PASTORIUS and SEAGULL II – January–May 1942

On 26 January 1942, following the United States entering the war after the Japanese attack on Pearl Harbor, 4,508 US troops and engineers were landed in Belfast. When Hitler was informed, he gave consent to von Ribbentrop to plan a response in case the Americans attempted to establish bases in neutral Eire as they had in Iceland and Greenland. There was also concern as they had learned of a secret British plan to pressurise de Valera to allow British troops to use the port of Cork.

As the Abwehr's earlier operations in Eire had all failed, the Foreign Ministry liaised with them in planning Operation OSPREY (FISCHADLER). Overall control of the operation was by the Reich's Security Headquarters while the Abwehr was responsible for the technical planning and training. 100 volunteer commando troops, designated the *Sonder Lehrgang Oranienburg*, included 70 non-commissioned officers and 30 privates who were specially selected by Clissman based on their knowledge of Irish and English culture and the English language. Commanded by Dutch SS Hauptsturmführer Van Vessem, they were given training in English, British weapons, and sabotage using explosives and incendiaries. Two IRA volunteers from the Friesack Camp were to be sent as guides and liaison with a group of Brandenburgers. The plan was for them to be parachuted into Eire if the Americans moved south and train IRA members and any Irish soldiers willing to fight. The operation was shelved when the American troops did not move south.[1]

According to an American report on German intelligence, Amt VI was convinced that the capturing of their agents in Ireland had provided British Intelligence with everything they wanted to know about Amt VI's office on Berkaerstrasse, Berlin. They suspected that the Irish agents would have talked about the organisation, personnel, sabotage training and missions.[2]

While this account investigates the Abwehr saboteurs infiltrated into Britain, there were others sent to the United States and details of their story are worth including as there are similarities with the experiences of those already described and that effort adds details by association to missions to England.

The Abwehr had had agents in the United States from as early as 1937 who had been instructed to commence sabotage activities only when hostilities began between the two countries. The Federal Bureau of Investigation was aware of the spy ring but took no action until 30 July 1941 when they rounded up known German agents.[3]

In January 1942, Alfred Hitchcock's film *Saboteur* was released, the American equivalent of *The Thirty-Nine Steps*. The hero, Robert Cummings, works in an aircraft factory and is accused of sabotaging his works and causing the death of his best friend. Cummings is the fall guy for a clever ring of Nazi spies, headed by Otto Kruger, an above-suspicion American philanthropist. Cummings goes on an inter-state chase after Norman Lloyd, the real saboteur, while he is also being pursued by the FBI. On the way, he picks up Priscilla Lane, a reluctant 'travelling companion' who initially hates him and intends to turn him over to police at the first opportunity. However, she eventually realises Cummings is innocent. It is possible that this film gave the Abwehr ideas about attacking factories in the United States.

Keen to take action, the Abwehr planned a series of major sabotage attacks. On 13 June 1942, four German saboteurs were dropped by a U-boat near Amagansett Beach, on Long Island, New York. They wore naval uniforms in the hope that, if captured on landing, they would be treated as prisoners-of-war. After burying their uniforms, explosives, incendiaries and detonators, they changed into civilian clothing and made their way inland. Although they were stopped by a Coast Guard patrolman, he accepted a $260 bribe to keep quiet, and they caught the train to New York. When the patrolman returned to his office, he reported the incident and a search of the sand dunes where they had landed uncovered their hidden cache.

The contents of the boxes were listed in one of Rothschild's reports and may well be what was in the cases dropped into the sea by other saboteurs destined for Britain:

1. Fuse Lighter; 25
2. Electric Detonator; 25
3. Electric Match; 50
4. Wooden Block containing 5 threaded Detonators; 25
5. Wooden Block with a red pencil line round the outside containing 5 threaded incendiary igniters; 5
6. Dummy Detonators; 5
7. Dummy threaded Detonator; 5
8. This brass Adaptor; 2
9. Glass ampoule containing sulphuric acid; 11
10. Brass and Plastic Incendiary Device wrapped in paper, on which is written 'Fu F.O. MIUNTAN (?) H2SO4 EBOINT (?)'; 10
11. Pen and Pencil Delay Mechanism with 6–7 hours delay; 2
12. Pen and Pencil Delay Mechanism with 2¾ – 3¾ hours delay; 2
13. Pen and Pencil Delay Mechanism with 11–13 hours delay; 1
14. Clockwork-Mechanical-Striker Delay Mechanism [...]; 10
15. Metal Button for setting the Clockwork-Mechanical-Striker Delay Mechanism; 10

16. Detonator for Clockwork-Mechanical-Striker Delay Mechanism; 10
17. Roll of safety Fuse; 4
18. Role of Detonating Fuse; 1
19. Bomb camouflaged as Lump of Coal; 4
20. Block of TNT; 20. In the box in which the TNT was packed there were bits of cardboard on which was written in pencil 'HARNISCH'.
21. Can containing abrasives.

1. <u>FUSE LIGHTER</u>. This is constructed of rolled paper with one end open to permit the insertion of safety fuse. The friction caused by pulling the button at the closed end is sufficient to ignite a quantity of match composition which in turns ignites a safety fuse. The fuse lighter is probably a standard commercial type.
2. <u>ELECTRIC DETONATOR</u>. These are of sufficient strength to detonate the blocks of TNT (see No. 20). The detonators are contained in 30 calibre copper shells and have untinned copper leg wires insulated with cotton wrapping, covered by black waterproof material.
3. <u>ELECTRIC MATCH HEAD</u>. There is a female thread at one end to accommodate a detonator or igniter. At the other end there is a pair of wires leading into the tube, connected with a filament coated with match composition. If this device is connected to a source of electric power (torch battery) it will set off a detonator or igniter.
4. <u>WOODEN BLOCK CONTAINING 5 THREADED DETONATOR</u>. These have been specially designed to fit other pieces of the sabotage equipment. They contain sufficient charge to initiate the explosion of blocks of TNT.
5. <u>WOODEN BLOCK WITH RED PENCIL LINE ROUND THE OUTSIDE CONTAINING 5 THREADED IGNITERS</u>. This block is identical with the previous one and can only be distinguished by the red pencil line along one edge. The 'detonators', however, which it contains are in reality igniters. The distal end of the 'detonators' has an opening painted over with a thin film of cellulose. There is a band of rend paint round the centre of the 'detonator' barrel and under this paint two or three holes have been drilled in the tube. The distal half of the igniter is filled with thermit, while the proximal end contains a mixture of potassium permanganate, antimony sulphide and metallic antimony.
6. <u>DUMMY DETONATOR</u>. This detonator contains no charge and is for the purpose of training. The letters 'Ub' probably stand for Ubung (practice).
7. <u>DUMMY THREADED DETONATOR</u>. This also contains no charge and is for instructional purposes.
8. <u>BRASS ADAPTOR</u>. This allows a detonator or igniter to be used with safety fuse as one end of the adaptor has a female thread to accommodate the detonator, while safety fuse can be crimped into the other end.
9. <u>GLASS AMPOULE CONTAINING SULPHURIC ACID</u>. This acid is used with incendiary device No. 10.
10. <u>BRASS ANND PLASTIC INCENDIARY DEVICE</u>. This device consists of a small brass tube filled with potassium chlorate and sugar. Into this tube

there fits a smaller celluloid tube in which there are about five holes covered with a parchment-like material. In this inner tube there is a cavity into which about 0.5 c.c. of sulphuric acid is placed. When inverted, the sulphuric acid penetrates through the parchment covered holes in approximately 65–70 minutes. After penetration, it reacts with the potassium chlorate and sugar, producing a flame, about three inches in length and sufficient to ignite a detonator or igniter. The device has a base made of brass into which the brass tube screws. The other end is threaded to accommodate a detonator or igniter. It is obviously intended for use with other equipment as the brass base contains an outside thread which had no function other than to permit the whole being inserted into some type of bomb. Further confirmation of this exists and there are three small holes in the brass bass which are probably intended as a key-way.

11, 12, 13. PEN AND PENCIL DELAY MECHANISM. This delay mechanism is identical with the pen and pencil sets given to SNOW and SUNDAE by the Abwehr, even the label on which the delay time is written is in the same handwriting as that on SUNDAE's samples. This device has been described in detail in 'German Sabotage Equipment (Technical)'. The variation in delay is effected by a variation in the thickness of the celluloid in the pen.

14. CLOCKWORK-MECHANICAL-STRIKER DELAY MECHANISM. This delay mechanism, which incorporated a 13-jewel movement Swiss watch originally intended for a wrist watch, can be set up to 14 days. It is based on the mechanical striker principle as in the earlier types used in the Eastern Hemisphere by saboteurs such as ARKOSSY and SNOW. Presumably, the technical deficiencies experienced with the standard 21-day clockwork-electric delay mechanism, frequently used in the Eastern hemisphere, have now resulted in this new type being designed. The serial numbers are of the form K1ys, K and 1 being dummies. The designation K1 may, therefore, be encountered when reference is made to this type of delay mechanism by Abw. II.

17. SAFETY FUSE. The only difference between this safety fuse and the types with which we are familiar is that it has a covering of two layers of synthetic rubber or flexible plastic. It burns at the rate of one foot in thirty-four seconds.

18. DETONATING FUSE. This has a core filled with fulminate of mercury and paraffin wax, being wrapped around with interwoven white and red thread. Although it is quite flexible and easily detonated, it is not sufficiently powerful to detonate the TNT blocks.

19. BOMB CAMOUFLAGED AS COAL. This consists of a block of compressed TNT weighing about half a pound, covered by a plastic material somewhat similar to plastic wood. All the bombs were shaped in the same mould. The plastic wood was painted black and is a rather poor imitation of real coal. There is a hole through the 'coal' part going into the middle of the TNT, through which the detonator is inserted.

20. BLOCK OF TNT. The block was cast, probably as a somewhat larger slab, from which the blocks were then cut by sawing with a mechanically

driven circular saw. In one end of the block, there is a hole for the insertion of the detonator. The blocks are obviously intended to weigh 1 kg although some are slightly underweight.

21. <u>CAN OF ABRASIVES</u>. The can is made of paper and contains about 1 kg of a mixture of steel filings, sand and silicon carbide.

The main feature of the equipment is the very large amount and diversity of types that the saboteurs brought. Although they were also given instructions in the manufacture of home-made explosives, incendiary material and delay mechanisms, it is evident that the stocks they brought were intended to last a considerable time.

The incendiary igniter, which is, in fact, an ordinary detonator modified to act as an incendiary, is interesting and useful. The brass and plastic incendiary device is conveniently small and easily hidden or camouflaged. The saboteurs pointed out that the pen and pencil delay mechanism which SNOW was told to use against high explosive stores, was a useful incendiary weapon if set off without its detonator when a considerable flame issues from the end of it. The 14-day delay mechanism is well made, though the writer had difficulty in fixing the detonator into the hole in the block of TNT owing to the awkward shape of the delay mechanism itself.

The 'coal' is much inferior to our own offensive department's efforts, though presumably it would not be noticed if it were put in a coal bunker of a locomotive, where it would get covered in coal dust.

The can containing abrasives is probably the most interesting item brought by the saboteurs. There was no point whatsoever in equipping the saboteurs with abrasives because these are so easily obtained within the country. At the same time it shows for the first time that Abw II are interested in the types of sabotage normally committed by disgruntled workmen and are instructing their agents in this method of interfering with production. This sort of sabotage is in one way a greater menace than that carried out with the high explosive and incendiary bombs; because it is easy to assume, when sand or other abrasives are put into lubrication systems, that it is the work of dissatisfied persons who are neither sympathisers with the enemy nor in their pay.[4]

One imagines that Rothschild sent copies of his report with its photographs and sketches to the boffins at Brickendonbury and Aston House and probably to the District Security Officers to provide guidance should similar finds be reported around Britain.

Three days after these supplies had been buried, on 16 June, four more German saboteurs were landed by U-boat off Ponte Verde Beach in Florida from where they made their way undetected to Jacksonville and then Chicago, Illinois and Cincinnati. Research by David Johnson shows that George Dasch, the leader of the Long Island team, had decided to defect before he left Germany but there was disbelief when he rang the New York police station demanding to speak with J. Edgar Hoover, the FBI director. Instead, Dasch went to the FBI headquarters in Washington, D.C. to speak to Hoover personally. Eventually, he was allowed to speak with the

Assistant Director of the manhunt who was only convinced when he was shown the contents of the briefcase with details of the mission and $86,000. This led eventually to the arrest of the seven other German agents who, under interrogation, confessed that the Abwehr had prepared them with three weeks' intensive sabotage training at Quentzgut. They had been given instruction in the manufacture and use of explosives, incendiary devices, primers (blasting caps) and various mechanical, chemical and electrical timing devices.

Their mission, code-named Operation PASTORIUS after the leader of the first German settler in America, was to sabotage American war industries. Their targets included hydroelectric plants at Niagara Falls; aluminium plants in Illinois, Tennessee and New York; the Horseshoe Curve, an important railway pass near Altoona, Pennsylvania, and the nearby railway repair shops; locks on the Ohio River near Louisville, Kentucky; a cryolite (mineral used in aluminium manufacture) factory in Philadelphia; Pennsylvania Station in Newark, New Jersey and the Hell Gate Bridge in New York.

There had been a plan to destroy a dam holding New York's water supply, but this was shelved as it was thought impossible for a small group to blow it up. They were also instructed to spread a wave of terror by blowing up bridges, railway stations, water facilities, Jewish-owned department stores and businesses and public institutions. They were issued with almost $175,000, fake birth certificates, Social Security cards, draft deferment cards and driver's licences. In return they were paid, depending on their previous employment, between 200 and 600 Reichmarks a month. This would stop once Abw II learned that they were imprisoned or executed but their wife or nominated relative would be given an unspecified lump sum if they died on mission. If they were successful and returned to Germany, they were promised a well-paid job for life.

President Franklin D. Roosevelt established a military tribunal to prosecute them. All eight were found guilty; six were executed, and the two defectors had their sentences reduced to thirty years for one and life imprisonment for the other. In fact, they only served two years as they were deported to Berlin in 1946.[5]

Given the nature of their sabotage mission, Rothschild was sent to Washington to be briefed on this Abwehr operation. His report shed light on their training methods at the 'Sabotage School' and the statement that the men had been instructed to 'trust nobody and kill any man who turned traitor'.

The submarine that dropped the first four agents had apparently run aground, and the US Coastguard's stupidity led to its escape. One saboteur was reported to have admitted being a secret agent in a bar after drinking too much and it was believed that a third group of saboteurs had arrived but had not been apprehended. Perhaps that was a deliberate deception to increase US citizens' vigilance about potential saboteurs.[6]

One German prisoner reported that Admiral Karl Dönitz, the Nazi U-Boat commander, had been so incensed on hearing of the failure of the mission that he refused any help to Abwehr II for months.[7] Rothschild reported

...a decision had been reached not to send submarines on pure sabotage expeditions in the future, but to include one or possibly two saboteurs among the normal crew of a submarine going on an operational trip. This technique was the one employed in landing the German agent JANOWSKI in Canada. For this and other reasons, it is most unlikely that in future saboteurs will be landed with large stores of sabotage equipment. The saboteurs will be instructed to purchase their sabotage equipment within the country concerned and will only bring with them such things as detonators, which occupy little space and cannot be manufactured by amateurs.

This sabotage expedition was better equipped with sabotage apparatus and better trained than any other expeditions of which the Security Service has heard. The German Secret Service attached the greatest importance to the success of the undertaking and were fortunate in having technicians among its members. Two members were mechanical fitters and were therefore in a far better position to commit sabotage to machinery than the usual type of saboteur employed by the German Secret Service.[8]

When news that Operation PASTORIUS had failed and that Codd had been arrested in Dusseldorf on charges of extravagant behaviour and imprisoned, Operation INNKEEPER was aborted. Codd's story can be read in Hull's and Stephan's books.[9]

Just before Christmas 1941, Brady, Walsh, Cushing, Private Patrick O'Brien and Private William Murphy were released from Friesack and provided with 'entertainment' in Berlin before being sent for intensive explosives training at Quentzgut Camp and then a wireless course at the Abwehr School at Stettin, close to the Baltic coast. Although Hoven expected Cushing to lead the group, Haller refused to send him on any mission, considering him 'a rank opportunist, without backbone of moral fibre, a loud-mouthed braggard with little courage or intelligence, whose reliability was highly doubtful'. Murphy was described as 'a colourless individual' who had irritated his German minders due to his volatile behaviour whilst drunk. 'O'Brien was only intended as a companion for the others. Mentally, he was subnormal and seemed to live in a dream world all of his own.'[10]

Only Walsh and Brady showed potential. Walsh, code-named Vickers, had been captured in France in 1940 fighting with the British Expeditionary Force and had been recruited at Friesack. Haller considered him 'a mature, determined and quiet person, who seemed to have genuine Irish nationalistic feelings, to which was added an adventurous streak. Mentally he was above average; his weakness was an overfondness for drink. His tech abilities were good, and he passed his WT training and sabotage course in Quentzsee with flying colours. While he was training, Abw II proposals that he should go on a sabotage mission against the UK were accepted by him without apparent reserve. He asked little financial reward, and received, like the others, RM 12 to 24 per day.'[11]

In May 1942, the month before Operation PASTORIUS, Haller discussed with Dr Koerfer from the Economic Group Electricity Supply a revised Operation SEAGULL. They devised a plan to sabotage the Lochaber hydro-electric power stations at Fort William and Kinlochleven. Opened in 1909, the latter generated electricity for an aluminium smelting works which supplied most of the material needed by Britain's aircraft industry.

Walsh was chosen for this mission and told that a Luftwaffe attack in 1941 had failed due to the nearby mountains interfering with the bombing run. What the Germans did not know was that to prevent attacks on the works, wires had been erected across the valley to deter low flying aircraft and camouflage netting erected over the pipeline. Security guards were also in place. Irish labourers had been employed in digging the tunnels feeding the hydro-electric scheme and quite a number had married and settled in the area. German prisoners-of-war had helped build the roads in the area.[12]

Walsh was told he was to be flown to Norway with Brady, code-named Metzger, and then infiltrated into Britain. Brady also made a good impression on Haller who described him as 'a strong Irish nationalist, and claimed to have contacts in IRA circles, although he was evasive about names and addresses.'[14] Using false identification papers in the name of Thomas Dunphy, Walsh was to be parachuted from a Focke-Wolf Fw 200 'Condor' at a spot he chose himself in the North Midlands. The wireless set and explosives were to be dropped separately but attached to his parachute by a thin cord so as to be close by when he landed. He would be supplied with secret ink to communicate with an address in Portugal supplied by Abw 1. Provided with £8,000 in cash, he was to find accommodation in Glasgow, meet up with his Irish friends and set up a three-man sabotage team. They were to use specially made explosives to blow up the 13-km pipeline which carried the water from Blackwater dam to the turbines in the electricity plant at the works. Should he find it impossible to reach his main target, he was given a secondary target, a smaller power plant at Kinlochleven, also connected with the aluminium works.[13]

As increasing numbers of American troops were arriving in England, Haller considered sending Brady by submarine to Northern Ireland or England to learn about the number of US forces, their training and equipment, intelligence he would transmit back to Germany by radio. It was also suggested he would establish a network of IRA agents and carry out sabotage attacks as directed from Germany.

In July 1942, both men were sent on a refresher course at Quentzgut. As part of Walsh's preparation, Dr Konig, their explosives instructor, took him to visit the Eder dam in Hesse, about 150 km east of Dusseldorf, which supplied water to two hydro-electric power stations. He was given instructions as how best to destroy the pipelines. Both the Eder and the Mohne dam, about 50 km away, supplied water and power for the nearby Ruhr industrial area and were on the RAF target list. Despite being heavily defended by anti-aircraft batteries, Barnes Wallis's bouncing bombs dropped by Lancasters successfully breached both dams on 17 May 1943.[15]

In mid-1941, Brady agreed to be trained for a different mission. He was to go to Northern Ireland with a South American passport in the name of James de Lacy. He was provided with £8,000, $3,000, three British identity cards but no ration books, essential for anyone wanting to live unnoticed in Ireland. He was to be parachuted into the area south-east of Ballycastle, County Antrim, and find employment in Harland and Wolff's shipyard in Belfast. He had to recruit a team of four or five sub-agents, if possible IRA members, and undertake small-scale sabotage in the shipyard. He was also to attack important 'targets of opportunity' in the immediate vicinity.

In *Hitler's Irishmen*, Terence O'Reilly claimed the Abwehr knew little about conditions in Northern Ireland as they received none of their newspapers. Sending an IRA sympathiser into the Harland and Wolff shipyard was a lunatic concept:

> ...it was famous throughout Ireland as a hotbed of extreme unionism, where in the past any Catholic employees had frequently suffered injury or death at the hands of their Protestant 'co-workers'. Although the exigencies of wartime had obliged the shipyard to hire large numbers of Irishmen from south of the border, these were regarded with deep suspicion even at cabinet level. Any attempt by Brady to set up a group of saboteurs in the shipyard would, if he were lucky, have merely resulted in denunciation to the authorities. Yet Brady did not point this out to Haller.[16]

Both Walsh in Scotland and Brady in Ireland were to liaise by wireless sets and coordinate their attacks once contact with the Abwehr had been established.[17] Neither received any parachute training. However, shortly before their take-off for Norway, the pilot of the Focke-Wulf was ordered by Haller to return to Berlin as Walsh had been reported telling Cushing, a fellow Irish prisoner, that he planned on landing to hide the money the Abwehr had given him for the mission and then turn himself in to the British authorities. Always suspicious of the Irish prisoners' true loyalties, the Abwehr had bugged the communal flat where the Irish prisoners were staying and overheard their conversation.

Walsh, Cushing, O'Brien and Murphy were sent to Sachsenhausen concentration camp and survived the war. The British brought no charges against Walsh as MI5 believed his claim that he had no intention of carrying out his mission. Returning to Ireland, no more was heard of him. Brady was returned to Berlin and given more wireless training for another mission but not to Britain.[18] According to Thomas Strogan, one of the other Irish prisoners at Friesack who had volunteered for wireless training, Brady told him when he returned from Norway that he had been given several thousand pounds to take with him. Strogan identified other Irishmen who undertook Morse, wireless and high explosive training and claimed that some of the other Irish prisoners were sent to fight on the Eastern Front.[19]

Brady fought with the Waffen SS in Eastern Europe and, following the Russian advance, went into hiding before handing himself in to the British authorities in Berlin in 1946. Returned to Britain for a court martial, he received a 12-year sentence.

Stringer's file details his experiences at Friedenthal until May 1945 under Skorzeny's command, who was using the alias of Dr Wolff. An SD officer named Ludwig organised a group of about 200 men divided into cells of five or six. Stringer's group was taken to Hals, a villa near St Ulrich, a village in the Tyrol Mountains, Austria, where they buried arms, ammunition, wireless sets and sabotage materials. There was no indication that they were a stay-behind team to engage in attacks of the Allies' supply lines should Germany fall but, given the SD's plans for Spain, France, Belgium, Holland and Denmark, it is quite possible. The men were given civilian clothing and told to return home, something Stringer would have found difficult. He reported that when the men dispersed, they were told to look out for a newspaper advertisement which would read: 'SOLAR – Ladies underwear found at railway station. Owner please apply Box No...' On making contact, they would receive their instructions from Ludwig.[20]

Stringer made his way to Brussels where he also surrendered to the British. During interrogation by Sergeant Adeline, he revealed details of a sabotage dump in Austria. On 17 August 1945, accompanied by Adeline, Captain Hatton Groome of the Civil Security Section and Special Agent Austin Lewis of the US Counter Sabotage Section, they visited St Ulrich to locate explosives, radio sets and other equipment hidden by the Germans. According to Groome's report,

> ...we found, in a mountain chalet situated in the mountains within three miles of a farmhouse known as Hals, buried under the floorboards of the cowshed, the following articles; this was due to STRINGER's locating the dump and suggesting I dig under the floorboards: -
> 25 packets each containing 5 kg Plastic explosive.
> 12 packets each containing 300 rounds rifle ammunition
> 5 packets each containing 250 rounds pistol ammunition
> 10 Nipolit charges
> 4 Nipolit potato masher grenades
> 4 German egg grenades
> 8 G.A.C. Time Delays
> 2 coils (appr. 25 metres each) prima cord
> 2 coils (appr. 25 metres each) safety fuse
> 6 incendiary flares
> 1 box containing 16 pocket Incendiaries
> 20 booster charges (small)
> 10 100 cm. lengths BZE, safety fuse and detonator assemblies
> 2 lumps explosive coal
> 6 boxes (50 each) BZE 4.5 sec Pull Igniters
> 6 boxes (50 each) ZAZ 35 Pull Igniters

They found empty wooden boxes in which food stores had been hidden but failed to locate the hidden radio sets, machine guns and small arms. They also found Wagner's burnt out car. Groome took photographs and brought back an incendiary flare and 2-hour time delay detonator as evidence and rendered the rest of the cache harmless.[21]

Stringer was subsequently court-martialled and sentenced to 14-years but was released in 1950.[22]

The IRA's ability to reactivate its sabotage campaign against the British had been minimised, not only by the German agents being captured or handing themselves into the authorities but also by the action of the Royal Ulster Constabulary and British Army in Northern Ireland in rounding up suspected members. By August 1942, six IRA men in Eire had been executed, all but one for murder. Two IRA volunteers were shot dead while resisting arrest, and three died on hunger strike; 400 had been imprisoned and about 1,000 interned, 600 in one round-up.[23]

Another Irish agent destined for Britain was James O'Brien from Wexford. According to O'Reilly, he was a civilian captured on a British freighter and imprisoned at Friesack. Recruited by Hoven, he was provided with wireless training in Berlin and taken to the French border with Spain in the summer of 1942. His instructions were to make his way first to the Irish Legation in Madrid and then to Ireland. However, he went to Portugal and contacted the British authorities in Lisbon to whom he told his story. It appeared G2 and MI5 knew of his movements from intercepted postal messages.[24]

Hoven had arranged for him to be employed by a German firm which had a subcontract in France. Whilst on a business trip, he was allowed to escape.[25]

This was to be his cover story. He was to go to Donegal and to transmit from there weather reports, and reports about the armed forces in Northern Ireland. He was to construct his own transmitter. Before departure he was to be given £1,000 and crystals for his wireless set. Unfortunately however, he elected to cross the Franco-Spanish border before he had received either the money or the crystals. His excuse was that the man failed to make the rendezvous. He notified the Germans of what he had done before leaving ... he was eventually repatriated. We have considered the possibility of using him but in all the circumstances we are inclined to turn down the proposition.[26]

According to Liddell, the code O'Brien had been trained in was very primitive, and from this it was inferred that the Germans had never invested much hope in him.[27]

Moving on from the Irish situation in the early years, Friedrich Praetorius, alias Walter Thomas, admitted that between 1935 and 1938 the only agents he was aware of were those run by Dr Pheiffer of Bremen and three agents run by Lips [?] in France, including Dr Hartmann von Juechem. These three were arrested by the French before the war. He admitted that the Abwehr had a number of agents in England, then, 'from 1938 business sharpened':

a) A young German student named ALLNOCH was persuaded to send PRAETORIUS reports on industry in England while attending the LONDON Polytechnic.

b) A German business man living in London named UNLAND was suggested as an agent by DIERKS of I/M and, whilst visiting his hometown of HAMBURG in 1938 was introduced to PRAETORIUS to whom he agreed to send reports on industry in England – for a consideration of £25 a month; he moved to DUBLIN just before the war, but it is not clear whether this was to evade the Nazis in Germany, the law courts in England or the war in general.

c) A young German studying at a German Commercial School in London was suggested as a likely agent by a civilian named KRAUSE working in I/M and introduced by him to PRAETORIUS in Dec 1939; this German, named SCHUETZ also agreed to send industrial reports to PRAETORIUS from England and for this purpose was sent back to LONDON as the LONDON agents of REMY & CO, remaining there until August 1939.

d) At SCHUETZ's suggestion a friend of his called EIBNER in LONDON was contacted by mail and met in BRUSSELS in 39/40. He too agreed to send industrial reports & returned to England whence he wrote occasional reports to PRAETORIUS via Portugal until 1942.

e) A Swedish parson's son named GOESTA was recruited and sent to BIRMINGHAM in ca. Aug 39 to provided industrial intelligence – he returned to HAMBURG via Sweden in ca. May 40 and was later dropped into England via parachute.

f) Lastly a Canadian engineer working at the SPERRY GYROSCOPE Co. in LONDON was recruited and used by I/L.[28]

When war started, he admitted that the Abwehr was 'very badly supplied with agents abroad and those that were there had no WT [Wireless Telegraphy] or SW [Secret Writing], so that censorship alone put a stop to their reports.'

S/W was not used until late in 1940 when an officer was attached to Ast X for this purpose as a representative of Ig. Efforts were now concentrated on despatching agents to the U.K. and to the U.S.A. or to adjacent countries where observation would be of value. [...]

INVASION OF ENGLAND

Before the problems outlined above could be resolved and acted upon the more immediate needs of dealing with England arose: a conference was called in KIEL in about July 1940; those present included: -

Admiral CANARIS	BERLIN
Oberst PIEKENBROOK	BERLIN
Kapt WICHMANN	HAMBURG
Major PW	HAMBURG
Major RITTER	HAMBURG
Major SENSBURG	PARIS
Hptm. WENZLAW	BRUSSELS
Kpt. MUELLER	KIEL

CANARIS gave the order at this conference that all possible efforts must be made to recruit and train agents to be dropped by parachute on England and that such missions would be known as Unternehmen LENA [the name of a senior Abwehr officer's wife]. So far as PRAETORIUS remembers some 6–8 agents were despatched in the course of the ensuing months though he can only name 3: – GOESTA, JACOB(SEN) and [redacted]. (The last named proving a great success as WT was maintained with him right to 1945.) At the time it was expected that these agents would only have to be of independent means for some 6–8 weeks as by that time the invasion of England was expected to be an accomplished fact; they were therefore provided with money to cover such a period and the supply of money to [redacted] presented (later on) unforeseen difficulties which were only overcome by BERLIN invoking the assistance of Japanese diplomatic channels. [...]

Training System

The principles laid down by WICHMANN and fostered by PRAETORIUS were that the officers in charge of agents should spend as much of their time was possible with their charges so as to get to know them personally and be able to judge their characters and reliability. In conformity with this policy agents were not sent off to a central training school but were trained by the personnel of Ast X. Even the training in WT work, including operation, morse, codes and wireless construction, went counter to this policy for it had to be done by the technical personnel of I i or of WOHLDORF WT station and during this training the agent was apt to get to know his WT instructor better than his master-to-be, thereby destroying some of his confidence in his master. Other technical training was given by Von RAFFAY of I g.[29]

A post-war MI5 report claimed that 'The Germans no doubt intended to use pigeons with saboteurs or invasion troops from this country and were training them for that purpose; we believe, though that they were never sent.' Instead, the Abwehr agents were supplied with wireless sets, their messages to be received at Wohldorf, a wireless listening station about 20km north-east of Hamburg, known as Funk-Leit-Stelle-Uebersee. Headed by Oblt Schlottman, its code name was DOMAENE.[30]

The general training and briefing carried out by the officers in charge of agents was done in a variety of places: agents were accommodated at random in hotels and each officer or department had a room or suite of rooms which were usually rented in a block of offices. In this way, the chances of agents meeting were reduced to a minimum. The following were the training 'centres' which PRAETORIUS recalled.

a)   I H office in the house of Dr KOCH of ?35 Blumenstrasse
b)   I M An office in a business house at 6, Esplanade.
c)   I g An office in the offices of the Insurance firm of BERKMEYER situated near the HAMBURG Bourse.
d)   I Wi and later I i An office in the Pferdemarkt, HAMBURG with the cover name of 'Bibliographisches Zentral Archiv'
e)   An office in a business house called 'Handels Agentur Uebersee' situated 'Am Grossen Burstah
f)   I Wi PRAETORIUS knew of BOETTERN and STEGEMANN long before the war and sometimes used an office: using the address as a mail drop. From 1941 until the air bombardment in 1943 the whole of I/Wi was housed in this firm's office, only retaining one room at the Ast.

g) I Wi BOETTERN, early in the war moved to COPENHAGEN and ran a firm known as the 'Dansche In-und-Export Co' which PRAETORIUS also used as a mail drop,

h) I Wi A room in the offices of 'BECKER & FRANK' which was a subsidiary of REMY & Co – making pharmaceutical goods as contrasted with REMY's chemical products. A Dr MUTZ was the head man in this firm, to which Hans BLUM had belonged earlier.

i) I M This department, for the benefit of its 'Schoffe-Befragungs-Dienst' had two offices in STELLA Haus, Reedings-markt, HAMBURG from 1937/38 – 1945. On the offices doors were the names :- Von BREYMAN & Co' and 'MUELLER's Schifffahrtsdienst'.

In addition some agents were sent to an office in LUEBECK run by the I/Wi officer KLINKISCH; whilst I also had an office for WT training in BREMEN which had no connection with the Nebenstelle there.

As regards technical subjects PRAETORIUS asserts that photography was not taught as the equipment was not available and that 'micropunkt' was only shown to agents but never used.[31]

The first two Abwehr agents successfully infiltrated into England in the summer of 1940 are not mentioned in most British accounts of the German espionage service. Charles Wighton, a British journalist, collaborated with Günther Peis, an Austrian who had transcribed and translated Abwehr II's War Diary. Compiled by Lahousen's staff while he was in office from 1939 to 1943, it was included in a chapter in *Hitler's Spies and Saboteurs*.

Two Nazi-supporting Danes, a 26-year-old mechanic, Hans Schmidt, and a 24-year-old electrician, Jorgen Björnson, both from villages near Haderslev in South Jutland, had been working in Germany after the German invasion. Both spoke German and good English but with a strong accent.

When they offered to join the Wehrmacht, they were directed to Abwehr II's headquarters in Hamburg. Considered excellent material for sabotage training, they were asked if they would be prepared to fight for Germany in England. When they agreed, they were sent to Dr Rantzau's shipping office. Perhaps the financial reward, the potential excitement of the mission and a clandestine life in England led them to accept several weeks of wireless telegraphy training.

Following this intensive preparation, the two men were sent to a Luftwaffe school not far from Hamburg, where they were instructed in the details and characteristics of various types of British aircraft, and told what to look for at British airfields. They were also given elementary instruction on how to make weather reports.

By this time, it had been decided in Berlin that they would also undertake sabotage, and they were hurriedly shown how to manufacture explosives from ordinary substances easily obtained from British grocers' and chemists' shops. They were given instructions on how to use these explosives with the various types of fuses disguised as British-made fountain pens and pocket flashlights, which they would carry with them.[32]

The Abwehr provided them with British clothes, dispatch-case wireless sets, fake identity cards, ration books, £400 each in British notes and a cover story to use should they get caught. They were also told how to behave under interrogation by the British Intelligence Service and to claim that they were Danes who had escaped the German occupation because the Gestapo was after them. Fake records were made to show they had disappeared from a Copenhagen factory after the German occupation.

In early August 1940, on their way to Brussels to meet the Luftwaffe pilot who would fly them across the North Sea, they made a successful practice wireless transmission to Hamburg to confirm they knew how to contact Abwehr HQ. The pilot, who had lived in Oxford before the war, showed them maps of the area and located a drop zone in a wooded area outside Salisbury. This was not far from the RAF airfields they were expected to send information on in advance of Operation SEALION, which, they were told they should expect in September. Avoiding the built-up area of London would reduce the chances of his plane being shot down by British ack-ack.

As their flight was dependent on the weather and the moon, they had to wait. The pilot wanted a dark night and no low cloud so he could see the countryside. Accommodated in a Brussels boarding-house, they waited but after five days, Schmidt disobeyed instructions and went to see Randzau, who was staying at the Metropole Hotel, to report that Björnson had developed a relationship with the chambermaid at the boarding-house and was worried that he might brag about their intended mission.

Rantzau's response was to tell Schmidt not to mention their meeting and act as if nothing was wrong. A phone-call to the Abwehr office in Brussels led to two officers being sent to trail Björnson and his lover down the Boulevard Adolphe Max to be able to identify the girl. The following afternoon, she did not turn up for their rendezvous at a café in the Place de Bruckère. When he discovered that she had disappeared from the boarding-house, he denounced her to Schmidt as a typical Belgian woman.

Pretending to be the Gestapo, the Abwehr had arrested her and her father, charging her with interfering in German affairs. After intense questioning, the father was told that they would both be shot if either of them talked about their arrest and ordered him to lock her in her bedroom for the next fortnight. When Lahousen told Canaris of the incident, his response was, 'there's trouble as soon as you let women into espionage affairs.'[33]

As the conditions for the flight were still unsuitable, the two men were sent to Paris and ordered to enjoy themselves but to avoid doing anything to attract the Gestapo's attention. A week later, the flight was on. Taken to an airfield outside Chartres, a converted black Heinkel with all its bombing fitments removed flew them over the Channel and dropped the first enemy parachutists in England.

Schmidt's first transmission was not until the early hours of the following morning. Rantzau was pleased to be handed the message, 'Both landed safely in dropping area arranged. Will report further later.' The Hamburg wireless operator assured him that it was typical of his earlier transmissions and unlikely to have been sent under duress. Atmospheric conditions or other disturbances meant the next message could not be understood, and it was not until at an unscheduled time the following morning that Schmidt reported, 'Now at point 5 miles south-west Salisbury. Björnson's left foot badly injured. Lying in small wood. Danger of being discovered. You must help us (repeat) help us.'[34]

The wireless experts confirmed it was Schmidt's message, and if he had been captured, MI5 would not have been able to crack the code so quickly; even if they had, they would have insisted he kept to his scheduled transmission times. The Berlin chiefs sent Schmidt questions which, when answered, convinced them of the need to help. A message was sent to 'Johnny', SNOW, to provide assistance and he reluctantly agreed to help. What is uncertain is whether the British wireless listeners picked up his communications but when SNOW met Rantzau in Lisbon a few weeks later, he was able to report the full story.

Wighton and Peis made no mention of Schmidt and Björnson having been given any parachuting training, but it is likely they did. Despite a strong breeze and semi-darkness, Schmidt made an almost perfect landing in an open field. Having hidden his parachute and rucksack in some bushes, he went to look for Björnson.

Half an hour later having searched in vain, he saw a group of oak trees and heard a voice calling in Danish, 'Help me. I'm trapped. Help me.' Looking up, he saw a dark bundle which had to be Björnson. Climbing up the tree, he eventually found him hanging upside down in the upper branches. Crawling along one of the branches, he cut some of the parachute straps and lowered his fellow agent onto a lower branch. When his foot touched it, he cried out in pain. Eventually, Schmidt managed to get his colleague to the ground, but it was clear that he could not walk.

Finding a clearing in the wood, he retrieved Björnson's and his own parachute and rucksack and made a tent. Schmidt left his friend semi-conscious with no pain-killers, and walked across the fields to the village of Stratford Toney. Using the Ordnance Survey map he had been given and eating his German chocolate, he tried to reach Salisbury. Determining that he would not be able to make it and get back before dark, he returned to Björnson. On learning that he needed medical assistance, he made a meal of cold tinned meat and cold tea from a flask and at 0300 hours, his scheduled transmission time, he sent an urgent request for help, keeping it short to avoid detection.

The next day, after more iron rations, he made his way to Salisbury. Desperate for proper food, while looking for a food store or snack bar, he bumped into his first British policeman. Keeping to his cover story, he showed his identity papers and was directed to a snack bar near the cathedral. Worried that the policeman was suspicious and would inform his colleagues to check up on him, he decided against it, walked back into the countryside and, unable to get back to Björnson, slept in a haystack.

The following morning, he found a café, bought some tea, toast and fishcakes and then stocked up with bread, half a pound of butter and three ounces of bacon at a general store. Worried that the shopkeeper was going to report him, he walked back to the woods. On the way a woman car driver stopped and gave him a lift.

There was no reply when he whistled a Danish song. Björnson was unconscious and clearly had a fever. Because it was an emergency, he erected the aerial and transmitted another message. Half an hour later he received a personal message from Rantzau telling him not to worry and that he was trying to arrange help.

The next morning Hamburg sent the following message:

Schmidt will proceed to Winchester to arrive station at 2.30 P.M. G.M.T. this afternoon. In main hall with be a dark, small man in brown suit and brown soft hat. He will carry a Manchester Guardian. Schmidt will address him as Dr Roberts. Later he will reveal himself as Johnny.[36]

After cooking a meal, he tried to find Winchester but discovered that all the road signs had been removed. Lahousen did not know of this defensive measure the British government had put in place. When he eventually found the Winchester road he hitched lifts and was dropped in the town centre. Rendezvousing with 'Johnny' was tense but, once identification was made, he was told to take the offered cigarette and the piece of paper behind it. On it was an address in Salisbury where they would meet that night as Johnny was worried he might be being watched.

Instead of waiting for the next train, he hitched to Salisbury and met 'Johnny' as directed in a large villa on the outskirts. There was an unidentified Welshman present, possibly G.W., and the three of them shared soup, a capon and an excellent Cheddar cheese washed down with a beer, which he claimed tasted terrible. It was arranged that Björnson would be taken to a doctor 'who would cause no trouble' leaving him to continue his mission on his own.

So, after his first sleep in a British bed, he rose early and walked back to tell his friend and Rantzau the news. Burying all evidence of their presence, he helped Björnson across the fields to the nearest road. The rendezvous was at 0900, but the first car did not stop. At 0917 Johnny showed up, helped Björnson to get in and drove off. Schmidt never saw him again and learned later that when he recovered he was arrested and spent most of the war in an internment camp. Whether it was Camp 020 or O20R is not known. There is no file on him in the National Archives.

Schmidt followed Rantzau's instructions and went first to Southampton, then made his way along the South Coast to Brighton, sending weather reports twice a day and the number and types of planes seen on the airfields he had circled in red on his Ordnance Survey map and any evidence of damage. He also reported what he saw of the Battle of Britain from the fields of Kent and what he heard getting to know British troops in the pubs; he was able to forward useful intelligence to Rantzau, some of which caused consternation, notably large concentrations of troops and much armour in the proposed invasion area.

At the end of October, Rantzau was worried that Schmidt's transmissions would be detected by the British so he ordered him to cease and go to live in Wales for his own safety. Although directed to commit acts of sabotage, there is no sign he did.

Although an unnamed Welsh Nationalist sympathiser provided a safe farmhouse in a Welsh valley, he did not enjoy rural life and sent a message requesting more active work. Sent to London, he spent the rest of his money in hotels and boarding houses until, shortly before Christmas, he sent a request for more money. Rantzau arranged for him to meet a Japanese agent at the bus station in Shepherd's Bush carrying a copy of *The Times*. On rendezvousing successfully, he was told to follow him by bus to Victoria Station. When the agent left the newspaper on his seat, Schmidt took it to the men's toilet and opened it to discover £1,000 in £5 notes.

Friedrich Obladen, a German businessman who worked for Ast Hamburg, admitted during a post-war interrogation that in summer 1940, he planned a German commando for Kapt. Wichmann to be used in *Unternehmen Seelowe*.

I learnt later that in preparation for *Seelowe* agents were parachuted into England. WICHMANN, I was told, personally protested to Admiral CANARIS that it was a crime to drop any more agents into England simply to deceive the English. There were men enough in England waiting for German Troops who failed to show up.

I do not know whether (Ast) Hamburg dropped agents into England. It was rumoured that an agent who was injured in landing by parachute signalled by W/T for help and another agent was landed to assist him. I also heard of a case where a Japanese passed money to a German agent in a London omnibus I cannot vouch the truth of these incidents, nor whether (Ast) Hamburg was implicated; most unlikely that it was.[37]

Getting work on a farm, Schmidt went round livestock sales and transmitted intermittently for the rest of the war, providing details of concentrations of Canadian troops around the Southampton area before the Dieppe raid in August 1942. One message read: 'Just married. Leaving on honeymoon. Uncontactable for 14 days.' He also reported an important military exercise in the same area when the British were attempting to fool the Germans into thinking that they were planning to open a Second Front in France. In response to a message in late 1943 which read: 'Now father of 7 lb son,' Lahousen replied, congratulating him on being the first German agent to father a child in the course of his duty.[38]

Before D-Day he reported on the build-up of troops along the south coast which the Germans erroneously believed were going to invade the Pas de Calais. Details of American troop concentration, damage done by VI and V2 rockets were sent and his last message in early April 1945 was just before Field Marshal Montgomery's 21st Army Group closed in on the Hamburg wireless centre. Lahousen later heard that Schmidt was living in London after the war with his wife and family.[39] Why SNOW did not report him and why the British wireless detectors failed to locate his transmissions is unknown.

One result of this mission was that Lahousen considered that all subsequent operations into Britain had to be by boat. There was no mention that giving agents parachute training would improve their chances of landing safely. Masterman reported two agents, George Graf and Kurt Goose, code-named GIRAFFE and GANDER, who had been parachuted into England with wireless sets. Goose was dropped in Hampshire on 3/4 October 1940. Both were captured and turned but their wireless sets could only transmit, not receive, so their usefulness was limited.

It was revealed after the war that both Canaris and Lahousen had been anti-Hitler and supported a German resistance. In his War Diary, Lahousen later admitted using captured British time-pencils for the explosives in the failed Hitler assassination attempts on 13 March and 20 July 1943. Ironically, he was promoted to Major General and transferred to the Eastern Front. When Canaris' link to the latter attempt was identified, he was removed from power in February 1944 and executed along with many other plotters. With the leaders of what was called the 'Abwehr Resistance' out of the way, Lahousen was replaced by Wessel Freytag von Loringhoven. In France, the Abwehr's subsequent sabotage operations were centred on the Hotel Lutetia in Paris. Research by Sebastien Albertelli revealed that

> In the summer of 1942, envisaging the eventuality of an Allied landing in France, the Abwehr began to prepare by recruiting locally for future agents and by creating sabotage schools. A centre was installed in the château Rocquencourt, north of Versailles. It oversaw several schools in Vaucluse (La Montagnette), in Sarthe (Le Tronchet, Antoigné and Maulny), near Orleans (Château d'Etang), near Angers (La Roche), near Toulouse (Riquet) in Bayonne and Marseilles.[40]

The sabotage training camps at Rocquencourt, La Montagnette, Antoigne and Maulny were mentioned by several captured French agents but, as yet, nothing has come to light on the Abwehr's other camps and the agents trained there.

10

Operation LENA: Infiltrating pre-invasion Nazi agents into England, September 1940 – The 'Brussels Four'

Operation LENA, the infiltration of pre-invasion spies into Britain, started in early September 1940, a week or so after Schmidt and Björnson's mission. In Terry Crowdy's *Deceiving Hitler*, he claims Canaris gave responsibility to what became known as the 'Abwehr Spy Offensive' to Ritter, alias Rantzau.

> Rather than providing the day-to-day intelligence being reported by the likes of SNOW's Welsh network, the Lena spies were to be trained as forward scouts for the invasion troops, locating potential invasion beaches and landing sites for parachuting gliders. They were then to make contact with the invading forces and act as guides through the countryside.
>
> Ritter set quite a narrow limit on the type of people suitable for this mission. They were to be aged between 20 and 30, in good physical health and possessed of some technical knowledge. The man chosen as talent scout for the mission was Dr Praetorius. Nicknamed the 'Pied Piper', he trawled his net over the occupied territories looking for suitable candidates among hothead Nazi stooges and disaffected young men who could be blackmailed or otherwise cajoled into undertaking what would be a perilous mission.[1]

The first four were landed near Dymchurch on the south coast of England on 3 September 1940 unaware that it was one of the exclusion zones, and security passes were needed. This was at the height of the spy paranoia that raged across the country where enemy agents and fifth columnists ready to support an impending invasion force were thought to be everywhere. As a result, people were a lot more vigilant and reported anyone or anything suspicious to the police.

Belgian Henri Lassudry, and three Dutchmen – Karl Meier; Stoord, sometimes spelt Sjoert, Pons; and Charles van den Kieboom – had been brought from Le Tourquet, near Boulogne in two single-masted French fishing cutters, *La Mascotte* and *Rose du Carmel*. Once they were close to the Dungeness coast, they used rowing boats to reach the shore. Only Meier could speak English well, Pons and van den Kieboom could only understand when it was spoken slowly, and Lassudry could not speak the language.

The 26-year-old Lassudry, using the alias of a German named Joseph Waldberg, was a committed Nazi from Mainz and had been engaged in espionage for the Germans in France before the invasion. The 23-year-old Meier had been born in Germany, took Dutch nationality, studied in the United States and had lived in Birmingham before the war. A fervent Nazi, his English was good, but he had no experience of espionage.

They were frightened by a patrol vessel so Meier claimed they put their cypher wheels, wireless codes and maps in a weighted bag and dropped them overboard. On landing near the Grand Redoubt at West Hythe, they let their boat drift away on the tide, buried the wireless transmitter on the beach, hid their food and belongings in an empty boat and slept.

When Meier went to get a drink and some cigarettes in Lydd, he found the Rising Sun pub closed at 0930 and knocked on the door asking for a champagne cider. The cider was advertised outside but not being local he did not know that production had been suspended. Mabel Cole, the landlady, told him to return when it opened at 1000 but he could buy cigarettes at the shop across the road. She was further surprised when he knocked his head on the low ceiling beams when he went out.

On returning to the pub, he was charged 'one and a tanner' for his drink, which confused him, so he just told the landlady to take it from a pile of coins he offered. He then started chatting with one of the locals and asked him about the number and location of troops in the area. As the local was an Air Raid Warden who had been warned about strangers, he asked Meier for his identification papers. Having none, Meier was reported as saying that he was a refugee and 'we arrived last night,' thus implicating his colleagues. The police were called and after three hours of questioning at Dymchurch Police Station, he revealed Waldberg's whereabouts. He was reported to have told the police, 'You've caught me, and I don't mind what happens to me, but I don't want to go back to Germany.'

Waldberg in the meantime had set up his wireless set and sent two messages, expressing concern that Meier might have been arrested. He was about to transmit the third when he was apprehended walking across farmland near the railway line to Lydd with his set, five batteries and a Morse key.[2]

The 26-year-old van der Kieboom was a half-Dutch, half-Japanese receptionist at what he initially claimed was the YMCA in Amsterdam but later admitted it was the Victoria Hotel, a building used by the Abwehr. Pons, 28, was an unemployed Dutch army ambulance driver. Both had been engaged in illegal currency and jewellery smuggling, which had been noticed by the Nazi authorities. They both claimed that they were subsequently blackmailed; either agree to be sent to England or be sent to a concentration camp. They chose what prospective spies called *Himmelfahrt* – the ascension into heaven.

Van den Kieboom and Pons were also unsuccessful. They were stopped and questioned by two privates in the Somerset Light Infantry who were driving past them as they carried their bulky equipment along the coast road. Suspicious of their credentials, the police were called. Whilst waiting for them to arrive, Pons told some locals who had approached to see what was going on that he was a Dutch refugee and asked where he was. Van der Kieboom was given permission to visit the toilet where it was later discovered that he had hidden his codes, map and secret ink.

All four were taken for questioning at Dymchurch Police Station and once their confessions were signed, they were sent on 6 September to Camp 020 for further interrogation. All four had identification papers with the triangle on them that SNOW had given the Abwehr, thus proving they were German agents.

Stephens was keen to find out about their training, their mission and whether other agents were imminent. Nothing to indicate that they were saboteurs was found in their possession, only £130 in £5 and £1 notes, wireless transmitters and receivers, a loaded revolver and a sheet with the contact details of about a dozen people in Britain. No doubt MI5 made appropriate enquiries. They also carried blankets, biscuits, chocolate, a jack-knife and a pocket compass. Claiming initially to be Dutch refugees escaping Nazi oppression and hoping to sail to Canada, they later admitted being sent by the Abwehr. MI5 described them as 'The Brussels Four', a group of spies 'rather alarming in its local magnitude'. Having little spycraft, Pons claimed that his mission was to find out 'How the people is living, how many soldiers there are, and all the things'.[3]

Interrogation of the others found that they were to sleep rough, mingle with the locals in pubs, on buses and trains and collect intelligence on coastal troop positions, frequency of patrols, location of landmines and weather conditions as well as to report on British morale.

At the start of September, each of them had been led to believe the invasion was coming very soon. When the Wehrmacht followed, they were instructed to signal by handkerchief any approaching forces. 'Ich bin hier mit einem Sonderauftrag der Deutschen Wehrmacht.' (I'm here for a special misson for the German armed forces) they would say, followed by the password: Elizabeth.[4]

The four men admitted staying for five days at Chateau de Wimille, run by Kapitan Platz, assisted by Major Seynsburg. It was described as

...a large mansion some distance from the village of Wimille, near Boulogne. It is situated in the valley of the Denacre, a stream that runs into the sea at Wimereux. It is about ten minutes' walk from Wimille. The mansion is a two-storey building, surrounded by park-land. Containing about fifteen to twenty rooms, built of white stone with brick facings and a dark slate roof. There is a terrace on the side of it, showing white. It stands in an isolated position, quite close to a secondary road. The Chateau and grounds are guarded day and night by a military guard in plain clothes. In the immediate vicinity, there is a platoon of troops who probably furnish the guard.[5]

Whilst there they had been given 'a month's cursory training in Morse and cryptology, were shown how to use their transmitters, and given a few sketchy lectures about the structure of the British army. The German Intelligence Service, poorly run at the best of times, had been taken by surprise by the speed and success of Blitzkrieg, and these invasion spies had been a very quickly organised response.'[6]

The Joint Intelligence Committee, claiming to have 'a significant item of interest', issued the code word 'Cromwell' to the Home Guard in the Kent marshes, the order to prepare for an imminent invasion.

When Liddell was informed of their arrival, capture and interrogation, he reported:

> They had been instructed to report on British defensive measures on the coast near Dungeness and on army reserve formations in depth from Dungeness to Ashford and thence to London. They said that there was a concentration of mounted troops equipped with mules at Le Touquet. This information was confirmed to some extent by SIS sources. They have been told that an invasion would take place before the middle of September. In the meantime, they were to report anything they could with the small transmitting sets in their possession. They were to work in pairs. Each pair had £60 in English currency and food for seven days. They were given no contacts in this country. [sic] In fact they were singularly badly directed and to anybody with any knowledge of conditions in this country it should have been apparent that none of these people could hope to succeed. All of them had been misled about conditions in this country, probably as an inducement to them to come over.[7]

Van der Kieboom was persuaded to transmit a message to the Germans saying Pons had been shot and that he and the others had gone into hiding. Having admitted being German spies, there was no admission that they had been sent on a sabotage mission. Stephens considered them unsuitable for use as double agents so they were taken to the Old Bailey for trial on 19 November 1940 under the Treachery Act. This had been rapidly passed through Parliament and been given royal assent on 23 March 1940 to outlaw under the penalty of death conduct 'designed or likely to give assistance to the naval, military of air operations of the enemy.' Using the Emergency Powers (Defence) Act banning disclosure of any information with regard to any part of the proceedings, the story was kept out of the press. Although only Meier admitted his guilt, Pons escaped the death sentence, claiming that he had been forced to work for the Germans.[8] Waldberg appealed, claiming his defence lawyer had recommended he plead guilty, not realising the consequence was hanging. He claimed that his real name was Henri Lassudry, a Belgian citizen, who had been forced to work for the Abwehr as they had threatened to arrest his father. Despite the appeal, he, Meier and van der Kieboom were found guilty. Hours before Meier left Pentonville Prison, he wrote to his mother. 'I know that it will be a shock to you to hear that I have passed away when you receive this letter. I certainly believe that you will understand that it is better for me to die for my ideals.'[9] The letters Lassudry wrote to his parents and girlfriend were not sent.

Ian Cobain's research into official secrecy revealed that Sir Alexander Maxwell, the permanent under-secretary at the Home Office, expressed concern to Viscount Swinton, the head of the Security Executive responsible for MI5, that such an important case had been held in secret. Instead of the British public blaming the

Home Office, he wanted Swinton to be accountable. Swinton had to explain the importance of the double cross system in the war effort. 'The combined work of all the services has built up, and is continually adding to, a great structure of intelligence and counter-espionage. A single disclosure, affecting one individual, might send the whole building toppling. Even in passing sentence, a judge may inadvertently err.'[10]

At 9.25 on 10 December, after Meier and Lassudry had been hanged in Pentonville prison, MI5 issued a two-paragraph communiqué for Fleet Street and the BBC informing them that the two men had been apprehended shortly after their 'surreptitious arrival in this country', with a wireless set and a large sum of money; that they had been tried and convicted, and hanged that morning. The communiqué added: 'Editors are asked not to press for any additional facts or to institute inquiries.'[11] Seven days later, a second notice announced the execution of Kieboom. Pons remained interned.

To reduce media interest in the trial of enemy agents, MI5 suggested courts martial in military establishments followed by execution by firing squad would reduce the number of journalists, the need for a 24-hour advance notice of execution and coroners' juries.

An MI5 history of the Security Section stated that the interrogation of these first agents to be infiltrated into England 'filled in many gaps in ISOS information and enabled the first general picture of the main lines of Abwehr activity against us to be drawn.'[12]

Two days after the arrival of the Brussels Four, the first of two other agents arrived, this time by parachute. The 27-year-old Swede, Gösta Caroli, and 26-year-old Dane, Wulf Schmidt, had been prepared in Germany for a mission in the English Midlands. They were both Nazi supporters and had been friends in training but had been given little practice in parachute jumping. Caroli was flown out from Chartres in a Heinkel 111 on 6 September 1940 having been told to release his wireless set separately. Wanting to ensure he had it with him when he landed, he tied it to his chest with a belt. Jumping from 5,000 feet, he landed in a field on Elms Farm, near Yardley Hastings in Northamptonshire. As he came down more quickly than expected, the wireless set hit his chin and knocked him out. When he regained consciousness a few hours later, he dragged himself to a ditch and slept.

A farm worker spotted his feet and found him tangled up in his parachute. When the farmer, Cliff Beechener, arrived with a shotgun, Caroli admitted that he was a Swedish citizen and a German spy. Taken to the farmhouse; he was detained until the police arrived. He was then taken to Camp 020.[13]

When Liddell got to hear about Caroli the following day, he noted in his diary:

A parachutist descended during the night from a height of 15,000 feet; he had been stunned by his wireless set and was found lying in a ditch at Denton, Northants, at 17.30 hours yesterday. He was dressed as a civilian and was in possession of a German automatic and a wireless set which could transmit and receive. It was of a similar pattern to that now in possession of SNOW. The man's name is +++++++ [blanked out, Summer written in ink]. He is a Swede of German origin. He had been dropped by a Heinkel plane and had embarked at Brussels. He had intended to land at Birmingham and thought that on landing he was somewhere near Stratford upon Avon. It transpired that he had been in England as late as December 1939 when he stayed with friends at Boughton. He was in possession of his National Registration Certificate. He had been trained at Hamburg; Hinchley-Cooke took down a statement from him at Cannon Row [Police Station], and he was then sent on to Latchmere.[14]

Also found on him were £200, a map of the area as well as the loaded German pistol. Whether MI5 knew of his arrival was not mentioned by Liddell. Under interrogation, Caroli claimed that his mission was to investigate and report on fortifications along the South Coast and that the German invasion would follow the Luftaffe's attack on the RAF. He also mentioned a pontoon bridge across the Channel and that another agent was to be dropped to assist him. After being promised he would be spared execution, he revealed the location of Wulf Schmidt's drop, somewhere in the Fens, gave them his description and their planned rendezvous, the Black Boy Inn in Nottingham on 20 September. Successfully turned, Caroli was given the code-name SUMMER, sending messages back to Germany claiming that he had been in hiding since his arrival.

His interrogation revealed that he had been in England in 1938 and worked as a journalist, visiting industrial sites in the Birmingham area. Whether this was reated to future sabotage attacks or intended targets for the Luftwaffe to bomb is unknown. On trying to escape later in the war, he was interned.[15]

Boeckel acknowledged that Caroli had sent a few messages but when he stated that he was in danger and would endeavour to leave England, nothing more was heard from him.

All the LENA agents Boeckel met had received instruction in map reading, secret ink (aspirin method), the furnishing of weather reports and training in technical aeronautical matters, in Hamburg. Most of them were accommodated at Hotel Phoenix there. 'None of them spoke perfect English, but BERLIN insisted that they be despatched as rapidly as possible.'

Boeckel also admitted going to Madrid in October/November 1941 to meet Obst von Wenckstein, Freg Kap Lenz, the Commercial attaché at the German Embassy and the German Chamber of Commerce to investigate the possibility of sending agents to Britain by sea. He met Thiele of the Fichtebund who introduced two Falangists as possible agents but nothing came of it.[16]

As promised, Schmidt was parachuted from a Heinkel 111 bomber, specially painted black for dropping agents over Britain (a foolish 'camouflage' for any aircraft, day or night). In the early hours of 20 September, he landed in a field near the anti-aircraft battery for RAF Oakington, near Willingham, Cambridgeshire, but twisted his ankle and hit his wrist on landing as well as getting his parachute caught in telegraph wires. Having buried his wireless set, he managed to walk to Willingham in his smart blue suit, wash his swollen ankle at the village pump and, in excellent but accented English, bought a copy of *The Times* at a local shop. He also bought a replacement wrist watch as he had broken his on the Heinkel's strut as he jumped.

After breakfast in a local café, he planned to walk back to the field near the Half Moon Bridge where he had hidden his wireless set and suitcase. As he was crossing the village green, he was stopped by Private Tom Cousins of the Home Guard, asked to show his identity papers and taken to the Three Tuns public house where he was questioned further by Colonel Langton, the Home Guard Commander. Found to be in possession of £132, $160, fake identification papers in the name of Williams and a Danish passport, he was arrested and taken to Cambridge Police Station for further questioning.

Schmidt was taken to the 'London Cage' where, according to Liddell, he was assaulted by Lt. Col. Scotland and subjected to the use of drugs to extract a confession. Although 'rescued' by Stephens, he kept to his cover story for thirteen days until MI5 told him that Caroli had told them all about him, given them his description and their rendezvous. Angered that his friend had betrayed him and faced with the prospect of execution, he provided details of his recruitment and training and, like Caroli, agreed to work as a double agent. He was given the cover name of Henry Williamson and the code-name TATE. According to Masterman, he was the longest lasting double agent in the war.[17]

Born in Aabenroe, Denmark, he spent his youth in Argentina but returned to Denmark in 1931, joined the army and fought in the Cameroons. Interested in Nazi ideology, when he returned to Hamburg in 1940, he was recruited by the Abwehr. Introduced to Caroli during training, they became friends and agreed to be sent on a mission to England. Because of his injuries, he was unable to transmit the details of his mission, to report on conditions in the triangle between Birmingham, Cambridge and London.[18]

He reported being entertained by the Abwehr in Paris before his flight, where Ritter introduced him to Vera, another agent destined to be sent to Scotland. This was Vera Eriksen, also known as Vera von Wedel née Schalburg, Vera von Stein, Vera de Cottani de Chalbur and Vera Staritzky.[19] He stated that what he saw while he was being driven through London so contradicted what the Abwehr had told him about life in the capital, that he realised it was all propaganda. It is likely that the other German agents experienced the same disillusionment when they realised what conditions were really like in Britain.

...the streets swarmed with people, cars, buses, news vendors, and shops were open as usual, with fairly full shop windows. No one seemed to be suffering distress in the least. People stood and looked up into the sky where the last critical phase of the Battle of Britain was going on. He also saw that Buckingham Palace was still standing in its full glory. Not one bomb crater did he see during the trip.

He realised that everything he had heard was untrue. He started to question whether he should actually put his life at stake for such obvious lies.[20]

Major Karl Krazer, who worked in Abwehrstelle Belgium and was captured and interrogated after the war, shed light on Operation LENA, Caroli and Schmidt:

Unternehmen Lena was a reconnaissance operation which was executed by all Abwehr agencies covering Great Britain in preparation for *Unternehmen*

Seeloewe, code name for the invasion of the British Isles. The last mission connected with operation Lena, according to Subject, was undertaken in early September 1940. As proof for that Subject mentions the fact that all agents connected with operation Lena were equipped with summer-type radio transmitters. [...]

M Subject recalls two Agents who were parachuted into England during the month of September 1940. Subject describes one as tall, blond and blue eyed. He was a simple German soldier recruited from the ranks of the Regiment Kurfuerst. This man according to Subject was dropped by parachute some 240 km south south-west of Manchester. He was equipped with a Radio transmitter and allegedly captured by the British shortly after his landing. Subject does not remember this Agent's name.

Slightly later, still in September 1940 another man was parachuted into England from Abwehrstelle Belgium. Subject is unable to give this man's name, description or the location where he was dropped. Subject states that this man was presented to him as 'ANTROMACHE', and believes that this was the Agent's code name as well as the code name of the operation this agent was engaged in.[21]

The Germans contacted SNOW to arrange Caroli's rescue, which he told them he achieved, even though both were in MI5 hands. Provided with secure accommodation in Hinxton, Cambridgeshire, Caroli sent MI5-inspired messages back to Germany. According to Crowdy, he proved to be unstable and attempted suicide. In January 1941, desperate to escape his boredom in captivity, he almost strangled one of his guards, stole a motorbike and a canoe and drove to the East Coast, hoping to paddle across the North Sea. However, the motorbike broke down and he was recaptured near Newmarket. Had he escaped, he could have revealed Masterman's double cross programme and perhaps influenced the longevity of the war.

Keeping their promise not to execute him, he was interned at Huntercombe for the rest of the war. His set was played back to the Germans. Wichmann identified agent 3725 as having been parachuted in September 1940 by Abwehr Eins from Brussels. 'He was run directly by Abwehr Eins Berlin up to the spring of 1944, and only his wireless traffic passed through the Hamburg station. When Major BOECKEL was transferred to Hamburg, No. 3725 was also transferred. News was required and given regarding the Air Ministry and later about the effects of V.1. and V.2. There were often doubts as to whether the news supplied was genuine.'[22]

Boeckel claimed he was sent reports on the Royal Air Force and the aircraft industry, shipping movements, troop movements, unit and formation signs, the effects of German bombing, extracts from newspapers and magazines, and meteorological information. Although Berlin had doubts about his reliability, 'He received large payments for his services, once via the Japanese Embassy, and £20,000 when an agent IVAN of KO Portugal was being sent to America and a dollar credit for him in America could be acquired only by making £20,000 available in England.'[23] Having believed the MI5 deception, the Germans awarded Caroli the Iron Cross First and Second Class in abstentia.[24]

SNOW provided MI5 with details of the next agent's arrival. On 31 January 1941, Joseph Jakobs parachuted into a field near Dove House Farm, Ramsey Hollow, Huntingdonshire. Having broken his right ankle on exiting the plane, he was unable to walk. The following morning, two local farmers, Harry Coulson and Charles Badcock, spotted him after he had fired his revolver into the air to attract their attention. The Home Guard were alerted who caught him still wearing his jump suit. His parachute, harness, spade, torch and box of ammunition were found and an attaché case. Inside it were £498 in notes, forged identity papers, a blank ration book, wireless transmitter, headphones, batteries, insulating wire, codes, a Shell touring map and a German sausage. The map had pencil lines connecting Peterborough, Bedford and Cambridge and an X just south of Holme station, not far from RAF Upwood and RAF Warboys.

After a spell in hospital, he was taken to Camp 020 where he told TAR that he was a German citizen, born in Luxembourg in 1898 and had served as a lieutenant during the First World War. He was married with three children and practised as a dentist until having to join the Wehrmacht in June 1940. When his three-year prison sentence in Switzerland for selling counterfeit gold was discovered, he was demoted to feldwebel and transferred to the Army's *Meteorologischen Dients* (weather office). Recruited by the Abwehr, he was trained in wireless telegraphy and meteorology in Berlin and prepared for a mission in England to report on weather conditions around London. He was flown out of Schiphol airport and supposed to have been dropped near Peterborough. Whether Jakobs' story was true or a cover story is unknown, but his granddaughter claimed that he had not been given any parachute training.

There was no mention of any sabotage equipment being found or whether sabotage was included in his mission. There was also no indication that he received any sabotage training in Berlin. However, MI5 were suspicious and when he refused to be turned and transmit messages back to Germany, he was court martialled in camera because MI5 of course did not want details being released to the media. Within ten minutes he was found guilty of espionage, sentenced to death and was the last man to be executed in the Tower of London on 15 August 1941.

During his interrogation, he identified the woman in the photograph he had in his possession as his mistress, 35-year-old Clara Bauerle. She was a famous German cabaret artist who had performed in Britain for two years before the war and spoke English with a Birmingham accent. On receiving a wireless message to say he was settled in England, she was to be parachuted into the West Midlands to join him.

Whether this was just Jakobs telling lies is unknown as no mention of her appeared in any of the documents I have read. However, D J Cockburn and Alison Vale's investigation into the mystery of *Who put Bella in the Wych elm?* includes the possibility that it was Clara Bauerle. A body of a woman had been found hidden in a heavily pollarded tree in Hagley Wood, Worcestershire, in 1943. She had been asphyxiated. One suggestion was that she had been killed by a British officer trying to apprehend her who then disposed of her body in the tree. Giselle Jakobs, who researched her grandfather's life, disputes this theory as she reported finding Clara's death certificate stating she died in Berlin in 1942.[25]

Praetorius reported that early in 1942 there was a debate about how to get an agent named Karel Richter into England. He was a German Czech sailor who agreed to undertake a mission for I/Wi in return for full German nationality. Praetorius, Wichmann and others travelled with Richter to Paris to confer with the Naval Commander-in-Chief. It was decided to send him by boat from Holland to make landfall in the Wash but Berlin rejected the idea, preferring to parachute him just north of London. This was despite the Luftwaffe arguing that defences of London and the surrounding area were too dense.

On the night of 12/13 May 1941, 29-year-old Richter parachuted near London Colney, about 25 miles north-north-west of London. He hid his wireless set and equipment and spent several days in the nearby woods. On 14 May, when he emerged, two men got out of a lorry and asked him for directions for Hatfield. Unable to help, one of the men asked him where he was going. He said he was aiming for Cambridge but felt ill and needed to go to hospital. The driver spoke to a passing policeman who gave Richter directions and then questioned the strange foreigner. Richter told him he had come from Amsterdam by motorboat, landed at Cromer on 10 May and had been to Norwich, Bury St Edmunds and Cambridge. Unable to get accommodation as the hotels were full, he had slept rough. He denied having landed by parachute and having a wireless set. When his papers were examined and they did not match the details on his expired Czech passport, he was taken to Camp 020.

His forged identity papers were in the name of Fred Snyder, 14 Duckett Street, London, E1. This address was the headquarters of the BUF, which had been destroyed by German bombing. After interrogation, it was only when MI5 confronted Richter with Josef Jakobs who had trained with him in Hamburg, that he made a full confession. He admitted that, unwilling to face war at sea, he had deserted ship after returning from New York in December 1939. After visiting his family in the Sudetenland, he fled to Sweden en route to the United States where he hoped to settle. Having incorrect papers, he was deported. Arrested by the Gestapo, he was put in a concentration camp where he was recruited by Boeckel in November 1940. He was trained in air intelligence and wireless telegraphy in Hamburg and The Hague, and prepared to be sent by boat in January 1941 but adverse weather conditions in the Channel delayed his departure.

A second attempt was made on 9 May but when the motor launch which set off from Delfzijl was 8 miles off the coast of Cromer, 'Fritz', the leader of the party, decided that the swell was too great to allow a safe landing so the plan was aborted. Three days later, he was parachuted from Gartenfeld's plane with a wireless set, £550 and $1,400.

He claimed that his mission was to check whether Wulf Schmidt, known as agent Leonhardt, had been captured by the British and turned into a double agent. He claimed that he was to deliver the wireless set and £400 to Leonhardt who would rendezvous with him outside the barber shop inside the lounge of the Regent Palace Hotel, Piccadilly, at 1400 on the 15th, 20th, 25th or 30th of May or at 1700 at the Tate Gallery, or 1900 outside the main entrance of the British Museum. They would both be wearing only one glove on their left hand and he was to say 'Hello George, how do you do?'[26]

Leonhardt was Agent TATE. TATE kept the appointments but sent messages back to the Germans to say PHOENIX had not appeared and that he suspected he had been badly hurt or caught. The Germans then made alternative arrangements to send him the money.[27]

Richter admitted, though it was not included in his trial, that he had received training in Berlin and Hamburg, confirmed by Jakobs, which included using invisible ink to send messages and the general recognition of army defences. As well as sending meteorological reports, details of controls on roads and railway stations, he also had to

> ...obtain full details of the Grid System of Electrical Supply, particular attention being paid to sub-stations. He would then intimate that this information was considered to be so important that he, RICHTER, had been ordered to take back personally to Germany plans etc., thereby enlisting the aid of the second agent [TATE] in obtaining a boat or launch for his return via Holland. This part of the journey completed, he would immediately contact Dr SCHULZ [Praetorius] of the HAMBURG Abwehrstelle, when he would be asked to describe in detail the appearance, clothes, mannerisms and peculiarities of the agent in London. This would enable the German S.S. to obtain definite confirmation whether the man at present transmitting messages was their original agent, or whether he had been captured and another substituted. Dr. SCHULZ referred to the agent in London as a 'pearl', remarking that if this one were false, the entire string would be equally false – 'Das ist unsere Perle – ob sie echt ist, das wird sich herausstellen, und wenn diese Perle nicht echt ist, dann ist die ganze Kette falsch'. He traced his reasons for suspicion to a certain telegram despatched by the London agent last Christmas, containing the following wording: 'Greetings to the people at the Phoenix Hotel'. According to Dr. SCHOLZ, no real German agent would have referred in so many words to the 'PHOENIX' Hotel, a secret rendezvous of the Nachrichtendienst. He also said that the telegram contained too much.[28]

Details of the locations of electricity sub-stations, should they have reached Hamburg or Berlin, could then have been the targets for one or more future German-trained saboteurs or Luftwaffe bombers.

Richter also shed light on Feldwebel Schulz's S.S. operation in The Hague. An apartment at 131 Vondelstraat was being used to instruct enemy agents. As well as identifying Gaston, another wireless operator, he supplied descriptions of Major Merkel, alias Malten, Oberleutnant Hiller and 'Zebra', Schulz's subordinate.

Whilst in training he was given the cover-name 'Roboter' after the robot in *R.U.R.*, a play by Czech Karel Capek. Gosta Caroli was called 'Berling' from the Swedish novel *Gosta Berling*. Schmidt was called 'Leonhardt' and Caroli always called him 'Leonardo da Vinci'. Charles van den Kieboom was called 'Kirsch', an association between his Japanese blood and the cherry blossom of Japan. Stoerd Bons was called 'Piøert', Dutch slang referring to his attempted escape from the Nazis. Karl Meier was called 'Milch'. Joseph Jakobs was called 'Julius', thought to be because, like with Meier, it shared the same initial letter of the surname. Jose Waldberg was called 'Dubois', his mother's name after her second marriage.

He thought that 'wald' in German and 'bois' in French might have had some significance. John Moe was called 'Jack', an abbreviation of 'John' and Tor Glad was called 'Tege', the German pronunciation of his initials.[29]

He also claimed that if he did not get back to Germany by 12 July, 'Leonhardt' would automatically be considered by the German SS as unreliable.

Karel RICHTER's extreme fear of the Gestapo has greatly influenced him both in interrogation and in association with other internees. He is quite convinced that the Germans will successfully invade this country and examine all our records, in which he wishes to avoid compromising himself. He has stated quite openly that when this occurs, similar scenes will be enacted to those which took place in Poland. That the Germans will fail in this enterprise he cannot conceive. In consequence, his story has been extracted piecemeal, and can only be considered accurate when it has been possible to verify the details from another source.[30]

A transcript of his court case is included in his file. Despite claiming that he had no intention of carrying out his orders, he was convicted of espionage. His appeal to Edvard Benes, the exiled Czech President, failed and he was hanged at Wandsworth Prison on 10 December 1941.[31]

Three days after Schmidt's arrival, three men arrived in Plymouth harbour on the cutter *La Parte Bien* and proceeded to hand themselves into a naval patrol boat. Gerald Libot, Hugo Jonasson and de Lille admitted being recruited by Otto Voigt (Vogt), an Abwehr officer in Antwerp, for espionage work. An MI5 report identified a German Lieutenant Adolf Voigt as head of recruitment in Ast Antwerp.

He is described as tall, heavily built, with a grey moustache. He had been living in Antwerp for a number of years and in collaboration with his brother runs a well-known shopping agency. VOIGT maintains a number of talent spotters working in the port of Antwerp. These men bring their candidates for inspection before VOIGT at his private address in Avenue Hélene, Antwerp. If the candidate is accepted he then has to go to VOIGT's business address which is 100, Avenue d'Italia, where he is signed on.

Recruits of this kind are needed as crews for various fishing vessels and fishing cutters, normally requisitioned by Nest-Brest for the purpose of making trips to the English coast and landing agents there.[32]

Under interrogation, the three men claimed that they were to sail ships between French ports, the UK and Ireland and were on their way to Le Touquet but preferred to land in Plymouth. Although they subsequently admitted that part of their mission included sabotage, details were not included in their personnel files. It is possible that they dropped their equipment overboard before handing themselves in.

All three were interned in Camp 020 for the duration of the war. Libot claimed he was a member of the right-wing Belgian Rexist Party and a Nazi propagandist. Jonasson was from Sweden and had been given 2,500 Belgian francs to undertake a sabotage mission, details of which were not given. They claimed to have been drunk on route from Brest to Le Touquet where they were supposed to pick up some more agents. As they have no personnel files in the National Archives, little is known of their mission, but Hoare claimed that their interrogations provided information of considerable value on the personnel and activities of Nest Brest.[33]

A week later, Boeckel accompanied three agents to Norway for a flight to northern Scotland. In the early hours of 30 September 1940, a German seaplane landed in the Moray Firth and three passengers, Werner Walti, Karl Drücke and Vera Eriksen (sometimes spelt Eriksson or Erichsen), disembarked into an inflatable dinghy which they rowed to shore near Portgordon, just over 50 miles east of Inverness. Walti walked to the railway station at Buckie, a major herring-fishing port, and bought a ticket for Edinburgh. Drücke and Eriksen made their way to Portgordon Station where, at 0730, the stationmaster was suspicious of their bedraggled appearance, soaked shoes, ignorance of their location, asking for tickets to Forrest, not Forres, and Drücke opening a wallet stuffed with banknotes and offering far too much cash for the tickets.

Whilst provided with tea, Eriksen claimed to be a 27-year-old widow from Denmark and they had stayed the previous night at a hotel in Banff and had taken a taxi to a mile from Portgordon station. When Major Peter Perfect, the Scottish Regional Security Officer, arrived, the couple were searched and found to be carrying forged identity and ration cards with the red pyramid that SNOW had recommended the Abwehr add to their documents, a wireless transmitter and receiver set, a torch with 'Made in Bohemia' written on it, a revolver, ammunition, a coding device, graph paper, about £400 and a half-eaten German sausage. Given the evidence, they were arrested and escorted to London for interrogation.

A search of the coast found their knifed dinghy, a set of bellows and an aluminium oar which an RAF officer identified as being from a Luftwaffe seaplane. Walti's description was obtained from the Buckie stationmaster and sent to Waverley Station in Edinburgh and a search of the left luggage revealed his damp suitcase, which contained a genuine Swiss passport but with no entry permit, a revolver, £190, another transmitter and receiver, eleven Ordnance Survey maps of Norfolk, Suffolk and East Scotland and a map showing the location of Scottish aerodromes. The police were waiting when he arrived to reclaim the suitcase and, when questioned, he pulled out a Mauser pistol but was overpowered, arrested and also sent to Camp 020.

Interrogated by Lieutenant Colonel William Hinchley-Cooke, it was not until March 1941 that they signed confessions. They claimed that they were supposed to cycle the 600 miles to London but the choppy seas had swept their bicycles overboard before they reached shore. Their mission was part of Lahousen's HUMMER NORD I, which included reporting on shipping and, it was supposed, sabotaging RAF airfields prior to invasion.

Drücke posed as a French refugee from Belgium named Francoise de Deeker and claimed he was guaranteed passage to England only on condition he handed a wireless set to a man in the ABC cinema in London. Under intense interrogation, he kept to his cover story.[34]

Walti claimed to be a Swiss citizen and while working as a chauffeur, had helped Jewish diamond merchants escape from Belgium into France. Arrested by the Gestapo, he claimed he was beaten up and threatened with being sent to a concentration camp unless he undertook a mission to deliver a suitcase to someone in England.[35]

Eriksen claimed to be a long-lost niece of an Italian countess living in Kensington and that she had to go to London and 'hand over the wireless set to a man called Wilkinson, who was tall and thin with fair hair, who would call on her at the Dorchester Hotel within the next five days.'[36]

There are conflicting biographies of Vera Eriksen who had numerous aliases, but all agree she was born in Siberia. One source stated it was 23 November 1907, but she told MI5 it was 1912. Her father was Danish and her mother Ukrainian and she grew up in luxury in the Russian Tsar's court in St Petersburg where her father was an important official. However, following the Russian Revolution, her family were deported to Siberia. When her father was murdered by the Bolsheviks, her mother appealed to a former boyfriend, then a communist official, who provided papers, money and tickets for the family to go Paris.[37]

Research by author and journalist Adrian Searle found that her family moved to Denmark in the early-1920s and that, by 1924, she had become a professional ballerina, touring England in 1927. If these dates were correct, her claim to Hinchley-Cooke that she was only 27 was untrue. For additional income, she performed in the Folies Bergère where she is reported to have attracted the attention of Count Sergei Ignatieff, an 'unscrupulous' Russian double agent. During the 1930s, it was thought that she acted as his drug mule, carrying cocaine to various European cities, eventually becoming addicted. There were also suggestions that she spied on the Communists in France. In 1937 she was living with Ignatieff in Brussels, but, when she tried to break off the relationship, she claims he tried to stab her and then disappeared. At this point, her brother, a right-wing soldier, introduced her to Major Hilmar Dierks, the Abwehr officer in Hamburg responsible for infiltrating agents into Britain and elsewhere. They became a couple and she spied for him on the Soviets in Belgium and London between 1938 and 1939.[38]

There was no mention of Vera having had any contact with Dr Graff, the Abwehr chief in London, while she was in England. According to Wighton and Peis, one of Graff's agents known as 'Lady May', the German-born widow of a Scandinavian businessman, reported having found a potential recruit. She had met an elderly Italian countess in a small hotel in Kensington who had been an important figure in the diplomatic world and still had useful connections. She had inherited a small property in the Bavarian Alps but was having difficulty selling it and transferring the money to her London bank account because of German currency regulations.

Graff wrote to the countess, offering to help. He invited her to the Bayerischer Hof Hotel in Berlin and offered to arrange the sale and the money transfer if she would switch her allegiance from Mussolini to Hitler. She agreed and, to cover her expenses, he gave her £200 and told her that he would stay in touch.

When war seemed inevitable, Graff was instructed to 're-activate' the countess. Invited to the Doelen Hotel in Amsterdam, she readily agreed to his offer to finance her renting and furnishing a fashionable flat in Mayfair where she could renew her links with her influential friends by hosting lavish parties. He also offered to find 'a beautiful niece' to help her. While he knew some beautiful young women agents, he did not know of any suitable for this mission

Wighton and Peis made no mention of Vera's ballet skills, drugs or Ignatieff. They reported that her singing and dancing talents got her a well-paid job in a Russian restaurant in Paris. By the age of 18, her mother had taken her to Brussels where she worked in another Russian restaurant. Wanting a more independent exciting life, she moved to London, working in nightclubs and improving her English.

After a few months, it was claimed that a love affair with a Frenchman drew her back to Paris where she became well-known in theatres and cabarets for a double act with her lover. Reunited with her Russian friends, she was reported as being persuaded or blackmailed into working for the Russian secret police.

She acquired an admirer who regularly attended her performances. Treating her to champagne, he introduced himself as Herr Mueller, a German businessman selling German batteries in Holland, Belgium and France. Aware that she might be attracted by the man's money, her jealous lover attacked her one night at the cabaret table with a knife but was overpowered by Mueller. When the attacker was led away, Mueller took her to the hotel where he was staying with two friends. He confessed that his real name was Hans Dierks and introduced his friends as 'Karl Druegge' and 'Robert Petter', the cover names of Drükke and Walti.

Wighton and Peis identified the trio as important Abwehr officers who were operating a spy network in France and the Low Countries and which had played an important part in the collapse of France during the German invasion. Whether Dierks had been aware of her work for the Soviets is unknown but without funds, she accepted his offer of a new life and moved into his flat near the Rothenbaum-Chausse in Hamburg and travelled around occupied Europe with him. They quickly became lovers, and she learned that he was the chief of the Abwehr's naval section. On one occasion at the Metropole Hotel in Brussels, he introduced her to a Welshman who was described as one of the most important spies in England.

In August 1940, Dierks told her that he had to leave on a mission and was unable to take her with him. Worried about her future having left her friends in Paris and her mother in Copenhagen, in an 'outburst of hysterics' she accused him of making up the story to leave her for another woman. Breaking Abwehr rules, he told her the truth. As there was to be another great offensive, he had to be sent abroad; somewhere she could not go.

As Vera did not believe him and demanded to know the truth, he apparently said

> It is absolutely forbidden for me to tell you, but if you promise never to say anything, I am being sent to England with Richard and Robert, to carry out sabotage. You know that I'm an expert on naval matters, and I have been ordered to sabotage naval installations in England.[39]

Desperately upset and angry, she refused to speak to him and the following morning, having left for work, he had 'a curious presentiment' and went back to the flat and had to break down the door to find her unconscious having swallowed half a bottle of sleeping pills. He got her to the hospital in time and she eventually recovered but the Abwehr learned of her attempted suicide and the pressure Dierks was under. Sending him to England with his lover in such a delicate state might diminish his effectiveness.

Graff, who was back in Berlin by this time, had a brainwave. Ignoring Canaris's concerns about women being involved in espionage, Lahousen agreed that Vera should be sent to London as the Italian countess's long-lost niece and shelter Dierks in between the periods when he was engaged in his sabotage activities. The mission had to be postponed, and Vera was sent to the Abwehr's Hamburg training school where, while Germany completed the occupation of Holland, Belgium and France, she received intensive training in wireless telegraphy, Morse code, microphotography and elementary sabotage.

On 2 September, the night before the flight to Stavanger, the Abwehr threw a farewell drinks party for the four HUMMER NORD I agents at the Lowenbrau Restaurant in Hamburg. Having drunk copious amounts of Bavarian beer laced with Schnapps, Dierks drove them back to his flat and turning a corner at speed, the car overturned. He was killed and the others only slightly injured.

When Lahousen learned the news the following morning, his first reaction was to cancel the mission, but the invasion of Britain was imminent. Hitler was desperate for spies and saboteurs to be in place beforehand and angry with Canaris for not being able to provide an accurate picture of what was happening in England. As Lahousen had three fully trained agents, he decided to send them, despite their recent traumatic experience. They were flown to Stavanger that night and told that they would be landed by a flying boat off the northeast coast of Scotland and would have to paddle a dinghy to shore.

The following day they were driven to a small fiord and given practice in disembarking from a flying boat. They were provided with British clothes found in the British Embassy in Oslo, three bicycles found in the cellar of the British Consulate in Bergen, fake identity papers and ration cards, wireless sets, Morse keys, batteries, replacement parts for the sets, lists of sabotage targets, Ordnance Survey maps of Britain and names of people they could contact in England. They then had to memorise their cover stories and wait until conditions were right for the flight. Druegge was to be known as Drücke, a Flemish refugee who wanted to perfect his English and was bringing a wireless set for someone in London.

At 0100 on 30 September 1940, they were woken and within a few hours they were on their way to Scotland. Phil Coldham's research suggests the Abwehr gave Vera morphine before she got on the plane.[40]

Drükke and Walti refused to cooperate with MI5, were tried at the Old Bailey in March, found guilty of espionage and hanged in Wandsworth prison on 6 August 1941. Eriksen induced a miscarriage while in prison, thought by MI5 to have been Drücke's child, and refused to admit her role as an Abwehr agent until six months after her colleagues' execution. She reported that Walti was to operate on his own and that Gunnar Edvardson, a Norwegian sabotage agent, was to have joined them with a trunk-load of equipment.[41]

Eriksen's cooperation with MI5 was thought to explain why she was spared execution; but research by Searle and Phil Coldham suggests that on her first visit to Britain she stayed with Dierks' friend, the Duchess de Château-Thierry in her Baker Street flat, who had high-ranking RAF officers amongst her social circle. There were suggestions that she succeeded in photographing sensitive documents obtained clandestinely from unsuspecting officials. There were also reports that she gave birth to a son while in Britain the first time, but the identity of the father is unknown. Some suggest it was the result of a relationship with a British VIP who paid for the boy to be looked after in an Essex orphanage. Others suggest he was Dierks' son, but her records only show that a son was brought from an orphanage to see her in prison.

Agreeing to work as a 'stool pigeon', she was sent to an internment camp on the Isle of Man to report on fellow internees. Praetorius reported learning that her two colleagues had been arrested shortly after landing but it was not until late-1944 that Ast Hamburg heard that she was ill in an Isle of Wight internment camp. They sent her a food parcel but heard nothing more.[42] At the end of the war, she was deported to Germany, but an 'administrative blunder' allowed her to disappear, never to be seen or heard of again.

According to Wighton and Peis, when Lahousen was captured after the war, he was shown photographs of Drükke and Walti and told they had been executed. They had both been hanged in Wandsworth prison on 6 August 1941. When shown Vera's photograph he was told by a British officer that she had been given a false name and was living on the Isle of Wight. They also reported Graff stating that the Italian countess had been working for the British all along.[43]

In an almost identical operation to Walti, Drükke and Eriksen, on 25 October 1940, a German seaplane landed in the Moray Firth, about 15 miles north-east of Inverness, allowing Gunnar Edvardsen, the fourth member of Eriksen's team, and two other passengers, Legwald (Sigmund) Lund and Otto Joost, to get into an inflatable rubber dinghy with two bicycles. After thirteen hours rowing, they landed at Old Bar, Auldearn, near Nairn, and, according to Edvardsen's personnel file, walked to the nearest police station to hand themselves in.

When Major Perfect interviewed them, they all claimed that they were fleeing the Nazis. A search of their possessions revealed that they were carrying twenty-nine £10 notes with consecutive numbers, suggesting they had all been paid by one organisation, possibly the Abwehr, so they were escorted to Camp 020 for further questioning.

In Perfect's report, he suggested that 'it is time that someone gave these coast watchers a shake-up. This is the second lot of people who have come ashore, and the Police have been the means of affecting their arrest, and of course, if you ask the Police what the watchers are doing they say that they 'just get together in a hut and have a good gossip."[44]

The sand dunes where Edvardsen, Legwald and Joost claimed to have landed were searched and a knifed dinghy was found. When they were questioned about it, they were initially unable to explain it. Rothschild ordered another search to see if they had buried any sabotage equipment but there was no mention of a trunk-load of equipment. The 33-year-old Edvardsen claimed to be a Norwegian journalist who, after writing an article critical of the Germans in the *Dagbladet* newspaper, had had his house searched twice by the Gestapo. Fearing that what had happened to some of his colleagues in Germany might happen to him, he decided to flee the country.

He admitted meeting Lund, a 55-year-old Norwegian sea captain, in the Tony guest house in Oslo who told him that he had a divorced wife in Middlesbrough and thought he could get passage in a fishing boat across the North Sea. As he had assaulted a German policeman, he was keen to avoid imprisonment. Edvardsen told him that he was anti-German and wanted to escape. When Edvardsen saw Lund again in September 1940, he was introduced to 29-year-old Joost who claimed to have been born in Saarland, Western Germany, but spoke only German and French. When he joined a Socialist group in 1935, he was forced to work in France, joined the International Brigade and fought in the Spanish Civil War before escaping to Paris. With no identification papers and no job, he made his way first to Belgium and then, in August 1939, to Norway. He claimed initially that some fellow Norwegian soldiers were keen for him to escape to England. Later, he admitted that a Fritz Andersen took him to the Søstren Hotel in Oslo and told him that if he did not accept a mission to join one of the foreign brigades in Scotland, he would be denounced as a political refugee. He was to ascertain everything possible about its location, composition and movements and 'report to any German officer of any German unit which succeeded in landing in this country'.[45]

They claimed that, having purchased £315 of English bank notes, they left Oslo on 1 October 1940 for Aalesund, near Kristiansand, and set sail for Scotland on 17 October 1940. Joost claimed he first met Lund on the fishing boat *Boreas* and Lund claimed the boat belonged to Ingwald Furre and they had paid him 2,500 kroner per head for the trip.[46]

Edvardsen claimed that his experiences had convinced him to escape to England where he hoped to expose the truth about the German occupation to his friend, Thyge Lin, a former Norwegian Government official.

While all three were interrogated separately, some discrepancies arose in their cover stories. Under pressure, Lund admitted that they had left Aalesund in a seaplane so when he was brought into the room with Edvardsen, Edvardsen admitted that 'he had been lying and expressed his readiness to give a true version of the whole affair.'[47]

His revised story was that he had been working for four years for the *Sporting Life* with Georg Andersen in Oslo when the Germans invaded. On 10 April 1940, Andersen's brother Karl persuaded him to work for 5 kroner a day as well as food, cigarettes, etc, as an interpreter for an Austrian Mountain Battalion that had been sent to Northern Norway. Under pressure, he revealed that Karl, not Fritz Andersen, was really Fritz Anglemayer, an Abwehr agent responsible for infiltrating agents into Britain. He admitted meeting Dr Müller, the head of the Oslo Abwehr Stelle on or about 1 September at the Hotel Norge in Bergen and signed the German equivalent of the Official Secrets Act. Müller paid him 5 kroner a day for three months and his parents 500 kroner a month while he was away. He argued that he had no alternative but to agree as he could not obtain work in Norway because he had written against the Germans and the quislings, Norwegian collaborators. Anglemayer told him, 'The English fancied their coasts were very strongly guarded and the landing of persons such as himself would show them that it was possible for Germans to come over to England.' The plan was for him to be landed by boat in the Shetland Islands but his mission was not clear as the next few sentences in his statement were crossed out. When questioned about it being a sabotage mission, he denied it.

> EDVARDSEN strongly denies that the object of his visit to this country was to destroy bridges etc., and act as a saboteur. He states that he was told that he would in all probability be caught and interned, and the sole reason for his journey was to demonstrate to the British Authorities that in spite of their safeguards it was always possible for the Germans to land agents in this country. He says that Dr MULLER informed him that the Germans would be here within three weeks and that there would then be other work for him to do.[48]

He acknowledged meeting de Dekker (Drücke), Walti, who he also called Werner, and Eriksen in Bergen and detailed their journey by boat to Aalesund. The original plan was for him to accompany them as an intermediary with the crew of the fishing boat and return to Norway after they had been dropped. The four set off but could not reach shore because of a British patrol and returned to Norway. A seaplane was used instead but as there was not enough room for Edvardsen, his departure was delayed for a month. Anglemayer decided to send him with Lund and Joost.

> EDVARDSEN finally left Stavanger by seaplane on October 24th at 7.30 p.m. The seaplane came down about three hours later and LUND, JOOST and himself got into a rubber boat with three paddles. They were in the boat for thirteen hours before reaching land. He had with him some clothes, a lamp [torch], a camera and a revolver. They also had two bicycles [why not three?] in order to get away more quickly from the shore after landing. As soon as he landed, he threw his revolver away. After landing, the three decided to go to the nearest Police Station.[49]

By the end of December, Edvardsen had admitted that he had brought a pair of insulated wire clippers and that it was his intention to create alarm and despondency by destroying telephone wires and generally commit acts of sabotage. Stephens intended to proceed with prosecution under the Treachery Act and ordered another search of the beach to be made.

Joost admitted that 'he had been sent on a sabotage mission by the Germans and that he had hidden his sabotage equipment in the sand at Nairn. These articles were subsequently discovered by the Police in the place described.'[50] However, there was no mention in their file of any other equipment being found apart from the clippers.

> During the interrogation today, it was stated that I was to carry bombs with me. It is quite possible that I have joked [crossed out and replaced with boasted] and invented a story of this kind. Such an action would, however, be quite foreign to me, and there was no one on board who saw

any bombs. If I had any, I would certainly have been careful not to talk about the matter. [...]

It may appear strange that on both occasions I left without any special mission. This is, however, correct. On the first occasion, it is my impression that I was sent for the purpose of camouflage and that it would appear convincing when we said we were refugees, one from Belgium, one from Switzerland, one from Sweden and one from Norway. As regards the last trip, we were told to 'go and wait till we come'. LUND was to go to the Seamen's Home in Glasgow, and we others were to go further into Scotland. On the whole, it is my impression that it was not of great importance that anything should be done here (apart from those who brought in Morse apparatus). I think there is a good deal in what Karl ANDERSEN said, namely: 'that it will cause confusion when the English notice that the Germans are bringing people into this country'. Moreover, I had the impression that the more people Karl Andersen sent over, the higher his stock would rise. If it was one of the conditions that something should be done here in England, they would have tried to find people who know something about espionage or sabotage, instead of people like us.

When we left Norway, ANDERSEN said that in three weeks an aeroplane would be sent with 2 or 3 telegraphists, and they would presumably land at Portsoy [on Moray Firth coast, Aberdeenshire].[51]

Evardsen's interrogator described him as 'a wild type and reputed to be a saboteur, but for the time being, there is no concrete evidence to this effect.' In Stephens' opinion, they were 'short-term agents', part of what was called the 'Jitter War', the Germans' deliberate attempt to demoralise the British into believing that the German invasion was not only imminent but also that its success was inevitable.

Their mission appeared to have been to cycle across Scotland cutting as many telegraph wires as they could to create alarm in advance of a German invasion which they expected to arrive in the middle of November. One pair of wire cutters between the three of them could hardly be expected to create much damage. Losing their bicycles limited the extent of their operations and having no identification papers, believing they would not be needed once the German forces arrived, showed an astonishing lack of awareness of the prevailing security conditions in Britain. They also had no wireless set and were, therefore, unable to communicate with their base in Norway. They had apparently received no training and, apart from Lund, appeared to speak little or no English.

After almost four years' imprisonment, in June 1945 all three were deported to Norway. The files sent to the Norwegian authorities led them to sentence Edvardsen to two years' imprisonment and loss of civil rights for ten years. Lund and Joost argued that they had been press-ganged into working for the Abwehr.[52]

There was another Norwegian saboteur who was reported to have been sent to Britain. According to a post-war report on the German Intelligence Service based on interrogations of captured Abwehr, SS officers and agents, 'DAUFELDT of Abteilung Nord was responsible for the training of a Norwegian called PETERSEN who was destined to be sent to London via Sweden on a sabotage reconnaissance mission. This enterprise was not successful.'[53]

George Kronberger, an Austrian SD officer who operated in Greece between September 1943 and October 1944, defected to the British following the Allied invasion. He admitted working at Ottoladen from 1942, a training school for saboteurs and wireless operators outside Berlin. It had been set up on Himmler's orders to send saboteurs into Allied territory. Kronberger's Commanding Officer at Ottoladen was *Hauptsturmführer* Mandel, alias Muller but he identified *Hauptsturmführer* Hans Christian Daufeldt, code-named Dresscher, as responsible for sabotage operations against North European countries and Hstuf Langenbach, code-named Schneider, as responsible for sabotage in West European and other countries. It was Daufeldt who sent Petersen in April 1943 to discover whether 'there was any possibility of carrying out sabotage or other destructive work there and to return when he had seen how the land lay. He was to travel normally by plane from Stockholm to London and return by plane. 3 weeks after he had departed, DAUFELD said that he had returned to Berlin and that he did not think P. had been to London at all.' There was an SIS trace of an Oscar Pederson trained in sabotage work in Berlin but, as there were about sixty Norwegian refugees in this country called Pedersen or Petersen, MI5 did not investigate his case. 'From KRONBERGER's story it would seem very unlikely that PEDERSEN could possibly have gone from Stockholm to London and returned to Berlin in three weeks; rate of travel and travel control in this country would make a journey of that nature in that time quite impossible.'[54]

Another document refers to him visiting Sweden in the autumn of 1943 where he got in touch with the German Legation in Stockholm. He then returned to Norway where he planned to burn down the Norwegian Refugee Camp at Kjasaeter.[55]

Kronberger also mentioned being told by Frau Koppensteiner, who handled teletype messages in Vienna, that another agent called Klinburg was sent to England via Switzerland shortly before January 1944. They had met in early 1943 when Klinburg was in the SD's Sabotage Section office in Berlin. He was described as Austrian, probably from Vienna, aged between 26 and 28, about 1.7m tall, brown hair, small, delicate face, white complexion, very slim and delicately built, almost girlish and spoke English.[56] Whether he managed to reach Britain is unknown, nor whether he had been given a sabotage mission as there is no record of a Klinburg in the National Archives and his name did not appear in any of the Security Service histories.

Schmidt told his MI5 interrogators about another agent he had trained with in Brussels, Kurt Gross, spelt Goose in some documents, who spoke English fluently having studied geology in the United States but had returned to Germany and trained in espionage and wireless telegraphy with the Brandenburgers. He was parachuted in with a wireless set near Wellingborough, Northamptonshire, on the evening of 3 October 1940.

Following Brandenburger tradition, he wore his military uniform on landing but, once he buried his parachute, he changed into civilian clothes. Apprehended by a local farmer, he was handed over to the police. He had a wireless transmitter, a grid-type code and word key, a forged British passport, a National Registration card and ration book in the name of A. Phillips and £141 in English bank notes.

Interrogated at Camp 020, he claimed to have agreed to a mission to report on meteorological conditions, road blocks, defence positions and civilian morale in north-west England between Bedford and Liverpool, as he wanted to escape to America. He too was successfully turned and given the code-name GANDER. However, his contribution to the Double Cross deception was short as he only brought a transmitter, not a transmitter/receiver.[57]

In early 1940, Wilhelm Hollman and a group of fanatical Nazi members of the Brandenburg Regiment were preparing a spate of daredevil stunts in connection with the invasion of England. He claimed to be acting on behalf of Abwehr II, but neither Lahousen nor his Commanding Officer were aware his plans. According to Haller, he had made contact with the Hoven brothers and Clissman and made independent attempts to contact the IRA.

Guy Vissault de Coetlogon, a lieutenant in the Waffen SS and fervent Breton Nationalist, was given the task of recruiting fishermen to take German agents to England. When Lahousen found out, Hollmann was transferred from the regiment.[58]

Details of Hollman' plans were revealed in a post-war US intelligence report which Duncan Gardham, the *Telegraph*'s security correspondent, detailed in 2010. Hollman was described as 45 years old, 'but looks at least 50 ... a trifle stooped' with a 'gold right incisor tooth and 'very little hair ... Has long arms, very thin legs, blue eyes.' During the 1930s he worked as a secretary in the Jahnke Buro, a freelance intelligence unit run by Kurt Jahnke for Rudolph Hess, Hitler's second-in-command. According to Gardham's report,

...members of his group spent March 1940 training on embarking and disembarking from barges that had been constructed on the rivers and canals of Germany and the Low Countries and then towed down the Channel coast and concentrated on the beaches opposite Dover. The landings were planned along the English coast and in Scotland, and Southern Ireland but the attack would be centred around Dover.

The invasion would begin with a 'heavy aerial attack' followed by 'specially trained shock troops' who were to 'attempt to make landings with a view to seizing and holding strategic positions until the main body of German troops could be brought across the channel in barges.'

The informant, Werner Janowski, said his unit was to arrive under cover of darkness, wearing Allied uniforms, as others had during the invasions of France and the Low Countries.

The report, released to the National Archives, says they were 'to proceed along the cliffs to a point outside Dover where there were steps leading down to the beach and from this point they were to continue along the beach and regain the cliff head by means of some steps near the station in Dover'.

The unit was then meant to secure the docks and railway station and signal to the Luftwaffe that they were ready for the main invasion body to follow by barge into the port.

Training for the invasion continued through September and October 1940, with the unit under orders to 'prepare for embarkation at a moment's notice.'

The orders were never cancelled but by October the rank and file realised that the invasion would not take place that year, and when the barges were moved to Dunkirk, most were apparently destroyed in raids by the RAF during December.

The soldiers were right; Hitler had cancelled 'Operation Sealion' on 17 September 1940 after hearing that his forces lacked naval support after losses in the Norwegian campaign and air support as a result of the Battle of Britain.

An estimated 21 enemy agents were infiltrated into Britain in September and October 1940, including twelve on Operation LENA and, it was claimed, wrongly as it turned out, that every single one was captured.

On 1 April 1941, an electrician reported finding a dead man in a nearly completed air-raid shelter on Christ's Piece, Cambridge. He had been shot in the head and a Belgian-made Browning Automatic revolver was found beside the body. The police investigation which followed eventually involved MI5 in an embarrassing case. Press censorship ensured nothing was revealed to the public until after the war.

Documents found on the body identified him as 27-year-old Jan Willem Ter Braak, from Gravenage, Holland. A medal of the Virgin Mary, what the police called a 'Catholic charm', was found in his possession, as well as copies of the *Daily Mirror*, *Star* and *Evening Standard* for Saturday, 29 March 1941. Careful investigation of them found no markings. An out-of-date ration card gave his address as 58 St Barnabas Street, Cambridge, where it was found that he stayed from 4 November 1940 to 31 January 1941. The numbers on the card had been given to the Abwehr by SNOW.[59]

Subsequent evidence showed that he had rented an office with accommodation at 11 Montague Road, Cambridge, which he left without paying his bills on 29 March taking all his luggage, telling Miss Greenwood, his landlady, that he was going to join the Free Dutch forces on the coast and would be back the following weekend. Mrs Sennitt, his previous landlady reported him leaving every day between 9 and 10 after bread and toast and returning about the same time every evening. Bus tickets found in his possession suggested he had travelled to London, St Neots, Bedford, Huntingdon, Peterborough and Alconbury Hill. As there was an RAF airfield at Alconbury, there were concerns that he may have been engaged in espionage. There was no suggestion the visit to St Neots could also have included RAF Tempsford. The only mention in the file suggesting that he might have been engaged in any sabotage activities was from the Buckinghamshire Police but it was not noted by the Cambridgeshire investigation team, nor MI5.

When he was found, he was wearing four woollen vests and two pairs of long johns, which suggested he had planned to be out in the cold. The doctor called to check estimated that he had been dead for 24 hours. When his suitcase was searched, all that was found were clothes and a set of keys belonging to the left-luggage office at Cambridge railway station. When this was searched, another suitcase containing a wireless transceiver was found. A search of his lodgings revealed in a locked wardrobe two exhausted batteries, an accumulator which he would have used as an alternative power source, and an aerial. The set was the same design as that used by agents captured in Scotland. Based on interviews with people who had met him, he was described as aged about 27, about 6 feet in height and had a strong Dutch accent. He had told people that he had escaped with the Dutch Forces from Dunkirk, worked for the Free Dutch Press in Torquay and Oxford, and was writing a book.

TAR suspected that he had been able to communicate with the Abwehr until Christmas until the batteries of his set ran out, then communicated using secret ink. He surmised that he had been told to rendezvous with another German agent who was due to arrive on 29/30 March. When no-one arrived and he only had 1s. 6d. in his pocket, not enough for a meal, he shot himself.

Regarding the rented office, TAR surmised that Ter Braak had been told he was going to oversee other German agents following the expected invasion and needed an office in Cambridge as a rendezvous and a place to collate information. A folded parachute containing a harness, padded helmet and jump suit with Belgian chocolate wrapping paper, a piece of paper with a Brussels address and a broken aspirin in its pocket had been found beside a bridleway at Hill Farm, Haverham, near Bletchley, Buckinghamshire, on 3 November 1940. It was assumed to be Ter Braak's. It was of the same make as that used by Richter and the chute had two cords with clips for attachments like a suitcase. Their pistols were of identical make and pattern, suggesting they had both been sent by the same organisation. Investigations suggested he had landed on the night of 29/30 October. Searches with bloodhounds of woods and farm buildings in the area were undertaken and enquiries made but the parachutist had not been found. The Chief Constable of Buckinghamshire was criticised for not notifying MI5's Regional Security Officer of the incident.

When investigations were made with the RAF to determine the flight path of enemy aircraft over the Haversham area and whether it might be possible that someone was using an illicit high frequency ground-to-air transmitter to signal to overflying pilots, the results proved inconclusive. Enquiries made regarding transmissions made using the frequencies found on Braak's crystals between 4 December and 31 January failed to turn up anything.

MI5 thought that he was another of the Operation LENA agents but post-war interrogations of Ritter, Bensmann, Boeckel and Zebralla of Ast Hamburg and Ast Bremen led them to disbelieve this as the Germans claimed the operation ceased in October 1940. It was assumed therefore that he had been sent by Major Sensburg of Ast Brussels or by Aussenstelle Antwerp and was from the same control station as Karel Richter.[60] Regional Security Liaison Officers were informed of the case and the blame for failing to arrest Ter Braak was laid at thec door of the Assistant Aliens Officer in Cambridge. He was criticised for not following up two reports about Braak.

In early 1947, the Dutch authorities contacted their British counterparts for details of Engelbertus Fukken, the real name of Ter Braak. His fiancée, Miss Eeltje van Roon, had requested proof of death so she could claim on the life insurance policy she had taken out before his departure for Britain.[61] He was buried in an unmarked grave in St Mary's, Great Shelford, 3 miles south of Cambridge.

Thomas and Ketley claimed der Braak was a Soviet double agent who was murdered to prevent him betraying others involved in his work. There was no mention of this in his file but there were several redacted pages.[62]

In a confidential memorandum, dated 22 October 1940, Lieutenant General Mockler-Ferryman reported to Aldershot Command, Eastern Command, Northern Command, Scottish Command, Southern Command, Western Command, London District, 4th Corps and 7th Corps that

> It may now be divulged that a number of enemy agents have been captured during the last month. It is, however, most undesirable that this information should be published by the Press or discussed outside the Army, for as in the case of submarine sinkings, it is important that the Germans should be kept in ignorance of the fate that has overcome them, at any rate for an appreciable period.
>
> Four agents were recently landed from boats on the South East coast. They had in their possession wireless sets, ciphers and maps, and supplies of food and English money. They had received instructions to obtain detailed information of our defence works, stocks of food, aerodromes, morale etc.
>
> Wireless sets are often carried in small suitcases, which may be hidden or buried in woods or fields during the day time.
>
> It is known that the enemy is most anxious to obtain information about conditions in England, and it is must be expected that attempts will be made to introduce further agents, by sea or by parachute, at different points in all parts of Great Britain and not necessarily on the more obvious East and South Coasts.
>
> All ranks should be made aware that the danger of spies is a real one, and they should be educated to view with suspicion anyone, however plausible, who is inquisitive or appears to be hanging about for no particular reason.[63]

From the British point of view, there was an element of luck in the capture of virtually all the pre-invasion agents. Most Secret Sources provided evidence of names and times of arrival of some of them and captured agents provided further details under interrogation, but their general failure was attributed at the time to their own stupidity. There was also criticism of the Abwehr's poor selection process, the agents' weak language skills and their lack of training in British social customs. They were not professional agents; they were amateurs. Ordering a drink in a pub before opening hours, cycling on the wrong side of the road in Scotland and paying £10 and six shillings for something that was 'ten and six' were elementary errors.

While some in MI5 thought the Abwehr might have wanted them to be deliberately caught and work as triple agents, this view was outweighed by those who were convinced they were bona fide double agents. Those who refused to be turned were tried in camera, with no public in attendance, and executed, providing a great propaganda opportunity for the government to persuade the British population to be on their guard against potential spies and saboteurs. Even though there were 14 executions, Stephens was reported as being disappointed that there were not more.[64] According to Crowdy,

...mounting fear of a German invasion prompted a spy scare in Britain of epidemic proportions. The collapse of one European country after another before the Nazi *Blitzkrieg* could only have one explanation: in each country, there must have been a network of German agents behind the lines, aiding a German advance. A similar network, it was assumed, must exist in Britain, plotting to undermine the state. The myth of the German fifth column was born on a most un-British wave of public hysteria, stoked by the press and the politicians...

German spies were spotted everywhere, and nowhere. Police were deluged with reports of strange figures in disguise, lights flashing at night, burning haystacks, and paranoid neighbours hearing strange tapping through the walls. One avid amateur spycatcher reported seeing a man with a 'typically Prussian neck'; Baden-Powell, the original scoutmaster, insisted you could spot a German spy from the way he walked. Anyone and everyone might be a spy. Evelyn Waugh lampooned the frenzy: 'Suspect everyone – the vicar, the village grocer, the farmer whose family have lived here for a hundred years, all the most unlikely people.' The spies were said to be spreading newspaper on the ground to give secret messages to airborne Germans, poisoning chocolates, infiltrating the police, recruiting lunatics from asylums to act in a suicide squad, and sending murderous agents into the British countryside disguised as women hitchhikers.[65]

In 2014, German historian Monika Siedentopf put forward an alternative view of the failure of the Abwehr agents sent to Britain. In her book, translated as *Operation Sealion: Resistance inside the Secret Service*, she suggested that Herbert Wichmann was involved with Canaris in the failed assassination of Hitler in 1944 and in the discussions with the Allies at the end of the war in mending ties between Germany and Britain. Her thesis was that Wichmann thought Operation SEALION was badly planned and would harm Germany. He did not want relations between Germany and Britain to be irreparable and therefore deliberately sabotaged the invasion by sending men he knew would be likely to fail. Although they were enthusiastic Nazis, they were of low intelligence with poor knowledge of English and English life. Many were petty criminals and members of Fascist parties in Denmark, Holland and Belgium who were motivated by money.[66] This argument was confirmed in Lahousen's post-war interrogation.

Whatever the truth of the matter, the German invasion did not happen. In Wichmann's interrogation report, he claimed that he was called to St Germain in Paris in early September 1940 to report to Major Kleikamp of Heeresgruppe A. He met the High Command of Army Group A, Feldmarschall von Rundstedt, Generalmajor von Sodernstern, Oberst Blumentritt, Major Kleikamp and Oberst Freiherr von Vechtmar. At a conference attended by officers from Abwehr Berlin, Ast Paris and Abwehr organisations in France and the Low Countries, Colonel Hans Oster, (later Major General), Canaris's Chief of Staff and deputy head of the Abwehr's counter-espionage bureau, explained that the invasion of Great Britain was imminent. Plans and preparations for the Abwehr needed to be made which included him being in charge of Ast London. His staff were to be Korv. Dr.

Pfeiffer, Ritter, Wettstein, Obladen, Praetorius or Schauenburg, Trautmann and Karv. Kapt. Liebenschuetz.

Other persons I proposed were SCHUCHMANN, at that moment in Havre. To be G.C. of an Einsatzkommando, and Hptmann STRAMER from Hamburg, appointment uncertain.

Major TRAUTMANN was to be in charge of communications. He was to provide at least 3 mobile W/T stations, and had to provide the W/T sets to each kommando and one to the Ast, and the troops would receive normal Army W/T sets. Major FELDMANN of Ast Paris was to set up the Abwehr Kommando III, and he was to select the personnel from Ast Paris and Ast Brussels. With regard to II Kommando, these were to be transferred complete, when required, and WICHMANN knows nothing more about them.

Although WICHMANN was told to make his whole organisation mobile, no vehicles were provided, and he had to forage for himself from vehicle parks. When the invasion was cancelled, WICHMANN had not yet acquired a quarter of the vehicles he required.

For purposes of liaison, WICHMANN visited I/AD of Armee BOSCH, near LILLE, and of an army lying a little north of Rouen.

On September 25/26, an indoor invasion exercise took place at St Germain. Generaloberst HALDER, Chief of Staff of the Army, was present. The result was the discovery that the German Air Force and Navy could not guarantee the necessary minimum protection for the invasion to have a hope of success. WICHMANN notes that Oberst PIEKENBROOK, Chief of Abwehr I, was extremely sceptical of the invasion's taking place, from the very start. RICHMANN was never shown the plan, but understood that the point of attack was due to be between Eastbourne and Hastings, where the first bridgehead was to be established. Breaking out of the bridgehead, the troops were to move eastwards towards Folkestone and Dover, so as to free these ports first. Some 6/8 divisions were to be put into the first bridgehead.

WICHMANN states that the barges and other transports which it was proposed to use were quite unsuitable, and that there would have been manned by completely incompetent crews. The Navy had apparently not been properly consulted, and these half-baked plans had gone forward, only to be abandoned at the last moment.[67]

Hans-Joachim Rudloff, a member of the Brandenburg Regiment which had been ready to invade Weymouth, reported that 'it was common talk amongst the staff officers of the VIth Army that the invasion had been called off in order not to antagonize the British too much. At that time, everyone believed that the British would be ready to contract a compromise peace with the Germans when they saw that the situation was really serious.'[68]

11

Mrs O'Grady, sentenced to death for sabotage – August 1940–February 1941

The British government used the threat of invasion to ensure heightened anti-espionage and anti-sabotage activity. On 16 September 1940, Liddell reported that one Mrs O'Grady was in Holloway, the women's prison. An internet search reveals that Searle and Andrew Bradford had uncovered a fascinating story of this woman, Dorothy O'Grady, the first British woman to be found guilty of sabotage under the 1940 Treachery Act and sentenced to death.

Born in 1897 in Clapham, South London, Dorothy was adopted by George and Pamela Squire but, following the death of her adopted mother when she was 10, she was badly treated by her father's new wife, their housekeeper. After being trained for domestic service, she was convicted and sent to borstal in 1918 for forging bank-notes. The following year, while in service in Brighton, she was sentenced to two years' imprisonment for stealing clothes. When she was released, she worked as a prostitute in London for which she was convicted four times. On the day of her release, 16 August 1926, she married Vincent O'Grady, a 45-year-old London fireman.

When her husband retired, they moved to the Broadway in Sandown on the Isle of Wight where they ran the Osborne Villa boarding house. However, with the outbreak of war, he responded to the call for retired firemen to return to work in London, leaving Dorothy on her own. In August 1940, she was described as

> a 42-year-old lonely landlady, short, plump, with poor eye-sight and a squeaky voice. Quiet and reserved, she spent her time alone with her dog, and had no known friends; even her neighbour did not know her name. With no tourists visiting England's front-line for bed and breakfast, and without her husband, Dorothy doted on her dog, taking it for walkies on the beach every day.[1]

The Battle of Britain was underway and England was facing the threat of imminent invasion. Only about 100 miles from Le Havre, the Isle of Wight was considered vulnerable. As Sandown had views over the Solent, the approach to Southampton and the naval base of Portsmouth, its strategically important coastline was designated an exclusion zone with restricted civilian access.

The 5-mile beach in Sandown Bay was the likely landing site for the Germans so the 12th Infantry Brigade was stationed at Sandown barracks and the area defended by searchlights, anti-aircraft guns, mines, barbed wire, 'dragons' teeth', anti-landing-craft devices, concrete pill-boxes, iron rails, old First World War naval guns and trenches.

Unknown to the British, on 16 July 1940, in preparation for Operation SEALION, Hitler had issued a directive to the Wehrmacht to 'examine from its own viewpoint whether it appears practical to carry out subsidiary operations, for example, to occupy the Isle of Wight ... prior to a general crossing'.[2]

To detect enemy shipping and low-flying aircraft, an experimental Chain Home Low radar station was constructed in July on Culver Cliff, close to the Royal Navy's shore signals and wireless station. Modern weapons were installed in the Victorian forts of Culver Fire Command overlooking Sandown Bay. Sections were removed from Ventnor, Shanklin and Sandown piers to prevent them being used by the enemy as landing stages. All these things would have been obvious to Dorothy, who ignored the Defence Regulations on the route she usually walked Rob, her black retriever, sometimes at night.

On 9 August 1940, she was apprehended by 'squaddies' from the Royal Northumberland Fusiliers on the beach at Yaverland having ignored the 'No Trespassing' sign and crossed the barbed wire. As it was the third time she had been spotted, they told her they were going to report her to the police. Alarmed at the prospect, she offered them ten shillings to keep quiet and let her go. They refused and walked her 3 miles to Bembridge police station where her name and address were taken. A search revealed a torch, a small swastika badge under her coat lapel, cut-out Nazi paper flags, a pencil and notebook containing drawings and detailed maps of Sandown Bay. Her activities were described as a nuisance and, to warn other civilians about breaking Defence Regulations, she was summoned to appear in the Magistrate's Court in Ryde on 27 August charged with 'entering the foreshore, contrary to regulation 16a and acting in a manner likely to prevent or interfere with the performance of HM Forces'.[3]

Although she would in all likelihood have been given a severe verbal reprimand and a fine as an example, Dorothy did not turn up at court. When the police called at Osborne Villa, the place was empty, only a note on the door saying: 'No more milk till I return.' Her flight convinced the police that she was a 'fifth columnist quisling'. A manhunt was launched which extended across Southern England. There was a worry that she had found a way to avoid the tight security at the ferry ports where a permit was needed to travel. MI5 got a warrant to open her post to see if she was in correspondence with German Intelligence.

She had taken Rob to live in Latton House guest house in Totland Bay on the western side of the island and was using the name Pamela Arland, one she had used as a London prostitute. After Sandown Bay, Totland was in the middle of the Freshwater peninsula, the next most heavily defended part of the island. During her three weeks in hiding, she was spotted walking in restricted areas, cutting military telegraph wires in the Alum Bay area with her nail clippers and making maps using information about gun emplacements by paying small bribes to local schoolboys. The second time she was arrested at Alum Bay, she tried to bribe a policeman with cigarettes and chocolate.

> When these offers were refused she apparently made a suicide bid. In spy novels, professional spies always carry cyanide tablets to make the supreme sacrifice when caught. Dorothy didn't have cyanide. She took twenty ephedrine tablets from her handbag and swallowed them. No record exists as to the effect of this overdose; whether she needed medical treatment, or whether her life was actually threatened by it. So, we do not know whether this was the serious suicide bid of an undercover agent now unmasked.[4]

On 10 September, when the police had called at the guest house, they caught her reportedly trying to flush papers down the toilet. A search of her room revealed a notebook containing annotated maps of Sandown Bay and the western coast including radar stations, gun emplacements and military barracks.

Whether she had any Irish Republican sympathies or IRA friends is unknown, as is whether she had posted any previously annotated maps to a 'dead-letter box' in Lisbon. She told MI5 that she handed them over in the middle of the night to a German agent on the beach who had paddled ashore in a rubber dinghy from a waiting submarine. There was no evidence that she had a wireless set or sent encoded messages in secret ink. However, MI5 were conscious that the information she had collected was 'terribly accurate' and 'of great importance to the enemy' in the event of a German invasion. She told them that she had been recruited by several Dutch friends before the war.

She was arrested and charged under nine counts of the 1939 Defence Regulation Act, the 1911 Official Secrets Act and the 1940 Treachery Act. The first four carried the death penalty: conspiracy with intent to help the enemy; making a plan likely to assist the enemy's operations; intent to impede the British Armed Forces by cutting a military telephone wire; forcing a military safeguard; approaching a prohibited place for purposes prejudicial to the state; making a plan of potential use to the enemy; acts which might prove prejudicial to the nation's defence; sabotage and possession of a document with information purporting to relate to the nation's defence measures.[5]

One of the Isle of Wight detectives visited Liddell and told him that she had spent time in borstal and had convictions for prostitution. 'Her maps and diagrams are quite good and the details of gun emplacements etc. are correct. She still refuses to say whether she was acting for anyone in particular. She evidently dislikes this country. I am a little inclined to think that she might be the type of person who likes to be in the limelight.'[6]

Taken to Winchester for trial, her case was held in camera on 16 December 1940, the day after the hanging of Charles van den Kieboom. As there was no evidence showing that she had passed on the intelligence, she was tried, not as a spy or an enemy agent, but as a saboteur. The judge, Sir Malcolm Macnaghten, found her guilty of making a plan which could be of use to the enemy and of cutting a military telephone wire. Using the Official Secrets Act, she was also found guilty of entering a prohibited area and making a map that the Germans would find useful in a possible invasion. Given what had happened during the IRA's sabotage attacks and the country being at war, the judge told her she was to be hanged on 7 January 1941. Eighteen others received the death penalty during the war, but she was the only woman. Whilst awaiting execution, she was kept in Holloway women's prison in London.

Sir Edward Atkinson, Director of Public Prosecutions, considered that the sentence ought to have been carried out because if the sentence was commuted the news of her reprieve would not only send a message to the British public that her activities were innocent but also to the German Intelligence Service that the British were weak and sentimental.

The case hit the headlines in Britain and overseas, even as far as Australia and New Zealand. The *Daily Mirror* was reported as moving the story of America signing the lend-lease agreement, the export of military supplies to Britain to assist the war effort, to the second page.[7]

Liddell was aware of her case: 'Mrs O'Grady has been sentenced to death. Personally, I doubt whether she is guilty of anything more than collecting information. She probably pictured herself as a master spy, and cannot bring herself to say that there was really nothing behind it at all.'[8] Her post-war autobiography suggested that she was mentally unbalanced.

> The excitement of being tried for my life was intense. The supreme moment came when an official stood behind the judge and put on his black cap for him before he pronounced the death sentence. The man didn't put it on straight. It went over one of the judge's eyes and looked so funny that I was giggling inside and had a job not to laugh. It was hard to keep a straight face and look serious and solemn as I knew a spy should. I found it disappointing that I was going to be hanged instead of shot. My next disappointment was to learn they would put a hood over my head and tie my hands behind my back before taking me to the scaffold. This upset me. I protested, 'What is the good of being hanged if I can't see what is happening?'[9]

With no one to look after her dog, it was put down. O'Grady's lawyer appealed against the death penalty, arguing that the judge had prejudiced the case by misdirecting the jury. The Prosecution wrote to the Home Office arguing that 'if this woman is reprieved the knowledge ... would go to German intelligence ... a reprieve would serve as an encouragement to female spies'. The appeal proved successful and on 10 February her sentence was commuted to fourteen years' imprisonment. She was sent to Aylesbury Prison, Buckinghamshire.[10]

Searle's research uncovered a prison psychologist's report which indicated that she had an IQ of 140 but was

> a deeply troubled woman who regularly self-harmed, and had attacks 'in which she has to "obey people" inside her who encourage her to do harmful acts to herself'. She had enacted a pretend hanging by placing a chair on her cell bed, and sometimes slept naked under the bed. There was a palpable sexual dimension to her behaviour, which included tying herself in awkward positions for hours at a time. The prison medical officer, Dr Violet Minster,

said Dorothy inserted an alarming collection of objects into her vagina: a light bulb, more than 50 pieces of broken glass, a small pot, and 100 pins.

She also claimed that she was not really a spy, only pretended to be to make her life more interesting as she was a bored, lonely housewife without her husband. She claimed to have copied the maps from guidebooks and annotated them with information her lodgers might find interesting on walks around the island. She carried the swastikas to make her outings more exciting and had dared herself to cross the barbed wire into the restricted areas.

She served nine years before being released on compassionate grounds to care for her dying husband. Instead of going to see him, she went straight to the Fleet Street offices of the *Sunday Express* to sell her story. 'All my life I have never been anything, I have always been insignificant. I never had a close friend, not even at school. I felt tremendously bucked when I saw that they thought me clever enough to be a spy. It made me feel somebody.' She had been looking forward to being hanged as she 'wanted to know what it felt like'.

She spent the rest of her life in Osborne Villa, largely ostracised by the locals who were convinced she was a traitor and she died on 11 October 1985, aged 87. Her story inspired James Friel's 1992 novel *Careless Talk* and BBC radio play *The Spy Who Never Was*, in which Maureen Lipmann played O'Grady. When the Public Record Office, renamed later the National Archives, released her file, Barry Field, the Isle of Wight MP, investigated her case hoping to prove her innocence but admitted being staggered by the treachery she had sunk to. He believed that if her intelligence had been passed to the Germans, it would have altered the direction of the war.

In Searle's book on O'Grady, he suggests that there could have been a link between her and Vera Eriksen, who was thought to have been sent to Aylesbury Prison as a 'stool pigeon', to extract information from other inmates and to have settled on the Isle of Wight after the war.

During the O'Grady incident there was a sabotage attack on RAF Tangmere, an airfield near Chichester on the South Coast, about 25 miles north-east of Sandown. In September 1940, during the Battle of Britain, 602 Squadron (City of Glasgow) was transferred to RAF Tangmere, where it lost two Spitfires and their pilots to sabotage. Explosives had been placed next to the supercharger casing. In spite of a major investigation involving MI5, MI6, Special Branch and the RAF's internal security, the saboteur was never found. During the following January, another sabotage attempt was made whilst the squadron was stationed at Prestwick aerodrome in Manchester, but the explosive was found in time and no damage was done. Whether those responsible were IRA activists or German agents is unknown.

Getting accurate information about sabotage to planes has been difficult as the government was keen to play down any instances of such activity in case it generated copy-cat cases, gave support to Fascist groups or demoralised the British public into thinking fifth columnists were successfully destroying RAF property.

Following a query on the Aviation Forum, one member reported that in the Battle of Britain edition of 'Lost Voices' it was suggested that a pilot was killed when the parachute he used to bail out failed to open. All the parachutes had been re-packed by Irish labourers and the sabotage was blamed on those who had IRA sympathies. There were reports of other parachutes not opening, with the suggestion that a pin had been deliberately bent. Sabotage was mentioned as a possible reason for a 20 OTU Wellington bursting into flames on the ground at RAF Elgin.[11]

Following the crash of a Mosquito operating from RAF Banff in northern Scotland, an investigation team identified that a lock-nut had not been sufficiently tightened and a missing split pin had resulted in the aileron becoming detached. With police help, they discovered that an inspector working at one of the Mosquito shadow factories had links with the IRA. He was arrested and shot for sabotage.[12]

Another member reported that in 1940 a fifth columnist had been active at the Vickers aircraft factory in Broughton, Flintshire; but whether sabotage had been carried out is unknown as no further details have come to light. Edgar Brooks reported:

> One of the local furniture factories came close to being prosecuted for sabotage when it was found that one of the employees, instead of filling gaps in Mosquito wing joints with wood, as he'd been told, was stuffing them with paper, instead, then pouring glue over the top, hoping it would fail. Unfortunately for him, it was found that his method, because the glue soaked into the paper, was actually stronger than the approved system.
>
> There will always be someone, in any war, who thinks contrary to others; I worked with a man, 10 years my senior, who continually said that we'd have been better off if the Germans had won. [13]

In Edward Smithies' *Aces, Erks and Backroom Boys*, one contributor remembered that lubricating oil was discovered in the oxygen lines in a delivery of brand-new Blenheim aircraft, which would have caught fire or exploded in contact with oxygen.[14] In John Moffat's *I Sank the Tirpitz*, he reported that sugar was found in the fuel tanks of several Swordfish aircraft stationed in Scotland, which led to at least one crash. Which airfield it was and whether a saboteur was found was not recorded.[15] In Juliet Gardiner's *Wartime Britain 1939–1945*, she mentioned that in 1942 a Birmingham woman was convicted of sabotaging munitions for aircraft which would have exploded immediately on firing.[16] In Angus Calder's *People's War, Britain 1939–1945*, he mentioned a teacher being jailed for spreading defeatist opinions to his students and one man getting seven years for destroying telephone boxes.[17]

12

Arthur Owens, Gwilym Williams and the Welsh Nationalist Party (Part 2): October 1940–June 1942

Whilst the Abwehr had contacted Owens about their pre-invasion agents, there was no indication in Williams's file that they contacted him. That is not to say they were not given his or SNOW's details. They may have had to memorise them, but no evidence of such has come to light.

On 10 October 1940, Williams reported to TAR that he had been invited to the Athenaeum Court in Mayfair, not far from the Spanish Embassy in London, where he met Miguel Piernavieja Del Pozo, a Spanish journalist and observer in the *Instituto de Estudios Politicos*. Publicly forecasting a German victory had brought him to the attention of MI6, who described him as 'a dissolute and irresponsible young man, aged 26, of the playboy type'.

Del Pozo handed Williams a tin of talcum powder containing £3,500 in large-denomination notes 'from a friend in Madrid'. Williams made no mention of being asked to use it to support the activities of the three expected arrivals, but told Robertson that he was asked to supply a brief weekly report on the activities of the WNP and, as he acquired the information, a list of places in England and Wales where there were industries engaged in the manufacture of military materials and aircraft. Instead of using the Post Office, Del Pozo wanted it delivered by hand and suggested that to avoid having to make weekly trips up to London Williams should find an intermediary.

While Williams admitted that it was the largest amount of money he had ever seen, it may have been that he pocketed some as Masterman later reported him being given nearly £4,000. According to Liddell, when told he had to hand it over to MI5, Williams threatened to resign and John Marriott, Masterman's deputy, was needed to calm him down. Cash obtained in this way was deposited in a Bank of England account and used to pay double agents' wages and expenses. Depending upon their importance, they were given a percentage of what they were given by the Germans, with some getting as much as 10%; but what Williams was given was not mentioned in his file. Liddell considered him 'an unpleasant type and obviously on the make', an attitude not evidenced elsewhere in his personnel file.[1]

On the same day, 10 October, Liddell commented that they had obtained a Home Office warrant and were considering putting a microphone in Del Pozo's flat while he was in Glasgow, adding that 'SNOW was reported as beginning to feel his oats again after a long period of quiescence'. This was a polite way of saying that he was in keen need of female company.[2]

When Williams was asked by Del Pozo how the people of Wales were taking the war, he reported that he had told him that

> they've now got their backs up, and that their morale was one hundred per cent, particularly since the bombing of Wales had taken place. I told him that before the bombing commenced the people of Wales were mostly pacifists and many of them defeatists. They are still anti-English, but owing to the indiscriminate bombing that has taken place in Wales the people appear to have somewhat changed and have a greater leaning towards England. He did not comment on this.[3]

One imagines that this intelligence, when passed on to the Abwehr, would have diminished their expectations of being able to find a Welsh sabotage group. A few days later, as requested Williams took a report and a list of known factories in Wales to Del Pozo at the Athenaeum. This could have included the first list in Williams's personnel file as it had the name POGO written on the top. This was MI5's codename for Del Pozo.

Del Pozo told him that he had just returned from visiting an aircraft factory and an aerodrome in Scotland and that he thought it amusing that the British Consul and the BBC staff who accompanied him thought he would be valuable for propaganda purposes. Pretending to be a fool, he collected all sorts of valuable intelligence which he could sell to his 'friends', his German masters, in Madrid. They had invited him to visit Germany after the war, which he hoped would be soon.

Conscious that MI5 might open his post, Del Pozo recommended that Williams hand his reports to Mr Segundo, a porter in the Spanish Embassy. If this was done early afternoon, it would allow him to catch the return train to Swansea and avoid the cost of overnight accommodation. In a discussion about expenses, Del Pozo asked Williams for money to pay people for the information they supplied him, claiming to be paid only £20 a week, £4 of which covered the rent at the Athenaeum. He wanted to buy a car and live outside London where the cost of living was cheaper. As SNOW had to be asked for additional funds, Williams was unable to help immediately. When he apologised for only providing vague information about the factories, Del Pozo pulled a piece of paper from his pocket and read out the following:

> 'We are particularly interested in places where aeroplane parts are manufactured, in particular propellers and engines. We desire to know the location of factories, whether large or small as orders are changed to different factories. Sometimes the output of large factories is small and output of small factories large.
>
> We are also particularly anxious to know the extent of all supplies of aluminium and other material which arrives in this country from the United States, dates and quantity, the name of the steamship line in which they are conveyed, and how they are otherwise delivered.
>
> We need some information from men in the Army, for example, in Berkshire, Buckinghamshire, Oxfordshire, Bedfordshire, Northamptonshire,

Salisbury and Aldershot as to the names of regiments and numbers of battalions stationed in these areas.

We are particularly anxious to know where bombers that bomb Germany set off on their raids. We want to stop these quickly.

We want you to try and 'boycott' [meaning put out of commission] all factories and warehouses where food materials are manufactured and stored.'

I pointed out the difficulty of carrying out what is asked in the last mentioned paragraph, as I have no material with which this could be done. I told him that on the occasion of my visit to Antwerp last October our friends had promised to supply me with the necessary materials by means of an aeroplane or submarine. Owing to their failure to supply the materials I have been wasting my time for twelve months when I could have been making some move in this matter. I asked him to bring this to the notice of his friends in Madrid, which he promised he would do.

I now pointed out the extreme difficulty and risk that would be involved in trying to obtain the information that he required, but when time permitted I would endeavour to obtain it. I stated that I did not think it possible to obtain the information direct as I could not possibly approach the places from where such information could be obtained. It would be necessary for me to depend upon such information as could be obtained from men employed at these places, and soldiers in the areas. I pointed out that I would need to be very careful in approaching such people, and it would be necessary to bribe them well. He agreed that this would be so. I further told him that I could not promise to move in the matter at once owing to the necessity of my being available at home when our friends arrived. He informed me that he understood.[4]

When TAR was informed, he responded immediately by obtaining answers to Del Pozo's questions which the RAF and the Army were happy could be passed on to the enemy.

By the end of October, Williams had been provided with a car to facilitate his intelligence-gathering missions around Wales and his trips to London as well as a regular supply of petrol coupons to avoid the rationing restrictions. He was also introduced to Squadron Leader Arnold who helped him produce the following list of potential sabotage targets which had to be submitted for MI5's approval before being handed over to the Germans:

Bristol Aircraft Factory
The factory covers about 50 or 60 acres, and is situated at Filton, about 4 miles direct North of Bristol at a point about 6 miles on the eastern side of the Severn Tunnel. It adjoins the main line of the Great Western Railway between London and South Wales. Engines for Blenheim Bombers are various types of fighters are manufactured at this factory. These and other types of aircraft are assembled here. The factory is well protected by anti-aircraft guns.

ROYAL ORDNANCE Factory, Bridgend
Covers about 60 or 70 acres at least. Situated at a point about 20 miles due West of Cardiff, also adjoins the main line of the Great Western Railway between London and South Wales. Engaged principally in the manufacture of

explosives and other materials formerly manufactured at the Royal Arsenal at Woolwich. Appears to be easy to locate from the air, and as far as can be ascertained is not very well protected from air attack.

ROYAL ORDNANCE Factory, Pembrey

Covers about 40 acres. Situated near the main line of the Great Western Railway between London and South Wales at a point about six miles due West of Llanelly in South Wales; an important metallurgical town. It may also be located by proceeding West from Swansea for about 16 miles. The factory is used for the manufacture of shells and explosives, and shell filling. A large aerodrome is situated further West quite close to the factory, recently used for training purposes and is now part of the fighter command.

Aluminium Imports

Brought from U.S. and Canada to London, but sometimes also discharged at the Bristol Channel Ports – principally Bristol and Cardiff, thence conveyed by rail to Slough for smelting. Slough is situated between London and Maidenhead, about 6 miles due East [sic] of London. I have been unable to obtain any particulars as to the arrival of ships, as this depends to a large extent upon the state of the weather and other circumstances, which makes it impossible to establish times and days of arrival with any degree of certainty.[5]

This was accepted for sending but, as he was expected to report weekly, he was told not to send it all at once and that MI5 would endeavour to help obtain other relevant information. He also prepared the following report:

WELSH ACTIVITY

The Welsh Nationalist Party has a membership of about 20,000; a large number take no interest of any extent from a political or Welsh freedom point of view, but all are deeply interested in Welsh culture.

For many years, the party has put up candidates for parliamentary honours, but none has been successful at the Parliamentary Elections.

In so far as direct action against the English Government is concerned the only overt act was in 1936 when Professor Saunders Lewis, the Rev. Lewis Valentine and Mr D. J. Williams set fire to the bombing school, near Pwllheli in North Wales, as a political gesture after many appeals had failed, which were made to the English Government not to establish aerodromes in Wales. These three gentlemen, who are prominent Welsh Nationalist leaders, afterwards gave themselves up to the Police. They had a spectacular trial at the Old Bailey and were sentenced to nine months' imprisonment. The Party gained much sympathy and support for their aims by this political gesture, but no one followed the lead given by these ardent supporters of Welsh Nationalism. This no doubt, is due to the fact that the necessary material with which to commit acts of this kind is too difficult to obtain. I have no hesitation in saying that further acts of this nature would be carried out if the necessary materials were available.

Before the outbreak of war, the Party was not very progressive in its efforts to obtain Welsh freedom, but ever since hostilities began the Party has become strongly pacifist and is continually proclaiming that Wales desires no part in England's war. All possible encouragement and help are given to the young men of Wales to put forward Nationalism as one of the grounds for conscientious objection to military service in the English Forces.

At the Annual Conference of the Welsh Nationalist Party at Aberystwyth last August Mr Saunders Lewis, who has resigned the Presidency but still takes a very active interest in the Party's affairs, called upon the Executive to use its utmost endeavours to persuade the English Government to conclude an early armistice so as to reduce further bloodshed. Mr Lewis's speech on this occasion was well received and supported by many delegates representing the various branches of the Movement. The Party is now engaged in propaganda to emphasise the need for a free Wales so that peace for this country can be concluded.

In addition to pacifist work the Party is continually making protests to the English authorities concerning the construction of armament factories and aerodromes in Wales. Considerable stress is laid on the fact that the Llyn Peninsula – where the bombing school is situated – is being bombed and, as a result of this bombing, attention is being called to the leaflet, entitled 'Aerodrome today – bombing tomorrow', published by the Party when Saunders Lewis and the others sabotaged the bombing school.

At present much propaganda is being carried out in connection with the evacuation of English children into Wales. We in Wales feel considerable indignation because we are swamped with English evacuees. The Party is claiming credit for having always urged that safe areas in Wales should be reserved for the evacuation of children from bombed Welsh districts, and they are now sending petitions to the English Government to remove English children from Wales to safe places in England.

Concerning the possibility of an invasion the Party leaders are exercising great caution as to the action, they would be likely to take, as they have to be very careful owing to the severe penalties that can be imposed under the Defence Regulations. They emphasise that in the event of an invasion large numbers of English refugees would swarm into Wales and that necessary measures should be considered for countering this menace.

It is obvious that the leaders of the Welsh Nationalist Party will not commit themselves as to their attitude should foreign troops land on Welsh soil. Personally, I am of the opinion that some of the Party members will join the English in resisting but, if tactfully handled, I believe that a large proportion would at least be passive in [the face of] invading troops.

It may be gathered from the foregoing notes that the attitude of the Party may be defined as passive hostility rather than open resistance to the English.

I have worked very hard in an effort to build up a nucleus of people to render us assistance, but the task has been uphill as, in this connection, the Welsh mentality is so very different from the Irish and the ancient tradition of revolutionary struggle is nearly played out.

However, I feel that given the necessary means I can increase quite considerably the number of my compatriots who would be prepared to render assistance in the cause. In the present juncture, I must admit that there is little prospect of stirring up any effective resistance of a widespread nature in the Welsh Nationalist Movement as a whole. The most that we can reckon upon from the majority of really convinced Nationalists is goodwill rather than active support, the remainder appear to be leaning towards England. This is due, in some degree, to intensive propaganda by the English and the present bombing of Welsh towns, both these are bound to effect the weaker and muddle-headed members. It must be realised that as public opinion outside the ranks of Welsh Nationalists becomes more bitter against Germany, Party work for our cause, or even from a purely pacifist angle, becomes increasingly difficult, unpopular and dangerous.[6]

One imagines that he took a copy of this article and a selection from the earlier information when he went to meet Del Pozo in London on 7 November. However, on the train journey he read an article about Del Pozo's pro-Axis views in the *Daily Telegraph* that convinced him the police would be keeping watch on him and his contacts. Instead of going to the Athenaeum, he rang and arranged a rendezvous outside the Cumberland Hotel, from where they took a taxi to Belgravia Square where he was to be introduced to Mr Segundo at the Embassy.

On the way, I told Piernavieja that it was impossible for me to obtain the information he had asked for concerning aircraft factories, etc. as I could not visit the areas where such information could be obtained without a permit and such permits are not granted unless there are very good reasons for requiring them. It would be too risky for me to attempt to obtain by other means such information as was required. I pointed out to him that I had agreed to carry out acts of sabotage, but not espionage, and for this purpose I could have the co-operation of a number of Welsh Nationalists in North and South Wales, but it was impossible to carry out any acts of sabotage without the necessary material. I informed him that some of the men that would co-operate with me are employed on important work, such as Clerk to the Water Board and foreman builder at a Royal Ordnance factory. All of them are embittered men with anti-English views and are well placed so as to carry out sabotage work, particularly in the matter of polluting with bacteria water that is gathered at the large reservoirs in the Welsh mountains and carried by pipeline to places such as Birmingham. I told him that in the absence of necessary material I could do nothing. His reaction was that he would let his friends know what I had said, but he would like me to try and get some information as it is, he said, for the purpose of sabotage that they want to know. I again said that I could not possibly do anything unless I was supplied with the means of carrying out such acts and that the men who would do the work would have to be well paid for it. I handed him the report of 'Welsh Activity', told him of the Bristol Aircraft factory and gave him verbal particulars concerning imports of aluminium.[7]

After being introduced to Segundo, arrangements were made for the delivery of subsequent reports. They then went back onto the street, and Del Pozo brought out another piece of paper which included a request for the following information:

We want to know everything of interest concerning the South coast of England, for example, the positions of all regiments and where they are, what length and breadth of line they occupy, positions of reserves, tanks and big guns. We want details of the coast from Margate to the Isle of Wight, what parts of the coast are steep and flat and what you can find out about the beaches. We would like you to find out all you can about particulars of battalions, naval bases, aircraft and aerodromes all over England, giving their exact location.[8]

Having made notes, Williams told him that getting such information would be practically impossible and that a foreign journalist would have more chance. Before Del Pozo went off to Fleet Street to discuss the newspaper article, Williams stressed again that when he was in Belgium he had been trained for sabotage, not espionage. Once back in Swansea, Squadron Leader Arnold helped him to prepare the following aviation intelligence for MI5's approval:

The Polish and Free French Air Forces operate from an aerodrome near Gloucester.

The Manchester Airport is now a Royal Air Force Aerodrome, and raids to the Continent are made from this place.

At Hullavington, which is about fifteen miles due West of Swindon, is situated the largest aerodrome in England. It adjoins the Great Western Railway main line between London and South Wales. Fighter and Bomber Aircraft take off from this aerodrome. The Bombers, I am informed, take off for Germany and Italy from here.

I am also informed that Bombers take off from the North-East Coast of England and the East Coast of Scotland, but as these coasts of a depth of three miles are prohibited areas it is very difficult to ascertain definitely the exact locations of aerodromes.

As a result of my enquiries, I am informed that the French Free Forces, the Canadian Forces and Australian Forces are stationed at Camberley, which is situated about two miles from Sandhurst and about thirty miles in a South-Westerly direction from Marble Arch, London. (A note by this last paragraph read 'NOT APPROVED. As Camberley is full of New Zealanders and other troops, I do not feel we are justified in getting them killed.')[9]

The revised list duly omitted the reference to Camberley and, on the advice of MI5, included an acknowledgement of his source, 'an informant who is usually reliable, but I cannot, of course, give any personal guarantee to their accuracy'.[10] There was also a second edition of 'Welsh Activity', which included details of potential saboteurs and the approved details in response to his 'friend's' query about the South Coast.

WELSH ACTIVITY

A prophecy made by the Welsh National Party since the outbreak of war concerning the effect of the war on Wales is already being fulfilled. North and mid-Wales and indeed every part of Wales which is reasonably safe are rapidly being occupied by wealthy and leisurely English folk and Jews who are buying and renting every imaginable kind of dwelling at high rents. As far as can be observed these people are not grateful to Wales for the hospitality given them. They regard their sojourn here as a period of necessary boredom and have adopted a sneering tone towards these 'quaint' places and 'quaint' people. Resentment of their presence is fast growing, and much more so as Welsh workers are being forced in their thousands to seek work in highly dangerous areas in England – the very areas as precipitately abandoned by the vulgar English rich. The country responsible for plunging Wales into the war was England. The power responsible for the denudation of Welsh quarries and mines is England. When Wales' workers are deprived of their homeland; when her contribution to England's conscript army numbers hundreds of thousands; when she cannot even offer the shelter of her quiet countryside to her own mothers and children – the Wales of tomorrow – the only role left for her to play is that of unwell host to England's cowardly rich.

For our purpose, I can probably obtain the service of a number of Welsh Nationalists, apart from members of the Party, for any action, you may propose against the English if the necessary material and funds are made available. These men include the following:

An employee of a Labour Exchange in Merionethshire who also carries on the business of a local Post Office.

A friend of the above who lives near him is a garage proprietor and is also employed as clerk of the local Water Board.

These men are 100% Welsh, are strongly sympathetic to the Welsh Nationalist Party and have signed petitions advocating the use of Welsh in Law Courts, etc. They have not actually joined the party for fear it might reflect on their position as Civil Servants. They are well placed for such action as sabotage of water supply by pipelines from Welsh mountains to large English towns such as Birmingham etc. They are also in a position to supply valuable information concerning aerodromes that are being contemplated in the locality.

A resident of Llandudno, where he is in a position as a Dentist, is an embittered man with anti-English views. Provided he was well compensated financially I am of the opinion that he could be persuaded to do very useful work.

A man living near Wrexham who is very sympathetic towards Welsh Nationalism is a foreman builder employed at a Royal Ordnance Factory. He is a clever man and if well paid I believe that he could be used in connection with sabotage at the Government industries in that area in which he is employed.

I also know of a number of men in the Swansea and Brecon areas who are 100% Welsh and definitely anti-English. One of these is engaged daily in and about the docks; another is engaged in the metal industry. Both have access to places of great military importance. Another is at Breconshire where there are many new works for the manufacture of war material being erected.

All these men and many others that I know would be only too pleased to do all they can against the English. If you can supply the necessary material and funds, I will get in contact with them as soon as possible.

Margate to Ramsgate
Cliffs with beaches mostly with access to the cliff tops by tracks.
Ramsgate to Deal
Beaches.
Deal to South Foreland
Beaches at low tide.
Folkestone to Eastbourne
Beaches all the way.
Eastbourne to Seaford
Beaches only when the tide is out, except at Birling Gap.
Seaford to Newhaven
Beaches.
West of Newhaven to Brighton
Beaches only at low tide otherwise water is up to the cliffs.
Brighton to Selsey Bill
Beaches all the way.
Isle of Wight
Whole coast has beaches at low water even when backed by cliffs but east end has no cliffs of any importance.[11]

What percentage of his 'Welsh Activity' report was MI5 misinformation to add pressure on the Germans to fulfil their promise of sending supplies, funds and potentially more agents is unknown. It seems likely that Ford had briefed Williams well before he next met Del Pozo to hand over the report on 29 November. Afterwards, Williams provided TAR with a detailed account of the meeting. He reported telling Del Pozo that his chief had wanted to read his report before he handed it over and now insists on seeing all reports first. Also, as his chief, SNOW, was planning to visit the Germans in a neutral country in the near future, he volunteered to take any reports Del Pozo might want handed over, to which POGO answered, 'Very well.'

However, Del Pozo told him that he was returning to Madrid shortly and urgently needed the £100 he had given him on their first meeting to pay one of his contacts for 'a very special report' he wanted to take with him. When Williams asked Del Pozo about the delivery of sabotage materials and funds, he was told that the request had twice been put to the Germans, but they had yet to reply. He then added,

'Of course, that money I gave you was for sabotage work.' I told him that the money would be used for assistance in committing acts of sabotage, but the material required to carry out the work would have to be supplied as I could not possibly purchase the material in this country. I then said, 'Supposing whilst I was endeavouring to carry out acts of sabotage and it became necessary for me to suddenly leave the country, can you suggest how I could do so and can you tell me with whom I could get in touch to help me to do so.' He hesitated for some little time, and I asked him if he understood, he then said, 'You could go to Portugal and then it would be easy for you to get to Spain.' But I said it is very difficult these times for one to leave the country. To this, he said that I could ask my chief about it.[12]

Williams reported being asked for another passport-sized photo, identical to the one that they already had and informed that Del Pozo had been followed on several occasions but had successfully 'lost' them. This was because Special Branch was attempting to identify the others in Del Pozo's Spanish spy ring.

There was a discussion about a new type of high explosive which the English were using in connection with anti-aircraft shells which on exploding sent other shells into the air which then exploded themselves. Before repeating his urgent need for the £100, he read out a list of requirements about military strength and emplacements along the south coast.

TAR arranged for the money to be delivered to Mr Segundo the following day and to help supply relevant intelligence for Williams's subsequent report. His file contains correspondence relating to meetings with Del Pozo querying where the £5,000 the Germans had promised him was, reports to TAR, an account of a 560-mile round-Wales car trip detailing the military defences he had seen, and a bill for £1 18s 9½d for 19 gallons of petrol. Del Pozo's demands for £500 to pay for information about a new aeroplane engine were arranged.

On 7 January 1941, the Abwehr II War Diary mentioned Spanish sources referring to the blowing up of a munitions train between Newark and Melton Mowbray, Leicestershire. The veracity of this report has yet to come to light, but the note beside the entry suggests it was usual Abwehr II guesswork as no evidence was produced.[13]

There was nothing in GW's file related to sabotage until 9 January 1941 when, following a meeting with Del Pozo, Williams underlined part of his report telling TAR that Del Pozo had told him that when the £5,000 arrived, 'we would buy a car and get some material for sabotage work together'.

A new code was agreed to let Del Pozo know the day of their next appointment. Before the name Thomas was written on the telegram, an initial letter would represent the day of the week. L = Monday, T = Tuesday, M = Wednesday, J = Thursday, V = Friday, S = Saturday and D = Sunday.

He asked me what I thought of the bombing of Ireland; I stated that I thought the Germans were not doing any good by it. Then he informed me that the Germans had not bombed Ireland, but that the bombing had been carried out by the R.A.F. using German unexploded bombs that had been dropped in this country and that it had been done so as to try and arrange a conflict between Ireland and Germany, so that England could invade Ireland to protect her and thus obtain Naval bases on the West coast of Ireland which would be the only effective way to deal with the German blockade of England as England cannot deal with the blockade in any other way. The Germans, he continued, would probably accept responsibility for the bombing of Ireland to prevent England obtaining the West Coast Naval bases.

I asked what he thought of the British successes against the Italians; he replied, 'Oh, the Italians are nothing, the Germans are only using them because it suits their purpose.' (He spoke of the Italians with utter contempt.)

During the course of conversation, he informed me that he was to have a meeting with General de GAULLE on Thursday, and remarked that the General 'is a friend of ours'. I asked who he meant by 'ours' and he said, 'we, Spain'.

... In conclusion, I have no hesitation in saying that this man is definitely still pro-German and, in my opinion, would do anything to help Germany against this country. He became quite elated during that part of the conversation when mention was made of the prospect of receiving material for sabotage work and the purchase of a car to be used in connection with the carrying out of acts of sabotage. He evidently proposes to work in conjunction with me in committing acts of sabotage against this country. Of course, I must leave it to you to suggest ways and means to counteract such proposals. I would, however, suggest that we await further developments in this direction.[14]

While waiting for the money to arrive, MI5 provided Williams with relevant information for him to describe the recent military developments across Wales, a lengthy political diatribe against the English and an argument that an early peace would be in Wales's best economic and social interest – just what the Germans wanted to hear.

By the end of January, he had produced the following report based on a field visit he made to his local reservoir, presumably to show the Germans the detail he could provide should they allocate such a target for sabotage action. Whether he received any help from his friend on the Water Board was not specified.

The Swansea Waterworks

The Swansea Waterworks are situated at a place called Cray (Crai in Welsh) which lies beyond the Swansea Valley in the uplands of Breconshire. The reservoir covers a large area and contains sufficient water to supply the whole of the inhabitants of Swansea, which number about 160,000, and some of the neighbouring small towns. Ships that enter the port of Swansea are also supplied with this water.

Cray is a very small agricultural village, sparsely populated, about 30 miles in a northerly direction from Swansea and about 10 miles in a north-westerly direction from Brecon.

The reservoir is in close proximity to the main road – numbered A4067 according to the Ministry of Transport's numbering – on the east side and the London, Midland and Scottish Railway runs parallel to it on the west side. Both the railway and the road run through the Swansea Valley from Swansea to Brecon.

The reservoir is only a short distance from the road and is surrounded only in part by iron railings about six feet in height.

Access to the water's edge from the road is easily obtained by walking down a gradually sloping grass-covered bank. No precautions have been taken to prevent anyone from approaching the water. There are a number of notices adjacent to the reservoir indicating that fishing is prohibited.

From the air, I would say that such an expanse of water situated in a mountainous country ... could not fail to be easily seen.

As far as I could see, there are no anti-aircraft or other defences, except occasional road barriers, within many miles of this reservoir.

The water is conveyed to Swansea by means of a pipeline.[15]

When he saw POGO again at the end of the month, there was no mention of the three German agents whom Williams presumably thought had already entered the country.

In Williams's discussions with Del Pozo in early 1941, there was no indication when he was to be given the poison to use in the reservoir, only that it would be provided by a Spanish doctor. When TAR asked Williams for a detailed account of all his contacts with Del Pozo, he provided one querying whether, if MI5 considered Del Pozo to be traitorous and arrested him, he would have to give evidence in court thus giving the Germans a chance of identifying him as a double agent. Given the possibility that Del Pozo might prompt the Germans to infiltrate more agents, sabotage materials and funds into Britain which MI5 could intercept, the game was allowed to continue.[16]

Williams provided further reports in February and, in response to TAR's request, a more detailed report on the Cray Reservoir:

The water flows subterraneously from the Reservoir to a Purifying Plant situate about 2½ miles distant on the Swansea side of the Reservoir. Thence by subterranean pipes to Swansea.

The Purifying Plant is a concrete structure surrounded by loosely coiled wire, and four men are employed as watchmen by the Swansea Corporation. … The Plant is situated quite close to the main road in a desolate and mountainous area. An observation post has been constructed near the Plant from which anyone approaching can be seen. I got into a conversation with one of these watchmen – a man about 48 to 50 years of age – who informed me that they had been issued with rifles and would use them against any unauthorised persons approaching the Plant. The rifles were kept in the observation post and were not carried during the day, but were at night. The man was dressed in ordinary civilian clothing and wore nothing to distinguish him from any other person. This man also informed me that eight soldiers patrol the immediate vicinity of the Reservoir, four by day and four by night. I passed some time away in close proximity to the Reservoir but saw no one else about there.

The pollution of water could be affected quite easily without going anywhere near the Reservoir. This could be done from the main road which passes over a number of small bridges built over mountain streams that feed the Reservoir, and the contamination of any of these streams would be as effective as if the contamination material had been placed in the Reservoir. In fact, it would be easier as there would be no danger of detection.

The employment of watchmen at the Purifying Plant and soldiers at the Reservoir is probably a recent innovation as I did not observe anyone at either place during my visit on the 2nd ultimo. Under the circumstances an attempt to damage the Reservoir or Purifying Plant would be undertaken with considerable risk of detection. The possibility of causing damage to the pipeline would be extremely difficult on account of its depth below ground surface.[17]

MI5 would not allow such an attack to take place, given the enormous loss of life. Ironically, the next item in Williams's file was a detailed account for Lord

Rothschild on the effects of a three-night Luftwaffe bombing raid on Swansea which left almost 400 dead and then subsequent attacks across Wales in March.[18]

Given the vulnerability of reservoirs across Britain, a plan was put in place to defend them against attack. On 22 April 1942, the Ministry of Health contacted 'water undertakers', now called the Water Authorities, regarding:

Security and Anti-Sabotage Arrangements.

1. I am directed by the Minister of Health to inform you that he has been in consultation with the Security Service (M.I.5) concerning the protection of the more vital points of water undertakings against acts of sabotage by enemy agents who may obtain unauthorised entrance by stealth, or by persons of enemy sympathies who may have obtained employment in the undertaking.

2. A vital point has been roughly described (vide the paragraph headed 'Guarding of Vital Points' in Circular 2079 dated 1st July 1940) as a point or work which is easily attacked and at which serious damage could be caused which could not easily be repaired.

3. Public utility undertakings may at any time be subjected to –
   (i) Armed attack by sea-borne or air-borne troops.
   (ii) Acts of sabotage committed by persons who have obtained unauthorised entrance by stealth or by persons of enemy sympathies who have obtained employment in the undertaking.
   The former is an operational matter for the Military authorities. The latter alone is dealt with in this letter.

4. The Minister will shortly be in a position to furnish information and general advice made available to him by the Security Service as to the methods of sabotage which might be adopted by enemy agents or person of enemy sympathies and to suitable counter-measures. This information will be based on experience of methods which have been used by the enemy to damage public utility undertakings in countries which have ultimately been overrun.

5. In the meantime, it is requested that, if this has not already been done, a member of the staff of your undertaking should be appointed as Security Officer to be responsible to the management of the undertaking for seeing that all practicable security measures are effectively carried out. The large undertakings may find it necessary to nominate Assistant Security Officers to carry out the Security officer's instructions and to act for him in his absence. Names and addresses of the individuals nominated as Security officers should be sent to this Office as soon as possible.

6. The Security Officers and their assistants, managements, and those employees who are likely to receive from the Security officers secret information and instructions will be required to sign a declaration under the official Secrets Acts. The necessary forms will be sent to you in due course.

7. The information and advice on counter-measures referred to above will be sent, through this Office, to all Security officers; advice on the following subjects will be included: -
   (i) Passes.

(ii) Prevention of unauthorised entry.

(iii) Entrance – control of visitors

(iv) Entrance – control of lorries and cars.

(v) Use of dogs for night patrol work.

(vi) Camouflage used by the enemy in introducing bombs.

8. Lectures by representatives of the Security Service on the various counter-measures will be given in due course to Security officers, and regional meetings will be arranged for this purpose. It is hoped that representatives of the Security Service will visit certain of the more strategically important undertakings and make recommendations of the spot.

9. The Security Service have asked that enquiries arising out of this letter should not be addressed to them directly but should be submitted to this office in the first instance.

10. An additional copy of this letter is enclosed for the Engineer of the water undertaking.[19]

SIS's surveillance of Del Pozo continued and they reported they 'he was devoting his time exclusively to the girls at Café de Paris and acquired such a reputation as a drunkard, waster and buffoon' that he was recalled to Spain.[20]

Nothing further was heard from him until the end of March when the British Embassy sent a telegram informing MI5 that he had been arrested in Spain as a member of the outlawed fascist Falangist party, imprisoned for six months but had escaped and was in hiding in the German Embassy. Not wanting to lose Williams's services, MI5 instructed him to continue reporting to them on the Welsh National Party and on what was happening at the docks and industrial areas, especially munitions and aircraft factories. This intelligence would be used by Rothschild to identify weaknesses in security to allow measures to be taken to strengthen them. The following report on key Welsh industries could have equally been used to improve counter-sabotage measures.

On Tuesday 8 April I paid a visit to Milford Haven and found this place to be a hive of industry, there were numerous Naval and Merchant ships and fishing trawlers to be seen about the docks and Haven. In the Haven, there was a large number of Cargo ships waiting to move off in convoy. This little town has become of considerable military importance as Oil Tankers are anchored in the Haven and petroleum discharged by sub-marine and subterranean pipeline to huge subterranean storage tanks on the left side of the town (looking in shore) quite near the docks and Fish Market. These storage tanks, I am informed, are well below ground level, well-guarded by soldiers and also well camouflaged with grass growing over the whole area with sheep and cattle grazing there. Further inland about two miles distant, still in the Haven, there is a large Mine and Shell filling Factory, the mines and shells being subsequently stored below ground ready for removal when required. There have been no enemy raids on this town but mines are sometimes dropped by enemy aircraft causing shipping losses inside and just outside the Haven. I was told that ships sometimes leave at night and steer rescued crews brought in during the early hours of the morning.

On Wednesday 9 April I visited Southerdown in the Vale of Glamorgan, not far from Porthcawl. Here I observed hundreds of new aircraft, both fighters and bombers, parked in fields adjoining the highway. There were no restrictions upon passage along the road except that people were not allowed to loiter in the vicinity of the fields. People in cars could proceed as slowly as they liked and would be able to make a mental note of the location of the fields and numbers of aircraft. This I suggest would be very useful to the enemy.[21]

By the end of May 1941, Masterman decided to reactivate Williams' links with the Germans by cleverly picking up where he had left off with the Spanish. He instructed him to meet Segundo in the Spanish Embassy, enquire about POGO's whereabouts and tell him that he was awaiting further instructions as to who his new master might be. MI5 wanted to know who the Germans had sent or were planning to send as a replacement. When Williams spoke with Segundo, he was advised to speak with Louis Calvo.

Before doing so, Williams met Masterman with Richard Brooman-White in the Bachelors' Club in London who told them that Calvo was a Spanish journalist who worked for *La Nacion*, an Argentinian newspaper. Broomam-White, an economics and foreign language graduate from Cambridge University, also worked as a journalist, writing on politics and foreign affairs for Scottish newspapers. When war broke out, he was a Second Lieutenant in the Dunbartonshire Light Anti-Aircraft Unit, Royal Artillery, but resigned due to ill-health in 1940 and worked in MI5's Security Section as head of Section B1(g), which dealt with Spanish espionage. In June 1940, he was put in charge of their 'Celtic Movements' Section so was particularly interested in finding out what else Calvo was doing apart from journalism. Consequently, his mail was intercepted and his phone tapped.[22]

Williams was told to ring Segundo, pretending to be very worried about having spoken with him, and asked him not to mention anything to anyone. When he did, Segundo told him to call back in five minutes and speak to Mr Villaverde, the Secretary, and discuss the case with him. Two names in a few hours was very good work. Masterman advised him to ring back and apologise that he would not be able to visit as he had to catch the train back to Wales. Brooman-White suggested he wrote to Calvo enclosing a stamp-addressed envelope, explaining his problem and asking to meet him and also seeing if Williams could find a Spanish-speaking friend to better explain his predicament to Segundo. It was also thought possible that the Spanish would investigate Williams and either denounce him as a German agent or employ him.

To help entrap Calvo, Williams was given a folder entitled Plan IV. This was a directive from the Air Ministry to draw aerial attack away from urban industrial and military targets to aerodromes. To avoid civilian loss and reduce damage to the war effort, the Germans were encouraged to bomb aerodromes, which were better defended to resist such attacks. According to Masterman, a number of documents were constructed and placed in a folder which was supposed to have been stolen.[23]

Williams was to tell Calvo that it had been given to him by someone in one of the Ministries who wanted £25 for it. Although it was old, it was useful intelligence and was worth much more. TAR permitted him to tell Calvo about his work for POGO but to stress 'if possible the importance of the fact that he had originally been trained in sabotage' and that he could get 'military and economic intelligence about South Wales'.[24]

After meeting Calvo in Sloane Street, he insisted on going to Hyde Park where their chat about POGO would not be overheard. When it became apparent that Calvo was willing to take over the intermediary role with the Germans, Williams reported he could

> open up and take him into my confidence. I then told him that apart from coming to this country to obtain first-hand knowledge of the extent of German bombing, Del Pozo had produced such proof as to enable me to satisfy myself that he had been instructed to get in touch with me by certain German sabotage experts who I had previously met. I went on to say that the work I did for Del Pozo was not connected with sabotage, but with the activities of the Welsh Nationalist Party and the defences and military works in Wales. I informed him that I was one of a number of Welsh Nationalists prepared to do anything to hinder the English in every possible way because we are strongly opposed to being governed by the English. I went on to relate an imaginary story of English financiers closing down various works in Wales and allowing the Welshmen to starve whilst they, the financiers, were having a damn good time in England on the money that had been made for them by these Welshmen who were now starving. I told him a lot of other piffle which appeared to have impressed him as to my hatred of England and all that is English. This seemed to have afforded him some pleasure as he said that the Welsh are very much akin to the Spanish, particularly those in the north of Spain. He then asked where I had met the German sabotage experts. I informed him briefly of my visit to Belgium in October 1939, what had taken place and how it had been proposed by the experts that I should be supplied with funds and material to enable me to carry out certain sabotage work in Wales. I had actually been in communication with my friends at an address in Belgium, but owing to the invasion of Belgium this had to be discontinued.[25]

Calvo told him that Del Pozo had been sent to England by the Falangists but, as a result of his 'un-neutral' press articles, the British, Italian and German authorities complained and the Spanish Press Attaché had him shipped back to Spain on 3 February. The boat he took from Liverpool was torpedoed off the Azores, but he was rescued. Although imprisoned in Spain, Calvo told Williams that Del Pozo's father was very influential in Spain so he had probably been released.

When Williams told him about the contents of the Plan IV folder, Calvo was tempted by the offer but needed to get the go-ahead from his superiors before engaging more directly with him. Later they had drinks where Williams was introduced to a Spanish doctor who was practising at 19 Harley Street and a number of others who appeared to know South Wales well, especially the Gower. Robertson and Brooman-White's plan had worked.

Nothing developed with Calvo until the end of July 1941. Before that, Williams continued to submit reports to Rothschild about the political and industrial situation in Wales. After meeting him on 24 July, he sent an account of the meeting to TAR. He admitted giving Calvo some Welsh Nationalist newspapers and then discussing a number of war-related topics including the point that his friends in the WNP who had been willing to undertake the sabotage had now become lukewarm because there had been nothing from the Germans and there seemed no likelihood of ever being sent any explosive materials or funds. He suggested £500 would cover the necessary payments. At the end of the letter Williams asked TAR whether it was OK 'to give a note to CALVO asking him to send it to my friends, and reminding them that they had not carried out their part of the matter that had been agreed upon in Antwerp of which I am still prepared to carry out my part if they will let me have what is necessary. This suggestion is made with a view to an opening of direct communication between the other side and myself.'[26]

At TAR's suggestion, he wrote a letter to Del Pozo, pointing out how disappointed he was not to have seen him, how pleased he was to have met Calvo and adding that he was willing to continue with the arrangements, hoping it would be forwarded to the Germans.

On 10 May 1941, a Messerschmitt crashed in a field near Eaglesham, south of Glasgow. The injured pilot was apprehended, telling the local farmer that he was Captain Alfred Horn. Taken away by the Home Guard for questioning, he then claimed to be Deputy Führer Rudolph Hess on a mission to make peace with Britain and that he had run out of fuel only 16 miles from the runway on the Duke of Hamilton's estate of Dungavel, South Lanarkshire. He demanded to meet the duke, whom he believed to be the leader of a political party ready to make peace with Germany.

Hamilton, Scottish Unionist MP for East Renfrewshire, was one of a number of British MPs invited to the 1936 Olympic Games in Berlin and had met Hitler, Hess, Ribbentrop, Göring and members of the German aristocracy. Sympathetic to the neo-Fascist Nordic League and the Right Club, Hamilton was monitored by MI5. The Nordic League, also known as the White Knights of Britain and the Hooded Men, was formed by two Nazi agents in 1935. Led by Archibald Ramsay, the Conservative MP for Peebles and Midlothian, it included members of the British aristocracy and was described as the 'British branch of International Nazism'. The Right Club, founded by Ramsay in 1939, was an attempt to unite right-wing patriots against Jewish influence and included the Duke of Windsor and the Duke of Westminster, plus other leading aristocrats and conservative politicians.

When Churchill learned that the Duke of Buccleugh, a major Scottish landowner, had attended Hitler's 50th birthday party in 1939, he was removed from his position as keeper of His Majesty's household and replaced by Hamilton. The Duke of Buccleugh and the Duke of Kent were reported to have been involved in a car accident not far from the crash site on the morning after Hess arrived. Local gossip has it that they had been part of a reception committee.

Hess claimed to have brought a plan for a negotiated peace whereby Germany would withdraw from its occupied territories leaving German police in control. Britain would be allowed to retain her empire and Germany would be allowed to focus its attack on Russia, policies supported by royalty and aristocracy. Some suggest the plan included a proposal to assassinate Churchill. However, when Hess met Hamilton the next day, Hamilton claimed not to know him. Denying he had been sent by Hitler, Hess was refused diplomatic immunity and imprisoned.

When Calvo next met Williams, he asked him what he thought about Hess's visit. On replying that he had not the faintest idea, Calvo told him

> it was definitely in connection with the invasion and that he had come to make all arrangements with their agents and friends among the Scottish Nationalists and those sympathisers in England and Wales including myself. He must have had all the names and addresses with him in the plane, but failing to complete his purpose he had burnt the plane and the list of names and addresses but that was definitely his purpose in coming over here.[27]

Lee Richards, a psychological warfare historian, reported finding no mention of a Scottish Nationalist angle in the bulk of the Hess files he investigated in the National Archives in Kew. However, he identified Donald Fraser-Grant, a Scottish Fascist, as the main presenter and scriptwriter of a clandestine radio station called 'Caledonia', which broadcast from the Berlin Olympic stadium. The station was part of *Büro Concordia*, a joint German Foreign Office and Propaganda Ministry operation that incited its Scottish and other listeners to undertake acts of sabotage, passive resistance and strike action.[28] A transcription of the 'Caledonia' broadcast on 26 August 1940 reads:

> Neutral correspondents in Britain are complaining about the Censor. Names of Harbours, docks and railways are cut out by the authorities. Newspapers and BBC News Bulletins are severely censored. But there are occasions when correspondents do get the truth into the newspapers.
>
> It is reported that the British Government has asked American newspapers not to publish news of the very desperate situation in which we are now. The general opinion in America is that the position is hopeless and that it's too late for America to come to our aid.
>
> The papers and the BBC only publish what Churchill wants to be known.
>
> If people knew the truth about our defences, they would realise what a fool's paradise we are living in to hope to win the war. If the truth were known, the war would not last another day.
>
> During the last few weeks and the last few days terrible damage has been done – Ramsgate: wrecking of gas works and aerodromes. We are only told a fraction of what goes on. Some areas are receiving continuous air attacks. A.A. Defences are suffering from too much work.
>
> Our efforts must be increased to acquaint people with the facts, to save our country from utter destruction.
>
> This war is the result of capitalism – we have known nothing but unemployment, hardship and poverty from capitalism. The English will not allow their country to be destroyed. We can and will save our native land by getting a separate peace for Scotland.[27]

While it is possible that the Germans had already contacted the Scottish Nationalist Party or were hoping to, no mention of this was found in Owens' or Williams's personnel files, nor in Masterman's account of the double-cross operations. That is not to say that it did not happen, given the support the Germans had given to the IRA and were expected to give the WNP. There may well have been overtures to the more extreme nationalists in Scotland willing to take on sabotage operations. It is just that such direct evidence has not come to light.

Founded in 1934, the SNP initially sought a Scottish assembly for Scottish affairs, but there was not the same level of disaffection with the concept of the United Kingdom as in Ireland. Scottish regiments, engineers, bankers, medical people and diplomats worked all over the British Empire. Successive British Prime ministers, generals, civil servants and senior political figures originated north of the Border and large elements of the Royal Navy and Royal Air Force were stationed in Scottish bases. There was little practical support for any movement in Scotland that advocated disunity.

There was some support for Nazism in 1939. Andrew Dewar Gibb, the SNP leader, told party members at its conference that 'Imperial England had no right to criticise the actions of any other country'. Hugh MacDiarmid, the nationalist poet, argued that the SNP ought to follow the Nazi model and in 1940 wrote a poem in which he said he would hardly care if London was destroyed by bombs. In 1941, Brooman-White was informed that Arthur Donaldson, the leader of the SNP, intended to form a puppet government in Scotland if the Germans invaded Britain, similar to Vidkun Quisling's government in Norway. He was reported as telling an MI5 agent that his movement was contemplating spreading confusion by false reports and minor acts of sabotage and was planning to start a whispering campaign to spread rumours of shipping losses. Using the Defence Regulation 18b, Donaldson was interned without charge for six weeks. Whether the proposed minor acts of sabotage were ever undertaken is unknown.

In the early years of the war, the SNP encouraged passive resistance among their supporters, rejecting conscription. Leaders of the movement were detained, members who disclosed their views were ostracised, and the direction of the movement was effectively stifled. Small-scale sabotage activities would have had little impact as the ports where Royal Navy ships and submarines were based along with civilian and military airfields were well protected. By autumn 1940, much of Western and Northern Scotland had become dotted with armed training camps. Naval forces, army units and patrolling aircraft were stationed at or very near any settlement with any military, economic or transport significance. Having a very limited physical infrastructure such as alternative road and rail routes made it unlikely that small-scale subversion would have made much impact in Scotland. For any nucleus of disaffected individuals to have remained undetected by the authorities for long in any region seems unlikely.

During the war, the SNP movement was small and lacked the manpower or influence to destabilise anything. The Scottish political situation was in no way comparable to the larger proportion of Ireland's population who were by then much more sympathetic to the call for a united Ireland. One imagines that those who advised the Abwehr and those British citizens with any Fascist sympathies would have recognised this.

Decrypts of messages sent to Berlin by Eduard Hempel, the Head of the German Legation in Dublin, showed they were mostly about Irish neutrality, but some in 1943 were reported to have infuriated Churchill. One proposed a German-Scottish alliance as a 'weapon in the fight against the gross materialism of the capitalist-communist union of English, Americans, Bolsheviks, etc.'. There was a request for war material to be sent from Ireland to take advantage of a general panic in England so that a republic in Scotland could be declared. There was also a proposal to establish a Celtic union with headquarters in Dublin.

MI5's investigation suggested the memo was as a result of disinformation by the Scottish Independent Movement, which it described as 'of little moment'. Professor Christopher Harvie suggested it had been generated by Tom Johnson, the Scottish Secretary, hoping to gain more power from parliament as he was concerned about a potential rise of 'a sort of Sinn Fein movement'.

Douglas Macleod, a BBC radio broadcaster, reported in 'The Thistle, the Shamrock and the Swastika' that Radio Caledonia had been encouraging a 'Scottish Socialist Republic'. There had been sixty-five disputes in the Scottish coalfields in the first three months of 1941; the Clyde shipyards had been paralysed by an apprentices' strike and there had been a strike in the Dumbarton aviation works. There were also reports of workers on go-slows and production defects. Whether there was sabotage and German agents involved was not reported.

In the report Williams gave Calvo to be forwarded to Del Pozo was a note pointing out that he had not received the £25 he had been promised for his last report, that he was disappointed that the three men he had been told would be arriving had not turned up and that he had gone to a lot of trouble to find accommodation for them. He also warned him that his Welsh friends were losing patience and that he would probably lose them unless they got a move on.

There was nothing in Williams's file indicating that he was aware that the three saboteurs had been arrested but one imagines that he would have wondered whether, if they had landed safely with their sabotage equipment, they would have attempted to contact him.

During his next meeting with Calvo another Spaniard appeared whom Williams called the 'Bullfighter'. From the description he gave to Masterman, he was identified as Angel Alcazar de Valasco, an ex-bullfighter and new Spanish Press Attaché, who, like Del Pozo, was a member of the Spanish Falangist Party and was suspected of being in Britain to facilitate espionage.[28] Calvo's link with Alcazar prompted Brooman-White to take a keen interest in Williams's links with a potential Spanish spy ring. According to Masterman, Brooman-White wanted to use Williams 'in a blitz campaign in order to hang CALVO and ALCAZAR, and blow himself in the process'.[29]

There were two reports in Williams's file, one heavily edited by Brooman-White that focussed on the military intelligence Alcazar would be particularly interested in and another heavily edited by Rothschild, whose aim was to ensure that the report would result in the Germans delivering their most up-to-date sabotage technology and, potentially, fully trained saboteurs. Rothschild's idea was that once these new agents were caught and interrogated, they would also be able to shed light on the most recent developments in the Germans' sabotage training methods and identify their targets. One imagines that some of that knowledge would then have been passed on to George Rheam, the Commandant at Brickendonbury Manor.

In early August 1941, Masterman acknowledged a further complication in GW's case. John Drew of the Home Defence Executive wanted Williams to be primarily used to pass over what were termed 'Sullivan' documents. These were the papers reported to have originated from James Sullivan who 'acquired' them from the office of a British Cabinet Minister but which he had to replace by 10 a.m. the following morning. They contained military intelligence which Masterman considered would tempt Alcazar to purchase, to sell them himself to the Germans and the Japanese. The result appears to have been that Brooman-White and Rothschild's reports were merged and Drew's 'Sullivan' documents about military intelligence included. There were two reports, the second containing all of Rothschild's edits and most of Brooman-White's.

Swansea, 6 August 1941

Dear Mr Calvo,

As requested by you I have made it my business to obtain certain information for you to send to my friends. I trust you will appreciate the difficulty that I have encountered in getting this information, as it is work that is altogether different from that which I agreed to undertake for my friends when I met them at Antwerp. Such work as I then agreed upon I am still quite prepared to carry out if my friends let me have sufficient material for the purpose and funds to pay those who I would require to assist me.

When at Antwerp my friends and I came to an understanding as to how the material was to be received by me. I am still waiting for material. They know that I cannot work without it neither can I work on my own, so I am obliged to obtain assistance for which it will be necessary to pay well. The work that I am asked to do now is not at all the kind of work that I agreed to do, in fact, it is altogether strange to me, but however I shall do my best.

I may tell you that I am chiefly concerned with what is happening in Wales and am prepared to do all in my power to obstruct the English in the manufacture of war material in Wales and the use of our country as Airfields. I know other Welshmen who are willing to assist me in all I undertake to do in this matter, but, as I have already said, I must have materials and money for the purpose.

At present, I am only able to inform you of what is taking place in a small area in Wales, but if I had sufficient means, I could go all over Wales and do something really worthwhile.

The following are particulars concerning the things you asked me, and I shall be glad if you will send this report to my friends so that they will know exactly how matters stand.

AIRFIELDS.

There is a new Airfield on Fairwood Common, which is just outside the town of Swansea on the way to the Gower Peninsular. It is situated just beyond where the road forks – one to the North and the other to the South. The South Road, for the distance that it runs through the Airfield, is closed to private vehicles, but people travelling in public vehicles are permitted along the road. The North Road is open to all traffic, and many aircraft can be seen near the run-ways and hangars. On high ground called Cefn Bryn, about two miles distant to the north-west, landing lights are exposed at night to mislead enemy aircraft.

At Pembrey, about 14 miles West of Swansea, there is a large Airfield which is extensively used for instructional purposes.

There are large Airfields at Stormy Downs, situate between Pyle and Bridgend, just off the main Cardiff to Swansea Rod, and at St Athans, situate about 8 miles West of Barry Down.

About 3 miles North of Haverfordwest, in close proximity to the Haverfordwest – Fishguard Road, a large Airfield is in course of construction and nearing completion.

FACTORIES.

At Pembrey, in close proximity to the airfield, is an Ordnance Factory used principally in the manufacture of explosives and shell filling. Quite close to this factory are steel works where military material is manufactured.

Near Glyn Neath, about 10 miles north-east of Neath, a Synthetic Oil Plant is being constructed and nearing completion.

A large Carbide Factory is being constructed on land which adjoins the main line of the Great Western Railway between Port Talbot and Bridgend.

At Bridgend, adjoining the main line of the Great Western Railway is an Ordnance Factory covering thousands of acres where material is manufactured similar to that at Woolwich Arsenal. There are thousands of people, male and female, employed day and night for seven days every week.

At Port Tennant, on the east of and adjoining the Swansea Docks, there are two Magnesium Works in full operation.

At Milford Haven there are (1) a Flax Factory nearing completion, (2) a Mine and Shell filling depot situate just inside the Haven, where mines and shells are filled and stored underground. (3) Petroleum storage tanks of immense capacity and built underground immediately in front of the Railway Station. These tanks are covered with earth upon which grass grows and where sheep and cattle are allowed to graze. (4) Engineering and other works surround the Dock where all kinds of ships are repaired. This town is a hive of industry.

In the Swansea Valley, running north from Swansea Docks, there are numerous steel and other works where the military material is manufactured in full swing. There are also numerous collieries. Anti-aircraft defences are few.

SHIPPING.

Cardiff, Swansea, Newport and Barry, all in the Bristol Channel, are now extensively used by ships which formerly were dealt with at Liverpool and

Bristol. Convoys of military vehicles and guns of various kinds are brought on certain days of the week to Singleton Park, which skirts the bay at Swansea about 2 miles west of the centre of the town, and are loaded in ships at Swansea Docks for shipment to the Far East and elsewhere. Troops are also taken by the same. Ships from Swansea and other ports in the Bristol Channel proceed to Milford Haven to be convoyed. Many captured ships are used in this connection; they are re-named with two-word names, the first of which is always 'Empire'.

In connection with the movement of ships, it is always very difficult to obtain definite information as to their arrival, but I sometimes receive news of their departure about twelve hours before they leave the docks. This news could be immediately transmitted if I had a wireless transmitting set.

FOOD.

The supply of necessary foodstuffs is still fairly good but appears to be getting less each week, particularly in the large towns. Beer, tobacco and cigarettes are very scarce. Shops exhibit notices indicating that they have no cigarettes, sweets and chocolates. Public houses open only for part of the permitted time each day because they have not sufficient beer to supply their customers during the whole time.

Most of the wealthy Jews have quitted the large towns and taken refuge in the country districts where they have taken over all available accommodation. These people visit the surrounding farmhouses and buy up butter, eggs and poultry for their own use at any price. This is done clandestinely as producers are liable to heavy penalties if found selling goods in this way.

The particulars furnished above are as definite as I can possible supply, but as I have already said, this is not exactly my line. What I am more anxious to do is something that will discourage the English in using Wales for their military purposes and at the same time do something that will be of real assistance to my friends.[30]

Apart from Rothschild, Brooman-White and Drew wanting their input into Williams's reports, there were also the Double Cross additions. Masterman wanted Williams to build up a channel of communication with the Germans, particularly using the Spanish diplomatic bag, as part of their deception game. Passing documents this way, although it took over a week to get to Madrid, was more effective than having a wireless operator spending hours encoding and transmitting. He recognised that they had to await the German response, not knowing whether they would respond to the offer of sabotage or be more interested in the military, economic and political intelligence. Four options for Williams's future were put forward:

a)   That we should continue to run G.W. ourselves without outside instructions, and adjust his work according to circumstances as they arise. It will be remembered that many gents have developed in ways unexpected at the outset, and have, for example, changed both in grade and in method. If at a later stage we get positive orders to blow G.W. in order, let us say, to destroy CALVO, that is that and we must obey, but we are a long way yet from committing ourselves to any such course. Incidentally, we should be absolutely satisfied that G.W.'s evidence would be conclusive, and that CALVO would perish as desired before we make up our minds to the sacrifice of G.W. At present, the outcome of the CALVO proposal is very dubious.

b) That we should instruct G.W. to report on August 8th in the manner already approved in principle by us – i.e. he should bring a certain amount of information, suggest that he is temperamentally and by education better suited to sabotage than to espionage, and enquire how far his 'Sullivan' documents have been appreciated. We shall then see, from the answers given to him, in which direction the Iberian-Teutonic cat seems disposed to jump; the delicate question as to how to force the sabotage card after that is a matter for us to decide.

c) That in his sabotage prospectus he should refrain from giving personal and geographical details since the handing over of these may involve us in difficulties and may have unfortunate repercussions. In other words, we should accept Rothschild's form of prospectus and not Brooman-White's.

d) That in the meantime Drew's new 'Sullivan' documents should be discussed and prepared in case of need.

Finally, the recent discussions convince me that the less other sections know of the manner in which we work double-cross agents the better; suggestions made on half-knowledge are not really helpful, and it seems to me essential that we should leave the fullest control of our agents in our own hands, so long as they are our agents and unless or until we get positive orders from higher authority for their use or destruction.[31]

Little transpired in the next meeting Williams had with Calvo except that Alcazar appeared again but left after handing over a note. Williams reiterated his willingness to engage in sabotage. In the discussion in the 'Bachelor's Club' afterwards with Masterman and Marriott, Williams was told to use Brooman-White and Rothschild's reports to type out another.

He expressed concern that the details included could lead to the Germans attacking Welsh targets and killing his friends or other good Welshman. His motto was 'Wales for the Welsh' and he would 'far rather prefer to sabotage factories from inside when he would know how much damage would be done and would be able to regulate to a certain extent the loss of lives. By a process of hard work and many acts of sabotage he feels that he would be able to persuade the English that it was not much good building factories in that part of the world'.[32]

There was also an understanding that the intelligence included in the reports ought not to be revealed to other agencies. Without mentioning the Army, Navy or Air Force, there was an unstated awareness that they might object very strongly if they learned that the Germans were being provided with such sensitive data. The word treason was not mentioned, but it is likely Masterman knew he might have to justify himself in very high quarters should knowledge leak out. The revised report for Calvo was as follows:

Swansea, 6 August 1941

Dear Mr Calvo,

As requested by you I have made it my business to obtain certain information for you to send to my friends. I trust you will appreciate the difficulty that I have encountered in getting this information, as it is work that is altogether different from that which I agreed to undertake for my friends when I met them at Antwerp. Such work as I then agreed upon I am still quite prepared to carry out if my friends will let me have sufficient material for the purpose and funds to pay those who I would require to assist me.

When at Antwerp my friends and I came to an understanding as to how the material was to be received by me. I am still waiting for material. They know that I cannot work without it neither can I work on my own, so I am obliged to obtain assistance for which it will be necessary to pay well. The work that I am asked to do now is not at all the kind of work that I agreed to do, in fact, it is altogether strange to me, but however, I shall do my best.

I may tell you that I am chiefly concerned with what is happening in Wales and am prepared to do all in my power to obstruct the English in the manufacture of war material in Wales and the use of our country as Airfields. I know other Welshmen who are willing to assist me in all I undertake to do in this matter, but, as I have already said, I must have materials and money for the purpose.

The following are particulars concerning the things you asked me, and I shall be glad if you will send this report to my friends so that they will know exactly how matters stand.

In area Senny Bridge (near Brecon) military transports bearing placard white and red, divided horizontally, with ITC/SWB on it.

Saundersfoot Bay, half mile north of Saundersfoot village, in valley, 100 yards by 80 yards area of coast mined. [There then follows a list of points regarding naval gun positions, movement of troops to the Middle East, etc.]

...I am informed on good authority that there is considerable discontent among the Shipwrights and Riggers at Milford Haven caused through the introduction of a 'clocking in' system by the employers whereby the men have to 'clock in' on arrival at the yards to commence work and 'clock out' from the yard upon ceasing work. Prior to the introduction of this system, the workmen recorded the time that they were employed by daily work sheets. Under the new system less work is done and discontent is caused by reason of the fact that the men instead of ceasing work where they were employed now have to go back to the yard to 'clock out'.

I am informed that there are 187 Shipwrights and riggers belonging to the Shipwrights Union, at Milford Haven and it was touch and go recently whether there would be a stoppage of work. The matter is under consideration by the officials of the Shipwrights Union in conjunction with the employers, but I do not know the result.

In the Swansea Area work seems to be proceeding quite normally. Things in general have been quiet again in this area for some time but Haverford

West has had two night raids. I have been unable to ascertain the extent of the damage.

In general; South Wales is not quite so busy as it was in the pre-war days due to the policy of factory dispersal which was actively pursued after the heavy raids of last year. This has not proved in some cases, e.g. steel works, but assembly plants have gone to other areas. Some for instance are now located in Shropshire and others in Gloucestershire.

A few new factories are going up, however, in particular one near Glyn Neath and another between Port Talbot and Bridgend. It is stated locally that a carbide factory is to be erected at Bridgend adjoining the main line of the Great Western Railway, but there are no signs of this at present.

At Pembury there is an ordnance factory and adjacent to it a steel works.

In the Swansea Valley running north from Swansea docks there are numerous steel and other works, some of which are not working. Air raid damage has not been serious lately. One raid early in May damaged the County Hall at Cardiff, and a good deal of damage was done to civilian property at Skewen and in the suburbs of Swansea. The worst raid recently was one at the end of June when Cardiff, Penarth and Barry were attacked. Barry and Penarth docks were damaged. A steelworks at Newport was also hit in this raid. [Then information about food, cigarette shortages and wealthy Jews, as above.]

I would like to re-emphasise, as I have previously stated on a number of occasions, that the collection of information is to me both difficult and dangerous. I have no training to guide me as to what is important or what are points of interest to my friends, but I know the dates of convoy sailings are obviously of great interest. You will realise that it is extremely difficult to ask questions without arousing suspicion. Furthermore, I have no means of getting such information across quickly and there is so much delay that by the time it arrived it would probably be useless.

The reports I am now submitting are not perhaps of great importance, but the documents I have recently handed over would, no doubt, have been most valuable if I had not had to keep them in my possession for so many weeks.

I feel, however, that I could be of far more use concentrating on sabotage activities and, in this field, I am sure I could do some good work. When I met the Commander in Antwerp, I told him that about 20 of my Welsh Nationalist friends would be prepared to help in this kind of activity, provided the personal danger were not too great. Since then the position has been considerably altered by a number of factors: some of the men have been called up for military service, other have become embittered by the bombing of Welsh towns and are no longer prepared to help Germany. I have, however, still got a small nucleus of associates in whom I would place confidence and, if I were given funds, I might be able to enlist more.

It may be helpful if I give some outline of the spheres in which I think I could work. I have two entirely reliable friends in Swansea. One is a small business man who has not got any particular facilities for working but is a man of absolute discretion and considerable courage. The fact that he also has a motor car which he is ready to place at our disposal is helpful. The other man is an immigration official, who is 100% Welsh National and anti-English. He can quite easily obtain access to buildings in and about the docks. If he were supplied with suitable material and delayed-action fuses, it might be possible for him to insert them into cargoes which are awaiting shipment. In the course of his duties, he has to board ships that enter the docks and could also enter warehouses at the docks where merchandise is stored preparatory to loading and after being discharged from ships.

It is becoming very difficult indeed to get hold of the raw materials for making incendiary bombs and even more difficult to obtain high explosive. I recently tested this out and felt very nervous because although I was at a chemist's shop where I was not known, fortunately for me as I felt the chemist was suspicious. He refused to sell me things I asked for and said I must get a permit. He said this in what I took to be a suspicious way. I said I would get a permit from the Police, but did not go back as I thought it was too dangerous. I only did this to test whether it would be possible. It is obvious that the regulations about buying things from which high explosives or incendiaries can be made have been tightened up a great deal. In order, therefore, to carry out sabotage on a ship or on pipes leading from a reservoir, which I think would be the easiest, I must be supplied with the material to do it. This means incendiary material in the case of ships, and high explosive in the case of reservoirs. I do not know exactly how big an explosion a given quantity of high explosive will cause and therefore do not know whether it would be possible for me to place sufficient high explosive in a crate or package to do real damage to a ship. On the other hand, I could place an incendiary bomb in one of these, and providing that the cargo was suitable selected, which I think can be arranged, a serious fire should result.

I am familiar with the means by which water is supplied, and it would be quite easy for me to blow up a section of the pipes leading from the reservoir. These pipes are not guarded and in some cases are only just under the surface of the ground. They pass through lonely spots where one could blow them up without any danger. Would the blowing up of a pipe, some of which are six inches in diameter, be of any value? How much explosive would be needed to do this?

The only other man who might be of help is one who, when I last heard of him was working as a carpenter in the Royal Ordnance Factory near Wrexham; and I have not seen this man for some time, and it is possible that he has gone to another job; I do not know him very well, and I would not like to put a definite project to him without checking up a little more fully on his present attitude to the war. I would not consider him worth mentioning had it not been for the fact that if he is still in his job at the Royal Ordnance Factory he would be in a position to do such valuable work. In this connection, I need more expert guidance. All I know at the moment from my colleague is that the Ordnance Factory fills anti-aircraft shells and that there are hoppers in which large quantities of powdered explosive exist and to which my colleague has access during night shifts.

I am told that food stores are being built in the neighbourhood of Colwyn Bay and he might possibly be useful there also.

As regards the rank and file members of the local Welsh Nationalist branch of which I have just been appointed a secretary, I do not think that in their present state of mind we could rely on them sufficiently to give their active support. The best man was Owen Ap Owen, who I have succeeded as secretary, and who has now been imprisoned by the English because he refused to enlist to serve in their war against you.

I would point out that the main handicap is the difficulty of obtaining necessary materials. When I was in Antwerp, I was instructed in preparing a mixture with potassium chlorate and sugar for the purpose of incendiarism. Under the existing regulations and restrictions, however, it is impossible to obtain potassium chlorate from a chemist without a grave risk of arousing suspicion. Also, I have little confidence in the delayed action by means of sulphuric acid in a bottle, and this is certainly not suitable for planting in ships' cargoes. It seems to me that this is the most profitable line for me to develop through my immigration official friend and I am confident that, if I am supplied with material and really effective delayed-action apparatus, I could get some good results.

The final difficulty, and perhaps the most important is the delay mechanisms. We must have delays of some sort or other which will give us sufficient time to get away from the scene of the sabotage, and in the case of a ship so that it will be well on its voyage before anything happens. As I have already stated the purchase of unusual chemicals is now extremely difficult, if not impossible, and in any case, I have not got sufficient technical knowledge to make a delay, therefore these would have to be supplied too.

As regards the detonators I think I can pick up some of these from the collieries in Wales. Miners frequently take detonators home and even sell them to their friends.

I have the possibilities of committing sabotage on three different types of objectives. First, one of my colleagues is an Immigration Officer at a port and during the course of his duties aboard ships would have opportunities of placing an infernal machine in the cargoes. Secondly, another of my colleagues is in an Ordnance Factory in Wales. Thirdly, I have another colleague who has considerable knowledge of reservoirs, the pipelines leading from them and their pumping systems, and also the systems of guarding them. I also have some knowledge of these. I have carefully considered the best methods of committing sabotage.

Summarising what I have said above, I have got the people and know of places where sabotage can be carried out, but I must have the material, and particularly the delays with which to do the job. Whoever supplies these must, of course, see that they are suitably disguised.[33]

It was noticeable that the plan to pollute the reservoir was changed to blowing up the pipeline, a method which would incur no loss of life. It is also worth including those sections of Broomam-White's report that were omitted from the final version.

Another absolutely reliable friend is the secretary of a branch of the Welsh Nationalist Party who has a large house in the hills in Breconshire. He is a rather timid individual, and this limits his usefulness. However, his house is in an out-of-the-way place, and he is extremely well-known and respected throughout the district; it would, therefore, be an ideal spot for storing any materials that you might send me. For this purpose, I can easily obtain his consent.

In another part of Wales, I have two good friends near Aberystwyth. One of them is employed in the local Labour Exchange and has access to an airfield which is being built near there. The other is clerk to the local Water Board. It is some time since I made contact with them and I know they are depressed and disillusioned at the time they have to wait before getting instructions. I am, however, quite confident that they are willing to do all they can in the matter of sabotage against the English.

I would remind you that I have been kept waiting so long for the equipment you promised that unless you are prepared to let me have some without further delay I shall find it practically impossible to do anything to assist you as the longer I have to wait for material the greater becomes the difficulty of obtaining assistance and access to military works once they are in operation. It is not so difficult to approach them before they are completely constructed.[34]

The meeting at Calvo's apartment the following evening was described by Williams as a 'séance'. There was no mention of sabotage, just a request for information on rationing, shipping, the armaments industry, submarine warfare, the invasion and Eire.

After a trip to a garage where Williams was provided with free petrol, they went to see the 'Bullfighter', whose conversation with Calvo was translated as 'Everything is now all right. The money will come along in about a fortnight, either in Dollars or English notes. It will come in the Spanish bag.' A submarine did make its way to a bay indicated on a map by Del Pozo, but could not get near enough to effect a landing.[35] When asked if he meant Oxwich Bay, Calvo confirmed it. Williams did not mention being surprised by this news that the Germans appeared to have supported his sabotage plans. What was also strange was the fact that he had not been involved in the arrival of the U-boat, the potential landing of more agents and the transfer and storage of supplies. According to a captured German agent in Brazil, he identified Williams as the head of German espionage in England who supplied new Abwehr agents with identity and ration cards.[36]

A further conversation with Alcazar ensued which was translated as 'Hess came to Scotland with instructions concerning the invasion. Something went wrong before he was able to land so he burned all the papers, otherwise someone from Scotland would have come to see Y [?] with definite instructions as to the part I was to take ... After the victorious conclusion of the war by Germany, who would also control Spain, you will be invited to Spain where you will be introduced to Senores Franco and [Ramon] Suner [the German Foreign Minister] and you will have a good time.'[37]

Before he left, Williams was told not to include names at the beginning or end of subsequent reports and to put them in an unaddressed plain envelope.

He was also to bring an invoice for all the costs he had incurred on their behalf. As he had been requested to submit another report in two to three weeks, he asked TAR 'that sufficient data of a fictitious nature be furnished me to enable me to make out a report covering the matters upon which information is required, so that I may gain further confidence with my friends, which, ultimately, may lead to better things'.[38]

Another detailed report was written, a list of divisional signs was provided and some torn pieces of paper purported to have been rescued from James Sullivan's waste paper basket in the Home Defence Executive were added to the plain envelope for Calvo. Alcazar was not present at the next meeting so there was no money and Calvo claimed not to be able to discuss a salary. When asked if he was given money by Del Pozo, he said he had but that he handed it over to his chief, Mr SNOW. Letting slip Owens' code-name was a mistake. Calvo was interested in contacting him but Williams claimed not to have seen him for some time. Whether he knew that the SNOW case had finally been 'terminated' on account of him triple playing TAR is unknown.

On SNOW's return from Lisbon he handed over to MI5 the £10,000 Rantzau had given him and detonators hidden in toilet soap, time clocks hidden in a talcum powder tin, shaving soap and torch battery and an acid delay hidden in a fountain pen and pencil. These would no doubt have been passed to Rothschild for examination. MI5 then spent several days interrogating him to determine whether he had, as he alleged, told Rantzau that all his traffic was controlled and the whole of his undertakings were known to the British. A note in his file stated that, 'What exactly SNOW did or did not give away or admit to the Germans we cannot tell, though we can make surmises. The riddle of the Sphinx and the doctrine of the Trinity are simple and straightforward affairs compared to this case.'[39]

Unable to trust SNOW further, to avoid him divulging what he knew about the double cross, he was eliminated and his case was closed. This was MI5's expression for having him imprisoned in Dartmoor. To explain his absence, a message was sent to the Germans apologising for his inability to continue working for them as the stress of his work had caused him to suffer a nervous breakdown. Major Boeckel reported receiving a message in February or March 1941 signed 'Radio Operator of 3504' stating he was too ill to continue work and asking to whom his transmitter should be handed. He presumed SNOW had been discovered and abandoned the connection.[40]

Rantzau claimed after the war that he had only given SNOW £500 and thought he had taken the money and ran. Masterman changed his mind about SNOW and gave him £500 when he was released from prison. Instead of moving in with Lily, he met another woman, took her surname and moved to Ireland where he ran a radio repair shop until he died in 1957.[41]

When Marriott learned that SNOW's name had been mentioned, there was concern that Calvo would pass this name on to Alcazar, Del Pozo's boss, and MI5's deception game would be exposed. High-level discussions took place about whether to arrest Calvo, Alcazar and their contacts during which Masterman reported the difficulties that would ensue. Alcazar could expose Williams's role and the use of the Spanish diplomatic bag to send documents to the Abwehr would be lost. As Williams was considered at that time to be Masterman's second most important agent, if his cover was blown it was thought that the Abwehr might start to question the loyalty of their other agents.[42] Masterman's argument won the day and both Calvo and Alcazar continued their work in Britain under close surveillance by MI5.

Although a number of meetings took place where Williams handed Calvo more MI5-inspired reports and 'Sullivan' papers, there was no subsequent mention of sabotage. The content of the 'Sullivan' papers related to a convoy destined for Malta, which Williams subsequently claimed had led to a U-boat sinking HMS *Ark Royal*, the Royal Navy's aircraft carrier, in November. The Plan IV report encouraged the Germans to attack well-defended airfields rather than British cities.

Further attempts were made to arrest Calvo in early 1942, eventually with success. This time Masterman's objections were overruled. Under interrogation Calvo revealed the extent of a Spanish spy network across Britain and, according to his file, he was successfully turned and played a role in MI5's elaborate plan to convince the Germans that the Allies' D-Day landings included a large force invading Pas de Calais. This successfully persuaded the Germans to place several divisions in the wrong location, facilitating the bridgehead in Normandy.

With Calvo gone and there being no indication that there was going to be an army of German-sponsored Welsh saboteurs, Williams continued to supply Rothschild with military and other intelligence about South Wales until early summer 1942 when, according to TAR, he was

> informed on 28 May that his services were no longer needed. Even though his phone was removed and his car taken, he replied, 'I must agree that the services I am now able to render do not justify my retention in your employment, but I am most pleased to know that our association has been satisfactory to you. I only wish that I had been able to give greater satisfaction, but I don't think that the inability to have gratified such a wish is entirely due to any fault of mine. However, if at any future time I should renew acquaintance with my former business associates, or anyone in the same line of business, I can assure you that you will be informed immediately of the transaction.[43]

In Masterman's post-war account of the Double Cross system, he acknowledged that at the start of the war Britain was justifiably afraid that

> a great campaign of sabotage would be carried out by the enemy in this country. In truth and in fact very little sabotage was done or even attempted, but in the early days it was thought, and rightly thought, that the most important work of our double-cross agents might well be on the sabotage side, that is to say, they might help us to arrest other saboteurs resident in or sent to this island. G.W. was primarily a sabotage agent. His earliest tasks were to raise recruits among the WNP for sabotage in Wales, and he also discussed the possibility of poisoning of water supplies. G.W. himself in his dealings with the Germans always sniffed at the task of collecting intelligence reports which was demanded of him, and proudly pointed out that he was

by profession an expert in sabotage and that he felt it something of a slur on his reputation that he should be employed in what he considered a less honourable sphere of activity.[44]

He went on to argue that the end of Williams's career as a double agent in the attempt to limit the success of any German sabotage operations was a great loss 'for he was by far the best channel we ever had for the transmission of documents, and his value in this respect might have been a growing asset. Moreover, his "elimination" placed others of our agents in danger and imposed a policy of extreme caution upon us.'[45]

Williams returned to his private detective work but eighteen months later suffered a debilitating illness from which he died in 1949, aged 62. Humphries' summary of his wartime contribution was that 'he had the Abwehr jumping through hoops and helped Britain win the intelligence war'. He was 'an ordinary man who did an extraordinary job for his country, one that could have been more productive but for the shadow cast over his operations by Calvo's arrest. Not for a moment did Rantzau seem to suspect that Williams was anything other than the fanatical Welsh nationalist collaborator he pretended to be. After Owen's termination, Williams was regarded by the Abwehr as their last man standing in Britain.'[46]

Rantzau was transferred to less important duties having lost SNOW, but as far as the sabotage story is concerned, Williams had played his role admirably.

Thomas and Ketley's research into the *Gruppe Rowehl* reported pilot Knemeyer dropping agents into Central and Southern England.

> … one from Normandy to west of Bristol on a great moor where the famous English prison [Dartmoor] stood. The same night the bombers flew their big raid on Coventry's ball-bearing factories. [14/15 November 1940 when 21 factories were destroyed and about 1,100 people killed.]
>
> Everything in Southern England was lit up by the searchlights looking for our bombers. Near Bristol we ran into heavy flak and were in the searchlights for a long time. Ruhnke was my observer. Gartenfeld flew with us to see the agents jump, and we had 'gondola' Do 17 or Do 217 [?]. I put one down from Brussels, in the Midlands near Birmingham; he was Norwegian. The one on Dartmoor was a South African student.[47]

The identity of these two agents and whether their missions included sabotage is unknown. No reference to any agent being dropped on 14/15 November has come to light. However, according to Farago, Ritter told SNOW that he suspected another agent destined for Manchester had not made contact. He had been parachuted on the night of 7 September 1940 but his mission lasted less than five minutes as he landed in the Manchester Ship Canal near Birkenhead. Ritter also reported that a South African agent had not made contact after his drop and suspected that he too had drowned in a canal because of the wireless set attached to him.[48]

Boeckel identified an agent of Ast Bremen named KROPF who was despatched in November 1940 by Tornow from a Brussels airfield. He was instructed to go to Ashbourne, Liverpool. SNOW was to give him a wireless set but reported a man drowning in the Mersey. According to Gartenfeld-Staffel, Kropf was dropped further south.[49]

Josef Starzincky, a Polish agent working for the Germans in Brazil, was captured in 1942 and sent to Camp 020. During his interrogation, he provided details of four agents he trained with who were destined for England. Two were identified as Jakobs and Schmidt. One was reported to have been dropped near Bristol and never heard of again. The other was a German born in California who was about thirty, 1m 65cm tall, dark hair, and spoke English with an American accent. He had been dropped in Scotland, south of Glasgow. Walsh, mentioned earlier, was to have been dropped south of Glasgow but his mission was cancelled. He was Irish.[50]

Major John Gwyer, who interviewed Starzincky, admitted that MI5 initially suspected the agent dropped near Bristol to be GANDER and the other to be CORBS, a South African who was thought to have drowned. Gwyer thought the muddle could be explained if GANDER and CORBS were the same man. There was no mention of them having a sabotage mission but he suspected that they were the agents expected by SNOW and GW.[51] MI5 suspected that Corbs could have been a US citizen who had been dispatched by Ast Hamburg to England in 1941.[52]

Although Masterman claimed that all the German agents infiltrated into Britain during the war were captured, evidence shows he was unaware when he first published his account of the Double Cross system that a number had evaded detection. Of the thirteen infiltrated as part of Operation LENA, he reported that the seventh escaped immediate arrest and made his way to London, where he was caught the day he arrived. He had handed a Soho waitress food coupons together with his money in payment for a meal. Suspicious, the waitress called the police. Number 8 also escaped arrest on arrival. But in purchasing a railway ticket to Bristol, which the clerk told him 'would be ten and six', as mentioned earlier he handed over 10 pounds, 6 shillings. The police were called and he was arrested. Who these agents were has yet to come to light.[53]

13

Three Cuban saboteurs land in Fishguard, Pembrokeshire, South Wales – November 1940

At the height of the O'Grady incident, eight men landed in Wales. During a severe storm on the night of 12 November 1940, a French fishing boat, MV *Josephine*, took shelter in the fishing village of Fishguard, Pembrokeshire. When the Dutch captain, Cornelius Evertsen, claimed to the Immigration Authorities that he, his four crew and three passengers were refugees, they were escorted to London for questioning. Under pressure, when Evertsen changed his original story and admitted being paid by the Abwehr to land three Cuban saboteurs in England or Dublin, they were all detained under the Aliens Order and taken to Camp 020. 'Tin Eye' got to work on them, presumably trying to determine whether they were the three men Williams was waiting for.

The crew members, Peter Krag, Arie van Dam, Theophile Jezequel and Juan Martinez, admitted working for the Abwehr but only as sailors. Their Cuban passengers were 34-year-old Pedro Hecheverria, an ex-foundry worker from Santiago; 37-year-old Nicholas Pazos-Dias, a mechanic from Havana; and 41-year-old Silvio Ruis Robles, a linotypist from Vera Cruz, Mexico. They claimed to have fought with the International Brigades in the Spanish Civil War but had fled to France following the success of General Franco's Nationalist forces.[1]

Robles's account was more detailed than that of his compatriots. According to his story, he met the others in July 1940 while he was interned at a camp in Guermantes, Seine-et-Marne, about 30 miles north-east of Paris. When the Spanish and Latin American prisoners were faced with deportation to Spain or unoccupied France, the three of them asked to speak with the Cuban Consul as Cuba was neutral. They were allowed to visit Paris on 12 September where they were given some financial help by the Consul. However, unwilling to work in Germany, face possible execution in Spain or internment in southern France, they looked for work with a Hungarian acquaintance who had been interned with them. He gave them 100 francs (about £5) and offered to help. Three days later, he introduced them to a German lieutenant named Schim or Schimmler, who told them that he was looking for three young men who would be willing to work in England for the Germans.

All three claimed that they saw this as an opportunity to escape France as they supported the Allies. Having accepted Schim's proposal, they were given 2,000 francs to buy clothes and told to get photographs taken of themselves. To draw them in, the next day they were given 400 francs each and on 17 September they were introduced to Kapitanleutnant Witzke, who had met Williams in Antwerp. He gave them a further 400 francs. The following day they were given 200 francs and a train ticket to Brest, where they were provided with accommodation and 40 francs a day.

On 20 September they met 'Leo', a German interpreter, and 'Lebel', who drove them to a villa outside Brest and taught them sabotage. Their file did not include details of the training. At night, they were given 40 francs and told to go into town and enjoy themselves. Whether MI5 questioned them about the sabotage methods and the materials used is unknown as there was no mention of it in their file.

A week later, having packed their bags, they were driven to Le Touquet near Boulogne and boarded MV *Josephine*, where Witzke and 'Hubert', another German officer, gave them their final instructions. If caught by the British, they were to say they were refugees destined for Dublin and the boat had come from Douarnenez as it was less suspicious that Brest.

They would be landed off the west coast of Britain and were to carry out sabotage in the neighbourhood of Bristol. [The exact targets were not specified.] Each would be given £50 Sterling to maintain himself until he could find work in England. On arrival, they should report to their Consul as refugees from Germany and ask for employment, preferably in a factory since this would give them plenty of opportunities to carry out sabotage; in any case, whatever employment they chose, they were to be sure it was in the neighbourhood of Bristol. If by any chance they left England for a neutral country, they must go immediately to the German Consul and report, asking the Consul to write to Dr Schneider, bei Schunck, Heinstrasse 9, Hamburg, notifying their arrival. WITZKE promised them a large monetary reward and future employment with the victorious Germans.[2]

Gottfried Treutlein, an Abwehr interpreter in Brest, admitted interrogating the three Cubans, arranging their supplies and accompanying them to the quayside.[3] However, bad weather and the boat's engine breaking down meant they were brought back to Brest. Waiting for the boat to be repaired and finding a new captain and crew delayed their departure until 5 November.

When they eventually set out ROBLES and his companions were given £50 each and a suitcase with dynamite and explosives. These consisted of dynamite bombs, other dynamite contained a) in green-pea tins, which had a cardboard-plugged aperture in each lid, through which a hole could be made for the wick, and b) in cardboard packets of flour in which the wick could be inserted anywhere, detonators and fuses. Each man was also provided with an F.N. revolver and 24 rounds of ammunition. According to their statements, the Cubans threw their explosives overboard when they were only 40 miles from Brest, but Captain EVERTSEN suggests that they only did this when they were on the point of putting into Fishguard. All three were in possession of Cuban passports.[4]

Yet again bad weather affected their progress, and, according to another MI5 report, Pazos-Diaz developed an abscess, which the captain considered needed medical treatment; in addition, both he and Hechevarria were sea-sick.

> HECHEVARRIA and PAZOS-DIAZ claim that they disposed of their incriminating sabotage material when the 'Josephine' was one day out of Brest. ROBLES did not dispose of his until the boat was much nearer Fishguard. A possible interpretation of this is that HECHEVARRIA and PAZOS-DIAZ were much too sick to care about what happened and that ROBLES, when he realised that his companions had disposed of their sabotage material and were unlikely to be of much use, decided to do likewise rather than carry on the mission alone.[5]

Evertsen offered them the chance of landing at Swansea Bay, but as his two colleagues were too ill, Robles refused to land on his own so the captain proceeded to Fishguard. The *Josephine* was searched twice, the incriminating evidence reported as found was a German flag, a loaded Browning automatic revolver and a round of ammunition. In a separate file on camouflaged sabotage material were photographs of high explosives hidden in tinned vegetables and packets of starch and a safety fuse hidden in a cloth belt.[6]

> On arrival in this country ROBLES and his companions were supposed to apply to a local Labour Exchange for work, preferably in factories where it would be easier to commit acts of sabotage. Bridges were to be another objective. Bristol or Liverpool were apparently to be the sphere of their operations. They were told not to try to communicate with Brest or Germany except that, in the event of their succeeding in leaving England and wishing to return to Spain, they were to go to the nearest German Consulate and ask the Consul to write to Dr. SCHNEIDER, bei SCHUNK. Haynstrasse 9. Hamburg.[7]

Masterman was not entirely convinced that they had been sent to support Williams. They made no mention of him during their interrogations. If they had been instructed to contact him, they were not prepared to admit it. There was no evidence to suggest that they were questioned to identify specific targets in the Bristol or Liverpool area, but it is possible that they would not have been told until they had settled in and received instructions from Williams or SNOW. In a post-war memo J. M. A. Gwyer wrote

> ... the only things which link them all to G.W. are first that they arrived at about the right time, secondly that they were to work in about the right area, thirdly that the SNOW traffic, though not clear on this point, refers to men rather than a man who were to assist G.W., and fourthly that the Cubans were overwhelmingly unlikely to succeed in their mission without some local assistance. I doubt if we shall ever clear this matter up unless and until we get a full statement from RITTER. In the meantime, I doubt whether it is worth to retain our hold on the Cubans, who being persons of low intelligence are unlikely at this stage to be able to tell a full or straightforward story however much they may wish to.[8]

The three Cubans, the captain and crew, were interned initially at Camp 020. Pazos-Diaz died of tuberculosis in Liverpool Prison on 20 April 1942. Robles and Hechevarria were deported separately to the United States in early 1946. The English currency they had brought with them, just over £100, was not returned as they had admitted that it had been given to them by the German Secret Service. The loose change and Spanish and French currency was returned, along with their personal possessions. The Home Office paid the deportation costs and gave each man £1 subsistence.[9]

The loss of the three Cuban agents, potentially several others and GW's reports of declining support amongst the WNP must have given the Abwehr cause to doubt the wisdom of continuing their plans in Wales. They must have realised that large-scale sabotage operations in Britain were out of the question and therefore focussed on small-scale attacks.

Whether the Abwehr had learned of Camp 020 and arranged for the Luftwaffe to attack it in the hope of releasing prisoners is unknown, but

on 30 November, an air-mine landed on the roof and exploded, which caused severe damage, but only one person was killed, a German prisoner named Bruhn. The secret bugging equipment was destroyed, as was the officers' mess, offices and lodgings; the telephones, water and electricity were also put out of action. For a while therefore, all interrogations were held in the mortuary. The necessity of a reserve camp in some other place was realised, as was the need for the storage of spent agents. One important part of the agreement with those who took on the work as double agents was that they would avoid execution. Therefore, a new institution was built, Camp 020R in Huntercombe, outside Oxford.[10]

During the interrogation of Gottfried Treutlein, a Bavarian who had been working for the Abwehr for five years before being captured, the man admitted that whilst working in Brest between June 1940 and summer 1941 he interviewed the three Cubans and escorted them to the harbour before their departure. He was helping Witzke run some Gruppe II boats and 'on one occasion successfully landed a Dutchman or Belgian in the UK'.[11] Although MI5 requested he provide more details, there was no further indication as to the man's identity in Treutlein's file.

In a report to Security Officers, they were told that in March 1941 a cargo of frozen eggs had arrived in Britain.

Some of the tins of eggs were placed in storage near the port of arrival. A few days ago, a labourer noticed that one of the tins appeared to be exuding a grey powder. He opened the tin and found it was filled with this grey powder and also found a fuse inside. This was handed to the police who passed it to B.1.c for examination. The tin of 'eggs', which superficially was identical with the genuine tins, but on closer inspection proved to be a fairly well made copy with certain small but significant differences, was packed tightly with a mixture of fine aluminium dust and calcium sulphate. The fuse consisted of a time clock and electric igniting device. Fortunately, the fuse had not operated, though there is no doubt that it was placed on board with the object of creating a fire.[12]

14

MUTT and JEFF: Plan GUY FAWKES – April 1941 to August 1942

Humphries' last comment about the Abwehr regarding Williams as their last man standing in Britain was not quite true. Two Norwegian saboteurs were successfully infiltrated into Scotland in late spring 1941. Whether he was fully aware of their subsequent activities is unknown as both handed themselves over to the British authorities within hours of landing and agreed to work as double agents. Their personnel files provide insight into their training, their mission and the extent of their double cross.

The earliest document in their case was a memo dated 7 April 1941 which H. J. A. Hart wrote to DGSS, the director general of the Security Section, stating that he had been rung at 1030 by Major Perfect in Edinburgh informing him that two enemy agents had been landed by sea plane in the Moray Firth. They had then rowed a rubber boat ashore at Crovie, near Gardenstown, Aberdeenshire, and, after cutting it up, at 0930 called at the nearest fisherman's cottage and asked to be taken to the police. They were dressed in blue ski-suits, Wellington boots and leather helmets and had with them two Rudge Whitworth bicycles and all their gear. This consisted of a wireless set in a suitcase, rucksacks and loaded 'Venus' and 'Allies' automatic pistols and ammunition.

Both were described as Norwegian, and willing to talk. The first was called Helge John Niel Moe, born 31 May 1919, in London, 5 ft. 9 inches tall, who worked in his father's ladies' hairdressing business in Oslo and spoke perfect English but with a Lancashire accent. The second was Tor Gleid, later written as Glad, born in 1916, the same height as his partner. He only spoke a little English.[1]

Hart instructed Major Perfect to fly to Crovie and ensure that proper enquiries were made to find out whether any others had landed with them and whether any others were due to land. All those who they had seen or spoken with were to be identified and told that they had not seen German spies. There appeared to be a deliberate policy to avoid the public being aware of the Germans infiltrating agents into Britain. The two men were taken by train in separate carriages to London and then to Cannon Row Police Station. TAR and Stephens were informed, an urgent investigation within the Norwegian intelligence community was ordered and MI6 were asked to check whether they had any intelligence on the two men, particularly Moe.[2]

The police officer who took them into custody reported them stating that they had come to Scotland to work in the interests of Germany by committing acts of sabotage and sending information by wireless but wanted to hand themselves over to the British authorities and give them whatever information they needed. The search of their belongings revealed what the first captured Norwegian saboteurs were provided with by the Germans. On Moe's person were found:

£97 in Bank of England £1 notes.

Five 20 and two 5 U.S.A. dollar notes.

Norwegian passport No. 2368 1766–34 dated 22 June 1934.

Diary containing visiting cards in name of Jack Moe, Oslo, list of names and addresses and small Norwegian flag.

Page of notepaper with Norwegian writing (Moe stated this was directions for making explosives and incendiary material for sabotage purposes).

Registration certificate (1919) in name of Helg Kristoffer Moe dated 13.5.1919.

Traveller's Ration Book No.CA 567243.

Letter in Norwegian.

Paper with writing in Norwegian (Stated by Moe to have been written by his mother to the Norwegian Prime Minister in London).

Chocolate, pocket knife, fountain pen, propelling pencil, 2 cigarette holders, box of saccharine tablets, box with two rubber preventatives, 1 bullet (said to be souvenir of war in Norway).

1 comb – broken.

Purse containing 6d. piece, farthing, Norwegian 2 ORE piece and an American coin.

R.F.C. brooch.

Small key which operated lock of case containing wireless transmitting set.

Wallet containing photograph of woman and child.

Certificate of Registry of Birth of Helge John Nel Moe dated at St Marylebone, London, on 7 July, 1919.

He was wearing a leather belt and when it was removed he said 'There are fuses inside'. The seam of the belt was opened and three lengths of fuses found.

In Haversack

Gent's raincoat.

Gent's toilet bag in leather holder.

Shaving brush. This was voluntarily produced by Moe who removed the handle and showed 7 detonators in the hollowed inside.

Small leather case with reflector or mirror containing piece of paper with the address: Trond Strup Vigtel, Brooklands, Dumfries, Scotland.

Ditmar cine camera in leather case.

Tin Crystallosetter

Camera folding stand.

2 books on Ditmar camera.

Box containing 20 rounds 7.65mm. ammunition.

Book of instructions on short wave transmission.

4 boxes containing exposed and unexposed films.

2 empty film boxes.

Pair clippers with insulated handles.

Pair scissors.

Newspapers 'Fritz Folk', 'Allers', 'Bragd'.

Magnifying glass with handle.

1 lemon.

Empty chocolate box.

6 boxes safety matches.

Pipe.

Tobacco pouch containing small phial

Norwegian ration card.

Cigarette case.

Sheath knife, propelling pencil 3 unused envelopes, paper wallet containing photographs.

Signalling hand lamp. Moe stated he had repeatedly flashed the lamp when making for land in the dinghy, but no one on shore had answered.

Small black notebook containing visiting cards and letter.

Box Talcum powder, 'first aid' box.

Rough sketch of part North Scotland (Moe stated it was sketch of landing site).

Large Norwegian flag.

Cap, hat, small piece of soap, 1 pair shoes, 4 shirts, 2 undervests, 6 handkerchiefs, 2 pairs socks,

In brown paper parcel

Gent's 3-piece brown suit (in jacket pocket: cuff links, studs and handkerchief. In trouser pockets: box containing one rubber preventative, handkerchief and safety pin).

Gent's tie.

In small attaché case carried on rear carrier of bicycle

Gent's 3-piece blue suit (in vest pocket: silver cigarette case)

Bakelite case containing cuff links, studs, black bow tie, brass finger ring, badge with Swastika [underlined]. Pairs short pants; 3 pairs long pants; 3 undervests; 3 shirts; 1 tie; 1 bed sheet; 19 collars; 1 pair socks; 3 handkerchiefs; 1 reel thread; 1 bottle mixture wrapped in copy of 'Dagbladet' newspaper. (Prescription: Menthol Liq.crb. det.20: Lin.set.c.glycerine Sol. Cet.alum 2%).

Similar items were found on Glad, including a clothes brush. Glad stated that 2 detonators had been inserted in each end of the brush handle. He also had a Zeiss camera, exposure meter, 3 unexposed films, 3 exposed films, exposed 8 mm cine film, a box containing packets of flashlight powder, and visiting cards in the names of Tor Glad and Oslo.[3]

The case carried on the rear carrier of Glad's bicycle was opened and found to contain a complete wireless transmitting set and an envelope containing a book of crossword puzzles. Glad stated that the set was to be used for sending their messages to Norway and that the crossword puzzles supplied the code.[4]

There was no mention in their files that the fountain pens were examined or that they mentioned that they could be used to conceal the parts of a time pencil.

An undisguised British time pencil was about the size of a fountain pen and had three parts. A thin copper tube at one end contained a glass ampoule of copper chloride. The detonator was in the middle. When the copper end was pressed hard, the glass broke. It was not advisable to bite it as the chemical burnt one's mouth. The released acid started to corrode a steel wire. When it snapped, it released a spring-loaded striker that fired a percussion cap that ignited the plastic explosive. What determined the time you had to get away safely before it blew up was the concentration of acid. A coloured strip was stuck on the side of the pencil. Black meant, in theory, that they had ten minutes' delay, red thirty minutes, green six hours, yellow, twelve and blue, twenty-four. Saboteurs had to make sure the glass broke before they made their getaway.

It is worth noting that MI5's description of their bicycles was far more detailed than that of the two men's physical appearance, enough to make any wartime bicycle fanatic within the intelligence community jealous. While there was no attempt to disguise their nationalities, photographs were taken to show how cleverly their sabotage equipment had been hidden.

In Moe's file are numerous reports, following Stephens informing him that anyone found guilty of breaking the British Treachery Act would be hanged. From their own accounts and intelligence obtained from various Norwegians already in Britain, it transpired that Moe had often visited England to see his grandparents in Ashton-under-Lyne and in June 1939 had trained as a make-up artist at Max Factor's studio at Denham, near Uxbridge. He returned to Oslo before the invasion where, as well as hairdressing, he worked at the J.A.R. Film Studio. Three months after the German invasion, he was more or less unemployed and admitted joining the Norwegian Nationalist Socialist Party in the hope of getting paid work.

He met Glad in July and was persuaded to be trained with him as a 'V-Mann' (*Vertrauenemann*), a German agent, and be sent to Britain as a spy. Glad had had a variety of jobs after leaving school and in 1939 was interviewed by Dr Mueller, the head of Abwehr II in Norway, whose official headquarters were in Klingenberg gate in Oslo. When asked to help to identify British agents in Southern Norway and spy on Norwegian loyalists, Glad claimed that he made no attempt to do this and was dismissed after a week. Although he received pay for this work, he claimed he did nothing and was later given a job in the Quisling government's postal censorship office, where Moe began working a few days later.

Moe was sacked after three months for providing a Norwegian loyalist with a list of anti-Nazis the Germans wanted to stop from being employed. Glad left the following month, claiming that the work was boring, and spoke with Carl Andersen who suggested that he ought to be trained as an agent and be infiltrated into England. When he agreed, Andersen suggested that he went with someone else, so he suggested Moe. Dr Mueller supported the plan.

Their intention, Moe claimed, was to learn as much as they could about the Abwehr's modus operandi so that they could pass on all their intelligence to the British when they arrived. He was given the code-name JACK and Glad was called TEGE, T.G. being his initials. They were trained in using Morse and wireless telegraphy in Oslo and told to use the code-name EMIL for England and OTTO for Oslo, to include the name Henri in each message; but if they were captured by the British and forced to operate under duress they had to omit Henri and use any other name. This information was no doubt acted upon in MI5's subsequent wireless transmissions.

Surprisingly, there was little detail about their sabotage training, only that they had finished their wireless training by March and whilst they were waiting for the next full moon, 47-year-old Herr Koschwitz instructed them in the preparation of incendiary and explosive mixtures in an office at Andersen and Andersen's import/export company in Johansgate, Oslo. This was Abwehr II's unofficial headquarters. 'He gave them formulae to copy and learn by heart and on one occasion took them out to a place near Fornebu Aerodrome where they made an incendiary mixture as an experiment. These formulae are in Moe's pocket book.'[5]

The apparent lack of questioning about their sabotage training suggests that some in MI5 were not too interested in the technical side. Moe could show them what Koschwitz looked like as they had taken a cine-film of him. It was clearly a much less secure training programme than at Brickendonbury.

Moe and Glad were not their real names, and it appears that they never told MI6 them. Wighton and Peis identified Moe as Jack Berg and Gleid [sic] as Olav Klausen, a sergeant in a Norwegian sapper regiment. As Glad already knew about how much explosive to use on the weakest points of bridges and trains and which vital machinery to target in a factory, it was Moe/Berg who needed extra tuition.[6] Captain Mueller provided them with a final briefing.

> On the sabotage side, they were to attack targets of opportunity, but above all, anything which was vital to the British aircraft industry. They were also told to attack railways, armaments factories, food stores or petrol tanks, for the U-boat successes were rising, and anything that the saboteurs could do would tighten the stranglehold on Britain.
>
> On the espionage side, they were instructed to find out as soon as possible all details about the identity cards, ration books, and other documents for refugees from occupied Europe. They were also given an assignment which throws a curious sidelight on how little the Germans knew about conditions in wartime Britain. From some source or other Berlin had received a rumour that the population of London was being evacuated to Scotland in preparation for a German invasion, which in the spring of 1941 still remained a possibility. The two young men were told to report on this in detail.
>
> On a longer-term basis, the two Norwegians were ordered to concentrate on reporting troop movements, and as far as possible to function in the areas around the Clyde and the Mersey, from where they could report by radio the departure of important troop convoys for overseas. In addition, they were told to establish the whereabouts of as many as possible of the Norwegian refugees, and the addresses of relatives in Norway.[7]

The information the British obtained from them was that, after their training, they were taken to Stavanger where Dr Mueller showed them maps of different sabotage targets in Scotland, Aberdeen and Edinburgh being the most important, and told them that after dealing with these places they were to use their own judgment and 'do their best'. Their chief task was to commit acts of sabotage in food dumps and transmit by wireless any information they could pick up regarding troop movements, the effect of air raids on civilian morale, and even weather reports. They were also to pay special attention to any new aerodrome they might note. To ensure the payment of bonuses they were advised to give two days' notice by wireless of any plans for sabotage and keep newspaper cuttings as proof of success, to be handed in at German Headquarters after the invasion.[8]

Each had been given 500 kroner a month during training and they were told that the same amount would be paid into their bank account while they were overseas. The £100 and $110 they were each given they claimed was enough to last the two months until the Germans invaded; bonuses depended on the results of their sabotage. One target specifically mentioned was bringing down electricity pylons. If they needed more money they had to send a message to Oslo, and in an emergency to Stavanger.[9]

The day after a farewell celebration of lobster, smoked salmon, caviar, foie gras and champagne at the end of March 1941, they left in a Bloem and Voss flying boat for Scotland. However, bad weather conditions and thick sea mist caused the pilot to return to Stavanger. When informed that conditions were right, Koblischke, the Abwehr officer responsible for training Norwegian agents, had just told the two men to get ready when he received a phone call from Oberleutnant Grothe, the head of Abwehr III, the counter-intelligence section in Oslo. He was told that a German, calling himself Werner Meyer, had been arrested by the coastguards just south of Stavanger in a boat which he claimed to have stolen to escape from Scotland. Keen to get up-to-date information on conditions on the Scottish coast, Koblischke went to see Meyer; however, although he provided useful intelligence, Koblischke was unconvinced that Meyer was a real refugee.

He claimed to have been born in Frankfurt/Main, a leader in the Hitler Youth, imprisoned for two years for stealing cars and released in 1939 on condition that he worked on a German weather ship in the Arctic. Captured by a British naval ship, he was interned at various prisoner-of-war camps before escaping from one near Aberdeen in late March. Being a staunch Nazi, he wanted to return to Germany and join the Wehrmacht.

After intense questioning in which Koblischke pretended to have been in Scotland and to have recognised Meyer in one of the camps, he confessed that he had been coerced into becoming a British spy. After being sent to a school to learn the elementary requirements of being an agent, he was transferred to 'a large house somewhere in the Midlands' with students of other nationalities, where he was taught wireless telegraphy, codes and the use of invisible inks.

Koblischke presumably was unaware of the location of the British training schools, and the name of the school was not mentioned. From there he was sent to a camp somewhere in the north-west of Scotland where he was taught how to sabotage railways and machinery. He also revealed that he had been taught how to use magnetic mines and thermite bombs and had brought with him in his kit-bag a British time pencil. Wighton and Peis identified it as the same type used by the Abwehr in their assassination attempt against Hitler when one was placed inside a brandy bottle full of explosives and handed to Hitler's adjutant during a trip from Berlin to the Russian front.[10]

Finally, Meyer claimed to have been sent to a camp near Aberdeen, taught how to handle a small sailing boat and then towed far out to sea by a British motorboat and left to navigate his way to Stavanger. Told to hand himself in to the Norwegian authorities and volunteer for the Wehrmacht, it was hoped that his poor health would mean he would be released so that he could go to Hamburg and place the message, 'Come to me all ye who labour' with his address in the *Hamburg Fremdenblatt*. This would result in a British spy contacting him with a wireless set. He was then to get a job in the Bloem and Voss shipyard in Hamburg, report on their submarine construction and carry out as much sabotage as possible.

Further questioning revealed what Norwegian refugees might expect at the Royal Victoria Patriotic School and what the situation was like on the Aberdeen coast, vital intelligence for the two spies, which convinced Koblischke to land them further south in the Firth of Tay, once conditions were right. Meyer was reported to have been sent to a concentration camp in Germany.[11]

As MI5 had doubts about the veracity of the two Norwegians' cover stories, lengthy interrogation sessions followed and their files include witness statements from Scots who had come into contact with them when they arrived, detailed accounts of their life stories, descriptions of all their family and friends and all the German officials and instructors they had had dealings with. Although Moe claimed not to be able to remember the names of all the other German agents he had met, he gave the names and addresses of all the Norwegians he had to contact in Britain, details of which had been written on a piece of paper hidden inside his shaving case.

Thinking that there might be a German invasion imminent, Operation 'Mr Mill's Circus' was activated. Cyril Mills, the son of the circus owner, arranged for captured enemy agents to be sent to North Wales. The two Norwegians were handcuffed and driven to a safe house in Colwyn Bay in north-west Wales where they could continue their work in greater safety. To prevent agents from escaping and falling into German hands and revealing the double cross, Petrie ordered their minders to execute anyone making the attempt. In the event, no escape attempts were made.[12]

By the summer of 1941, MI5 had apprehended twenty-two enemy agents from whom valuable intelligence about the German Secret Service had been obtained.

NOTE ON THE DESCENT AND LANDING OF ENEMY AGENTS
Up to the moment of writing this note six enemy agents have descended by parachute; of these, five descended in the East Midland area of England and one near St Albans. Eight other agents have landed by rubber boats put off from aeroplanes off the coast of Moray Firth. Four others have been landed by dinghies from fishing boats of the coast of Dungeness in Kent. A further four have arrived from Norway in a fishing cutter at Wick, purporting to have escaped from the Germans in Norway.

Attempts have also been made to land agents and saboteurs at ports from small cutters which have run into bad weather. The cases of the 'La Part Bien' and the 'Josephine', which surrendered some ten agents of varying importance, are examples of this latter class.

It is considered that a summary of these cases may assist in preparing the appropriate measures for the detection and apprehension of German agents on their arrival in this country. This summary, together with certain further matter, will be found in the attached Appendices.

Appendix A summarises the cases of the parachutists who have so far come to notice. The evidence suggests that the favourite area for their descents is that of the Midlands (Oxford, Northampton, Birmingham, Cambridge, Peterborough and Bedford). Within this area, the successful agent is usually instructed to obtain information on aerodromes, factories, road obstructions and other defences. Occasional agents may still be dropped in this area for these purposes, though there is some evidence that the enemy consider this method for the insertion of agents unsuccessful and accordingly incline to favour small boat technique. It is anticipated, however, that in the weeks preceding an invasion large numbers of parachute-agents may be dropped – especially in the rear of channel defences, and aerodromes and flying grounds of particular operational interest to the enemy.

Appendix B summarises the case of the four spies who actually effected landings by small boat from a fishing cutter in the Dungeness area. It will be noticed that these landings were effected in September 1940 and no similar landings on the south coat are known to have been made since, though there are grounds for thinking that the enemy have by no means abandoned their intention of effecting landings here.

Appendix C summarises the eight cases of landings from small rubber boats put off from seaplanes in the Moray Firth.

Appendix D summarises a type of case new since the first edition of this note, namely that of Norwegian escapees. This class is, perhaps, the most difficult of all the German agents to detect, since there is a flood of genuine refugees from Norway reaching this country and there is good evidence that the Germans have penetrated some of the escape organisations. It appears that the Germans are willing to let bona fide refugees escape to act as an unconscious cover for a single agent inserted among them and the task of detecting the agent among the genuine refugees is extremely difficult, since they do not come with any of the suspicious gear or equipment which has assisted in the detection of other types of agents. It seems that one object of this type of agent is to establish himself among the Norwegians fishing in this country and so exploit opportunities which fishing would offer to act as couriers between here and the Germans in Norway. It is also considered possible that the Germans may intend that a number of agents should make their way into Free Norwegian Forces here, so as to operate as a 'Trojan Horse' in the event of invasion. Up to date, only four agents of this type have been definitely proved to be such on their arrival here, but there are some others who have been detained because the evidence, not amounting to complete proof, points strongly to their being enemy agents.

Appendix E summarises the type of equipment with which many of the agents have been supplied, including some notes on the German forgeries of British Identity Cards and Ration Books.

Appendix F summarisies the information available on the preparation, equipment and dispatch of fishing cutters from the German Intelligence Stations in Northern France. Not all of the fishing cutters which are in the service of the German intelligence Service are intended to land agents, since they have a number of other special important functions, e.g. the observation of convoys and other shipping movements.[13]

Hitler abandoned Operation SEALION on 17 September 1940. When MI5 realised the invasion was no longer imminent, Moe and Glad were returned to the capital and provided with accommodation at 35 Crespigny Road, Hendon, North London, where their wireless set was installed. Their MI5 case officer, sometimes known as an agent handler, was Christopher Harmer, and their minders were Messrs Corcoran and Rea. The two Norwegians were paid thirty shillings a week with £12 per week expenses for food and entertainment for the five of them. In order to 'supervise' their wireless transmissions, Ted Paulton, a radio expert, lived next door with his wife.

Who came up with the code-names of MUTT for Moe and JEFF for Glad is unknown. The original Mutt and Jeff were early twentieth-century American cartoon characters, one short and stout (MUTT), the other tall and lanky (JEFF), and these had come to be used to describe two bungling men and the idea of a good cop and a bad cop. (The names are also Cockney rhyming slang for 'deaf'.)

To explain why they did not report immediately to the Germans on any sabotage activity, MI5 officers concocted a detailed cover story running to several pages entitled 'The Adventures of Mutt and Jeff'. It provided the details which they could pass on to the Germans should any questions be asked.

The Abwehr believed the messages that they were sent by 'Jack and O.K.'. Landing at the foot of a cliff, they had shredded the rubber dinghy, smashed the oars and scattered the remains in the sea. It then took hours to find a way to get their bikes and rucksacks up to the top. Using the Ordnance Survey maps they cycled leisurely south-west, pleased to be able to buy whisky in village pubs. They buried their explosives and hid the bikes near a famous lake in the mountains north of Glasgow, presumed to be Loch Lomond. They then caught a bus into the city, bought clothes in a second-hand shop, took the train to Euston and contacted Jack's relatives. On 1 May 1941, Lahousen's diary reported. 'The two agents sent to England in the course of Operation Hummer III Nord have arrived successfully. They have reported from London with the special radio equipment which they took with them.'[14]

Expecting them to be detained at the Victoria Patriotic School, the Abwehr requested radio silence. The Abwehr never knew what happened during May but on 1 June a message was received saying everything was fine. On 10 June, as expected, they sent Oslo details about identity cards, ration books and other information related to Norwegian refugees in England. In response, they were ordered to proceed with their sabotage. When Rothschild investigated MUTT and JEFF's case, he was particularly interested in how they proposed to make explosives as the very small quantities of materials they claimed to need were not as readily available from the chemists as they had been led to believe.[15]

By the end of June, Oslo was told that they had set fire to a food dump, a munitions dump and a wood store used by an aircraft factory. Lahousen read reports in British newspapers of fires in Southern England which he attributed to Jack and O.K., but he turned down one of their requests: MI5 was keen to learn about the Abwehr's chemical ability so a request was made that the chemists in the Tegel laboratories send details about what chemicals could be used to kill horses and cattle in the fields.[16]

MI5 asked Captain Martin Linge, another escaped Norwegian who was helping train Norwegian soldiers in Inverness-shire, to be infiltrated into Norway on sabotage and other missions, to further question MUTT and JEFF and to give his opinion of the veracity of their statements. Linge had 'the lowest possible view of Jeff', who he thought, as an army officer, had committed a treasonable offence, and his attitude to MUTT was, in Harmer's opinion, 'clouded by his dislike of JEFF'.[17] Linge's opinion was that anyone who had had dealings with the Germans was not to be trusted. The term for Norwegian collaborators was quislings, and there was a worry that some, fearing that the Germans might lose the war, would use the same method as MUTT and JEFF to escape to Britain.

The Germans were told that JEFF was working as an interpreter for the Examination Authorities, initially in London and then in Aberdeen interviewing refugees arriving from Norway. At this time, large numbers of young men were using what was called the 'Shetland Bus service', fishing boats which brought them across the North Sea so that they could join the Norwegian Forces based in Britain. The boats returned with trained soldiers, agents and supplies for the Norwegian resistance. MI5 thought that any information JEFF obtained on this topic would be of great interest to the Germans. It would also help identify any German agents attempting to enter Britain with a red pyramid marked on their documents. Amongst the fifteen messages he sent, he also included false details about Allied agents operating in Norway.[18]

A plan was therefore put forward by B.1.A in consultation with the authorities at the LRC (London Reception Centre), called PYRAMID. The object was to make it appear that an escape organisation existed in Norway and that Norwegians who were helped out of the country by this organisation stamped their papers with a little red triangle.

> It was thought that if JEFF were to get a lot of vital information of this sort he must also necessarily have a certain amount of information about the names of Norwegians who had escaped and their boats and so on, and with the help of S.I.S. a certain amount of information on these lines was included in JEFF's report.[19]

This included details of the blowing up of the imaginary HMS *Stora*. In the eyes of the Germans, he came down to London especially from Aberdeen to send this information. The information was well received, and there was almost conclusive evidence that it was taken seriously, although this information did not come to light for some time.

Throughout this time, their wireless set was also being used in Plan OMNIBUS, another scheme being played against the Germans. Three other double agents were involved, all supplying information to deceive the Germans into believing that British commandos were planning a second attack on the Lofoten Islands in Northern Norway. It aimed to persuade the Wehrmacht to divert thousands of troops and equipment into one of the most remote, desolate and frozen parts of occupied Europe, while the real intention was to attack Vaagso further south, cut off supplies to the Germans further north and force the Germans into further extending their forces in Norway.

In order to gather supporting material for Plan OMNIBUS, MUTT and JEFF were each sent with a Field Security Police (FSP) sergeant to different parts of Scotland. JEFF went to Aberdeen, but in attempting to obtain information from a soldier in a public house he behaved very stupidly by writing down notes on what the soldier said and as a result both he and the FSP sergeant were arrested by the police as suspicious characters. He was recalled from Aberdeen and reprimanded. When he attempted to sell his brand-new Leica camera – unavailable in British shops at that time – and broke the curfew regulations by spending a night with a nurse called Joan, he showed that he was not going to be an easy person to control. Complete liberty was out of the question so Marriott took the decision to intern him.

> His past record, and particularly his work for the Germans before his present mission, was ample justification for his internment and it was thought that if the Germans could be informed that he had been posted far away (Iceland was in fact decided upon) there might be a good chance of continuing the case with MUTT alone, who was considered to be reliable. JEFF was accordingly interned in Camp WX, Isle of Man, on 15 August 1941, and the Germans were informed that he had been posted to Iceland.[20]

Lahousen's response was to ensure O.K./JEFF received the order not to undertake any sabotage in Iceland, not to contact any Abwehr agents, send useful information back to Jack/MUTT and try to spread as much defeatist views amongst his military colleagues as he could.[21]

In JEFF's file was a police report headed Secret which expressed concern that a man who had handed himself over to the police admitting that he was a German agent was subsequently found wandering around Scottish seaports to report on the security measures there. As it seemed over and above his mission to interview Norwegian sailors, this was another reason why MI5 felt justified in interning him.[22]

Whilst he was interned, Paulton, who had gramophone recordings of JEFF's transmissions, imitated his 'fist', the style he used in tapping the Morse key, and sent his messages. After a hunger strike, JEFF was transferred first to Liverpool Gaol, then Stafford Prison, later to Dartmoor Prison and finally to Peel Prison on the Isle of Man.

It is worth noting that JEFF wrote a stream of letters and petitions ranging from pleading to abuse to the Home Secretary, the Norwegian Minister of Justice, the Norwegian Intelligence Service, various departments of the War Office, the head of MI5 and the Lord Chief Justice about what he was convinced was wrongful imprisonment, something he continued with after the war.[23]

While MUTT was sending messages back to the Germans, using 'The Adventures of Mutt and Jeff' as their basis, Harmer ensured that they included the disinformation for Plan PYRAMID. On 8 August 1941, TAR and Simmonds went to see Mr Gleditsch at the Norwegian Embassy to discuss MUTT and JEFF. TAR was against JEFF being interrogated by the Norwegians as he was worried he might tell them about Plan OMNIBUS and, with the support of Masterman and Marriott, it was decided to send him to Camp 020 without the Norwegians' knowledge. Although MUTT was considered to be more reliable, it was agreed that Linge should give him a good talking to, that he had to be told in emphatic terms the importance of his work for the Allies and given the Official Secrets Act to sign.[24]

As their mission targets included sabotage attacks on food dumps in Scotland, the messages to the Germans prevaricated, initially explaining how circumstances had developed which prevented them from undertaking any attacks and when pressed, they were told that MUTT was about to be called up. However, although the Abwehr appeared to believe the stories, they insisted that MUTT should undertake at least one sabotage attack beforehand, adding that he needed to obtain replacement batteries for his wireless set.

The W Board was convened to decide whether double agents should be allowed to carry out acts of sabotage when called upon by the enemy to do so. It ruled that 'the balance of advantage lay in permitting them to a limited extent, in that this would help to build up the enemy's confidence in the agents and provide information about his choice of targets'.[25]

A small-scale attack was planned. It would encourage their masters to send funds in recognition of their work and potentially encourage them to send more information about other sabotage projects, saboteurs and equipment. On 20 September, two messages were sent to Oslo regarding MUTT and JEFF's sabotage objectives, both saying the sites they had chosen were far too well guarded to allow them to attack but that they had identified an alternative target in Wealdstone, North London. Masterman initiated Operation GUY FAWKES, the first double-cross sabotage operation of the war. He acknowledged that it was

a highly complicated and excessively difficult [operation] to conduct successfully. It must be remembered that to get full value on the German side lurid accounts of the explosion have to appear in the press, but the press very properly will only put in accounts which their reporters can send to them. In other words, the press have to be deceived by us as well as the Germans, and if the explosion or wreckage has not been considerable, the reports in the press will, if they appear at all, be correspondingly meagre.

He obtained the agreement of a high official at the Ministry of Food and the Commissioner of Police at Scotland Yard. As the Ministry of Economic Warfare had details about all the possible targets of the German attack, they were also contacted. MUTT had to study the following report and maps of the site and be helped to plan and carry out an attack to provide first-hand evidence in his messages.

OPERATION GUY FAWKES

It is intended to cause a fire to break out in No. 8 Buffer Depot, Wealdstone, being premises used by the Ministry of Food as a flour store. The premises were previously owned by the Wealdstone Joinery Works who gave them up two years ago.

The site is situated near the junction of Byron Road, Masons Avenue and Christchurch Avenue, Wealdstone. Its position and approximate dimensions are shown on the plan attached. From this it will be seen that the site has about 80 yards' frontage on to Byron Road and a similar street called Oxford Place and that there are three gates into the site opening into these two roads. On the north and east sides the two roads mentioned above form the boundary, on the south side, there is an office used by the Inland Revenue and on the west side premises used by Kodaks Ltd as a store. The portion of the boundary between the premises of Kodaks Ltd and the premises of the Inland Revenue has not been inspected and appears to be impossible to gain access without entering the site.

The site has on it a small office and several large sheds. All the sheds are constructed entirely of corrugated iron sheeting. One large shed is dome-roofed and has open sides. The closed-in sheds are used for stores of flour. Food is stored in the dome-roofed shed and also in the shed at the western end of the site where certain pine shelves for use in the Inland Revenue Building are stacked. The approximate positions of these sheds are shown in the attached plan.

The gates opening on to the roads from the site are kept closed; they are double wooden gates and about 5' 6" high, they are secured on the inside and do not appear to be very substantially built. The wall is made of corrugated iron sheeting like the sheds and is about 6' 6" high. In order to obtain access to the site, it would be necessary either to go through the Office or to break open or jump over one of the gates.

It has been ascertained that there are fire watchers on the site every night of the week. These fire watchers are paid by the Ministry of Food and they sit or sleep in the small office opening on to Oxford Place shown on the plan. On Mondays, Wednesdays and Fridays there are also fire watchers on the roof of the Inland Revenue building which forms part of the southern boundary of the site. These fire watchers are known sometimes to sit on the roof and might thus be in a position to see anybody obtaining access to the site by jumping over one of the gates.

So far as the Police are concerned, there are two Police Officers who are liable to pass the site during the night. First of all, there is the constable on the beat which includes Byron Road and Masons Avenue. It is not possible to say which way round he patrols his beat, but he is bound to pass at least two of the gates on to the site, and he may do this coming down Byron Road from the north or turning into Byron Road from Mason Avenue. In addition, there is the Patrol which is liable to pass the site during the night. This also includes Masons Avenue and Byron Road and it is impossible to say which way round the Patrol will move.

About 800 yards to the north-east of the site is Palmerston Road where there is an A.R.P. [Air Raid Precaution] Fire Station. The nearest Police Station is in High Street. There are telephone boxes at the junction of Byron Road and Masons Avenue about 15 yards away and also at Harrow and Wealdstone Station and in the High Street and Station Road, all about ¼ mile away.[26]

There was no reference to the prevailing wind, but one would have imagined that the discussions about the attack would have mentioned that the most common wind direction in Britain is from the south-west. Of the 365 days of the year, on average it blows from the south-west on 200 of them. This probably influenced the decision to place the incendiary bombs in the south-west corner of the depot.

Other factors that were unmentioned were the best time of day to launch an attack, the weather conditions, whether there might be an air raid warning, whether the Fire Brigade was out on a call and what to do about the security staff in order to avoid loss of life. There was also no mention of a getaway plan, but one imagines that this would have been discussed with MUTT. As this was to be the first recorded German act of sabotage on British soil, one has to admire the military precision of the planning.

On the earliest convenient date, not being a Monday, Wednesday or Friday, two incendiary bombs will be placed among the wooden shelves stacked in the shed at the western end of the site in the position shown on the plan. These bombs will be placed so as to ignite about 4 o'clock in the morning and it will be arranged that they are placed there on a night when there is no alert and if possible when there is a mist. Steps will be taken to give adequate warning to the fire watchers to prevent them being in the shed when the bombs ignite and also to warn the police.

The actual plan of operation will be the following:

The bombs will be placed in position by someone detailed by B.1.A (referred to hereafter as A).

The bombs will be carried, one in a Service Respirator [gas mask] Haversack and the other in a suitcase.

The bombs will have a delay fuse of between 10 and 15 minutes. They will cause intense fire and smoke but no explosion.

At 0340 hours, the Police Constable on the beat will arrive at the gate nearest Masons Avenue. He will pay special attention to the possibility of anyone being about in the Depot and also keep a look out for the Police Patrol.

At 0340 hours, a car will turn into Masons Avenue from High Street and proceed to the corner of Byron Road and Christchurch Avenue. On the way along Masons Avenue, a look out will be kept for the Police Patrol to make sure that the officer on the Patrol is not just about to turn into Byron Road. At the corner, it will turn up Byron Road and draw up opposite the gate nearest Masons Avenue. It should arrive there at 0341.

If the Constable at the gate has observed anyone about or has heard the Police Patrol coming down Byron Road he will step forward and say 'Can I help you?' This will mean that it is unwise to proceed with the operation at that time and the driver will therefore enquire the way to Harrow Weald and will be redirected to the High Street via Palmerston Road.

Correspondingly, if the occupants of the car have observed the Police Patrol coming down Masons Avenue and about to turn into Byron Road, the Police Constable on the gate will be warned, the car will drive on and the constable will continue patrolling his beat.

In either event, the operation will be postponed until 0400 hours when exactly similar events will take place.

If, however, there is nobody about, the Police Constable will not move, and A will get out of the car with the two bombs. He will then clamber over the gate with the respirator on. The suitcase he will give to the Police Constable as he passes and as soon as he is over the gate, he will proceed to the spot marked on the plan where the bomb is to be placed.

Assuming he manages to get over the gate, the car will immediately proceed up the Byron Road, will take the first turning on the left up Palmerston Road into High Street where it will turn right, taking a subsequent turn on the right which will bring it back into Bryon Road. Five minutes after leaving A, the car will come southwards along Byron Road again and will pass the gate nearest Masons Avenue.

Having obtained access to the site A will set the fuses and having done this, will place the respirator haversack and the suitcase amongst the wooden shelves in the position marked on the plan. He will be given a space of not more than five minutes to do this, during which the car will be driving around and he will be ready to jump into the car as it passes the gate.

If it is not possible to synchronise approximately the re-arrival of the car with A's climbing over the gate, there will be a rendezvous round the corner in Christchurch Avenue. If A succeeds in completing his mission in under five minutes he will await the car at the gate; but if either after the five minutes have elapsed the car has not appeared, or the car does not find A waiting, he will be picked up at the rendezvous in Christchurch Avenue. He should not wait here for more than three minutes, and if the car has not arrived by then, he will make a getaway on his own.

The bombs are being constructed to provide a large quantity of smoke which is bound to be noticed. In addition, there will be an extremely bright light similar to a powerful magnesium flare, and it will, therefore, be impossible for the fire to remain unnoticed.

As a precaution against anyone being injured the Police Officer will keep the shed where the bombs have been placed under observation until they ignite, and if anyone goes into it during this time, he will keep him away by engaging him in conversation. Once the bombs have ignited the Police

Constable will continue patrolling his beat until he observes the fire in the distance; he will then give the alarm.

It is possible that the Police Patrol will arrive at the gate between the time that A climbs over and the return of the car. In that event, the Police Constable will be instructed to keep him in conversation until the car returns, when the Divisional Superintendent will explain to him that all is well and will tell him to continue his patrol and say absolutely nothing.

As a precaution against the Police Patrol arriving after the car has driven away but before the bombs ignite, the car will stop round the corner in Christchurch Avenue, and the Divisional Superintendent will station himself on the corner in such a position that he can keep the gate under observation and if necessary will intervene. As soon as he sees the Police Constable at the gate walk away (i.e. when the bombs have ignited), he will return to the car which will drive away down Christchurch Avenue.

Generally, as a precaution against the Patrol interfering in the operations, the Divisional Superintendent is arranging for special instructions to be given to the officer operating this Patrol to keep a certain place away from the site under observation during the small hours of that morning. This, he says, will not arouse suspicion because he has a complaint on hand about a certain place covered by the Patrol. It is therefore in any event very unlikely that the Patrol will interfere but even should he do so, it should be possible to deal with him as set out above.

The Police car will be ordered to stand by at 0300 hours so as to ensure that it is not out at the time of the fire.

Once the fire has taken place, matters are to be left to take their usual course. That is to say enquiries will immediately be set on foot by the Police and will be dealt with by them in the normal manner. Immediately after the fire also a D Notice will be circulated to the Press in the following form:

'No mention to be made of a fire which occurred in No.5 Buffer Depot, Food Stores, Wealdstone, on [9].11.41.'

The above details have been settled with the Divisional Police Superintendent. The only steps which now remain are to establish contact with Fighter Command to ensure that there is no likelihood of air raids on the night in question, and to issue the D. Notice.[27]

There was no way that MI5 would let MUTT carry out the sabotage himself. That role was given to Sergeant Cole, an FSP officer. Given all the weeks of planning this operation, one would have expected the operation to have been carried out to the letter. However, an unexpected and unplanned event transpired which, while not affecting the outcome, interfered in such a way as to create additional negotiation work for MI5.[28]

On 9 November, Harmer informed TAR that Operation GUY FAWKES had been carried out that morning. Everything had gone according to plan except that when Cole had planted the bombs and got into the car, the driver stopped in Christchurch Avenue to wait for the explosion. Just at that time a War Reserve sergeant cycled down the Avenue, saw the parked car with someone inside, stopped to make enquiries and took down the car's number plate.

Superintendent Martin, who was not in uniform, had accompanied Cole but was out of the car watching the gate so Harmer was left to answer the sergeant's questions. When Martin returned, he was asked to show his warrant, and they were in conversation about it when the bombs went off. Forced to leave the area without the sergeant being sufficiently informed as to what exactly was happening meant Martin had to resolve the issue before a statement was submitted.

The sergeant raised the alarm immediately so that the Fire Brigade arrived much earlier than anticipated and quickly got the fire under control. The respirator had practically burnt out but the suitcase, which exploded after the first bomb, was less damaged, and the Fire Brigade found three canisters and the starter springs.

On his return, Superintendent Martin informs me that he has dealt with the sergeant effectively, who has now made a statement to the effect that he was cycling down Christchurch Avenue, saw the fire start and immediately went to try and put it out. He is quite satisfied that the sergeant will not say that he saw either the superintendent or our car at the scene of the fire.

With regards to the relics which have been found – these are at present being held by the police and the next stage will be for the Home Office to be notified and for them to send down a member of their Explosive Section to examine them. This should take place during today. After consultation with you and Rothschild, I told Superintendent Martin that there was no objection to this course, and we wanted this case to go along on the normal lines.

The D Notice is presenting great difficulties. I rang up this morning and asked the Military Advisor to the Censorship if this could be done, but he told me that this would be impossible without an adequate reason. When I stated that the reason was that a fire had taken place in circumstances which gave rise to the conclusion that it was due to sabotage, he said that this would not be an adequate reason to give it to the press, and it would merely serve to draw attention to the incident. After consultation with Captain [Guy] Liddell, who saw the D.G. [Director General], it was decided that we would not press for a D notice, but merely allow the normal references in the press to be inserted. I therefore rang the Military Adviser to the Censorship again who told me that he had already sent the following communication to the press:

'A fire which occurred at Wealdstone this morning (9th) presents special features and all stories are to be referred to the Deputy Assistant Director'.

I then explained to him that since talking to him before, we had decided that as a D notice was impossible, we would like normal comments to appear in the press and that so far as we were concerned anything that the D.A.D. passed could go on. I also asked whether if the police put on a similar stop, they would get to know that we had already done so. He replied that if the police wish to put it on it would go through the Ministry of Home Security and if they try to put on a stop he will see that they are not informed that we have made a similar request.

MUTT will report that the sabotage has been done in a message which, if all else fails, he will send blind today.

Top left: Admiral William Canaris, head of the Abwehr (Germany's 'Defence' Service) 1935–44.

Top right: Lieutenant-Colonel Erwin von Lahousen, head of Abwehr II (Sabotage Section) 1939–43.

Above left: SS Oberführer Dr Edmund Veesenmayer, head of Irish Affairs at the German Foreign Office in Berlin. Responsible for infiltrating saboteurs into Ireland, England, Africa and the US.

Above right: Major Nikolaus Ritter, alias Dr Rantzau, head of the Abwehr's counter-espionage service with oversight of sabotage activities against Britain.

Bottom left: Gwilym Williams, recruited by MI5 in 1939 to train as a German saboteur in Belgium and work in South Wales as a double agent.

Lieutenant Colonel Robin 'Tin Eye' Stephens, head of Camp 020, MI5's interrogation centre at Latchmere House, Ham Common, Richmond.

Major John Masterman, Chairman of the Twenty (XX) Committee which used captured enemy agents to send MI5-inspired messages to the Germans.

Victor, third Baron Rothschild, who founded Britain's first Counter Sabotage Section during the Second World War.

Left: Camp 020, Latchmere House near Richmond, where 480 enemy personnel were interrogated during the war, including most of the saboteurs sent to Britain.

Below: Cray Reservoir in the Brecon Beacons which the Germans had plans to poison with bacteria as it supplied water to South Wales. (Courtesy of Mal Durbin.)

Vera Erikson, alias Vera Schalberg, captured after landing in Scotland on 30 September 1940.

Karl Drűcke, captured German saboteur executed on 6 August 1941 (TNA KV2/19)

MI5 photograph of Eddie Chapman, Agent ZIGZAG (TNA KV2/458)

Water pipelines leading to HEP station at Fort William. Target for James Walsh, Irish agent. (Courtesy of Martin Briscoe)

Modern photograph of 35 Crespigny Road, Hendon, North London, where Norwegian double agents Helga Moe and Tor Glad were accommodated from 1940 and Eddie Chapman in 1942. (Courtesy of David Howard)

Buckingham Palace, one of the targets to be sabotaged. (Wikimedia)

Right: Fake sabotage damage to de Havilland's Aircraft Factory, Hatfield. (TNA KV 2/458)

Below: Ronnie Reed, ZIGZAG's case officer in front of the transformer house at de Havilland Factory, camouflaged to look as if it had been sabotaged. (TNA KV 2/458)

Helge Moe and Tor Glad, captured and turned Norwegian agents, code-named MUTT and JEFF (TNA KV2/1067)

Left: Helge Moe in captivity. (KV2/1067)

Below: Tor Glad's 1937 passport photo (KV2/1068)

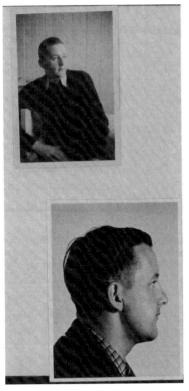

Tor Glad's British registration certificate issued in 1941. (TNA KV 2/1068)

Tor Glad before being sent to Britain in 1941 (TNA KV 2/1068)

Oxwich Bay on the Gower Peninsula, the planned location for German sabotage equipment to be dropped by submarine for Welsh Nationalists to attack targets in Wales.

Secluded beach near Portgordon, Moray Firth, where Swiss Werner Walti, Belgian Karl Drűcke and Russian Vera Eriksen/Schalburg landed by inflatable dinghy on 30 September 1940. (Courtesy of Gordon James Brown, Creative Commons)

Left to right: Pazos Dias, Juan Martinez, Karl Meier, Peter Krag; Theophile Jezequel, Charles van den Kieboom, Joseph Waldberg/Lassaudry, Stoord Pons Hoare. (Public Record Office)

Superintendent Martin told me that he would be bound today to inform all other divisions of the Metropolitan Police of the occurrence and warn them that special precautions should be taken in regard to buffer depots. I said that I was absolutely certain that this measure would have the enthusiastic support of the Ministries concerned.

It was a great pity that the Police Reserve Sergeant turned up when he did. Apart from this, there was no hitch whatsoever in the operation. I feel bound to remark that Cole did his job very capably and did not suffer in the least from nerves. Concerning Superintendent Martin, I do feel that we owe him a very special vote of thanks. He gave up a good deal of his time to arrange the details of this, his presence in the car was invaluable, and he spent the rest of the night investigating the results of the fire on the spot. He is also quite prepared for a good many of his police officers to have a lot of time wasted investigating the case without any complaint. When I left him in the morning, he said that he had enjoyed very much cooperating with us in this, and I think he really meant it. At any rate, he was most helpful and obliging throughout.

Finally as comic relief I should like to record that the fire watchers were both aged 70, that in the opinion of Superintendent Martin they would have been incapable of putting out any fire, that they showed every sign of having been sound asleep, that the room in which they were sleeping had an atmosphere which would have killed a normal man, and that one of them when questioned as to whether he had heard any noise in the night remarked that he had not and he could not understand how the fire occurred because he had passed that very place only ten minutes before. He then stated solemnly that the fire had taken place at 3.30 in the morning.[29]

The local CID, who were called in to investigate, discovered parts of incendiary bombs which they identified correctly as being material produced by the SOE. This led to a 'very delicate situation' in connection with the enquiry being made by Scotland Yard. Ultimately, however, the enquiry died out, and Masterman admitted that 'this first essay did, in fact, secure some at least of its objects'.[30]

While all the planning for the Wealdstone sabotage was going on, there were further worries about MUTT and JEFF. Reports from the Norwegian Embassy and intercepted German wireless messages indicated that, before they left for Scotland, they had told family and friends of their plans to sail to Scotland and that they had been sent by the Germans. What was not known was whether the Germans knew that their intention was to defect. There had been several months of silence from the Germans and MI5 was worried about what the Abwehr was thinking, particularly whether they suspected that MUTT and JEFF had been caught by the British and were being forced to play back their wireless set under British control. This helps to explain the importance of the Wealdstone sabotage in convincing the Abwehr that they were still at large and were continuing with their mission.

There were other reasons why MI5 was concerned. They wanted to continue their deception game with Plans OMNIBUS and PYRAMID and to prompt the Abwehr to send their men a financial reward for their efforts and hopefully drop more sabotage supplies, so that Rothschild could find out whether the Germans in Norway had developed any new sabotage technology.

The details of the Wealdstone sabotage were sent on 17 November in MUTT's seventy-eighth message. There followed some tense weeks until Oslo came back on air on 30 November, intensifying MI5's worry that the Abwehr doubted the veracity of the messages being sent.

There was then a gap in MUTT's file until the spring of 1942 when he informed Oslo that JEFF was returning from his trip to Iceland and that he was about to start his military training in Winchester. Before JEFF left, Harmer's plan was 'to adopt an ambitious sabotage programme, if necessary claiming acts of sabotage which are not in fact committed. I think this risk would be well worth taking to build up the Germans interest in the case.'[31] He recommended that in the middle of March MUTT should send the following message:

In the middle of April I will get leave, probably of nine days. I realise that I can obtain free travel to any part of England or Scotland and moreover I shall be in uniform so that I will be able to pass unnoticed. When you asked me about invasion intentions earlier on, I told you that the secret of this question was to be found in Scotland. Accordingly, if you can give me sufficient money to move about in Scotland, once I am there I will arrange to spend my leave in that part of the world. I can also, if I have money, buy a certain amount of sabotage material. If you really want me to carry out my orders there you must send me my money, and I suggest that you would be well advised to send somebody over to contact me at the beginning of my leave, he can then bring me some money, some more sabotage materials and also he would be in a position to take over the set and operate it when I am a fully-fledged soldier on active service. I say this because the working of the transmitter is becoming increasingly difficult for me, my leaves are short, it is difficult for me to use the transmitter and I have frequently to incur expense in travelling. This position will be very much more difficult as soon as I complete my training, which will be at the beginning of May. If you send somebody to meet me, I shall be able to render him invaluable aid because I can be in uniform and will be able to move about without questions and get him out of any difficulties and start him off on the right lines. If you are not prepared to do this, I feel I must warn you that the difficulties, the expense of working the transmitter and the troubles I have already had, will force me to close down.[32]

It was also recommended that he include information that he would be taking the wireless set with him so that he could continue transmitting from Winchester. There was then a gap of almost six months in MUTT's file. What he was involved in was revealed in Ib Riis's file. Riis was a German-trained Icelandic wireless operator who was landed in Iceland by U-boat, handed himself in to the authorities and agreed to MI5's proposal to become a double agent. Given the code-name COBWEB, he was assisted by SPIDER, the code-name of Jans Palsson, an Icelandic wireless operator who had been caught transmitting weather data to the Germans and, to avoid execution for treachery, agreed to continue transmitting for the British.

On 29 May 1942, the XX Committee held a meeting at St James's Street, attended by Commander Montagu, Major Foley, Major Robertson, Messrs Stopford, Marriott, Harmer and Reed, where they discussed a modification to Plan SPIDER, which they named Plan TARANTULA.

It had been conceived by the Commander-in-Chief of the Home Fleet primarily to assist convoy PQ 17 on its voyage from Iceland to Russia but secondly to bring the German Fleet out of its base in Norway 'to do battle'. According to a memo of the meeting,

> The Plan is to inform the Germans that a convoy is assembling in Iceland and that another is assembling at Scapa Flow and that it believed that these two convoys may in all probability be taking troops to affect a landing on the Norwegian coast.
>
> Note. It is known that the Germans are at the present moment in an extreme state of agitation for fear lest an attack should be made by us on the Norwegian coast.
>
> For the purposes of implementing the Plan the following has been agreed upon: -
> 1. The two agents who shall play the primary part in putting over the facts to the German Intelligence Organisation shall be
>   (a) Land SPIDER, whose business it is to report on the assembling of the convoy in Iceland, and
>   (b) MUTT whose business it will be to report on the assembling and departure of a convoy from Scapa Flow.
>
> It is believed that zero hour for the Iceland convoy will be 11 June and that in all probability, according to the wishes of C-I.C. Home Fleet, zero hour for the Scapa Flow convoy will be possibly zero hour plus two, three or four.
>
> Note. In actual fact, the convoy which is assembling in Scapa Flow will be a dummy one. It will give every appearance of being a genuine convoy in order to deceive air reconnaissance. It will in fact leave Scapa Flow when ordered and sail west about the Shetlands and will then go in an easterly direction as if in the direction of the Southern Norwegian coast.
>
> Land SPIDER's movements will be as follows: -
>
> He will be released from Camp 020 this afternoon (29 May).
>
> He will be taken by train by Mr Stopford and Mr Reed leaving London on 2 June.
>
> They will leave the U.K. by plane on the 3 June and will arrive in Iceland on the same day (it is hoped).
>
> They will re-establish W/T communication with the Germans and will report progress of the assembling of the convoy in Iceland. Their outgoing messages, which are the important ones from our point of view, will be intercepted and deciphered in this country, and the contents of the telegrams will be dispatched to Major Foley to all interested parties, namely M.I.5 (Major Robertson) and N.I.D. (Commander [Ewen] Montagu).
>
> As far as MUTT is concerned, he will be brought up to London on imaginary weekend leave on 6 June. He will report that the party of Norwegian specialists which has already reported on in his recent traffic, left

on 5 June for Thurso and are in all probability going from there to Scapa Flow.

This report should, it is hoped, have the effect of producing an air reconnaissance machine over Scapa Flow. In the event of nothing of this nature happening within three days of the message going over, a cable is to be sent to Stopford in Iceland asking him to put over information which will tend to confirm the belief that a convoy is assembling in Scapa.

JEFF who will in theory meet MUTT on 6 June, will take the key and send over messages about his experiences in Iceland, some of which will confirm the messages which have already been sent over by Land SPIDER dealing with ship movements in Iceland.

Arrangements have been made for details of reconnaissance over Scapa to be obtained from Colonel Stanford, M.I.5 from the beginning of March. These reconnaissances will be checked up against the departures of PQ convoys from Iceland.

The transport facilities for Stopford, Reed and Land SPIDER are to be arranged by Commander Montagu.[33]

The plan to lure the *Tirpitz*, Germany's 50,000-ton battleship, and a substantial portion of their naval strength, out of anchorage in Norway was cancelled. The messages sent by COBWEB, SPIDER, MUTT and JEFF were that the British Home Fleet had departed British waters for Iceland, leaving British water open to a major German naval raid.

At about the same time, Rothschild was sent to the United States to interview the eight captured German saboteurs. Based on their intelligence he produced a detailed report of their training and mission plan as well as a couple of paragraphs on

Abwehr agents in U.K. Captain MUELLER, an Abw. II official attending the course at Quentz Lake [sic], who is probably identical with Kapitan zur-See Herman MUELLER, told one of the saboteurs that he was in charge of sabotage activities in Norway, and that he had regular lines of communication between Norway and England, it being a simple matter to get agents to England from Norway. He only allowed his agents to remain in England for a few weeks after which he would recall them and send new ones. He said that several weeks before going to the Quentz School in April 1942, some of his agents in England had burnt down a warehouse full of supplies. This probably refers to the sabotage committed by two German agents from Norway which was unsuccessfully investigated [inconclusively added underneath] by Chief Inspector Greene of Scotland Yard.

At the completion of the QUENTZ course, MUELLER was to return to Norway where he would give a similar course to agents destined for England.[34]

While MI5 claimed to have apprehended all enemy saboteurs, this suggests some could have slipped under their radar. Whether Mueller trained other saboteurs and managed to infiltrate them into Britain is unknown. The attack on the warehouse would appear to have been another fake act of sabotage attributed to MUTT and JEFF, the details of which, for whatever reason, were redacted from their files. Theoretically, it could have been the action of other saboteurs who managed to enter the country unnoticed, commit their sabotage and then get picked up by a submarine or boat and return safely, but Wighton and Peis would likely have included mention of it if it had been in Lahousen's war diary.

It is worth including here Rothschild's second paragraph about Abwehr agents in the UK:

Dr VOGEL [probably Haller], an Abwehr II official, was said to run an organisation for recruiting British P/Ws of Irish descent for sabotage work in Northern Ireland and England. DASCH overheard VOGEL dictating a letter asking for the release of a number of P/Ws and stating that the records and personal histories of these men had been investigated, that they were known to be members of the Sinn Fein and IRA, and would be useful as saboteurs against England. VOGEL may be identical with Dr Jupp HOVEN [mentioned earlier].[35]

While it is possible that some reports of MUTT and JEFF's activities were redacted, Liddell reported another sabotage operation in Suffolk that was not mentioned in either of their files. On 13 August 1942, he commented in his diary, 'MUTT and JEFF have prepared a new sabotage act. Home Forces have passed a plan to make a fire at a camp near Barton Mills in Suffolk. This operation is being carried out in conjunction with SOE.'[36] Another note a week later indicated that the operation was underway, but further details have yet to come to light.

Although RAF Mildenhall was only 3 miles from Barton Mills, there was an RAF Maintenance Unit camped just outside the village on the road to Brandon. Nissen huts on the south side of the roads provided accommodation, but the workshops on the other side of the road were probably the target.[37]

15

Plan BROCK: August–October 1942

Another sabotage attack attributed to MUTT and JEFF was Plan BROCK. In August 1942, MI6 sent the Germans a message on MUTT's wireless set indicating that he and JEFF were planning to blow up some Nissen huts in the grounds of an old powder factory in a sparsely populated area of the New Forest in Hampshire.

In October 1942, Liddell informed the Director-General about their plan, which involved an explosion on Salisbury Plain in Hampshire. 'The objective is a food store on Army property and the Germans will be informed that the store must have contained ammunition as well since the explosion was a very big one. The Chief Constable of Hampshire, the RSLO and [Superintendent] Len Burt are in the know.'[1] Masterman added that evidence to make it look like the work of foreign saboteurs was to be deliberately left behind, including MUTT's Norwegian compass.

The task was allocated to Captain Leslie Wood, one of the explosives experts at Aston House. In Des Turner's account of Station 12, he quotes Wood as saying:

> The biggest fun job I had – MI5 asked me to lay it on – was a country job, a lot of people involved. They'd caught a German spy; they'd been waiting for him for months, while one of our operators learned to imitate his Morse exactly …One of their last messages, before they pulled him in, was that the Germans said to him: 'You are giving us information, but we want to see some action – what about these great food stores we've heard about? So our chap Morsed back, 'There's one of these big fat stores (fats, of course, were important in war) on Salisbury Plain. He gave them the location that we selected, and I said 'I'll see if I can blow it up and burn it at a fixed time;' night was selected. I took Sinclair Munro into my confidence, as I had to have somebody to help me. We found an old Dutch barn on the Plain, and we filled it up with what I called 'dog's breakfasts,' tar and all that kind of thing, and an explosive charge to blow the roof off and expose the flames. MI5 provided me with a racing driver, and he'd got some socking great racing car [Rothschild had a Bugatti]. He took the side of his car out and filled up

the back with soft Sorbo rubber and so on. The barn was at the bottom of a long dip on Salisbury Plain and the hill sloping up each way, and the road could not be closed for security reasons. The idea was to have a car on the top of the each rise and when they both blinked their sidelights, quickly, it meant that nothing was coming. I lit the fuse – it had to be a short one because it was beside a public highway. I ran straight for the road and this chap timed it perfectly. He drove slowly past, I put my arm in front of my face and dived head first into the car and we were off. And then boom! I thought, by gods, that's a bit bigger bang than I intended.

Actually, one of the chaps who was helping with this was young Rothschild, later Lord Rothschild, who came to spend the night with me beforehand, I've never forgotten it, because my younger daughter said to my wife, the next morning, 'Who's that nice man that played games with me after breakfast?' Vera said, 'Well, that was Lord Rothschild.' 'But who's Lord Roth?'

Anyway, Rothschild was in on this game and the lord lieutenant of the county, and they had a hell of a party arranged at his house, on the heights, whence we could see this enormous blaze. And sure enough, presently a German reconnaissance plane came over; they used to fly so high you couldn't hit them. All you could hear was a very, very high whine. It would be unarmed. So it was noted that this spy was doing his job. After that, of course, they could feed in slightly wrong bits of information. That's how intelligence worked in the war; you gave wrong information, but you also gave some right information that didn't matter too much, to feed them. I went back the next morning to have a look. My heart nearly stood still because, true, I'd knocked the roof off this barn, but a bit harder than I thought, luckily for me it had sailed clean across the road and missed all the telephone lines to the south of England. If I had hit those, my name would have been mud.[2]

As Liddell had also been involved in the operation, he accompanied Wood and Rothschild to witness the attack. His diary entry of 11 October provided additional details, some contradictory.

We met two officers of the police at the given rendezvous and they drove about quarter of a mile to the objective. This was about 12.15am. We drew the two cars up inside a field along the hedge. Meanwhile, guards were put out on the road to give us warning of any cars or cyclists. The SOE experts put in the explosives which consisted of nine pounds of Aminol, incendiary material and thunder rockets. The fuse was laid through the hedge on to the road. When this work had been completed, and we were satisfied that no cars, either way, could reach the site within a period of two minutes, the car which was carrying the SOE representatives pulled out onto the road opposite the end of the fuse and remained with engines running. We then came out and headed straight for an observation post about a quarter of a mile away. As we passed the first car, the fuse was lit. The SOE representatives and Victor Rothschild immediately jumped in and streaked up the road behind us. The explosion took place in about two minutes, ten seconds and was a formidable one. The incendiaries worked well, and a blaze of light went up which could be seen for miles around. There was an aeroplane somewhere in the vicinity which dropped a flare. We presumed therefore that the matter would be reported back to RAF headquarters. Not wishing to be in the vicinity of the conflagration, we made off after watching the fire for about five minutes. We reached Michael Ryde's house at Newbury at about 3 am. We heard later that the fire had been seen by a number of the Air Observer Corps and had been reported to the Andover police who had sent out two sergeants immediately. They had remained on site during the night. They had already ascertained that somebody had been seen in the vicinity of the hut several days previously. This was probably one the SOE men who was putting in the material. There was also a shepherd who might have given information since he was questioned discreetly by Michael Ryde in order to find out whether any of his sheep were left out at night. We had originally intended to use eighteen pounds of Aminol but felt that this might be dangerous if the whole hut was lifted into the middle of the road. We anticipate that the police will make enquiries with the military about the hut, when they will be told that it was taken over by GHQ Home Forces. Brian Mountain of Home Forces has been informed and will say that the hut was taken over for a special purpose and stored with certain Commando equipment. If the debris is carefully examined it is possible that a piece of German Bickford fuse will be found and a Norwegian compass or the remains of it. Len Burt, who is in the know, will be sent down as a special investigator. I am told that the explosion has disintegrated the whole hut and that a few loose thunder rockets have been found. Steps have been taken to get some notice of the incident in the local press.[3]

Like many of the earlier attacks, it did not go exactly to plan. Masterman acknowledged that 'the usual difficulties occurred'. The explosion was so effective that all tangible evidence of sabotage was destroyed. MUTT's compass 'which had been carefully left on the spot was stolen and disappeared. Some local sheep strayed too near the danger zone, and a soldier from a nearby camp was arrested and seemed unable to find any convincing story to exonerate himself.'[4]

As further clues had to be planted, a Special Branch officer was sent to convince the locals that it was sabotage, and appropriate accounts appeared in the local press.[5] Guy Liddell had been well informed of the incident:

We have got some further details about Operation BROCK. The Nissen hut was completely disintegrated, and pieces were discovered as far as 70 yards away. Within half an hour two policemen, a Home Guard officer, a Home Guard private and a shepherd were on the scene. Since then the police have been busily investigating the case. Interest appeared to be flagging when the Home Guard officer advanced the theory that the top of one of the sticky bombs had corroded through and set alight to all the rest. However, an expert from the War Office has now been down, and parts of the fuse have been found. At least five policemen have been engaged for the last twenty-four hours digging among the ruins and suspicion now falls on a private in the Royal Engineers who asked for a lift that night at about midnight and who has made a statement which has been proved to be incorrect. The intelligence officer of the 25th Division has also been called in and is showing a lively interest. An announcement will go into the press on Friday, and the Detective Superintendent of the Hampshire Constabulary is going to arrange for the local press to run the case hereafter. Photographs are available. Burt came to see me as he felt that the discovery of the German Bickford fuse and the Norwegian compass was working the local police into quite a fever. They now feel that they have a serious saboteur in the midst so I told Len Burt to soothe them down a bit.[6]

No doubt MUTT's wireless set was used to provide evidence of his latest success to the Germans. A note in his file reported Dr Mueller boasting to his Abwehr colleagues about their successes. Farago, who had access to Abwehr files, claimed that shortly after arriving in Britain, 'several reports about sabotage in Southern England appeared in the newspapers and they [MUTT and JEFF] promptly claimed credit for them in brash reports to Mueller'.[7]

16

Plan BUNBURY and Operations HAGGIS and PORRIDGE – September 1942–June 1945[1]

The next memo in MUTT's file was a report that both men were given their personal belongings back, but the list did not mention the contraceptives that MUTT had brought. Presumably he had intended to use them in Scotland, despite the fact that he had a girlfriend back in Norway. One imagines that his minders did not allow him free time to visit any houses of ill-repute so that he had time to think about his situation and planned to buy a diamond engagement ring for his girlfriend. As he had been unable to save the £50 estimated cost, Harmer suggested that he sold his expensive camera.[1]

As MUTT expressed a need for greater independence and the possibility of a paid job working for the Norwegians, a meeting was arranged to discuss his future with TAR. Wanting to be able to use MUTT's services at a future time, Harmer suggested that he be given government savings certificates which he could redeem after the war. TAR proposed that MUTT and JEFF's case be closed down as soon as possible after the present deception they were working on

> by announcing that JEFF intended to do an ambitious act of sabotage and then go off the air altogether. In that event we might hope that the Germans would suppose that JEFF had been captured and had given away MUTT, but that the matter had been given no publicity because we were unwilling to admit in the Press that there were saboteurs in this country.[2]

It was agreed that he would be given £7 a week until the Norwegians started employing him, that he moved out of 35 Crespigny Road to allow agent ZIGZAG temporary accommodation, and was given £50 in lieu of his camera, the last financial aid from MI5. The famous double agent ZIGZAG's sabotage work is referred to later. By the middle of October MUTT was living at 8 Dorset Chambers, Chagford Street, Ivor Place, NW1, but by early December, once ZIGZAG had moved out, he was back at Crespigny Road, being paid £2 a week with the same amount saved by MI5 to give him enough to enjoy some leave at the end of his training.

There was then another gap in MUTT's records until early 1943. A possible explanation for the redaction was found in Lahousen's war diary. He believed Jack had gone to Liverpool and Glasgow to report on the Allied convoys leaving for the Western Approaches. Sometimes his messages were considered to be very valuable but at other times they caused great consternation in the German High Command. When he claimed a large convoy, including Norwegian units, had left, the alarm was raised and all forces in Norway were put on alert to resist an attack. The next message reported them returning to port suggesting that it must just have been an exercise.

In October 1942, he reported from Tail o' the Bank overlooking the Firth of Clyde on the greatest concentration of ships he had ever seen, including grey-painted passenger ships with two or three funnels, at least one battleship, minesweepers, cruisers and other smaller craft. In mid-October, he reported landings being practised on the shores of Argyllshire lochs. As soldiers were being confined to ships, he reported learning from sailors in the pubs that everyone had been issued with Arctic clothing. Despite other reports from Abwehr agents that a major Allied operation was expected in the Western Mediterranean, influential figures in German High Command believed that an invasion of Norway was imminent.

In the last week of October, they were told that the convoy had left overnight. Luftwaffe reconnaissance planes from Norway were unable to spot what the Germans had dubbed 'Jack Berg's Convoy'. About a fortnight later, an Abwehr agent in Algeciras, overlooking the Straits of Gibraltar, reported more than forty troop ships and half a dozen battleships and aircraft carriers heading east under cover of darkness. MUTT's messages had played their part in the success of Operation Torch, the Allied invasion of North Africa.

To celebrate O.K.'s return to Britain, the two men reported a wave of sabotage successes and at the beginning of 1943 requested more money, explosives and fuses if their activities were to continue as they had been unable to locate supplies in British retail stores.[3]

In early 1943, MUTT was ordered by Oslo to sabotage an 'electricity undertaking'. However, MI5 considered that targeting a generating station supplying one of the major cities would cause too great an impact on the war effort so a minor town outside London was chosen. They devised Plan BUNBURY, named after a phrase in Oscar Wilde's play *The Importance of Being Earnest*, which refers to some mischief in the countryside. Initially, it was an attack on the electricity generating station at Basingstoke, Hampshire, which the Germans appeared not to know was insignificant and of little importance. As well as reinforcing MUTT and JEFF's status in the eyes of the Abwehr, MI5 had another purpose – 'to put the complacent utility bodies on the alert against enemy sabotage'.[4]

The 110-volt electricity generating station on Brook Street in Basingstoke was close to the gasworks but as Thorneycroft's factory beside the railway line was producing a range of military vehicles and the Bramley Central Ammunition Depot was only 2 miles north of the town, it appears that this proposal was abandoned; if the station had been put out of action, even temporarily, it would have significantly reduced production at these important sites.

As the key machinery that needed to be destroyed to halt production in any electricity undertaking was their transformers, magnetic bombs were needed to blow them up, and MUTT and JEFF did not have any. Whilst the SOE had developed magnetic 'limpet bombs' for sabotaging ships and 'magnetic clams' for industrial targets, MI5 was keen to get their hands on German sabotage equipment. To do this Oslo was asked to supply appropriate sabotage equipment to attack the power station and they were told that the optimum location for a parachute drop was the north-eastern coast of Scotland.

To create a plausible explanation for MUTT being in Scotland, the Germans were told that he had been given a job with the FSP in Aberdeenshire. This story was accepted, and they trusted him enough to arrange a drop of money, another wireless set and the requested sabotage supplies beside the Loch of Strathbeg, about 40 miles north of Aberdeen. What was called Operation PORRIDGE would confirm the Germans' continued belief in MUTT and JEFF being at large and on task.

Harmer made arrangements with Major Perfect, and the Lothian police force was informed about the flight of the German plane, the parachute drop, the possibility of a German agent arriving and the need for secrecy. In the event of an agent landing, it was agreed that MUTT would be allowed an hour to speak with him alone before he was arrested. Lahousen raised the issue of supplying MUTT to Field Marshal Wilhelm Keitel, chief of German High Command, who, intrigued by the two Abwehr agents' exploits, obtained the Luftwaffe's assistance.[5]

On 19 February 1943, MUTT received a message confirming that the drop was going to take place between 1000 and 0400 hours that night. MUTT, Paulton, Harmer, Inspector Christie, the Aberdeen City Police explosives expert, and other police officers were at hand to pick up the container. Harmer reported:

At about 22.30 MUTT took up position on the little track leading to the Loch about a quarter of a mile from the barn, dressed in the uniform of a Sergeant in the F.S.P. Superintendent Westland and I divided the night between us to keep watch with MUTT, everything was quiet until just after 02.30 hours.

At 0231 hours precisely, a plane was heard coming from the sea. The Germans had announced their intention of approaching from the South West, and the plane was therefore coming in the wrong direction. MUTT, however, flashed his torch in the sky which was completely ineffective because the plane suddenly emerged skimming the water of the Loch and plainly visible to the naked eye. On reaching the land side shore of the Loch it rose to about fifty feet and flew directly over MUTT and disappeared in a South-South Westerly direction. It was then not heard for three or four minutes. After this it appeared again flying down the Loch from the South West, i.e. in the direction from which it was intended to come. Once again it flew directly over MUTT at a very low altitude. It then made a sharp turn to the left and flew across the road between MUTT and the Loch and dropped a package which landed 130 yds from him and slightly to the south of the track. The plane then made off, and two or three minutes later we heard bombs fall at Fraserburgh, and the anti-aircraft defences opened up.[6]

According to Harmer, the package was not spotted as it left the plane, but the parachute was seen as soon as it opened and the package was collected. It was housed in a padded canvas case which in turn was in a canvas bag placed in a metal container. The metal container was attached by a handle to the parachute. The handle, however, was not placed centrally, so that the container was held at an angle. At the bottom end of the container as it fell was a brown paper parcel filled with sand which took the shock of the fall. The package contained, besides a Mains transmitter and receiver, several spare valves, a long length of aerial, a spare K.L.2 for the old set, two lengths of fuse for sabotage, a new crossword book for coding messages, typewritten instructions and £200 in green £1 notes.[7] Wighton and Peis claimed that high explosives and fuses had been sent, hidden inside Thermos flasks, that the valves and other spare parts for the wireless sets had been wrapped in rubber containers and that £500 in pound notes was supplied in four large leather wallets. Why there was a discrepancy is unknown.[8] When the local chief constable was informed of the successful operation, Harmer was told that a 7-year-old child had been killed in the Fraserburgh bombing and a hundred people had had to be evacuated when a bomb dropped on Peterhead failed to explode.

MUTT used the original set before he left Aberdeen to let Oslo know of the safe arrival of the package and thank them for the money and other items. Various articles from the *Aberdeen Evening Express* and *Press and Journal* which mentioned the bombing were posted to an agreed address in Stockholm as evidence. Without giving place names, they stated that an 11-year-old boy had been killed, but there was no mention of the parachute drop.

Paulton then escorted MUTT south, taking both wireless sets, and started transmitting from London. Before Harmer left Scotland, in appreciation for MUTT and Paulton being allowed to stay in the police station and for the help they were given, he promised a contribution to the police charity. He then discussed with the Aberdeen police the possibility of carrying out some controlled sabotage within the city and was assured that 'whatever our requirements it could be arranged without the slightest difficulty'.[9] Whether any explosions were subsequently carried out by the police in the Aberdeen area and their cause attributed to MUTT and JEFF was not mentioned in their files. While it may not have happened, it could be that, if it did, all references to it were redacted.

Wighton and Peis claimed that the two men, with new explosives and more money in their pockets, reported undertaking a new sabotage campaign targeting aircraft factories and other important installations using well-placed time bombs 'which achieved results out of all proportion to the limited resources required'.[10]

Requests to find out the secrets of the new British airborne radar devices the RAF was successfully using to attack German U-boats were encouraged with an offer of £10,000 deposited in a Swiss bank account. MI5 did not respond to this enticement, but they did send birthday wishes to Mueller as MUTT and JEFF had attended his party two years earlier.[11]

In the meantime, MI5 had come up with another idea for JEFF, code-named Plan PRUDENTIAL. The original plan was to tell the Germans that he had been recruited by the SOE and was being trained as an agent to be infiltrated back into Norway. While it would have captured the Germans' attention, Harmer was against this idea as it would involve having to provide false names of Norwegian agents. Instead, he suggested to TAR that JEFF befriended a British man training to be an SOE agent who offers to get him recruited. He gets an interview but is rejected. JEFF then gets his new friend to tell him about his mission and obtains

> various important details of the organisation for which he works. In this way, we can disclose to the Germans what they already know about S.O.E. and also support any small deception about the organisation, and at the same time avoid the necessity of giving details such as names, which in practice are impossible to provide.
>
> JEFF learns that a separate branch of the British Intelligence in Norway is being created, designed specially to help an Allied invasion from a military point of view. This is to consist of a small number of very skilled independent agents reporting on military matters operating in Norway, and a large reserve of agents to be sent to the country immediately before the invasion takes place. JEFF's friend, needless to say, will at a suitable time be transferred to this branch and trained as one of the first categories.
>
> After a suitable period, JEFF will then find out that his friend's mission does not include taking a W/T set with him. This is considered too dangerous as the British have too great a respect for the German powers of D.F'ing [using wireless receiving technology to identify the location of the transmission and arrest the operator]. He will, therefore, have no visible means, but will tour such places in Norway as he is instructed to visit, make reports and take them into Sweden. On the other hand, in case of urgency, he will receive various frequencies in which we will transmit to him blind at certain hours and on certain days...
>
> At a suitable moment, JEFF will overlook his friend's operational instructions and find out the call signs, frequencies and sufficient details about the code which we will use and report them to the Germans. Later, he will report that his friend has gone to a final training establishment and he has lost touch with him, and later still that so far as he can gather he has left and should be in Norway.
>
> When the next period for Norway deception arrives (presumably in the Autumn) we can start up with messages reputedly of an urgent character. These can be worded in as obscure a fashion as is necessary to safeguard other agents working in various districts of Norway, but at the same time can be so worked as to make the Germans think that something important is afoot.
>
> If this plan works in the case of MUTT and JEFF, it might be planted on the Germans as a new technique of the British Intelligence and thus enable us to operate transmitters to any part of Europe using a code which, on the information given by JEFF in this particular case, can be broken with reasonable certainty by the Germans.
>
> If you and Major Masterman think that this plan is worth doing, I will try and put it up in detail for S.O.E. and the Controlling Officer, as well as for S.I.S. I believe it would stand a very good chance of success and, moreover, I cannot see how it can ever be proved as a fraud. Further, I do not think that

either S.I.S. or S.O.E. could object on the grounds that it would give rise to an intensification of C.E. [Counter Espionage] activity in Norway since I doubt whether this is possible and in any case, we would never specify districts where their agents were working. We would merely in our messages refer to, for instance, District A or District B, leaving the Germans to suppose that the mythical agents knew to what these referred.[12]

Whether Harmer's proposal went ahead was not documented in their files. However, Operation HAGGIS was set up when JEFF announced his intention to try to carry out the sabotage of Basingstoke power station. The Germans informed MUTT on 17 April that when all was prepared they would send over ready-made material with instructions. They later announced that they would send them some more money at the same time.

JEFF made efforts to persuade the Germans to drop the sabotage material in the south of England, but when it became clear that this was going to take more time, it was arranged that it should take place after all at the old drop zone near Aberdeen during the period of MUTT's supposed leave. The Germans agreed for the drop to be between 26 May and 6 June so they were told that MUTT would be spending his leave from 21 May to 1 June in Scotland, with the primary object of receiving delivery of the sabotage material. According to Harmer,

On his first evening MUTT stated that he would reconnoitre the dropping place again, and in fact did so. There it was found that a new aerodrome was under construction, with a great many workmen about and controls. It had obviously become completely unsuited for an operation of this type, and the Germans were informed of this on 23 May and were given a fresh dropping place near Loch Meikle, East of Ellon, map reference Scotland sheet 31 540518. This the Germans agreed in their message of 24 May and gave as a time between 0230 and 0400 hours on the night of 27/28. MUTT then went on a supposed visit to Inverary, where he was supposed to report certain activity by Canadian forces. In order to fit this in, it was decided that he should not go on the air again until 27 May, the day on which the dropping was fixed. Unfortunately, however, conditions were very bad, and it was not possible to make the last-minute contact to confirm the dropping, but as it had been definitely settled in previous messages, we attended at the dropping place on the night in question. … No aeroplane came, and we returned to Aberdeen.

On the following day, we tried from fairly early to make contact but conditions were still bad, and we failed to do so. Accordingly, in the afternoon I decided to send Paulton back to London to try and make contact in his capacity as JEFF and arrange the dropping for us on Monday night. He went off on the evening train, and within a few minutes of his leaving contact was achieved, and the Germans informed us that the dropping must be postponed for a short while, and we were to give as soon as possible a new dropping place as near the coast as possible. On 29 May, we gave the Germans the third place, near the estuary of the River Ythan, map reference Scotland sheet 31, 547645, and asked for an immediate answer whether it was possible to carry out the operation at once. The Germans replied that they would have to discuss with their friends (presumably the LUFTWAFFE) whether the new delivery place would suit and that they would give us the new time as soon as possible.

As JEFF had gone to London, it was thought it would add an air of genuineness to the traffic if he, at the same time as MUTT was fixing up the new dropping place, was sending inconsistent messages about the failure to carry out the operation at the old dropping place. He therefore sent a message on 30 May, saying that he had heard from MUTT, who had waited at the appointed place and would be there the following night. Later on the same day, JEFF cancelled this message and said that he had heard further from MUTT, and the dropping must take place urgently.

On 30 May MUTT made contact in the afternoon and asked the Germans whether they had any message for him. They replied that they had not and that he should call again on the following day. He, however, told them to wait and sent them a message telling them, which was the fact, that the weather was good that evening – the morning had been very wet, but it cleared up about the middle of the afternoon and was very bright and sunny. MUTT said he would call again at 9 o'clock in the evening for a reply, and at that hour the Germans announced that the new place had been agreed and that delivery would take place that night between 1 and 2 o'clock, German summer time.

We therefore attended at the latest dropping place on the night of 30/31. There were present MUTT and myself and the two police officers who had been present on the previous occasion. About midnight a very bad ground mist arose which reduced visibility to a very short distance and made the identification of anything from the air, especially water, practically impossible. We, therefore, did not think it surprising that the plane did not come, although we heard a plane flying in the distance apparently north and south of us, at various times between 1.30 and 2.30 in the morning. The operation was abandoned at 4 o'clock, and we returned to Aberdeen.

At 0300 on 31 May the Chief Constable of Aberdeen-shire received the following message from the local Constable at Longside: -

'About 06.30 hours, 31.5.42, William Reid, farm grieve, Newton of Ludquharn, Longside, found in a turnip field about 200 yards N.E. of the farmhouse what appeared to be a deflated balloon or a parachute.

At 0710 the matter was reported to me and I made enquiry and found White German parachute marked as follows: -

LASTENFALLSCHIRN 25 KG
HMB No.12002501 AMFORDERZELCHEM followed by F. HERSTELLER –
HER TAGDER HERSTELLUNG 16.6.41.
WECHHONTROLLE 19.6.41.

Within the harness of the parachute, there is a light brown fibre attaché case 14" by 10", heavy in weight, has a lock which has a three-leg Isle of Man coat of arms on it. Round the case there is a string. Lying nearby is a battleship grey metal box, which is open at the top with a detached bracket for holding it up. This box measures 21 inches across, 12 inches broad, and 12 inches deep.

Everything has been left as found. Peterhead Police notified.'[13]

Before the attaché case was opened and the contents examined, Rothschild was contacted to make sure it was not a booby-trapped explosive device. Potentially it was what MUTT had asked for, money and sabotage material. In an undated letter from Brigadier Sir David Petrie, presumably sent to the Regional Security Officers, he informed them:

A German aeroplane recently dropped some sabotage equipment by parachute in the United Kingdom. Incendiary bombs, high explosive bombs and delay mechanisms were included. Photographs of these and of the attaché case in which the equipment was contained are attached.

The magnetic high explosive bomb has been previously noted, and it is illustrated in Figs. 40 and 41 of our booklet ENEMY SABOTAGE EQUIPMENT (TECHNICAL) II; the detonator container is shown in Fig.32; and the delay mechanism in Fig.28. The cylindrical incendiary bomb has no features of special interest. It is initiated by the safety fuse which can be seen attached to the main body of the bomb in the photograph.[14]

The next item in MUTT's file was a questionnaire, dated 5 June 1943, the contents of which suggest that it was produced by Rothschild. He had just returned from a meeting in Washington with the Federal Bureau of Investigation who had captured eight German saboteurs.

SUSPECTED ABTEILUNG II AGENTS
The Sabotage Section recently sent down a summarised questionnaire to be used as a guide in the questioning at interrogation centres in the U.K. of suspected saboteurs. The questionnaire, which is attached, may be of some use as a guide when questioning suspected saboteurs.

The following explanatory notes should be used in conjunction with the questionnaire:

Agents of ABT. II of the German Secret Service are concerned both with sabotage and propaganda, the latter being known as Insurgierung or J work. This explains question 4.

Diagrams of home-made mechanisms recommended by ABT. II to agents will be sent to you in the near future.

The following is a brief list of chemicals habitually recommended by ABT. II to their agents for use in making home-made sabotage equipment:

ENGLISH	GERMAN
Potassium nitrate (saltpetre)	Kalisalpeter or Kaliumnitrat
Sodium nitrate (chili saltpetre)	Natriumnitrat
Potassium chlorate	Kaliumchlorat
Sodium peroxide	Natriumperoxyd
Calcium sulphate (gypsum or Plaster of Paris)	Calcium sulfat
Potassium permanganate	Kaliumpermanganat
Flour	Mehl

Sugar	Zucker
Sulphur	Schwefel
Nitric acid	Salpetersaure
Sawdust	Sagemehl
Ferric oxide	Eisenoxyduloxyd
Paraffin (with 1 and 3)	Paraffin
Aluminium	Aluminium
Aluminium paint	Aluminiumfarbe

PERSONNEL.

Description of all persons connected with the agent's recruiting and training.

Which of these individuals had practical sabotage knowledge?

Did any have any professional knowledge of chemistry?

Name and descriptions of any individuals who attended the practical tests of sabotage given to this agent.

DETAILS OF SABOTAGE TRAINING.

Had the agent any previous technical knowledge, (machine tools, aircraft factories, ships etc.)?

Lectures received – laboratory instruction – practical work in the field.

Formulae of explosive and incendiary mixtures.

Was training specialised according to ultimate destination of agent?

Was training given by gaining access to premises by subterfuge or stealth, or by gaining employment?

Names of materials used, both in German and in English.

Instructions as to how materials were to be bought in the U.K. and cover reasons for their purchase. Quantities to be bought at one time.

Full descriptions and diagrams of home-made delay mechanisms.

Detonators – were these brought with the agent or were instructions given as to how they were to be obtained in this country?

Manufacture of fuses.

Was he taught how to manufacture his own detonators?

Was he taught the use of abrasives?

What was the attitude of ABT.II to the question of carrying and using firearms?

Camouflage of sabotage equipment.

Was he warned of any specific counter-measures to be circumvented, e.g. live fences and dogs?

DETAILS OF TARGETS GIVEN TO AGENT.

List of targets.

Was he shown maps or aerial photographs?

Methods of sabotage to each target.

Method of approach to each target.

Was he instructed to take employment in a factory in which sabotage was to be committed?

During training was emphasis laid upon self-destroying targets or upon self-destroying elements involved in such a target, for example a moving train which can be derailed by the loosening of a fishplate as an alternative to the destruction of a portion of a track by explosives? *

In addition to main targets, was he instructed to commit nuisance sabotage, such as putting explosive attaché cases in station cloakrooms?

Was agent shown targets in Germany similar to those he was instructed to attack?

In addition to sabotage, was the agent given other ABT.II assignments, i.e. anti-war propaganda, etc.?

TRAINING SCHOOL
Exact details of location and description of house, laboratory, garden, etc.
Length of training.

ACTION IN U.K.
How soon after arrival was the agent to start sabotage?

What cover was the agent to have in this country?

Was he instructed to obtain a job which could give him cover for the purchase of necessary chemicals?

Was the emphasis laid on home-made or professionally-made equipment? Was he expected to obtain H.E. [High Explosives] by theft or subterfuge?

Was he to announce intended acts of sabotage to his German Station beforehand?

Was he to inform his German Station of the success of his sabotage acts?

Was the agent to attempt to leave the U.K. when he had completed his sabotage assignment?

Names and descriptions of other agents being trained in sabotage and their probable destination.

* The significance of this question lies in the importance of discovering any change in the German sabotage training which may tend to show that they are spreading beyond their rather narrow preoccupation with explosive and incendiary bombs.

This appeared quite clearly to relate to our operation, and we accordingly went out to the spot and, after making due tests on the suitcase to make sure it was not an infernal machine, we opened it with the special apparatus provided by Lord Rothschild and examined its contents. They were as follows: -

£400 in £1 notes, done up in bundles of £100, with wrappers round them bearing certain initials.

Cardboard box containing six M.D. 1 magnetic clams filled with plastic explosive by S.O.E. and packed by them (the original S.O.E. wrappers and Scotch tape were still on them), and three plastic explosive charges specially prepared and used in a certain joint Combined Ops and S.O.E. undertaking which had taken place in Norway some time ago in connection with the blowing up of a pipeline.

Two 'M.L. flares' – standard S.O.E. equipment

Fourteen standard S.O.E. time pencils, with different delay times, in their standard cases.

One standard S.O.E. detonator container.

A certain amount of S.O.E. packing to prevent damage.

The spot at which the material had actually been dropped was some 10 miles from the place at which it ought to have been dropped. Moreover, we discovered that an R.A.F. mobile beacon had been at the bottom of the farm lane on the night before, and the pilot had no doubt mistaken the light given from this beacon for the flashes from MUTT's torch. However, it appeared in all the circumstances far too dangerous to acknowledge receipt of the package and MUTT, therefore, sent over a message on 31 May informing the Germans of the fog and that he had heard the aeroplane, and said that he would repeat the operation that night. The Germans replied that delivery had taken place at the red light signal at the described place and that repetition could not take place before the middle of July. MUTT made one further effort to make the Germans try again, at the same time repeating that the plane never came near him and adding that his signal was not red but white. On the following day he asked as an urgent question whether there was anything compromising in the suitcase, to which the Germans gave a negative answer, and he added in a further message that the pilot had not been at fault because the fog had been so bad.

The position so far as the Germans are concerned is, therefore, that if they believe MUTT, as I must assume they do, they will think that the material has gone astray and that it has fallen into our hands, together with the money. They are, therefore, bound to be to some degree nervous of repeating the operation and putting MUTT in danger, and if the pilot maintains his statement that he identified the dropping place and that it was a torch being flashed at him, they might even be suspicious to some degree of MUTT himself. It is thought therefore important that the Germans should be given as much information about the actual circumstances as is compatible with what might have happened in practice.

Accordingly when MUTT next communicates with the Germans he will inform them that on returning to his F.S.P. Section he found that the police had notified the military of the finding of the sabotage equipment and money and had asked them to keep a look out for an enemy agent. MUTT will also probably be in a position to say approximately where it was dropped and also to tell them that was dropped beside an R.A.F. beacon. This will give them the explanation of the red light and presumably dispose of any lingering faith they may still have in the pilot's statement. It is also suggested that an independent agent might hear some garbled story in Aberdeenshire about an agent having been dropped by parachute recently for whom the police are searching.

The one other point which remains is what is the position so far as publicity is concerned? As the County Police had been brought into this operation, they were able to instruct the local Constable, Sergeant and Inspector not to let anybody near the scene and we had removed everything within a few hours. The local police were evidently expecting us to order an immediate checking of identity cards and a general search of the neighbourhood. They were even contemplating calling in the military to beat a large area of forestation which was near the spot where the material had been found. We stopped them doing any of this and Inspector Hunter, at my request, gave them all a short talk telling them that in no circumstances must they talk about this incident.

The position, therefore, is that they do not know that we had prior knowledge of the dropping of this material, although they may very well think it rather odd that we did not make the routine searches and enquiries which would have been indicated by the finding of equipment dropped for an enemy agent. In my view, however, so far as this side of the matter is concerned, the less we do the better because it is very unlikely that they will arrive at the correct solution of the problem and their speculations will probably be taken up as exaggerated so that finally the story which will go around in the neighbourhood may be just as helpful to us as anything we can invent ourselves. There are, however, various routine matters which might be carried out, (a) to give the impression that this was not a controlled operation, and (b) in case some leakage about it may get back to the enemy. Lord Rothschild is anxious to circulate Security Officers at key points, R.S.L.Os [Regional Security Liaison Officers], etc. that sabotage equipment has been found in Scotland and that the equipment indicates the presence at large of an enemy agent, and asking everybody to be on the look-out. Another possibility is notification from I.B. Scottish Command to the local F.S.P. Section that this material was found in their region, in order to support the story MUTT will tell on his return. These matters are at the moment under consideration [15]

Before Lahousen was transferred to the Russian Front, he was informed that the drop had been successful, and the £2,000 and explosives were to be put to good use.

An anonymous report, very likely Harmer's, admitted that it had always been thought desirable to increase MUTT and JEFF's sabotage activities 'without impairing their value in terms of espionage'.[16] It appears that the proposed sabotage of the Basingstoke Electricity Undertaking had been shelved as there was no further mention of it in MUTT or JEFF's file. A search of the *Basingstoke Gazette* for August and September 1943 made no mention of any attack. Arthur Attwood's accounts of his wartime experiences as a Home Guard in Basingstoke made no mention of a sabotage attack, nor did John Leete in his *In Time of War in Hampshire*. Instead, a similar target but at a different location was identified, the electricity generating station at Prospect Row, Bury St Edmunds in Suffolk, East Anglia.[17]

Whether some of the redacted pages in their file give details of the reasons for this attack is unknown but Ronald Creasey, mentioned earlier, was reported in June 1943 to have stated that

the major part of the electricity supplied to the camps, houses, works and factories in Suffolk and Norfolk was supplied by the East Anglian Power Company. He suggested that an effective sabotaging of this plant at some appropriate future date might sabotage the American bombing plans at a critical moment, especially in view of the U.S. reliance on electricity. CREASEY was certain that very grave damage could be caused if this electrical concern could be put out of action but he could not say where the main power station was situated. He based his ideas on the new U.S. scheme for electric guiding systems on their airfields.[18]

Although it is undocumented, it is possible that this intelligence reached the Germans through one of Creasey's contacts or reference to it had been included in the disinformation fed to the Germans by one or more of the double agents. As the Germans had asked them to attack an 'electricity undertaking', MI5 decided to carry out their instructions to maintain MUTT and JEFF's reputation as successful German saboteurs; to obtain samples of the latest German sabotage equipment or more captured SOE equipment; to learn more about German sabotage techniques as well as to use the incident for propaganda purposes. While the media coverage could provide proof to the Germans that the attack had taken place, it would also raise awareness in factories across the country of the importance of increased security. MUTT's file contained the following details:

THE PLAN
MUTT and JEFF informed the Germans that they would sabotage a generating station at Bury St Edmunds in Suffolk. The selection of this target was governed by the following considerations:

It was consistent with JEFF's notional location in the Pioneer Corps.

The Electricity Undertaking belonged to a company with whom M.I.5 have had considerable dealings in the past, and in whose discretion we had confidence.

The local Chief Constable was known to be discreet and cooperative.

The Undertaking was small and unimportant. This was necessary as the authorities would never have agreed to staging an act of sabotage at a big Generating Station as this might have attracted the attention of enemy bombers.[19]

Another parachute drop of explosive supplies, code-named Operation PORRIDGE, was arranged, and MUTT and the police were ready and waiting outside Aberdeen to receive it. Although the location was correct, the parachute did not open. Consequently, the new transmitter and one magnetic clam were completely smashed. The remaining undamaged sabotage equipment consisted of six magnetic clams; three cylindrical incendiary bombs; two cases each containing five standard time pencils; two separate time pencils; a length of detonating fuse and fifteen detonators in a cylindrical Bakelite container. There was no mention as to whether it was SOE material. A note afterwards read 'see ZIGZAG'.

According to Harmer, the plan involved taking the General Manager and the local manager of the Bury St Edmunds power station into his confidence.

The active co-operation of the latter was essential and it was arranged that on a night when he was according to his normal custom taking his regular tour of duty as a firewatcher on the Works with two of his employees he should undertake to perform the following tasks:

Place one of the magnetic clams with live detonator and length of partly burnt safety fuse attached, on the pedestal bearing the Generator.

Place another magnetic clam (with magnets removed) on a disused condenser awaiting sale as scrap in an adjacent building to which it was not actually the practice of the staff to have access. This clam was to be initiated by the Works Manager with two standard time pencils connected to short lengths of fuse; with detonators crimped to their distal ends. The delay was to be approximately ten minutes in order to allow the Manager time to get back to the firewatchers' room before the explosion occurred.

The safety fuse which was used in conjunction with (1) above was a piece which had actually been supplied previously by the Germans to MUTT and JEFF and, before it was sent down to Bury St Edmunds with the rest of the equipment, a kink was deliberately made in it up to which the fuse was allowed to burn, thus providing in advance a plausible explanation for the failure of the bomb to explode.

It was arranged that the Manager, having returned to the firewatchers' room after initiating the time pencil, should thereafter follow as nearly as possible the exact procedure that he would have followed had an unexplained explosion in fact occurred, that is to say he and his colleagues on hearing the noise would immediately ascribe it to an aerial bomb, despite the absence of any previous air raid warning; and they thereupon were to ring up the A.R.P. authorities before making an investigation. When it became clear that the explosion was not due to an aerial bomb, they were to ring up the Police. The Police would make an investigation and if they came to the conclusion that an act of sabotage had been committed, would inform M.I.5, Regional Officer, who in turn would inform M.I.5 Head Office and ask for special sabotage investigators to be sent down to assist in the enquiry.

To lend colour to these proceedings it had previously been arranged for local Field Security Personnel to act the part of suspicious strangers in the district prior to the date for which the act was planned.

Press publicity was an essential part of the scheme, and it is necessary to appreciate that in the ordinary course press censorship in the United Kingdom imposes a rigorous and complete ban on any press reports on suspected acts of sabotage. On this occasion, a previous approach had been made to the Press Censorship authorities with a view to the ban being advisedly lifted and to provide in addition a previously agreed formula for a hand-out to the press on the subject. At this point it became clear that the press were unlikely to regard an explosion of the relatively small dimensions contemplated as affording a story possessing any particular news value, and the Press Censorship authorities pointed out that any attempt to stimulate their interest in what they would not normally regard as news would only tend to jeopardise the deception.

The following people know the true story: the Regional Commissioner; the Managing Director of the Central Electricity Board; the Area Manager of the Central Electricity Board; the Chief Constable of Bury St Edmunds; all M.I.5. Regional Officers so that they should have suitable stories ready in case they were questioned by local Police Forces; the Minister of Information and Chief Press Officer; one member of the Home Office; and certain persons in M.I.5. Head Office...

RESULT OF PLAN

The incident took place with complete success. The minor difficulties principally consisted in the unobtrusiveness of the unexploded bomb on the Generator which was persistently overlooked by all the local investigators until the Chief Constable had, in fact, led them to the place several times, whilst there was, of course, the difficulty of rendering plausible an explosion in a relatively unimportant part of the building with many vital targets lying open to the saboteur. An explanation for this necessarily had to be that the saboteur lost his nerve after placing the bomb on the Generator and threw away in the process of retreating from the scene the second bomb which he had already initiated, at what he thought was an important piece of machinery.

Statements were taken by the local Police from the persons directly concerned, including the Works Manager who had previously been told in general terms what to expect in the way of interrogation. Photographs of the scene of the explosion and of the unexploded bomb were taken [not included in MUTT or JEFF's file]. Special M.I.5 investigators visited Bury St Edmunds and conducted a normal investigation.

As had been previously indicated by Press Censorship, the press on visiting the scene were disinclined to pay any real attention to the subject, regarding the explosion as trivial and being probably influenced by local gossip which suggested that it had been caused by a gas explosion, this being one of the several entirely inaccurate explanations advanced by a so-called scientific investigator known to the local police. Only after some indirect prompting did any press notices appear, but in the result, they were fairly numerous if not very conspicuous, and they at least provided ample supporting evidence on which the Germans could check up MUTT and JEFF's claim. The security propaganda was largely covered by a letter from M.I.5. to Security Officers at all Electricity Generating Stations of which a copy is attached.

CONCLUSIONS

Although the opportunities for the Germans to check their agents' reports are now more limited than ever, and in no way more efficient, there is a plain advantage in a double agent periodically producing evidence to support his claim.

Although it is better when possible to engineer a relatively conspicuous fire or explosion which the enemy can check by aerial reconnaissance or by visual observation such opportunities are not easy to provide and press evidence with all the difficulties above-mentioned has then to be found as an alternative.

Whereas the security propaganda aspect could be covered by handing out an imaginary incident it will be clear from the forgoing notes on Press Censorship that such a course is fraught with grave danger and is likely to recoil on any subsequent plans of a similar nature.

The issue of deception has to be squarely faced. If, as in this case, the basic intention is to build up a double agent with the Abwehr, then the whole plan is founded in deception, and it should be recognised from the outset that friends, as well as enemies, must be completely deceived. If in the alternative overwhelming importance is attached to running no risk of any possible embarrassment with the Police Force on whose friendly co-operation so much depends, then any such plan requires to be separately contrived for the purposes of security propaganda when a wide circle of persons can be privy to the plan at the inevitable cost of rendering it the more likely to be recognised for what it is.[20]

Reg Stebbings, the manager of the power station, reported that the bomb that exploded had been placed on a condenser which had been out of use for some time. The large unexploded bomb on the generator was so well concealed that locals investigating the explosion, with no knowledge of the stunt, failed to find it. Detective Sergeant Clement Fuller, who attended the scene, reported two Scotland Yard officers appearing but seemed to make no further enquiries. Liddell reported on 7 August that 'Plan BUNBURY went off quite satisfactorily and everything is proceeding as arranged'.[21] The latter comment referred to ensuring that the media included reports of the attack. The Sabotage Section used it to raise awareness with Regional Security Officers, who probably warned 'electricity undertakings' in their part of the country.

At 0328 hours on 7.8.43, an explosion occurred in the premises of a small Electricity Undertaking in the Eastern Counties. Investigation revealed that this explosion took place near some plant which was not in use. Apart from this, an unexploded bomb was discovered attached to the pedestal bearing of the electric generator.

The unexploded bomb was one known as a magnetic clam. It is of British manufacture and has had a wide distribution in the Services. A number of these bombs are known to have fallen into enemy hands, and the one found attached to the generator was of this type. This bomb contains about 8 ozs. of plastic explosive and is usually set off by a chemical delay mechanism [time pencil]. In this case, ordinary safety fuse and a standard detonator were used instead of the delay mechanism and owing to a kink in the safety fuse it failed to burn up to the detonator...

Photographs of a magnetic clam, the chemical delay mechanism and a diagram of the latter are attached to this note. It should be noted that these clams are battleship grey in colour and are therefore difficult to notice when attached to electrical gear, which so often is of the same colour. [One wonders whether generators were repainted following this missive.]

To enquiries received as to whether any special security measures are needed to counter further possible attempts of this nature, the answer is that provided the normal security measures previously recommended by the Security Service are maintained at a reasonable level, no alarm need be felt...

The Security Service has never been in favour of relying too much on Home Guards, Police or other military bodies for maintaining security, and at the present time, when the man power shortage is so acute, this point needs re-emphasis. Physical obstructions which make access difficult, alarm systems, the periodic inspection of vital parts of the Undertaking for the presence of abnormal objects which may be camouflaged or uncamouflaged bombs, and the challenging of strangers are the main requisites for security against sabotage.

The investigation of the spot has so far been inconclusive.[22]

The photographs of the magnetic clam were not included in the file but there was a note from Rothschild with advice on removing them from the target and defusing them. It is possible that special bomb disposal training was provided for regional security officers.

MAGNETIC CLAM (HIGH EXPLOSIVE)

This bomb, known as a magnetic clam, consists of a metal container, approximately hemi-cylindrical in shape, with magnets at each end. It contains 8 ozs. of plastic explosive, and because of the magnets can be stuck against the target to be attacked. Through the aperture in the metal container, which can be seen in the first photograph, a wooden borer is inserted and a hole bored in the plastic explosive. The chemical delay mechanism with detonator attached (also shown in the first photograph), is inserted into the hole of the plastic explosive.[23]

When MUTT supplied the Germans with the details of the partially successful sabotage operation, their propaganda department exaggerated the story. At 2150 on 23 August, the German's Transocean radio circuit broadcast the following message:

When the big East Anglian [illegible] last week over 150 workmen were killed, and more than double that number wounded. Sabotage caused the explosion, and the culprit was caught. His name is (? Peter Blandfield) from North Africa. He had been imprisoned there by the Vichy authorities as a dangerous terrorist. He was released by the Allies when they occupied Oran and became a Free Frenchman.[24]

Guy Liddell had to deal with a number of repercussions from the police and the media.

9 August: Plan BUNBURY is going on, but there has been considerable difficulty about the publicity. The local CC [Chief Constable] is, however, trying to stir up the local press. Burt is on the scene and Victor [Rothschild] is going down tomorrow.

12 August: Rothschild and Burt came to see me about Plan BUNBURY. Burt thinks it desirable to ease up the police a little, who are suspecting the Irish and the Poles. There is great activity in the eastern counties and I understand that guards at utility undertakings have been doubled. The local press have got the story but do not think it worthwhile sending to London, as they feel it would not be passed by censorship. We are doing our best to grease the wheels but cannot do this too obviously.

16 August: So far BUNBURY has only got publicity in the East Anglian Daily Times.

17 August: BUNBURY has now appeared in the [London] Evening Standard in quite a lurid light. Mention was made of investigations by Supt. Burt.

19 August: When visiting SB [Special Branch] Langdon was confronted by Foster, Gill and 4 inspectors with the announcement of Plan BUNBURY. They said, 'Whatever your views about this case, we have come to the conclusion that it is either SOE or Lord Rothschild.' I am afraid Langdon did not put up a very good show. Although he did not commit himself positively, I think he left them with very little doubt about the origin of the outrage. Amongst other things, he is reported to have told them to keep it to themselves, which is of course a complete admission of guilt.

22 August: Peter Hope has got a reaction from the Assistant Superintendent in Newcastle about BUNBURY. He has been told to stick to the line given to him for communication to the CC [Chief Constable].

11 September: Wells has raised the question of putting something in the monthly HO [Home Office] police report on the subject of BUNBURY. He is reluctant to do this because he feels it wrong that the HO should mislead the police in an official document. I pointed out to that that we had faced up to this question long ago and made up our minds that in spite of the difficulties the question of the possible leakage of the truth had to be the first consideration.

22 October Last Sunday's *Sunday Chronicle* has raked up Plan BUNBURY again.[25]

An internal memo sent from B1a to B1c, the Counter Intelligence to the Sabotage Section, provided further insight into the impact of MUTT and JEFF's notional sabotage.

At our recent meeting, Marriott suggested that the dangers of sabotage in the UK were exceedingly low, and that it would almost be improper to try and stimulate security consciousness at factories and Public Utility undertakings through fake acts of sabotage. I have never considered that the faked acts of sabotage carried out for MUTT and JEFF had as a primary objective stimulation of security consciousness. The primary object was the maintenance of the German Secret Service's confidence in MUTT and JEFF. At the same time, BUNBURY had a beneficial result on security. To quote Captain Bennet of D.2: 'The Bury St Edmunds episode was a Godsend to us.'. it is evidently not realised by some members of B.1.A. who have not had experience of what I might call D. Division work, how extremely difficult it is to maintain even the barest minimum of security when nothing ever happens. ... The maintenance of security is rather like the maintenance of a fortune. Either one makes money or one loses money. It is rare that one can keep it without doing something about it.[26]

In MUTT and JEFF's case, it was concluded that 'friends as well as enemies must be completely deceived'.[27]

The deception plans for Norway continued. The initial targets of Narvik or Trondheim were rejected as being too far north and Stavanger was chosen instead. The Germans were told that Norwegian refugees had been questioned about Stavanger, that Royal Marines were receiving mountain training, that Norwegian currency was being stockpiled and that the landing would be on 1 May 1942. During April and May, Hitler diverted troops to Scandinavia, especially to reinforce Stavanger but whether this was a direct consequence of Operation HARD BOILED is unknown.[28]

Between August and November 1943, MUTT and JEFF were also reported to have been involved in Operation TINDALL This was another deception scheme that the British and Americans were going to attack Norway, with the supposed aim of capturing the port and airfield of Stavanger. Its real aim was to divert the Germans' attention away from the Allies' invasion of Italy by keeping the twelve divisions that the Germans had stationed in Norway in place. Messages were sent referring to five divisions camped in Scotland and dozens of gliders arriving at airfields and aerodromes and troop ships amassing in Scottish ports. To add to the deception, dummy airplanes and gliders were placed on airfields and aerodromes near Aberdeen.[29]

Although not mentioned in MUTT's file, Farago claimed that MI5 gave him credit for ordinary industrial, railway, marine and other accidents and drew such considerable quantities of sabotage material and funds that the Abwehr 'did not deem it necessary to send in other saboteurs so long as Klausen and Berg [MUTT and JEFF] appeared to perform satisfactorily'.[30]

By the end of 1943, another parachute drop was arranged. The Germans appeared to still trust MUTT and JEFF as they had agreed to drop more money, another wireless set and more sabotage material. MUTT's pay had been increased to £4 a week by this time as well as being provided with board and lodging and exceptional expenses, like the trip to Scotland to coincide with his and JEFF's Christmas and New Year leave.[31]

On 30 December, Oslo informed MUTT that the drop would be between 23.00 and 00.00 on the night of 2 January 1944. In order to enjoy Scottish traditional entertainment, Paulton accompanied him to Aberdeen where they enjoyed New Year's Eve together, with Harmer joining them on New Year's Day.

Although no reasons were specified beforehand, Harmer was mistrustful of the Germans as he arranged for the waiting personnel to be widely scattered around the drop zone; he was fearful that a bomb or booby trap might be dropped. Given the bombing of Fraserburgh that had taken place after the first drop, two Beaufighters from Longside aerodrome, near Peterhead, controlled the skies at between 2,000 and 3,000 feet, too low to be picked up by enemy radio but high enough and far enough away from MUTT that he would not see or hear them. As few people as possible in the RAF were informed of the nature of the operation and the pilots were sworn to secrecy. Although bad weather had prevented wireless communication on the day, the men were ready and waiting for the drop. Despite a strong westerly wind, visibility was very good but the plane had not arrived by 01.00 so the party left. Harmer was worried the pilot might have spotted the night fighters and had been put off. Wing Commander Ratten reported no signs of enemy planes.

The following day a message was received from Oslo saying that because of bad weather the flight might have to be postponed twenty-four hours but it would be confirmed between 16.00 and 18.00 hours. Radio communication proved impossible at that time but the party went out anyway. Snow showers and strong winds intensified as the night wore on. The two Beaufighters took off but no plane showed up and all the men returned to base.

On 4 January, the Germans sent another message explaining that bad weather had prevented the flight but that it would go ahead at 0100 the next morning with the same confirmation plan. All the men went out, the Beaufighters took off but despite much better weather conditions, there was no plane and the men returned at 0300 hours. Wing Commander Ratten informed Harmer that an enemy plane had approached the area at 1230, half an hour early, did a circle 4 miles off the coast, dived down to tree top level and returned to Norway at maximum speed. Various explanations were put forward as to why the pilot did not make the drop as promised with the RAF deciding that it was the unusual activity of the plane. Another flight was promised on 5 January and, despite there being no afternoon confirmation, the men went out and waited. The Beaufighters went up but the enemy plane did not arrive.

A message was received from the Germans cancelling the flight and promising another on the 6th. Although they were told that MUTT and JEFF's leave had ended on the 4 January, JEFF said that he would stay until the 6th but had to return on the 7th. Despite being told that they would deliver on 7 January, the men went out, the Beaufighters went up – no plane.

Harmer wondered whether the Germans were playing a game with him, whether they suspected MUTT and JEFF of being worked by the British and that they were wanting to irritate MI5. With no proof, he abandoned the plan, thanked the police and the RAF for their help and apologised for wasting their time. Although MUTT was left in Aberdeen under Ingram's supervision to see if he could renew contact with Oslo, Harmer asked the police to report on his movements.[32] MI5 believed that they had been compromised and so their case was closed.

The failed assassination attempt on Hitler in July 1943 led to Canaris's arrest and execution and Lahousen was transferred to the Russian Front. Senior Abwehr officers were not as convinced about MUTT and JEFF's claims of sabotage and espionage success and suspected that they might have been turned. It was argued that the British would never have allowed a bombing raid at the same time as the last drop just to maintain the fiction that the two agents were still active. In early 1944, psychiatrist and Abwehr wireless experts pored over all MUTT and JEFF's messages to check whether they were operating under duress. Trick questions were sent, but the replies convinced them their two Norwegian agents were still in operation.

When the Abwehr was taken over by Gruppenführer Schellenburg's SD in March 1944, Abwehr II's work was absorbed into Otto Skorzeny's Amt VI section, and their officers planned an operation to provide a definitive answer. A Norwegian miner with Nazi sympathies was trained and parachuted near the drop zone used by Jack and O.K. On landing, he was to bury his wireless set and, using the details sent in their messages, track them down without letting them know his real identity and then return to Scotland and transmit his report.

The plan failed when he broke his leg on landing, was arrested by the police and sent for interrogation. Wighton and Peis did not provide his name but stated that Jack and O.K sent a rude and angry message a fortnight later.

What did the Abwehr mean, demanded the two spies in abusive terms [unaware that the Abwehr had been taken over], by dropping another agent in their area without warning them? Did the fools in Berlin not realise that this sort of nonsense might easily have led to their capture by the British secret service? 'If any further operation of this type is attempted,' concluded the two Norwegians, 'we will immediately end our contact with the Abwehr.'[33]

This caused Schellenburg much consternation as it was not thought possible that the British Secret Service would inform Jack and O.K. of another agent's arrival. They presumed that they must have picked up the information from visiting the pubs near the drop zone. They were also convinced that the British would never have allowed them to send such an abusive message.

After numerous redacted pages in MUTT's file, the next reported in April 1944 that he had joined the army with a rank of Lance Corporal and, for cover purposes, he was to state that he served in a civilian capacity. Before he left MI5, they produced the following document for him to sign:

> I, Helge John Neal MOE, fully recognise that the activities in which I was engaged between April 1941 and January 1944 in co-operation with and under the instruction of Captain Harmer of the War Office were activities in regard to which the national interest imperatively requires complete discretion; that these activities, and all communications between Captain Harmer and me in regard to them, are covered by the Official Secrets Acts; and that any unauthorised disclosure on my part of any matter relating to them would constitute an offence under those Acts punishable by a term of imprisonment.
>
> I also recognise that information relating to these transactions would be of assistance to the enemy and that on this ground it would also be an offence under the Defence Regulations for me to make any disclosure of them.
>
> I solemnly undertake upon my honour to preserve complete discretion now and in the future in regard to the whole of these matters. Jack Moe.[34]

It appeared that Moe struggled with army life as, following discussions with Major Luke of B.1.A., the Medical Officer and the Company Commander and Colonel, he was released on the grounds of ill-health due to nervousness and stress. In August 1944, he was given £100 final payment, £20 army wages and a £30 contribution towards a return passage to Norway. A confidential summary did not mention the sabotage deception schemes:

> ... three parachute droppings organised by the enemy in order to provide MOE with sabotage material, radio equipment and money took place. Furthermore, he aided the British Intelligence Service in simulating messages from his companion who had had to be detained for conduct hostile to the Allied cause before he met MOE, and MOE's co-operation was generally indispensable to the whole operation. By his initiative and determination MOE succeeded in deceiving the enemy Intelligence Service, in presenting valuable information to the British authorities, and in providing a channel of important counter-espionage of deception value to the Allied Cause.[35]

MI5 continued transmitting messages about Allied troop movements to the Germans until early 1945, and it was not until several years after the war during a Norwegian Criminal Commission hearing in Norway that ex-Abwehr officials were questioned about Jack and O.K. that they realised that their suspicions about them were right all along.

MUTT settled in Oslo after the war, worked for the Texas Company, got married and had the remainder of his property returned. JEFF was released in June 1945 after four years' imprisonment and deported to Norway where he worked as a commercial representative but found himself accused of being a

German agent. He was arrested and spent a further seven months awaiting trial for espionage before his case was dismissed.[36]

There was a memo in the Sabotage Section file showing MI5's love of codes and symbols. ZIGZAG was given the letter A, MUTT and JEFF B, SNOW C, SUNDAE D, COCK E, SYRIAN XX F, ONIONS G, TACOMA STAR H, IMBER I, WROTHAM J and OLTERRA K. The others, details of which were not revealed in the file, were captured saboteurs who had been operating in Spain and Gibraltar.

By mid-1943, MUTT and JEFF had become the most important players in Britain's counter-sabotage section. They ensured the British received up-to-date sabotage equipment and money to fund their continued double-cross operation. There was the hope that they could encourage the Germans to send in more saboteurs whose arrival, capture and interrogation MI5 would manage. While there was intelligence obtained from the Most Secret sources and the XX network operating in Gibraltar, the eight recently captured saboteurs in the United States would help provide more.

An anonymous note in MUTT's file, probably Rothschild's, indicates that the author had been sent to Washington with the intention of obtaining that intelligence by using the previously mentioned questionnaire:

> Counter-sabotage differs slightly from counter-espionage in that information that we collect centrally in London is of considerable importance to other parts of the Empire and Allied territory. I will give two examples. We prepared a questionnaire for ABT.II agents which has had a certain distribution abroad. When I was in Cairo, I found that ABT.II agents were being interrogated almost exclusively on this questionnaire (copy attached). The local interrogating officers had absolutely no knowledge of the subject and without the questionnaire, as they were before I pointed out that it was already in the office, were completely impotent. Secondly, I think some of the information I took to the United States was of value to the F.B.I. in their interrogation of the eight saboteurs who landed there. Both the ABT. II questionnaire and the information I took to the United States contained material derived from the MUTT and JEFF case.[37]

Although MUTT and JEFF were unable to provide information on Abwehr II's headquarters, their training schools or their techniques, they helped with the identification of sabotage targets in Britain. As regards to equipment, an anonymous source, again possibly Rothschild, acknowledged they had been

> of constant value to the counter-sabotage section since the time when they arrived with camouflaged sabotage equipment and instructions for making of bombs from homemade chemicals, up to the present time when they are supplied with S.O.E. equipment, sometimes of a very specialised nature.
>
> It is not perhaps appreciated by some officers in B.1.A. how important it is for D.S.Os [District Security Officers] and other persons concerned with security to have up to date information as to what types of bombs the enemy are using, and what they look like. A significant amount of the information we have circulated to various parts of the world has been derived from B.1.A. XX

agents, and from letters received I am satisfied that our communications on the subject of counter-sabotage are appreciated and useful.

The identification of equipment used by the German Secret Service can also be of value to S.O.E. in determining which of their undertakings are compromised. This is a point which is at present under active discussion ...

I have dilated at some length on the subject of security as, with the exception of Colonel Robertson, I have no reason to believe that anyone in B.1.A. has had experience of the subject. It may, therefore, have been useful to indicate certain elementary principles.

A further point by Marriott at our meeting, and one which is painfully familiar to many sections in this office is the one concerning prophecies about the future based on experiences in the past. No enemy sabotage has occurred in England. Therefore, none will happen in the future. The first part of this proposition is true, but I wonder how many people would be prepared to dogmatise as to how little damage ZIGZAG [referred to later] could have done had he been so disposed. The second part of the proposition, even accepting the first (and ignoring the fact that enemy saboteurs have arrived, but have been caught), is not one which appeals to me at a moment when the whole trend of the war is changing, when the Luftwaffe is heavily engaged on many fronts and therefore less able to do industrial damage from the air, and when reorganisation of the German Secret Service appears to be in the air. Nor am I prepared to agree that all attacks in future will be of a para-military rather than a Secret Service type. There is no evidence in support of this contention.

Perhaps MUTT and JEFF have contributed to a greater extent than some people imagine in maintaining immunity from sabotage in the U.K. The German Secret Service is easily satisfied, and it appears that it is easily duped.

At the same time, I do not think the risk of enemy sabotage is great in the U.K., and I do not consider that security needs improvement. What it does need is maintenance at its present level (with certain technical modifications to meet the shortage of manpower), and as mentioned above, it cannot be maintained at its present level without occasional positive efforts.

When considering the possibilities of sabotage, it is as well to remember that information certainly exists in Germany which would permit of crippling attacks on our war potential. The fact that this information has not been used or even coordinated by the German Secret Service so far is fortunate, though it does not mean that use will not be made of it in the future.

The practical difficulties encountered during BUNBURY, and the views expressed by Director B and the Director General after its successful termination, make it quite clear that even to consider the possibility of further fake acts of sabotage would be a waste of time, unless they were carried out on purely military property or at sea. At the same time, the possibility of completely notional sabotage need not be overlooked.

From the Counter-Sabotage Section's point of view, it is not possible to consider MUTT and JEFF from the purely parochial U.K. angle. Although it may not be considered necessary to keep Allied countries and the British Empire fully informed about enemy espionage activities, this view is not held by the Counter-Sabotage Section in regard to sabotage, and we consider it one of our more important responsibilities to keep such places as Persia, Iraq, the Middle East, Gibraltar and Canada fully informed about enemy sabotage activities. The German instructions for attacking Diesel electric plants, provoked by false MUTT and JEFF information in the U.K. about the existence of such plants, will in the near future be the subject of a special recommendation to the Admiralty Dockyard at Gibraltar, which is served by a large Diesel electric station. The dangers of sabotage at the instigation of the German Secret Service are very great there owing to the number of Spanish workmen working within the Dockyard.

There are two special aspects of enemy sabotage equipment which are of immediate interest to this Section. First, because the armistice with Italy may make the Italians stop sabotaging our merchant ships in Turkey, Spain and Portugal, we are most anxious to know what techniques the Germans will use to continue this work, and I was intending to discuss with Harmer the possibility of MUTT and JEFF telling the Germans that they had an opportunity of sabotaging a British ship in dry dock, and asking for special equipment for this operation. Secondly, S.O.E. have recently sent some very special equipment to Norway. It is most important for us to know at the earliest opportunity if this equipment is compromised. MUTT and JEFF would seem to be the most likely source of information in that some of this equipment may be sent back to them if the sabotage angle of their case continues.

Finally, I should like to re-emphasise the dump concept mentioned by Harmer at our last meeting. If we could establish a dump [of explosives and sabotage equipment] in the north of Scotland from which MUTT and JEFF or other saboteurs coming to this country could draw, we should at least have some insurance against the possibility of further saboteurs arriving, perhaps even without the knowledge of MUTT and JEFF. Further, the accumulation of large stores of sabotage equipment would give us a greater insight into German sabotage weapons and the degree to which S.O.E. operations are compromised.[38]

In the 1990s there was an online Civil Defence report of a sabotage attack on English Electric's aircraft factory in Preston, Lancashire, undertaken by a team of Brandenburgers in 1943. The police and Home Guard's files were reported to have been removed. Enquiries with English Electric, Preston Historical Society and the Lancashire Archives have failed to reveal any details. While it could have happened and MI5 ensured that there was no media coverage that the Abwehr could pick up, there is also the possibility that it was another fake sabotage attack attributed to one of the captured agents. While MUTT and JEFF's files have many redacted pages which could have indicated their involvement, they were not trained at Brandenburg.[39]

17

Agent ZIGZAG and Operation THOMAS – December 1942–March 1943

The story of Agent ZIGZAG has been covered in several autobiographies, Wighton and Peis' work, the film *Triple Cross*, a French TV interview, Masterman's account of the double cross, a Channel 4 interview, Nicholas Booth's and Ben Macintyre's biographies and a BBC2 documentary based on the latter's best seller. However, while this account acknowledges this earlier research, it is largely based on the details of his involvement in sabotage that were found in his personnel file.

Eddie Chapman was born in Burnopfield, County Durham, on 16 November 1914, the son of a marine engineer. Largely left to himself as a child, he often got into trouble but left school and joined the Second Battalion of the Coldstream Guards. This included guarding the Tower of London. He got bored with his duties and after nine months' service he ran off with a girl he met in Soho. When he was caught, the military imprisoned him in the 'Glasshouse' in Aldershot for eighty-four days.

Dishonourably discharged, he settled in London and turned to petty crime, fraud and theft to fund his gambling debts and taste for women and fine alcohol. Hoare claimed that Chapman had been caught exposing himself in Hyde Park. He attracted women on the fringes of London society, indulged in violent affairs and had compromising photographs taken of them by a friend, which he used for blackmail.

After two months' imprisonment in Wormwood Scrubs for forgery, he joined the 'Jelly Gang', burgling properties and using gelignite to blow open safes taken from Odeon cinemas, Co-operative Wholesale stores and United Dairies. His luck failed on a trip to Edinburgh in 1938 when he was arrested, but he jumped bail and fled to Jersey. Followed by the police, he was arrested and sentenced to two years in prison. After escaping twice and being recaptured, his sentence was increased to three years, and he was in prison when the Germans occupied the Channel Islands in July 1940.

When he was released in September 1941, in the hope that he might be sent to England and escape, he and a friend, Anthony Faramus, offered to work for the Germans. To make their departure from Jersey appear realistic, Ast Paris arranged for them to be arrested by the Gestapo on a charge of sabotage and deported to Fort Romanville, a prison camp in La Bourget, a north-eastern suburb of Paris. They were the only Englishmen there; the others were people charged with espionage or sabotage against the Wehrmacht.

Frank Owen, the London-based correspondent for *Time* magazine, liaised with Chapman after the war to write his autobiography, in which Chapman described an early interrogation:

> In February 1942, I was again summoned to the commandant's office. This time, I met an attractive German-American woman accompanied by a young man. She was a brunette, with large brown eyes, a rosebud mouth, and well-manicured hands. Her clothes must have come from Schiaparelli or Molyneux. Obviously, she was the man's superior, for he treated her with deference. She asked all the questions. Her American accent was authentic, and she might have stepped down from a movie screen.
>
> What work did I think I could do in England? Was I prepared to carry out sabotage? Was it for money or hatred of the British that I wanted to work against them? I told her that I was only interested in money and that I disliked the British, chiefly for their prisons and their police. I explained, as I had done before, that I was wanted by them on several criminal charges, and that if they ever caught up with me, I would receive at least fifteen years. This seemed to satisfy her and her companion, and they left saying I would hear from them again.[2]

According to Crowdy, in April 1942, Chapman was sent to join the Baustelle Kersting, one of the Abwehr's most important sabotage training centres in Europe. Crowdy located the school at La Bretonnière-la-Claye, a chateau in St Joseph-sur-Loire, about 55 miles south of Nantes.[3] Most sources locate it at Chateau de la Bretonnière, Vigneux-de-Bretagne, about 12 miles north-west of Nantes. Officially it was a military engineering unit repairing roads and buildings in occupied France.

Under the control of 44-year-old Baron Rittmeister Stefan von Gröning, sometimes spelt von Grunen (who Chapman knew as Herr Graumann), Chapman lived a life of luxury in the gardener's cottage on a salary of 6,000 francs a month. In those days, he reported being able to buy butter at 90 francs a kilo, eggs at 24 francs a dozen and meat at 40 francs a kilo. As all the residents had noms de guerre, he was known as Fritz Graumann.

His sabotage instructor, 28-year-old Oberleutenant Herbert Vosch, had the task of converting him from a safe blower to a saboteur. Most secret sources identified Vosch's real name as Horst Barton and had him using the aliases Karl Barton, Hermann Vosch, Hermann Wojch, Herbert Wojch, Herbert Vosh, and Anton. Lessons were held in a room on the ground floor of the chateau specially transformed into a laboratory stocked with exotic compounds.

> Around the walls stood various chemicals in sealed glass bottles and on the small marble tables were scales with bowls for pulverising crystals into powder. ... My training consisted in making homemade explosives by mixing simple chemicals, chemicals which could be bought in any chemist's shop. For

some weeks I practised every day with him, making thermites and dynamites from simple ingredients. For example, potassium chlorate or nitrate mixed with sugar makes both a dynamite and a burning substance capable of giving off some 3,000 degrees of heat; potassium chlorate with oil makes dynamite. Many more such formulas were taught me. All of these I had to memorise; nothing could be put down in writing.

Another point which Vosch insisted was that I must on no account divulge any of these formulae to other persons in the Dienststelle. The number of people allowed to know such facts was limited, and each was sworn to secrecy.

An ordinary wristwatch was shown to me. Two wires were attached to it in such a way that when the hands turned they made contact with the wires. These wires were attached to a flashlight battery, from there to some burning mixture which contained a detonator and some gelignite. With this ingenious gadget, one could make a timed explosion for any period up to twelve hours. If a longer period was required, a seven or fourteen-day alarm clock was used. The wires were arranged so that when the spring expanded it made contact with them, and the same result was obtained.

I was taught how to wreck a train, and how to place a contact on the rails so that when the wheels passed over it the charge exploded. The contacts were cleverly camouflaged. Anyone inspecting the rails would pass on, unsuspecting.

For sabotaging a ship, a piece of coal was drilled and the hole filled with dynamite. This was then placed in the bunkers. Naturally, when the coal was shovelled into the furnace, the resulting explosion would wreck the boilers.[4]

Chapman's practice wireless transmissions were intercepted by listeners at Hanslope Park, a 'Y' Station in Buckinghamshire and passed to Bletchley Park. MI5 built up a file on Vosch which contains a list of the intercepted messages staff at Bletchley had decoded relating to him and Chapman in Nantes between the period 1 January and 12 August 1942. Vosch's real name was Karl Barton. Headed 'TOP SECRET U', the file revealed Barton had been congratulated by Abt II on being awarded the *Kriegsverdienstkreuz*, War Medal Cross. On 12 June, he sent the following message to Paris: 'All happenings such as attempted assassinations and acts of sabotage to be reported to Baustelle at this end without delay. Baustelle promises to support SO with its advice in the case of acts of sabotage.' The first reference to Chapman, termed FRITZCHEN, was on 18 June when Barton asked Paris 'For FRITZCHEN's training fifteen detonators and a few fuses (Gluehzuender) required. On 7 July, he wrote: 'In order to be able to discuss objectives (Ziele) with FRITZCHEN at the appointed time it is requested that a travel guide to London district be procured, in which connection it is considered probable that a guide could be found in one of the second-hand book stalls on the Seine.' The following day he reported 'Beginning of morning gymnastics, running, forward and backward rolls, swimming. Morning: Attention to FRITZCHEN's teeth. Regular agent (V-Mann) visits. Visit to Rittmeister von Groening in military hospital. Afternoon: intensive W/T training of FRITZCHEN.' On the 9 July, he had tuition in a new wireless cipher and physical training with special attention to rolling on the ground and on

17 July his sabotage and W/T training were 'recapitulated'. He had 'trial traffic'; he practised W/T traffic to Paris and Gefr. KERST brought an English W/T set for him from Angers. On 12 August, Barton had a 'discussion with V. COUSIN about suitable Breton agents for II in the event of further English landings. (16 letters corrupt). Gruppe ZAT (=II) NANTES requests permission to train V. COUSIN, who already has a knowledge of morse, in W/T technique and to make him familiar with the preparation of incendiary and explosive material. Further agents ready for employment will be reported shortly to AST Paris via Baustelle KERSTING'.[5] Chapman's messages always ended HE HO HU HA.

The seclusion of the chateau's grounds made it ideal for blowing things up.

'The garden was quite large and when we were going to do anything we simply went out and told the gardener to work at the other end of the garden' ... The Boys would sometimes cut down trees so that he could blow their stumps out of the ground. On one occasion, he mixed the wrong proportions and blew a trunk fifty metres into the air. 'There was a terrific row', Eddie recalled, because it nearly killed a man in a neighbouring property. We went and explained to the people in the neighbourhood that we were exploding land mines.[6]

As well as sabotage, Chapman admitted being taught wireless telegraphy, codes, secret writing and espionage skills.[7]

In July 1942, he was sent to a house outside Berlin where 65-year-old Professor Karl tested him on what he had learned about the manufacture and use of explosives. His sketch-map of the house and grounds is included in his personnel file. He was also shown other ways of making dynamite and fuses.

I made time explosives for his benefit with both fire and explosion, started fires with nothing but acid and a watch, prepared explosive coal for use in ships, and made many other small demonstrations ...

In August, a Panzer colonel came to visit von Grunen. During the meal, von Grunen asked the Oberst if he would like to see a homemade explosion, and if so, would he set a time for it. The Oberst looked at his watch and said he would like one for nine o'clock; it was then seven. We all set our watches by his, and I went out to make preparations.

Now, it is a difficult job to time an explosion to within a minute. I took some care, and placed my explosive charge under a tree, as near dead set to my watch as was possible. At five minutes to nine, we were sitting in von Grunen's study having drinks. Four minutes, three minutes to go – we were all examining our watches. Just as the Oberst said, 'Well, it's nine o'clock now,' there was a colossal explosion. I had used about ten pounds of dynamite. The tree was practically uprooted, and some windows in the chateau were blown in ... my reputation was enhanced accordingly with certain members of the German General Staff when the Oberst told his story.[8]

According to Booth, under Vosch's tutelage, Chapman was taught how to make home-made explosives using materials that could easily be obtained from chemist's shops.

Wojch showed him the best place to destroy a bridge, taking him around local railways to get a better insight. He was taught how to set explosives to wreck trains by putting charges on rail lines and how to hide wiring. For the destruction of a ship, he was shown how to hide devices in attaché cases. He learned how to pack clothes to muffle an alarm clock inside a suitcase, as well as how to make a coal bomb.[9]

His mission was to return to England with a wireless set and report back on weather conditions, the names, descriptions and location of American cars, the location of large numbers of British officers, direction of troop movements by train and the contents and destination of train trucks.

> By way of sabotage, I was given one thing to do, namely de Havilland's machine room at Hatfield where Mosquito bombers are manufactured. I was shown excellent photographs taken from the air of these works, showing the mounting hall, the machine room and the wood store. I was to blow up the machine room and if not possible, the wood store. This was to be done within the next two or three months.[10]

Chapman gave more detail in Owen's biography.

> These photographs were very good, and pencilled over the different buildings was a description of the type of work carried on in each. The various machine shops, mounting hall, offices, testing rooms and timber stores were all clearly marked. Then followed a larger photograph of the outlying district showing the approaches to Hatfield. There were views from various heights and angles. As I have said, it was suggested that I should try to blow up the boiler house, and if not, the electric powerhouse. As an alternative, I could set the timber stores on fire.[11]

If this sabotage was successful, he was promised 100,000 Reichmarks. Of all the possible sabotage targets in Britain, the reason de Havilland's factory was chosen was, according to Macintyre, because Reichsmarschall Hermann Göring, the head of the Luftwaffe, was

> ...particularly infuriated by the persistent little Mosquitoes, the mere mention of the plane could send him into a rage. 'It makes me furious when I see the Mosquito. I turn green and yellow with envy. The British, who can afford aluminium better than we can, knock together a beautiful wooden aircraft that every piano factory over there is building, and they give it a speed that they have now increased yet again. What do you make of that? There is nothing the British do not have. They have the geniuses and we have the nincompoops. After the war, I'm going to buy a British radio set – then at least I'll own something that has always worked.' [...]
> The de Havilland Mosquito – or Anopheles de Havilandus as military wags used to call it – had proved a lethal nuisance to the Nazis ever since it went into production in 1940. Indeed, its effect on the German High Command was positively malarial.[12]

Before he left Nantes, von Grunen told Chapman about the eight German saboteurs that had been caught in the United States. There had been a lot of coverage in the world press and Chapman acknowledged that they had gone through the same extensive training as him and that several members of his dienststelle knew them well. Before they left Paris, apparently one had talked to one of the women at a party held for them. Von Grunen must have disconcerted Chapman by telling him that they had been caught within only a few hours of landing, tried, sentenced to death and some were shot.[13]

The delay in sending Chapman was partly due to the Allied invasion of North Africa and the German's retaliation of taking over the unoccupied zone of France. Von Grunen and his dienststelle had been required in the operation.

Despite getting to know a number of Germans very well, Chapman decided that he would hand himself over to the British authorities as soon as he landed. He reckoned that the details he had written secretly into a notebook, an account of what he had learned about the Abwehr and his training, might guarantee him his freedom from fifteen years in prison. He was ready to double cross the Abwehr.

Eventually, on Monday evening, 14 December 1942, after von Grunen gave Chapman his final briefing with Oberleutenant Walter Thomas, the cover name of Dr Praetorius, at the Grand Hotel in Paris, he was told that he would be strip searched. Excusing himself to go to the toilet, he managed to tear the pages of his notebook into shreds and flush them down the toilet. Once the strip search was done, he was dressed in British clothes taken from captured soldiers.

The following day, he was given a wireless receiver and transmitter, two Bakelite boxes containing detonators, a tin containing 24 electric detonators and 34 rounds of automatic pistol ammunition, a .32 Colt automatic with two loaded magazines and one round in the breach, 4 packets of chocolate, 8 packets of grape sugar, 2 shirts and a handkerchief, toilet articles, a spade in a canvas bag, a torch, a wristwatch, a pocket compass, a box of matches with two specially prepared matches for invisible writing, an Irish Free State Travel Permit in the name of Morgan O'Bryan, a National Registration Identity Card in the name of George Clarke and a brown poison tablet.

He was then driven to Le Bourget airfield, near Paris, prepared for the flight and flown in a Junkers II over the Channel. At about 0230 on 16 December, he parachuted into a field near Littleport, about 6 miles north of Ely in the Cambridgeshire fens.[14]

Through Most Secret Sources, it was suspected from the message that Fritzchen was 'going on holiday' that he was about to be dropped but they had no indication where. Operation NIGHTCAP, the plan to collect him, involved asking Fighter Command to ensure that the likely aircraft was not shot down. The Regional Security Liaison Officers and police forces around the country were informed and a team of bloodhounds was on hand to hunt him down.[15] Lidell's diary for 1 October reads:

We had a meeting to discuss the arrangements for FRITZCHEN's arrival. Stanford is going to be at Fighter Command headquarters to watch the tracks for any suspicious planes coming in. The Regional Security Liaison Officers have been given full particulars and will mobilise the chief constables and a few selected Special Branch officers under the direction of Len Burt and his subordinates.

Camp 020 is in the picture and will be given a brief for interrogation. I saw Sir Alexander Maxwell [under-secretary to the Home Office] this afternoon about the case. It was decided that FRITZCHEN should go to Camp 020 and that he be detained in the first instance under the Arrival from Enemy Territory Act. It seemed unlikely that circumstances could arise which would necessitate his being brought before the Advisory Committee but if we were faced with such an eventuality the Home Office will do everything in their power to safeguard our interests. We propose to turn FRITZCHEN round immediately if his case has not caused too much publicity. We know a good deal about him already. He is probably an Englishman called Eddie Chapman. He has an identity card and a card permitting him as an Irishman to work in this country. He has had a large sum of money spent on his teeth. He is six feet tall and has been carefully trained in wireless, secret ink, sabotage and parachute jumping. He will be wearing a special kind of kit, details of which are known and will be dropped somewhere in the vicinity of London between now and 9 October.[16]

In Masterman's *The Double Cross System*, he also admitted knowing about Chapman.

Details of his training had been discovered from secret sources. We even knew that he could be identified by certain false teeth, because his departure from France had been postponed as the result of an accident during his parachute training, and the dental repairs had found their place in secret sources. We knew indeed a great deal about him; we knew that he would be in possession of two identity cards; we knew the details of his equipment, and we knew that an act of sabotage would be his primary assignment. What we did not know was whether he was really on our side or on that of the Germans.[17]

Chapman wore British-issue army landing boots for his parachute jump and carried a wallet in his pocket taken from a British soldier who had been killed at Dieppe four months earlier. He had two fake identity cards,

...and a letter from his girlfriend Betty, which is genuine. His pack contains matches impregnated with quinine for 'secret writing', a wireless receiver, a military map, £900 in used notes of various denominations, a Colt revolver, an entrenching tool [to bury his parachute] and some plain-glass spectacles for disguise. Four of his teeth are made from new gold, paid for by Hitler's Third Reich. Beneath his flying overalls he wears a civilian suit that was once of fashionable cut but is now somewhat worn. In the turn-up of his right trouser leg has been sewn a small cellophane package containing a single suicide pill of potassium cyanide.[18]

Masterman only mentioned that he was dropped by parachute near Ely, bringing with him an intelligence questionnaire and a wireless set. According to Farago, he landed at 2 a.m. on 20 December near Wisbech, Cambridgeshire, carrying his sabotage formulae, wireless code and cover address in his head, his Afu wireless set and £7,000 in a waterproof bag.[19]

Using the 'entrenching tool' to bury his parachute, he carried the wireless set to the nearest farmhouse, claiming to be a downed British pilot. The police were called, and he was duly interrogated, arrested, strip-searched and taken in a Black Maria to Camp 020. Having been issued with prison clothing, had his photograph taken and been given a medical examination, he was interviewed by Stephens, who was so convinced by his story that by 2.30 pm the following day he recommended to TAR that he should be used as a double agent.

Two days after arriving, Chapman signed a statement acknowledging his criminal past and giving a detailed account of his imprisonment in Jersey, training in France and Germany, everything he knew about his Abwehr contacts, how he was to contact them and details of his mission, all of which confirmed what was known from Most Secret Sources. He even wrote a letter to Stephens offering to be used as a double agent:

I started this affair and I will finish it. Many things can be done in France – sabotage etc. – reports of movements of troops – a trip to all Germany's principal towns is to be organised for me – I need training quickly – 'only in what you want to know'. I can arrange radio transmission for you. If you like an agent can come safely along with me, only you must have confidence in me – allow me to arrange things – otherwise the whole thing is going to be spoilt – Do not bring or arrest any of the two agents, who I have mentioned yet – The whole game can be done in one blow – How I can tell you – Don't think I ask anything for this. I don't – you have a thousand pounds enough to finance my mission to France. If any more is needed the German Government will supply it – It seems very strange the working of two different governments – one offers me the chance of money success and a career – The other a prison cell – There is not a great deal of time left to arrange things – Two months – Three months – A prison cell naturally breeds confidence – Am I misquoting – when I say a prison cell like poisoned weeds – Breeds darkness and despair.
To conclude speed is a very early need.
Votre serviteur,
(signed Eddie Chapman)[20]

Four Camp 020 officers wrote a letter in support of Chapman's offer. Masterman agreed, impressed with the 'apparent candour and completeness' of his story. TAR was persuaded and gave him the code-name ZIGZAG. Ronnie Reed was appointed as his case officer and Lance Corporal Allan Tooth and Sergeant Paul Backwell as his 'minders'. Until MUTT could be found alternative accommodation, he was put up in a room in a nearby riding club from where he could broadcast his first message. The Abwehr celebrated his safe arrival and, when he received their first message, B.1.a celebrated their latest double agent.

Masterman was convinced by Chapman's behaviour and demeanour that he was on the British side.

ZIGZAG's case was of absorbing interest for a variety of reasons. He had been most carefully trained even to the point of having to practice in being dropped by parachute. He had worked for a long period in the Nantes Stelle and had, therefore, a fund of information about enemy radio transmissions. The tasks set him were first and foremost to sabotage the de Havilland works at Hatfield where Mosquito light bombers were made. On this the Germans placed the greatest importance. In addition, he was to send daily weather reports, particulars of the movement of American troops, and information about American divisional signs and shipbuilding. He was also to report on internal transport in this country. For all these purposes, he had been supplied with £1,000 and explosives materials. What made his case particularly interesting was that his work was to be completed in a few weeks, and he was then to return either by shipping as a seaman to Portugal, or by way of Ireland, or by means of a submarine which was to be sent for him. He was promised £15,000 for the de Havilland sabotage and was told if he brought it off and returned, the Germans would probably send him to control a special sabotage undertaking in the United States.

The case, therefore, presented new features and new problems. If full advantage was to be taken of it, ZIGZAG would have (apparently at least) to carry out this act of sabotage, and also to return to the Germans. If he did this he might be able to communicate with us from Nantes, and we might also control and prevent extensive sabotage by German agents in America; but it was essential, if he were to return, that he should not know or guess the knowledge which we had through secret sources. The possibility had at all times to be considered that he might, on return to enemy territory, be persuaded or forced to reveal his association with British intelligence. Speed was also a necessity. Dr Graumann [von Grunen] who was ZIGZAG's spy master, had shrewdly but perhaps unwisely told him that if he fell into British hands, and the British tried to use him, it would take a long time, for the Germans could rely on 'red tape to stop the ball rolling.' Consequently, a quick decision had to be made, and ZIGZAG was put on the air at once.[21]

The explosive devices Chapman brought with him were handed over to Rothschild whose counter-sabotage section produced a portfolio of photographs of captured sabotage equipment. Those attributed to Chapman included a booby-trapped attaché case, a bomb disguised as a piece of coal, an X-ray photograph of a bomb disguised as coal and a photograph of a piece of coal he had prepared.[22]

The £1,000 given to him by the Abwehr, as with all other money confiscated from agents, was was deposited in a special bank account and used by MI5 to support the agents' new lifestyles. Once MUTT and JEFF had been moved out, Chapman, Reed and his two 'minders' moved into 35 Crespigny Road. Various social events were organised. Owens mentions him buying himself some excellent quality new clothes, going out regularly to the theatre, cinemas and restaurants, even to a Christmas pantomime.[23]

In Backwell and Tooth's first report, they acknowledged that they were dealing with a 'peculiar fellow. He appeared quite happy and was a mine of information, sometimes reading classical literature, often quoting Tennyson or holding forth on the various methods of destroying pylons, bridges and petrol tanks.'[24]

Over the next fortnight, the wireless set was used to establish a link with the Abwehr in France. His first message was 'I landed 2 miles north of LITTLEPORT near ELY. Then took train to LONDON. Buried gear, contacted friends. F.' Regular reports on bomb damage were sent. The conversations led the Germans to believe that he had met up with an old friend, found accommodation and was planning the attack on de Havilland's. To make the content of his messages more authentic, he was provided with a detailed cover story, one that he had to memorise as it would be tested by Reed and Tooth and MI5 officers simulating an Abwehr or Gestapo interrogation. Should he return to France, he would be debriefed in the same way British agents were on returning from 'the field'.

Reed generated the story Chapman would use if he was forced to admit he had been working with MI5. He was told to say that they had his wife in custody and would shoot her if he didn't comply with their instructions. This story covered the period from his landing in a field near Littleport to his departure for Lisbon in March 1943. Based largely on the truth, except for his arrest, interrogation and sabotage, extracts from it shed light on his visit.

After arriving by train at Euston, he arranged to meet up with Jimmy Hunt, one of his criminal acquaintances in London. In his biography, Chapman mentioned he was to offer £5,000 to his 'very old buddie, Freddie, if he would help me. Any other person who did the same was to be suitably rewarded. If any of these people decided to return with me to Germany, then German nationality and protection were promised them.'[25] It seems likely that using 'Freddie' in the book was to protect his friend's identity.

Not wanting to be spotted by the police, he rendezvoused with Hunt in a flat on Sackville Street where, omitting to mention his stay in France,

I told him that when I was imprisoned in Jersey, I had decided to work for the German Intelligence; that they treated me extremely well and had promised me a considerable amount of money if I would carry out a mission in this country. I had brought £1,000 with me and had been promised another £15,000 if I succeeded in sabotaging DE HAVILLANDS. It was an invaluable opportunity for Jimmy to obtain quite a lot of money and the protection of the German Government to get him out of the country. I showed him the radio transmitter which I had brought with me and said I required some place where I could work this. Jimmy told me that he had been considering renting a house in Hendon from someone called Lockington at 24 Beaufort Gardens, and that while he had not yet agreed to do this it was possible for him to expedite the transaction and to move in at the weekend. Meanwhile, however, it would be advisable for me to stay at the flat in Sackville Street and keep pretty quiet.[26]

The story he told the Germans was that he moved to a house in Hendon and set up his wireless set using the aerial they had provided. Hunt lived at 39 St Luke's Mews in North Kennington where he was supposed to run an engineering business, but this was where the safes they had stolen from the United Dairies and Co-operative Wholesale stores had been taken to be blown open.

After explaining that he needed to buy the appropriate ingredients for his sabotage, Hunt agreed to purchase what was needed from nearby chemists and give him the remaining gelignite he had from before the war. Chapman did not consider this to be enough so, according to his file, they decided 'to break into a quarry at Sevenoaks which we knew had a good stock of this sort of thing'.[27] According to Owen's biography,

> A few nights later we went down to Sevenoaks and forced open the magazine of this quarry. There were several hundred sticks of gelignite and a couple of hundred detonators. Freddie had a car and seemed to experience no difficulty in getting fake petrol coupons. On our return to London, we bought two suitcases and fixed up thirty pounds of gelignite in each, making use of a wrist watch and batteries for the time explosion. Freddie watched this with some anxiety when I explained the finesse required and told him that if one mistake was made the whole joint would be blown sky high.[28]

To create a more realistic story, in early January, Backwell took Chapman to local chemists to buy explosive materials, and they practised making small-scale explosives and burning mixtures, and using time bomb mechanisms in the house. Reed was subsequently asked to provide a list of their purchases and the addresses of the chemists they had visited.

> The reason for this is that we have an arrangement by which all chemists in the UK are supposed to report any abnormal purchases to us via the Home Office, and we are anxious to see whether ZIGZAG's particularly abnormal purchases, including as they did a request for something by its German name, occasioned the slightest interest.'[29]

One would assume that when Reed reported to Rothschild that Chapman had bought potassium permanganate and saltpetre from Boots the Chemists in Harrow, moth balls from an ironmonger's in Golders Green and kalium [potassium] from a chemist in Hendon, officaldom banged on the doors of the owners, reminding them of the government's requirement to report any such purchases.

Rothschild met Chapman twice using the name of Mr Fisher. They 'talked for hours, and got on famously, the crook and the peer, two men with nothing in common save a shared interest in loud bangs.'[30] They discussed booby traps and incendiary devices, coal bombs, train bombs and various ways to scuttle a ship. Chapman detailed the German techniques for making fuses out of wristwatches, ink bottles, and electric bulb filaments. He showed Rothschild how to conceal a rail bomb with a butterfly, how to hide dynamite in blocks of marzipan, and how to make a detonator from a patented stomach medicine called Urotropin. The transcript of Rothschild's conversation with him about his sabotage training at La Bretonnière was found in Vosch's file.[31] When they met the day before the attack on de Havillands, they discussed a plan to further convince the Germans of his credentials, the placing of exploding coal in the ship he would travel on to Lisbon.

Reed queried with Lt Cholmondley why the photographs of de Havilland's works as Chapman had reported them were quite different from the ones he was shown before he came to England.

The four large huts at the back of the factory, near the aircraft on the landing ground were not in the photograph which he was shown, neither were the huts immediately in front of the swimming pool, which I see from the plan are called 'R.A.F. huts.' He was asked if he could find out when the latter buildings were erected. Otherwise Reed would have to ask Group Captain Archer and his contact at de Havillands.[32]

One imagines Cholmondley provided a response, but it was not documented in Chapman's file. The following day, Reed contacted Colonel Stanford asking him to arrange for Fighter Command to send him the tracks of any enemy reconnaissance aircraft that approached de Havilland's factory from that day onwards, adding that 'the notional sabotaging of this place has been arranged for the night of 29/30 January, and we shall be extremely interested to know what attempts are made by the enemy to photograph the results.' MI5 wanted the aerial photographs to reach the Germans.[33]

On the same day, Reed added a memo to Chapman's file headed 'Sabotage arrangements' in which he noted that when Turner had enquired about the date of the notional sabotage, he pointed out that 'if we wished for darkness during the first part of the evening and for the moon to rise later it would be necessary to erect the camouflage material before the end of this month.'[34] When Cholmondley acquired a moon calendar, they realised that it was essential that the 'attack' had to take place within the next few days. Otherwise the moon would be too bright. According to Owen,

Two power plants supplying the factory were selected for the fake explosion. Their destruction would bring production at the plant to a virtual standstill, and that would surely satisfy the Germans. Also, the power plants seemed the easiest buildings on which to work. They were away from the main, more heavily occupied buildings. There were fewer workers to notice the elaborate camouflage work and question what was going on. They were located at a point within the factory grounds that an accomplished saboteur and burglar like Chapman could conceivably reach and enter with a package of explosives.[35]

On Thursday 28 January, a message was sent to the Abwehr stating that the plans for WALTER were complete and that Chapman would attack the two sub-stations the following night. WALTER was the German code-name for the de Havilland factory and THOMAS their code-name for his operation. Reed made arrangements for ZIGZAG to visit

these two sub-stations on Friday morning and it will not be necessary for him to be provided with an identity card for this visit as S/Ldr Gatey will be seeing Mr Street, the Security Officer at DE HAVILLANDS to tell him that a Mr SIMPSON and myself will visit him at 11 a.m. on Friday morning to see over certain parts of the factory. I asked Gatey if he would tell Mr St Barbe that if any enquiries were made after the sabotaging by any responsible bodies, he should say that something had occurred, but that it was very small and not worthwhile reporting. The same line should be taken by Mr Street in dealing with enquiries from the local press to the gate at the factory, and any people requesting information on occurrences at DE HAVILLANDS should make al their enquiries to Mr Street, the Security Officer.[36]

As Chapman had reported that all the English newspapers were available to read at the Dientstelle in Nantes, TAR discussed with Colonel Villiers and Colonel Stanford how best to obtain a press report on the sabotage. TAR agreed to visit Robert Barrington Ward, the editor of *The Times*, and arrange for him to include an article in the following Saturday's edition.

> As, however, no sabotage will really have taken place, and any statement to the Press that it has done so will be untrue, it is thought that this is going to be very difficult. I asked F/Lt Cholmondley if he could arrange for a reconnaissance photograph to be taken on Saturday morning so that we should have some idea of how the damage appeared from the air.[37]

Barrington-Ward was not persuaded by TAR's argument, despite the importance of the operation and the necessity of it being given newspaper coverage being stressed. He also ignored Tar's comments that all official authorities concerned had been informed, and the site would be camouflaged to give the impression of an explosion.

> Barrington-Ward was very sympathetic, but he pointed out that, though he would like to help, the suggestion that he should insert what in fact was a bogus notice in 'The Times' cut across his whole policy. Not only the reputation but the public utility of 'The Times' depended entirely on the principle that it should never insert any items of news which it did not believe to be true. Though the suggested notice about the explosion (of which I gave him a copy) was a small thing in itself, its insertion would be clean contrary to this first principle which 'The Times' observed. He promised to think the matter over and let me know this afternoon if it were possible to insert the notice or not.
>
> I discussed with him the possibility of working the matter through the Ministry of Information. He thought that this would be a mistake in that the Ministry of Information would either have to deceive the representatives of the press (which might have unfortunate repercussions on the Ministry) or alternatively tell the whole press more of the story than it was desirable that it should know. He therefore advised me, in the event of a refusal of 'The Times', to attempt a private approach to some other newspaper such as 'The Daily Telegraph' or 'The Daily Express'. If his reply is in the negative, we should both regard the negotiation as not having taken place and that he would 'forget' about the story.
>
> Later telephone message: 'The answer is respectfully No.'[38]

With *The Times* refusal, TAR went to see Arthur Christiansen, the editor of the *The Daily Express*, and his discussion with him was more successful.

As Chapman's mission included the sabotage of the de Havilland's factory, someone, possibly Masterman, came up with a novel idea, fake or notional sabotage, an attempt to convince the Germans that Chapman really did sabotage the factory when in fact he didn't.

The creation of this illusion was allocated to Jasper Maskelyne's Camouflage Experimental Section. He had been a stage magician in London in the 1930s and his 'Magic Gang' included an architect, carpenter, art restorer, electrical engineer, stage set designer, painter and a decorator.

When war broke out in 1939, Maskelyne joined the Royal Engineers and volunteered his gang's skills in ruses, deception and camouflage to the War Office. Impressed by his ideas, the Camouflage Experimental Section was sent to the North African desert where they were occupied cutting out pieces of plywood, painting them and fastening them onto jeeps, trucks, tractors and boats so that, from a distance, they looked like tanks, aeroplanes, submarines and even battleships. They also did it the other way round too. Tanks could be made to look like trucks and Royal Navy boats to look Italian or German.

They were said to have misled German bomber pilots into thinking Alexandria, the Mediterranean Egyptian port, was 3 miles away from its actual site by creating a mock-up of the port's night-lights in a bay 3 miles away. They made fake buildings, a lighthouse and anti-aircraft batteries. To disguise the Suez Canal, they set up searchlights and built a revolving cone of mirrors that created a nine-mile wide wheel of spinning light. To fool Field Marshal Rommel into thinking that the attack on El Alamein was coming from the south, two thousand fake tanks with fake gunfire were constructed in the south. They built a fake water pipeline, a fake railway line, broadcast fake radio conversations, and produced fake construction noises to create the impression that Montgomery's army was not ready for an attack. They were though. A thousand of his tanks attacked from the north disguised as trucks.[39]

RAF Tempsford, the airfield in Bedfordshire, from where most of the Allied secret agents were flown out from to be parachuted or landed in occupied Europe and from where two squadrons supplied the resistance movements throughout the war, was said to have been designed by Maskelyne to give overflying Luftwaffe pilots the impression it was disused. Some farm buildings were altered to look unoccupied; hangars were camouflaged to look like arable fields; new buildings were given thatched roofs or had painted tarpaulins covering them to look like farm buildings. The runways had patches of green and brown painted on them to look overgrown and a black line across one resembled a hedge. While cattle grazed on the fields and ducks used the pond during the day, the planes only ever took off, weather permitting, after dusk on the nights either side of the full moon and returned before dawn. There were anti-aircraft batteries, but the Gunners were said to have been instructed never to shoot any overflying enemy plane unless it was coming in to attack. Retaliation would have identified it as an active airfield. The plan worked and not one bomb was dropped on 'Churchill's Most Secret Airfield' throughout the war.[40]

To give an overflying German reconnaissance pilot the impression that the de Havilland factory had been sabotaged involved similar illusory work. Colonel Sir John Turner, the head of the Air Ministry's camouflage section, was involved in the planning, and it may have been he who asked Maskelyne to make it look as if it 'had been blown to Kingdom come'.[41] He vetoed the initial plan of laying asbestos sheets across the roof of the factory and then starting a large fire which could be spotted by German reconnaissance planes. It would have created a tempting target for the Luftwaffe. His plan was 'to erect a veil of sabotage so convincing that it would seem, from the ground as well as the air, as if a very large bomb had exploded inside the factory power plant.'[42]

According to Farago, 'Maskelyne used a big relief canvas to cover the entire roof of the powerhouse. Painted on it in Technicolor was the damage that had supposedly been wrought below. In one of his magic factories (of which he had three), he built papier-mâché dummies that resembled the broken pieces of the generator. He strew them, as well as chipped bricks, battered blocks of concrete, smashed furniture and other such props all around the place until it looked thoroughly wrecked to observers from the air.'[43]

Macintyre's research revealed that four models of sub-transformers were created out of wood and papier-mâché and painted metallic grey.

> Meanwhile, the real transformers would be covered in netting and corrugated iron sheets painted to look like a 'vast hole' in the ground … the walls of the smaller building would be draped with tarpaulins, painted to look like the half-demolished remnants of a brick wall, while the other walls would be covered in soot, as if blackened from an explosion. Rubble and debris would be spread around the compound to a radius of 100 feet.[44]

On 28 January, J.F. Furness of the Air Ministry sent Robertson photographs of the proposed sabotage with some useful suggestions which had to be added to Chapman's story.

> I enclose herewith two fudged photographs of what will be seen with some variations on Saturday morning. In case the Hun manages to get a low-level photograph, it is important for the saboteur to remember the following:
> (a) In the true place, he only had explosive to attack 2
> (b) In the untrue place there were only two transformers, and he dealt with them both, getting [over?] the fence around them.
> (c) He hid his explosive underneath the transformers. If he tried to lay them on top, he might electrocute himself as the high-tension wires are connected on the top.
>
> I would like a copy of my photographs you take afterwards. I also want to know when we should clean up.
> One more point. In the true place the gates will apparently have been blown. To avoid excessive curiosity, I am arranging for a screen to be erected beyond i.e. outside the gates so that no-one can look over. I leave it to you again to warn those in the know at De Hav that any talk must be met with the answer that it is a test to see if high altitude photography can pick up minimum damage as a check to some of our photographs taken over occupied or German territory.[45]

As Chapman would be expected to describe the site and situation of the works when he returned to France, a preliminary visit was arranged during which he made notes from which he could write up a report. This also provided him with accurate details for his wireless transmissions.

On 29 January, Reed reported that he, Chapman and Mr Horsfield visited the factory that morning and were shown round by Mr Street, de Havilland's Security Officer.

> We first inspected the real sub-station near the power house, and ZIGZAG said he thought that 15 pounds of explosive on the main transformer in the centre would suffice to destroy it. We passed on to the main power house and boiler rooms and ZIGZAG was intrigued to note that the pressure in the large boilers was 210 pounds per square inch. He thought that a large box of explosives on top of one of these would create more damage than a 4,000-pound bomb. ...The principal difficulty lay in the fact that the tall chimney associated with the power house would continue to smoke immediately after the incident and that we had found it impracticable to demolish this...
>
> ZIGZAG suggests that his cover story should be that he entered the factory with Jimmy HUNT by passing through this gate after breaking open the padlock and replacing it with another one so that no guards who were patrolling the factory would have any suspicions by seeing the broken lock. ZIGZAG would then make his way to the real sub-station, and Jimmy HUNT would be detailed to place the explosive charge in the transformers of the notional sub-station. He thought that about one hour's delay would be satisfactory.[46]

A series of notes were provided for Chapman to memorise and recount to the Germans when he met them again.

The visit to De Havilland, Hatfield

> Had a look round at Kings Cross and St Pancras Station areas, and saw a few lorries (W.D.) [War Department]. A no. of troops were travelling with full kit individually and not in parties.
>
> On arrival at Hatfield Station asked the way to Comet Hotel and were directed. Took a bus past the factory a short distance and walked back slowly, pausing to talk now and again to myself with my back to D.H. Works and then facing the area. Most extensive study was made of the whole area. It is well protected in most places. Best entry is in the neighbourhood of the Comet on the main road. Defences at back of private houses not known. Other sector for possible entry is road down side of factory and field at right angles to the main road. (Shown on sketch).
>
> We walked the whole length of the area along the main road, observed all entrances and buildings. Rough sketch is appended.
>
> The following points have been noted.
> 1. No. of aircraft on the field: 25
> 2. Locations of entrances marked on sketch [see illustrations]
> 3. Types of buildings.

4. Positions of boiler rooms
5. Fuel storage

There are three boiler rooms. 'A', almost opposite the Comet. 'B', in the buildings away from the main road across the landing field. 'C', amongst the main buildings near the main entrance. This is the largest.

Near the boiler room 'C' are coal and wood storage dumps.

Cars parked are plotted on the sketch as 'P'.

Some hundreds of yards from the area in the St Albans direction are four pylons or radio masts. They were not inspected at close quarters and their connection, if any, with the factory, is not known.

Types of buildings cannot accurately be assessed. Buildings bordering the main road appear to be offices and are marked as such on the sketch on both sides of the road.

A subsidiary building marked 'S' on the other side of the 3rd class road in the Welwyn Garden City direction has a boiler room. The importance of the building is not known.

The area with boiler room 'B' was inspected at a distance. Cars were parked in the vicinity, some aircraft on the ground nearby, and one building looked like a hangar. Judging from the noise, one of the buildings was used as an aero engine test bed.

Main entrance area. In addition to offices and large boiler room, it is thought that the mounting sheds may be behind the offices. (These are marked 'M'.)

The entrances are guarded by police and other officials, and it is likely that all regular workers there are known by sight, and any stranger would be carefully checked. [...]

E. [Eddie] would like the opportunity to scout around the area after dark, and suggests between 6 pm and 8 pm. It was explained he could not go alone, and that discovery would upset all plans for the job.

Things that must be known are:
1. times that shifts change.
2. size, position and nos. of boilers in each boiler house, and whether they are outside or not.
3. Types of guards, their numbers, methods of patrol, and areas they patrol.

During the visit, few people showed any undue interest in our presence. One labourer glanced at us two or three times when we were in one place near the building, but carried on his work, and we remained only a minute or so.

A visit we paid to a café backing on to the factory. No important conversations were overheard.[47]

There was a reference to a tracing of the works, which showed the sub-station containing the mains transformer shaded in red and the notional sub-station, near the swimming pool shaded blue.[48] Following their recce, they decided that thirty pounds of explosive would be needed. According to Chapman's cover story, this was packed into two suitcases.

...on the night arranged we went up there at about 7 o'clock and parked the car round behind a garage in front of the factory. We had some coffee in a nearby café and then crept through the gardens of a house at the at the back of the 'Comet' and slipped through the barbed wire at the unguarded gate. Jimmy made for the transformers near the swimming pool, and I tackled the one near the power house. We left one hour's delay on each of our explosive mixtures and came straight back to London in the car. I should have told you that, before we made any reconnaissance at the DE HAVILLAND factory, there was a dance at the 'Hendon Way' where I met the director of a subsidiary factory of DE HAVILLAND which is at the moment situated in Burnt Oak. I could not ask questions about its exact location, but DE HAVILLANDS were holding a staff dance at the 'Hendon Way' and people had come from the Hatfield area and from other parts of North London to join it. I met one of the girls at this dance, who was called Wendy HAMMOND (description of [his wife] Freda's friend) and I arranged to meet her again at the 'Hendon Way' the day after the one we had arranged for the sabotage. She told me that there had been an awful mess and that the people at the factory were trying to hush it up and say that nothing had occurred. She was a discreet young woman, and I could not get much out of her, but it was clear that there had been considerable damage and that no one wanted to admit it...

Although I am sure there was a pretty bad mess at DE HAVILLANDS we didn't get much newspaper publicity for it, but it is clear they had to publish something in the Daily Express on Monday, though I think it was cut out by the Censor later on because I bought two copies of the Daily Express and, while it was in the early edition, it had been removed from the later one. I suppose the Censor kicked up a row about it being mentioned at all.

It appeared that Reed felt the de Havilland case was not as dramatic in the public eye as it could have been.

It would be of the greatest importance in maintaining security in this country if we could have one 'sensational' sabotage case. During the whole of this war, we have had to maintain security at factories and other establishments connected with the war by propaganda methods. One real case of a saboteur being arrested [and tried in the courts] would do more than all this propaganda put together. It occurs to me that if the Germans are satisfied with CONKIE's [?] work, it would be reasonable, on Abwehr standards, for ZIGZAG to say that there were great opportunities for further sabotage in this country, that he had obtained accommodation and help (of a non-active variety) from certain of his gang, and that he thought he could do good business if two colleagues could be sent over. From the American sabotage case, it is clear that Abteilung II believe that successful sabotage on a big scale needs a group of about four saboteurs.

A possible disadvantage in this proposal is the psychological one that ZIGZAG may have some effect for some of his past colleagues at Nantes and would not like to see them strung up indirectly due to him.

An alternative method would be for him to put the above story across on his return to France and for him to come back again with a bunch of German saboteurs. If he was prepared to do this, any psychological objection that there might be to the former plan would not apply, because he would not be prepared to do this if he minded letting down some of his friends.

Given the row between the U-bootdienst and the Abwehr following the American sabotage case, I think there might be difficulties for the Abwehr in landing a group of saboteurs in the USA again. The only way they could do it within a reasonable time would be by submarine, and I doubt whether they will be permitted to put more than one, or at the most two, agents on board a submarine on routine work. The American plan, therefore, seems to be somewhat speculative and long-range. Indeed, the evidence that it was ever contemplated is not particularly strong. The other two plans outlined above would have all sorts of advantages from our point of view, and I wonder if you would care to consider them.[49]

The day after the attack, Reed wrote a memo for TAR saying that, 'as ZIGZAG could easily have brought LEO to England with him, and that there was the possibility that once back in German hands, he might be able to return with some German saboteur', he was concerned about the possibility that the men he brought back could be executed as spies. TAR replied saying, 'I sympathised with him entirely in this view, and I said that although I could give him no assurance so far as this country was concerned, I was pretty certain that we would take every possible step to see that his wishes were granted.'[50]

On the same day, Reed took TAR and Colonel Turner to the factory to see the results of the Camouflage Experimental Section's work:

The camouflage experts had arrived at dusk the previous evening [29 January] and the whole of their work had been finished by 11 p.m. in spite of an inky blackness. The camouflage was excellent and the impression gained was that aerial photography from any height above about 2,000 feet would show considerable devastation without creating any suspicion. Four replicas of the sub-transformers had been constructed of wood. Two of these were lying on their side in the real sub-station as if they had been blown from their position, while the real transformers had been covered over with netting and corrugated iron which was painted on top so that aerial photographs would show that there was a hole where they had previously been. Odd rubble and brick was scattered in the precincts of these transformers and the large wooden green gates which had been locked to the courtyard where the transformers were situated, had been removed and a pair of smashed green gates had been substituted as if the blast from the explosion had blown them outwards. The walls surrounding the transformers had been blackened, and tarpaulins had been placed over the wall next to the transformers as if the bricks had been blown away and this temporary erection had been installed to keep out the rain.

In the position of the notional sub-station, the other two transformers were lying as if damaged, surrounded by chaos and the wall of the nearby brick building had been covered with two tarpaulins, one apparently to keep out the rain and the other one painted as if a large hole had been blown in the wall. The wooden fence surrounding these transformers was lying smashed on the ground, and the earth had been disturbed as if by an explosion. The whole picture was very convincing, so much so that the operator in charge of the small boiler house near the swimming pool had arrived that morning in a state of great excitement because he thought that his machinery had been hit by a bomb during the night.

Mr St Barbe said he would arrange for the de Havilland photographer to take photographs of each of the two sites and send them to Group Captain Archer. Major Robertson asked Colonel Turner if he could start to clear away the broken transformers from the real sub-station on Monday, and also remove the whole of the rubble and broken piping from the notional substation that same day. It was thought necessary to leave the tarpaulins in position and later these would also be removed, and the brick wall painted to appear as if it had been rebuilt.[51]

There was no mention in Chapman's file that the Germans sent a reconnaissance plane to confirm the reported damage. Poor weather conditions were mentioned which could have prevented it. However, in Owen's biography, when Chapman was back in Berlin, he reported being shown aerial photographs taken two days after his 'attack', which amazed him as they exactly resembled those he was shown by the British.[52]

Two days after the 'attack', C. A. Harris, another FSP officer, reported visiting all the public houses and workers' cafes near de Havillands and hearing no rumours that the explosion was caused by sabotage. 'Construction work is in progress on a hangar north of the factory, but there is no indication that any sabotage has taken place in the district.'[53]

On 2 February, *The Daily Express* published the following article on the back page of the 05.00 edition, which went to Lisbon and other overseas destinations but not in the editions circulated in in the UK. Chapman's file includes the original copy of the newspaper with the article torn out as he took it with him to Lisbon. 'Factory explosion. Investigations are being made into the cause of an explosion at a factory on the outskirts of London. It is understood that the damage was slight, and there was no loss of life.'

On 8 February, the Germans informed Chapman that he had to change his plans for returning to France. As they were unable to pick him up by submarine, he had to make arrangements to get to Lisbon by boat. According to the cover story concocted by Reed, he paid Frani Daniels, who worked in a shipping office, £200 for the necessary papers. In fact, MI5 arranged his voyage as an assistant steward on board the 1,000-ton *City of Lancaster*, which he had to desert when it docked at Lisbon and make his way to the address of a safe house he had been given by the Abwehr.

To explain why Hunt did not escape with him, Chapman initially was to explain that it was too suspicious for both of them to try to get away at the same time. Reed recommended him telling the Germans the story that Hunt had been arrested and charged with possessing gelignite under the Explosives Act and a second charge of suspicious behaviour in the neighbourhood of Hatfield. As evidence, Reed arranged for an article to be inserted in the *Evening Standard* on Friday, 12 February which read: 'Gelignite Inquiries. A man was questioned at Shepherds Bush Police Station in connection with the possession of gelignite.'

Further deception included a report that a police van had been seen in Crespigny Road which deterred him from sending messages as he was suspicious that they might have detected his wireless transmissions. He was also told to tell them that he had collected all the documents he had been asked to take back to the Abwehr, ration cards, identity papers, etc. As these would be particularly useful for them to make fake copies of, it was thought the German authorities in Lisbon would make a greater effort to ensure he got back to France. However, he was later to tell them that he had had to throw them overboard when he learned that his possessions were going to be searched by Portuguese customs officials.

Masterman ensured that Chapman was well prepared for any German interrogation. Using what had been learned from Camp 020, a check-list was drawn up on ways in which to withstand interrogation, which might include the use of torture – something Stephens did not resort to – drugs, and humiliation, which he did. It would be interesting to know whether any of the captured Abwehr saboteurs ever used any of Masterman's strategies: 'Always speak slowly, this enables hesitation to be covered when necessary; create the impression of being vague; do not appear to be observant; give the impression of being bewildered, frightened or stupid, feign drunkenness or tiredness long before they actually occur.'[54]

Before Chapman left, he was interviewed by Mr Thurston, an American FBI officer, but the substance of their discussions was not documented. Maybe it was felt he might be useful in providing advance warning of another sabotage attack in the United States or providing names of potential saboteurs.

Aware that his future was not guaranteed, Chapman left £350 with Reed asking for it to be paid in weekly instalments of £5 to his wife. He also gave him a written request that if he did not return to England, once the Allies defeated the Germans, MI5 should obtain the £15,000 he had been promised and ensure it was shared equally between his wife and daughter. In return, he promised to do his best to obey their instructions. How MI5 was to acquire the money was not discussed.

MI5 instructed him to memorise a lengthy questionnaire dealing mainly with wireless stations at Bordeaux and Paris but also on the Abwehr in France and Germany, their training methods, their agents, etc., intelligence which he could pass on should he succeed in returning to England. Rothschild sent Reed two questions to ask Chapman and a memo requiring him to ensure that, once back in German hands, he needed to note the German sabotage undertakings and methods:

1. What targets do the Germans really think it would be a good idea to sabotage in this country? Supposing one was going to settle down here with a nice resident sabotage organisation, one would want a lengthy programme, and details of the targets in order of priority would be of great interest. The question of the vulnerability of particular targets must come into any list because obviously, one cannot do much to a place like the Valentine Tank Factory. Associated with this question is, how do the Germans decide which are the most important targets for sabotage.

2. The chemicals that the Germans seem to recommend mostly for home-made sabotage equipment re saltpetre, which is potassium (Kalium) nitrate, chili saltpetre, which is sodium nitrate, potassium (Kalium) chlorate, and ammonium nitrate; together with such things as flour, sugar, aluminium, etc., which can be easily obtained. Supposing that stocks of the first-named chemicals run out in this country, what alternatives can be used.

3. ZIGZAG should say that detonators cannot be got in England now without great risk. What are the way in which saboteurs coming to this country with detonators would have them camouflaged? What objects that people normally carry about might contain detonators or small pieces of sabotage equipment? ZIGZAG should come back with camouflaged sabotage equipment of as many types as possible.

4. If ZIGZAG returns to this country, he will obviously not be able to bring an enormous amount of sabotage equipment with him and in view of the increasing difficulties of getting stuff when over here, perhaps some regular method of supply through diplomatic channels could be arranged.

Summarising the above matters in an easily memorisable form, what we are interested in from the sabotage point of view is: 'Target, other chemicals, camouflage, steady supply.'[55]

In response to Rothschild's two questions, Chapman reported that the reason he had been given revolver practice while in France was to shoot his way out of any difficulties he might have encountered when arriving in Britain. The 'detonators are required for all explosive mixtures but are not required for any of the incendiary material ... any of the substances which he had suggested for causing fires should have the addition of kalium and sugar if it is difficult to start them burning. The acid fuse made in the ink bottle with the cardboard top can be placed in this mixture of kalium and sugar to give satisfactory delayed action.'[56]

He later told Reed that detonators could be placed in cigarettes, in bars of soap, or even worn as earrings or cheap brooches and that dynamite could be camouflaged as bars of marzipan or almond icing.

It could also be placed in tubes of shaving cream – half the tube being filled with cream and the other half with dynamite – or in jars containing honey and labelled 'honey'. ZIGZAG noticed that there are considerable purchases of honey going on in the black market in France at the present time and does not think that this would appear suspicious.

I gave ZIGZAG his questionnaire on sabotage which you suggested, and he says that the subjects which were discussed with him were air-screws, rubber refineries, shipping, sugar refineries, large clothing depots and aircraft production. I said I was grateful for this further information but that it was so very general that it was hardly of the same value that the specific objectives would be if he could obtain information about them when he returned.[57]

When the RAF analysed aerial photographs of the works, their remarks were inconclusive. The only indication of sabotage that an enemy observer might identify was that the roof seemed to be incomplete near the south-east corner and that a low extension appeared to be under construction at the south-east end of the pavilion. Two objects about 6 ft square were seen on the ground near the extension, but they couldn't be identified exactly as transformers. A number of unidentifiable objects seen in the yard meant that it could have been subject to a sabotage attack.[58]

Reed was astute enough to imagine Chapman might be questioned about his method of sabotaging the transformers so asked Commander John Senter, head of the Security Section, to get his technical people to investigate the aerial photographs to determine the quantity of explosives needed to cause the observable damage.

> You will notice that in the first site, (A, B, and C), the doors which shut off the brick walled enclosure were apparently smashed, and the large mains transformers are lying on the ground near the camouflaged ones. In the second site (D, E, and F), two large transformers are shown amongst a good deal of ruin with a hole in the wall which was produced by means of tarpaulin sabotage.
>
> I should be very interested to know from your experts how much explosive they would consider to be necessary to produce the amount of damage which you see in the photographs were it really to be attempted: a) if it were sabotaged by means of gelignite, and b) if it were attempted by home-made mixtures. In the case of a) could you also let me know how much space the gelignite would take up and if it would be possible to carry the amount required in a suit-case.[59]

The response was worrying. Although one of the technical officers rang up Reed to explain, a Major T.G. Roche was equally astute in writing a letter in case MI5 had to enact another notional sabotage in the future.

> Our technical people say that the <u>damage</u> to the units shown in the photographs could easily have been done with 20 lbs of explosives. They make, however, one reservation. The photographs show two of the units to have been overturned. Our people will not pledge themselves that this would necessarily have occurred, since this depends on weight, height, centre of gravity, method of fixing and other factors, on which they cannot express an opinion without seeing the objects. A further reason for their hesitation arises from the fact that you subsequently told Major Goodwin that the 'plot' provided 'for the charge being placed under the units', and we have no practical experience of placing charges in that position. Our procedure evolved by experience and practice is to place the charges on the side. A small charge placed on the side blows a hole in the transformer tank, the oil pours out and probably catches fire. The transformer may or may not be over-turned, according to the quantity of explosive used and the factors referred to above, but the transformer is destroyed.
>
> I attach for your information a copy of a report on two trials recently carried out. The second trial is the most lifelike, as in that case the transformer was filled with oil. The transformer was smaller than the units in your problem, but you will see that in the trial 1½ lbs of P.E., placed on the side, was sufficient to put the unit out of commission.

Our technical people also say that they are a little puzzled by photographs E. and F. If the 'plot' had provided for the charge to be placed on the side, the transformer might have been thrown over leaving the base undamaged as shown in the photograph. As the 'plot' provided for the charge being laid underneath they would expect to see damage to the base of the transformer.[60]

Roche's report was not included in Chapman's file, nor was there any indication as to whether the gelignite could be carried in a suitcase. This letter arrived too late for Reed to discuss it with him as he left for Liverpool at the end of February and set sail for Lisbon on 5 March.

In Owen's biography, Chapman describes meeting Dr Braun, an Abwehr officer, in Lisbon who asked him if it was possible to sabotage the ship. When he told him it was, Braun replied,

'Good. For that you will be well rewarded. Meet me later and I will give you some explosive coal. The ship is carrying Welsh coal, and I will prepare it for you.'

The reason for this distinction was that Newcastle and Welsh coal differ in grain. Should suspicion of sabotage have arisen, the coal would have been examined, and if a piece of Newcastle coal had been found in a Welsh bunker the plot would have been discovered.

I went out and ate a meal, and later met Braun and his companions once again. He handed me two lumps of coal about six inches square. I examined them. They were beautifully made. No one could have guessed that, far from being harmless pieces of coal, they were really infernal machines. A bag was given me, I placed the coal in it and hung it between my legs.[61]

However, according to Masterman's account,

While the ship was at Lisbon, ZIGZAG made contact with the Germans and eventually deserted as arranged, but there were moments of very great anxiety. We learned from secret sources that he was leaving on board pieces of coal given to him by the Germans and containing high explosive as a parting gift to the ship, and it was naturally impossible to be absolutely certain that ZIGZAG had not actually placed this coal in the bunkers, in order to set himself up with the Germans, without warning any of his former shipmates. An officer [Reed] was hurried out to Lisbon, and it was discovered that ZIGZAG had given the coal into the charge of the captain and that the proposal had come in the first place from ZIGZAG himself. He then returned into the charge of his German masters, and for the time disappeared from our ken. [The Germans gave him 100,000 Reichmarks for this bright idea.][62]

The prospects opened up by his return to the enemy were impressive. He maintained himself that as a reward for his work he would be allowed to tour Germany and then take up a position in the Dienstelle at Paris, Nantes, or Angers; also, that he would certainly get another sabotage mission either to the United States, or perhaps, in charge of a large band of saboteurs to this country. He also believed that he could set up an organisation in France on fifth column lines, which would stay behind if the Germans evacuated France and which, of course, he would be able to hand over lock, stock and barrel to the Allies. His own plan included the suggestion that he should undertake the assassination of Hitler as a one-man effort, but this proposal, with more than our customary caution, we declined to encourage. Perhaps we missed an opportunity, for ZIGZAG was an enterprising and practical criminal.[63]

Chapman did not place the exploding coal in the ship's bunker. He handed it to the captain and told him to pass it to the port security officer when he returned to Liverpool. He then told the Germans that he had placed it as instructed. There was no way for the Germans to check his story. Unidentified ships blew up at sea all the time.

Receiving very large payments for acts of sabotage that he did not commit must have been especially pleasing. According to Macintyre, Chapman's fame spread far and wide.

> From the lowest bars of Europe, the story of how a top German spy had tried to sabotage a British ship, reached German High Command, the FBI, and the highest levels of the British government. A copy of the Zigzag file was sent to Duff Cooper, the former Minister of Information who now supervised covert operations as Chancellor of the Duchy of Lancaster, who in turn showed it to Winston Churchill. Cooper reported that he had 'discussed Zigzag at some length with the prime minister who is showing considerable interest in the case.' MI5 was instructed to give the case the highest priority and to inform Churchill immediately 'if and when contact is re-established with Zigzag.'
>
> J. Edgar Hoover, the FBI chief, was also watching Zigzag's trail … Chapman was fast becoming a secret star worldwide; in Washington and Whitehall, in Berlin and Paris, his exploits, real and unreal, were discussed, admired and wondered at.[64]

Accounts of Chapman's experiences in Portugal, France, Germany and Norway, where he lived a life of luxury as a sabotage consultant, can be read in his biographies by Owen, Booth and Macintyre. Shortly after his return to Britain, in November 1944 MI5 disposed of his services following some indiscreet remarks he made when he returned to his old haunts and friends in the criminal underworld. He married his pre-war girlfriend, got involved in gold smuggling in the Mediterranean, mixed with blackmailers and thieves and became honorary crime correspondent for the *Sunday Telegraph*. He died in 1997 aged 83, and Reed described him as 'one of the bravest men who served in the last war'. We have not quite finished with this extraordinary figure. He returns (to the UK) in chapter 20.

18

Agent PRINS, Potential Dutch saboteur – December 1942

Johannes de Graaf arrived from Gibraltar on SS *Llanstephan Castle* at Gourock, near Glasgow, on 24 December 1942. Interrogated by an immigration officer, he admitted to being born in Canada in November 1918 and in 1932 being brought by his Dutch parents, who were naturalised Canadians, to live in Holland where they lived at 131 Valirusstraat, Amsterdam. He worked in Amsterdam as an accountant for N. V. Ltd Electro, which made oxy-acetylene gas.

When war broke out, he was interned in a concentration camp in Schoorl but was released by the Germans after a fortnight by telling them he was more Dutch than British and had spent most of his life living in Holland.

Returning to work, in August 1941 he was visited by a Dutch police officer who had instructions to take him to the police station. He did not indicate what for but on the way he gave the policeman the slip, returned home and told his parents that he had to leave Holland. He went to stay with Lucien Moreels, a Belgian he knew in November 1939 who worked for the French Deuxieme Bureau, their intelligence section, and gave him details about the load carrying capacity of certain bridges. After fourteen weeks in Belgium, Moreels helped de Graaf to get into France and, with the aid of an underground organisation, he spent six weeks in Toulouse and in February 1942, crossed the Spanish border near Port Bou on the Catalonian coast.

When he got to Barcelona, he reported to the British Consul and spent two months waiting to be sent to Madrid. After reporting to the British Embassy, he worked for eight months there as an accountant and produced a cheque for £25 as proof, signed by Major Haslan, said to be the Assistant Military Attaché. On 12 December, he was driven in a diplomatic car to Gibraltar and immediately put on a ship for Britain.

The interrogator expected his British passport to have Consular endorsement and noted that his date of birth had been changed from 9 November 1918 to 9 November 1925. De Graaf claimed it had been done by the Consul to avoid him being picked up by Spanish police. Claiming that he wanted to join the Royal Canadian Air Force, the officer commented that he appeared to have left Holland to save his own skin rather than for any patriotic reasons.

When he was searched by a Security Control officer, a tin, a bottle of Pyramidon, cotton wool, a sharpened match and small pointed sliver of wood with cigarette papers and Aspirin tablets were found in his pockets. In other documents, the word Pyramidon was redacted. His interrogation report noted:

> It is known that the Germans supply their agents with Pyramidon and the presence of this drug together with the sharpened wood was regarded as highly suspicious. It was considered that de Graaf's story and the purposes for which he had entered the U.K. were not satisfactory, and he was therefore served with Form 'B' under the Arrival from Enemy and Foreign Territory Order, and handed over to the Gourock Police who escorted him to Brixton Prison tonight.[1]

Transferred to the London Reception Centre on 30 December, he was interrogated by Lieutenant Sands whose report included more details about de Graaf's family background; the communication he had with a German SS officer to secure his release from internment; his means of escaping from the police; travelling to Belgium; and about Moreels.

Given MI9's interest in escape lines, he was quizzed at length about his escape to Spain, the people who helped him, particularly Jean, the organiser, Louis de Bray and Rev Caskie (who was being funded by MI9 to help evaders and others escape to Lisbon or Gibraltar) and the places he stayed. He provided names and descriptions of his contacts, including those he dealt with in the British Consulate and Embassy.

When questioned about the sharpened matchstick and sliver of wood, he claimed they were toothpicks. Dipped in Pyramidon it was said to ease the pain. Convinced by his account, Sands recommended that he be released to join the Canadian forces.[2]

Lieutenant Thompson got more details from him about the people he mentioned, particularly Moreels, whom MI5 already suspected of being a recruiting agent for the Germans. As there were discrepancies with dates and de Graaf being uneasy when questioned more intensely about Moreels and the others in the escape organisation, his release was delayed.

By the end of his fifth interrogation, he had confessed that he had worked for Moreels in 1939, and when he met Moreels' mistress, Laura, they became friends, and she gave him the name and address of her cousin, a Mr Thompson in London. He later confessed that this was wrong. It was J.A. Smeeton, 17 Victoria Street, S.W.1. While de Graaf doubted that Smeeton was involved in subversive activities; MI5 made enquiries and found that he had represented German firms in the late 1920s and early-1930s and had frequently travelled on the continent.

De Graaf also admitted that he had helped the Germans with information about fellow internees. To secure his release, he had been persuaded by a German called Bakker, either a SD or Gestapo officer, to join the Dutch Nazi Party and work in their Brussels party headquarters at 100 Belgian francs a day. While there he admitted learning Morse.

When he escaped the police, he went to see Bakker who provided him with the appropriate travel documents, nearly 7,000 Belgian and French francs, an unspecified number of Reichmarks and contacts within the Allied escape organisation. Assured that no harm would come to his elderly parents, he agreed to be sent to England as a spy and then return to Brussels with the intelligence he had gathered. He was under the impression that he would be flown to England and be back within a fortnight.

By 22 January, Thompson suspected him of working for a hostile organisation, doubted his explanations about his passport and statements about working for the Embassy in Madrid. This and having possession of secret writing materials led to de Graaf being sent to Camp 020 for further questioning.

Having to answer the same questions again allowed MI5 to cross-check his story, and any discrepancies were identified. Enquiries were made about the people he mentioned and it was noted that the escape organisation had been used by an Italian who was subsequently found to have been a German agent.

By mid-February, he admitted that, as well as being taught Morse, he was also given instruction in propaganda work, secret ink writing, wireless telegraphy, codes, messages, the use of fire arms and sabotage, prompting the comment that 'he has shown himself to be one of the best trained enemy agents who have so far fallen into our hands.'[3]

The plan to have him tried under the Treachery Act 1940 was made difficult because of his employment by the British Embassy helping them with processing other evaders wanting to reach Britain. There was also the question of a possible sabotage mission to be investigated.

By the beginning of March, he had admitted passing on information about the escape route to the Germans and responsibility for the arrest by the Germans 'of probably the most important British agent operating this route who was responsible for the very marked success which it had achieved in the course of the last year.'[4] The British agent's identity was not stated but Andrée de Jongh, known as Dedée, was arrested in January 1943 having made thirty successful trips over the Pyrenees bringing Allied airmen and crew, escaped prisoners-of-war and others wanting to escape Nazi occupation.[5] (She would survive Ravensbrück.)

TAR's undated report included the British Embassy's account of de Graaf's work with them over eight and a half months, following which they were sent a request to ensure all subsequent employees were from the Armed Services so that their security would have been cleared. De Graaf admitted that Bakker offered him a sabotage and propaganda mission in England, Denmark or South Africa. He chose the latter. Although no specific places were mentioned, 'the sabotage was to be done in ammunition factories, ammunition trains, food dumps, oil and petrol dumps.'[6]

He claimed to have rejected their contract for South Africa and found work with the British Section as a means of going to England instead. Stephen's memo included a note saying that de Graaf admitted that his sabotage targets in England were the same as for South Africa,

But they mentioned specifically the dry docks in big cities, mentioning Southampton, Newcastle, Londonderry and Aberdeen. The explosive was to be put on the side of the dry-dock and fastened to it with a time fuse. They said that a load of about 2 or 3 kilos of explosive should be enough to blow a hole in the dock wall.

Further instructions regarding locks, etc., to be blown, would have been received in the reply from the Zurich address, in the manner as for the W/T ... De GRAAF admits the German SS discussed with him an espionage mission to South Africa directed towards sabotage and anti-British propaganda ... De GRAAF was trained as a saboteur by KUNTZEL, an agent of the German S.S. in Brussels.[7]

He later admitted having ten lessons finishing in early December at an address in rue Veydt, Ixelles, Brussels. When he was not being taught, he admitted spending a lot of time in Kuntsel's company. They frequently discussed sabotage, which considerably increased his knowledge and understanding. He provided MI5 with details of the formulae, targets, methods of attack and sabotage materials, on which C. P. Hankey produced a report. One imagines that copies were sent to Rheam at Brickendonbury and Rothschild at Wormwood Scrubs.

High Explosive.
90 parts Potassium Chlorate powdered and mixed with 10 parts oil by means of a glass spoon. This preparation put into a tin or box, ready to be attached with a detonator.

3 parts Potassium Chlorate and 1 part sugar are powdered separately, and after being very carefully and thoroughly mixed, are put into a bottle, then placed in a tin or box, ready to be attached with a detonator.

Incendiary.
3 parts Jeweller's Rouge (which DE GRAAF terms 'Karpoet Mortoem') and one part Aluminium are mixed. This incendiary can be used for burning metal, but must, however, be accompanied by an exploder.

This mixture is what the Germans call KOPTAL 31.

Delay Mechanisms.
Dried peas in a glass.

A delay mechanism can be made in the following manner. Pack dried peas or beans into a thin glass or bottle, cover with Sulphuric Acid, seal the glass or bottle. The peas or beans expand, and cause an explosion when the glass is smashed, which fires the charge.

Tin with dripping water and cork.

Although this method was not mentioned during his training, DE GRAAF explains it as follows:-

A cork to which a wire is attached floats in a tin containing water.

The second wire is attached to the bottom of the tin where there is a hole so that the water drips out. When the water has all gone, the cork touches the bottom of the tin and the circuit is completed.

Paper pencil time fuse.
Two parts Potassium Permanganate and one part Plaster of Paris to be ground and mixed. Water is added until a paste if formed, and this is poured into a paper tube about the size of a pencil. This can be used as a fuse burning at the rate of 1" per minute.

Soaked paper as time fuse.

A solution is made by dissolving 20 grams of Sodium Peroxide in half a litre of water. A strip of paper, 1" in width, is soaked in this, and when dry serves as a time fuse with a burning rate of about 5" a minute.

Electrical detonator.

Four parts Potassium Chlorate and one part wood charcoal are mixed with a few drops of Collodion to form a stiff paste, the resultant weight of which to be about 10 grams. The current from a pocket battery is sufficient to fire this.

Key Ring as time fuse.

Take an ordinary key ring about 1½" in diameter and attach a contact wire to one of the ends of the ring. Then place a piece of sugar in between the two rims of the ring. Insulate one of the rims at a point adjoining the piece of sugar, and attach the second contact wire.

On immersion in water the sugar melts, the rims come together, and contact is made.

The action can be speeded up or delayed by using other substances which dissolve quicker or slower than sugar.

Watch used as a time device.

The winding knob of a watch is connected with a battery. An insulated terminal is fixed on the face of the watch at the time it is desired to fire the charge. This terminal and the battery are connected with the detonator which is to fire the High Explosive.

Contact is made and the circuit completed when the hand of the watch reaches the terminal on the face.

Time fuse with sulphuric acid.

A bottle with a paper stopper and containing Sulphuric Acid is turned upside down, and is placed over the incendiary it is required to ignite.

The Sulphuric Acid burns through the paper and comes into contact with the initiating mixture of Potassium Chlorate and sugar, which in its turn would come in contact with and ignite the Thermite.

If thin paper is used a fuse of a few minutes is produced; thick paper increases the delay to a few hours.

DE GRAAF has informed us that there are, of course, thousands of ways of completing a circuit, so there is no end, he states, to the number of methods which can be used by a saboteur.

4. Destruction Targets.

The following are the targets discussed with DE GRAAF by the Germans:-

Ammunition.

He thought the Germans were especially interested in the sabotaging of ammunition factories and dumps. He was to enter into the factory and blow it up by means of one of the first two formulae.

If unsuccessful in this, he was instructed to sabotage ammunition trains leaving the factory, either by making friends with the loaders and introducing a dummy box of ammunition which contained H.E. or burning material, or a charge of explosive was to be laid by the side of the gap between the ends of the lines. The circuit would be completed when the train pressed the ends of the contact wires together.

The Germans did not say whether they were interested in any particular kind of ammunition.

Chemical and Industrial Factories.

As an illustration, the N.V.E. factory in Amsterdam, where DE GRAAF had worked, was given, showing that the most important parts of such a factory to be sabotages were the boiler room, and the engine room or machine room.

On one occasion during his training DE GRAAF was told to find out all he could about a certain factory between Antwerp and Brussels. This, he believed, was a test to ascertain how capable he was of obtaining information on his own initiative.

He was told that very little explosive was needed to do a god deal of damage to a factory.

Oil, Petrol and Benzine Dumps.

Besides ammunition, any oil, petrol or benzene dumps which could be found were to be sabotaged by means of burning material. DE GRAAF was not told where any of these dumps could be found.

Dry Docks.

Dry docks at Southampton, Newcastle, Aberdeen and Londonderry were discussed.

While no exact directions were given as to the size of the bomb to be used, DE GRAAF was told that as much material as possible should be used. He had experimented with an oblong tin about 6" x 4" x 3". An electric detonator could be used for this purpose, but the burning time-fuse would probably be more suitable. In this case, a slow-burning type of fuse would be used, approximately 10" in length, which would give a delay of about three or four minutes. This would be placed in a detonator which contained an explosive mixture of Collodion, Sodium Peroxide and Plaster of Paris, which in its turn would detonate the charge of dynamite. The fuse itself would burn under water, but the detonator and the box container would be sealed by insulating tape. There would be a hole in the top of the container in which the detonator would be inserted, and this would be made watertight by ordinary insulating tape.

Lock Gates.

In the case of Lock Gates on rivers or canals, dynamite was to be enclosed in a wooden box of such a size that it would float. It would be dropped into the water up-stream from the Lock Gate so that the current would carry it down until it lodged against the Gate itself. Locks at Singapore, Suez and Panama were discussed.

Piers under Bridges, etc.

Although just placing the bomb might be sufficient to cause destruction, DE GRAAF was told it would be preferable to lash the dynamite container to the pier.

Floating Docks.

The procedure would be to attach the container to the outer fabric at water level, so that the explosion would result in the destruction of the sides and the filling of the intervening space, resulting in the sinking of the dock.

To blow an oil tank.

Oil in a tank will not burn easily, as there is usually insufficient oxygen. It is, therefore, better to blast a hole in the tank wall by using H.E. the oil will then run out. Previously an extra detonator should be attached to the H.E. and to it a fuse should be made to lead to an incendiary. The fuse must be of sufficient length to prevent the incendiary from burning before the oil reaches it.

When the H.E. explodes the oil runs out of the tank, the fuse is then detonated and fires the incendiary which, in turn, lights the stream of oil from the tank, and thus the contents of the tank are ignited.

The H.E. can be any type of explosive, and no special type of fuse is required to explode it.

The mixture described as KOPTAL 31 can be used to burn a hole in the tank wall, instead of blasting a hole using H.E. in such a case the KOPTAL 31 will probably burn the oil in the tank. However, to make sure a secondary incendiary can be used.

Blowing up an office.

DE GRAAF was told that an office could be blown up by making a circuit with the telephone receiver, for instance. No details were given in this case, because DE GRAAF realised how easy it would be. The telephone would be wired so that the circuit would be completed when the receiver would be lifted from its base.

Sabotage Materials.

Black Time Fuse.

The proportions were to be 4 parts of Sodium Peroxide to 1 part of sawdust. These two ingredients alone were sufficient as an incendiary material, and 1 ox of this material was sufficient to produce a 4" flame which would burn for a few seconds.

DE GRAAF's instructions for obtaining the various materials mentioned in the foregoing are detailed hereunder:-

Dynamite.

He was to steal this if he could from stone quarries or any other place where it was likely to be used for blasting purposes. He was not to attempt to buy this and thereby draw attention to himself.

Detonators.

As in the case of dynamite, DE GRAAF was to steal detonators from mines or other places where blasting was carried out. He was told that he might be given some detonators to take with him. They would be concealed in small brass tubes which would fit into fountain pens or propelling pencils. The tubes were approximately 3" long and 1/4" in diameter.

Sodium Peroxide.
This was to be purchased from a chemist, the pretext being that it was required as a preservative for meat.

Potassium Chlorate.
He was to buy this from any chemist, saying that it was to be used as a gargle for sore throat.

Potassium Permanganate.
Same as for Potassium Chlorate.

Plaster of Paris.
It was not anticipated that this would excite interest, but if asked he was to say that he wanted it to repair a wall.

Collodion.
He knew it would be difficult to obtain this, and he would have endeavoured, first of all, to make friends with somebody who would be in a position to obtain it for him.

If manufactured detonators could not be obtained DE GRAAF was to construct a detonator consisting of Potassium Chlorate (4 parts), Plaster of Paris (one part) and Collodion (a few drops) mixed to a stiff paste and smeared about the filament obtained from the inside of an electric torch bulb. The filament would be fired by means of a 4-volt dry battery cell. Delayed action could be arranged by means of a watch, the hour hand of which would make electric contact at a prearranged time.

If DE GRAAF could not obtain standard Army or mine fuses, he was to make one consisting of a strip of newspaper of approximately 1" in width impregnated with a solution of 20 grams of Sodium Peroxide in half a litre of water. It was estimated that this fuse would burn at the rate of 5" a minute.

6. Tests
At least six tests were carried out by DE GRAAF in the neighbourhood of Antwerp, in the old fortifications to the north of the city, off the Breda-Antwerp road. They were as follows:-
Two with dynamite.
One with dynamite and Potassium Chlorate.
One with Potassium Chlorate and sugar.
One with dynamite under water.
Holes were dug in the ground, a foundation made of iron and earth, and the charges laid between this and concrete blocks, of about 40 kilos in weight, which were put on top. The aim was to split the concrete.

Detonators used were slightly thinner than pencils, and about 2" in length.[8]

In a signed written confession, he stated that the Germans seemed interested in railway lines and ammunition factories and he was expected

> ...to try to make friends with people in the factory and blow it up. As an example, they gave me the N.V. Electro factory, pointing out where the most important parts were. If I could not blow up the factory I had to make friends with the porter and substitute a case of ammunition by a chimney case containing H.E. After watching the trains leaving the factory and thus blow them up; I also had to blow up railway lines and cause an accident with the ammunition train. Besides ammunition factories, they were interested in chemical and industrial factories.[9]

Bakker gave him the cover-name of Prins and the wireless code-name of Le Compte. Three cover addresses were provided where he could send messages 'en clair' or in secret writing. These were the Moreels at 158 Avenue Karreweld, Brussels, H. or F. Ploteyzer, Seegartenstrasse 6, Zurich, and Calle Madrano 49, Barcelona. No doubt MI6 arranged with the Post Office to have all mail addressed to these recipients opened and copied and for their overseas agents to make investigations.

The addresses of two employment agencies in London were provided, and he was told that details of his mission would be communicated to him once his address had been notified to Zurich or Barcelona.

> The reply from BAKKER would contain secret writing which DE GRAAF was to develop in soda solution, as instructed. He would be put in touch with another German agent in this country [unidentified but ZIGZAG left for Lisbon in February 1943] and through this medium supplied with a transmitter, together with code book and full instructions for transmitting.[10]

In return for his mission, he was promised that his parents would not be persecuted but given 400 florins a month and, having returned to Brussels, he was told he would be given a position in the Dutch or German Embassy or Passport Control Office. Alternatively, he would be given a farm in the Rhineland with a house, all installations and livestock. Arrangements for him being paid whilst in England would be made once he established contact.

He provided further details about his wireless training and codes and although described as a most dangerous man, the Director of Public Prosecution ruled against a prosecution. Instead, he was sent to Dartmoor Prison for the duration of the war. In one report, he was described as

> one of the best, and most extensively trained agents, not including ZIGZAG, who have been sent here since the beginning of the war. B.I.C. have had an opportunity of considering the accounts of his sabotage training, and state that he knows virtually all there is to be known of the German curriculum of sabotage instruction including their most up-to-date processes and devices.[11]

Not only was his training much in advance of most of the agents sent into Britain and who had been captured, but also

> it compares favourably with that given to the highest grade enemy agents who have so far been captured in any and all parts of the globe. In short, DE GRAAF is, in our view, not only a traitor but a highly dangerous one, and is equipped with technical knowledge and training, which had he not been detained, would have enabled him to blow-up vital targets in this country and do incalculable damage to our war economy.[12]

In another report sent by J. P. de C. Day to Major Geoffrey Wethered, at B.I.B., MI5's Security Section, he praised the work of the L.R.C. The case was

> an illustration of how the L.R.C. Information Index can be of assistance in catching out would-be penetrators. For what my opinion is worth, I think that the manner in which the L.R.C. examiner and the L.R.C. Information Section between them contrived to expose the weakness in the story of this dangerous agent reflects the greatest credit on them.[13]

While there was some discussion about whether de Graaf was an Abwehr or an SD agent, a memo to Milmo and Rothschild argued for the former.

> the S.D. interest in sabotage is a comparatively recent development which has grown out of its original legitimate interest in political espionage. Hence, it has always attempted to work through collective movements, in such a way that its interest in sabotage may best be described as a secondary development of its preoccupation with subversive movements. Its activities in North Africa are representative illustrations. The despatch of fully trained individual saboteurs against specific targets in countries remote from the agents' home territory does not however, run true to S.D. form. On the other hand, the DE GRAAF case does, in general terms, bear the mark of Abteilung II.[14]

At the end of the war, he was released from Dartmoor and given back his passport, belongings and the £25 cheque. The cash was kept as with other German money to fund MI5's double cross operations. Although his brother offered financial assistance for him to go to Canada, he thought about returning to Amsterdam to live with his mother and sister but changed his mind and found work in London instead.

E. B. Stamp, one of the Security Officers, commented about the de Graaf affair that as well as being 'a most interesting case, it produced a considerable and useful body of counter-espionage intelligence'.[15]

19

More potential saboteurs – Agents September 1941–September 1943

There are conflicting reports about Robert Lejeune, no doubt due to him telling different stories to different interrogators. One source reports that on 15 January 1944 he went to the British Consulate in Barcelona and, on the recommendation of the Belgian chaplain, made a full confession that he was a German-trained saboteur destined for England. The Consulate had already received a report 'of unknown reliability' that he had been head of the Rexist Movement in Antwerp responsible for many arrests and executions of patriotic Belgians. Another report states that he reached Lisbon before handing himself in.

He was sent to Camp 020 for interrogation, and parts of his report about his sabotage training and his mission interested Rothschild. According to his report, he was born in Antwerp in 1921, left school at 15 and was working as a clerk for *Route Militaire* when Belgium was invaded. He claimed that he was recruited by Albert Hendrickx of the organisation to penetrate the Antwerp branch of the Rexist Youth Party, a right-wing Catholic group, and report on its members' activities.

When Hendrickx disappeared with some important dossiers, Lejeune was suspected by Simmoens, a pro-Nazi party official, of having stolen them. During their discussion, when he was told that Belgian men were being trained as saboteurs and sent to England, he claimed that he volunteered as an opportunity to escape. In March 1942, he visited Dr Keilholz in his fourth-floor office, code-named Memiko, at 82a rue de la Loi in Brussels. Keilholz agreed that, like Wyckaert, he should undergo training. Between May and September 1941, he attended a sabotage course led by Abwehrabteilung, Gruppe II.

Instruction was given by a certain BONNEAU or BONEAU, a native of Eupen-Malmady, probably Belgian but speaking with a German accent, aged 30–35, tall, fair, blue eyes, moustache, and by MAERTEN, naturalised German of Belgian origin, aged about 40, brown hair, medium height, moustache. These two individuals were assisted at times by a de BAKKER, a German or Dutchman.

Instruction was given at 174 rue Veydt, Brussels, in a laboratory which had probably belonged to a medical practitioner. It covered the preparation of various sabotage compounds, i.e. -

Inflammable material made up of from gips (19 grams) and aluminium (10 g.)

Inflammable and explosive material made up from KCl03 (3 g.) and sugar or sawdust (1 g.)

Inflammable material made up from chrome (green) (31 g.) and sawdust (10 g.)

Inflammable material, made up from 'Kalisalpetre' (20 g.) and sawdust (25 g.) and flour (10 g.)

Explosive material, made up from 'Amonsalpetre' (90 g.) and aluminium (10 g.) N.B. all formulas by weight. Aluminium means aluminium powder, extra fine, as used in aluminium paint.

A companion under instruction with subject was Jean Schmidt (? Smid), a Belgian-born at Boechout, aged now 21, normally resident at Chaussec de Gistel, Bruges.

BONNEAU ... lives at Avenue Jan van Ryzwyck 104 or 204, Antwerp, telephone 78303. According to subject, Guy WYCKAERT was given his training at this address.[1]

One report stated that at the end of 1941, Lejeune and Jean Schmitt, one of the other agents, left Brussels for Britain, but their mission ended in complete failure. They never got further than the demarcation line of unoccupied France, where they were turned back. Shortly afterwards the two friends were sent off to Germany together as industrial workers. What happened to Schmitt is unknown, but it appears that Lejeune returned to Belgium:

At the end of 1942, subject accepted a course in wireless transmitting. The course, which consisted of sending and receiving messages between adjoining rooms at the rue Veydt address, was discontinued before subject made any considerable progress.

During all this time, subject was told that the organisation was waiting only for an opportunity of sending him forward, and he was paid at first 100 francs a day, rising to 5,000 francs a month.[2]

Bossart was assisted by Opdebeek, sometimes referred to as Damaert, and Bemers. Georges Hollevoet, aliases Gustave Holvoet and Georges Hullin, was a Belgian who organised the agents' departures. Assisted by Louis Debray, they had successfully penetrated local SOE and escape organisations that helped get people from Belgium to Spain. This allowed the Abwehr to send a number of its agents to England. Lejeune admitted being introduced to Andre de Smit, mentioned earlier, who he thought was a trained sabotage agent.

Another MI5 report described Opdebeeck [*sic*] as a heavy pipe and cigar smoker and Chief of Gruppe II's Nest Lille in Summer 1943. He worked closely with Abwehr Gruppe II, Brussels where he recruited agents for sabotage in the Lille district.[3]

Another report stated that Lejeune's first attempt to leave was in July 1942. Hoelvoet accompanied them as far as Vichy but, frightened by a French control point, they returned to Belgium. Another attempt in January 1943 failed when they could not get beyond Lyons. The next attempt in September was led by Debray, who had taken Wyckaert. a clergyman who was a prominent member of the escape line, and seven Dutchmen. One of the group was Rene Clauwers, whom Lejeune described as the head of a sabotage group. Despite the clergyman and five Dutchmen being arrested, Lejeune succeeded in reaching Barcelona.

As mentioned earlier, the Belgian consulate treated both men with suspicion. It appeared Clauwers had second thoughts so Lejeune wrote a letter for him to give to the German consulate asking to be repatriated. Lejeune never saw him again and assumed that he went back to Belgium.

Subject's mission when leaving Belgium was to 'sabotage anything and everything', whether he entered the Army, a war factory, etc. from the beginning he was determined to come clean as soon as he entered Allied territory.

He was not to correspond until he reached the U.K. or an alternative destination when he was to write to P.O. Box 506 Lisbon, with an inner envelope, addressed to Robert Dumont, 186 Bd. General Jacques, Brussels. He was then to use the following code:-

Je suis bien	je travaille dans l'industrie
Je suis tres bien	industrie de guerre
Je suis ici	en Angleterre
Je suis ce pays	Canada
Si loin de vous	Congo Belge
Avec des amis	je suis a l'armee
Je fais du sport	je travaille avec resultats
Je suis malade	difficulties[4]

There was no mention of him receiving any remuneration while in the UK, from which MI5 assumed that the Germans' means of paying their agents had broken down. The fact that Lejeune's parents had remained in Belgium seemed a sufficient guarantee for the Germans. One imagines that, like de Graaf, arrangements for him being paid would be made once he established contact. 'He was told he might be contacted in the UK, and that his contactor would approach him saying: 'C'est vous Robert, je viens de la part de Jean.'[5]

His claims to be a Belgian patriot were questioned by Milmo as he failed to tell the people who helped him travel down the escape line that they faced death and execution by the Germans. Under further pressure he provided details of his sabotage training, materials and the mission that he was meant to undertake in 1941. Rothschild was understandably particularly interested in the materials.

Notes on Appendix B
1. The word formula is really incorrect. 'Formula' refers to the relative amounts of elements such as chromium, oxygen and potassium. In a particular chemical compound such as potassium chlorate, the formula of potassium chlorate is $KCLO3$. What the saboteurs are taught is home-made incendiary or explosive mixtures, such as a mixture of potassium chlorate and sugar.

2. Pave V. Presumably the railway charges are fired by safety fuse as the direction by which the saboteur is to escape is given. Does the saboteur light the safety fuse to try and make the explosion coincide with the passage of a train over the part of the track concerned?

3. Pave VII. This bomb is known as a clam rather that 'a magnetic clam bomb'.

4. The hole is actually for the standard time pencil. Capsule is probably an inaccurate translation of the German Kapsel which means detonator. The detonator is inserted into the end of the time pencil (fig. 4 Red).

5. The chemical delay fuse is either grossly inaccurate drawing of the usual time pencil (see fig. 76) or is a new type with which we are not familiar. Although we have sent time pencils down to Camp 020 before I attach a further couple (in safe condition) which perhaps could be shown to LEJEUNE to see if this is what he was trying to draw,

   If it is not I enclose a drawing done by a saboteur captured in the Middle East of a Russian time pencil and we should be much interested to know whether this is more like the object that LEJEUNE has attempted to draw. (3) is the detonator and not a capsule.

6. These are home-made mixture and not formulas. There are certain minor mistakes due to faulty memory, but in general LEJEUNE has remembered his training quite well.

7. Page VIII. The word calcium chlorate is a mistake for potassium chlorate because of the confusion caused by the German for potassium being called Kalium.

8. Page XI. The ink bottle and watch delays, and the spiral railway switch are recorded in Red. At figs, 29, 34 and 44.
   The railway switch involving both rails is new.

9. Page XIII where were the clams to be placed for sabotaging gasworks?

10. Was removal or loosening of fishplates mentioned during training?

11. What kind of bomb was to be used to sabotage pylons and what delay was it to have?

12. Page XIV. What kind of delay was to be used when sabotaging the railway target?

13. How was the hangar to be sabotaged?

14. LEJEUNE made three attempts to get to this country in 1941, 1942 and 1943. Were the suggested targets the same in each case?

15. Was there any change in the type of training given in July 1941 as compared with February 1942?

16. Has LEJEUNE any information on the type of sabotage training which was being given to post-occupational agents? If he had, we should be interested to have answers to the following questions: -

    (a) Types of sabotage equipment likely to be used. Was emphasis on home-made or professionally-made? Were the agents to be provided with dumps of sabotage equipment in the coastal areas?

    (b) What targets were specially emphasised?

    (c) Was there any suggestion that these agents should set off demolition charges placed in position by Army engineers before retreat?

    (d) Does LEJEUNE know where the nine Dutchmen who were trained in Antwerp were to be used?

    (e) Does Ast Belgium control the post-occupational network in Holland?

17. A possible explanation of the 'acts of sabotage' which LEJEUNE was instructed to commit during training is this. Unknown to LEJEUNE the bombs were innocuous, possibly having dummy detonators. If this latter were the case the detonators would have the letters Ub on their ends. The exercises would be more realistic of the guards on the targets were not warned beforehand though there would be a danger that the trainees would be shot of this were the case. It is more likely that the guards were warned and told that the trainees did not know that their bombs were innocuous. It will be noted that LEJEUNE never actually saw any of his bombs explode during these exercises. Obviously, successful sabotage to the hangar containing machinery at Schaerbeck would only be of value to the Allies.

18. Although it does not occur in this report, it may be worth mentioning that the word safety cord does not exist and should be safety fuse. For details of various types of fuses, see fig. 60 in Red. ...

Plastic explosive was to be used against railway lines with a half hour delay. Saboteurs usually use a long 'Blitzschnur' [detonating cord] in sabotaging railways otherwise the get-away is hazardous. He can either light the fuse and simply destroy the line, or can calculate the time taken for the fuse to detonate the charge so as to catch a passing train. In the case of 'Blitzschnur' this delay would naturally be short...

Page VII. It is correct that the 'hole for capsule' is intended to mean hole of the standard time pencil, as described by B.I.C.

    The drawing is, as suggested, misleading. The pencil mentioned by LEJEUNE is exactly like the shorter of the two submitted by B.I.C., except that, in the case of that seen by LEJEUNE, the white metal covering had a number of holes in it, as he has indicated in his sketch. He does not know their purpose.

    d. B.I.C.'s suggestion is correct.

    e. Exact placing of bomb for destroying gasworks was not mentioned, but LEJEUNE assumes the bottom of the works would be the best place.

    g. Removal of fishplates never mentioned.

    h. Pylons were to have been sabotaged with clam, placed at bottom of pylon. Delay half an hour in this case.

    i. Delay in sabotaging rail target was half an hour in this case.

    j. Plastic, with time pencil.

    k. Sabotage mission the same on all three occasions when he was made to attempt to reach England, the last one only being successful.

    l. no change in training.

m. Post-occupational saboteurs had two missions – to destroy communications immediately after the Germans had retreated – before Allies arrived in the area and to carry out similar work in the area once it was occupied by Allies.[6]

In answer to questions about other students, he claimed that they were trained in Antwerp by Bonneau and Marten, but mostly by Bonneau and that they received the same instructions. Emphasis was placed on ready-made explosives. One student named Boucher was thought to have a quantity in the garden of his house in Lille. Their targets were mostly communications.

He believed two Dutchman, Dulek and Deden, he met whilst training in Antwerp had been sent to Russia. Two others, Xavier and Koll, told him in about January 1943 that they were to be sent to England in a fast motor-boat to carry out sabotage of an unknown nature. Whether they were sent he claimed not to know but pointed out that both were upset at being given this mission, as they were anxious to get out of the Service, Xavier especially, as he was going to be married. Neither names were mentioned in Hoare's book, and they do not have personnel files in the National Archives so, if they did get sent, they might well have avoided detection. Interned until the end of the war, Lejeune was flown back to Belgium in May 1945.

The Abwehr had not given up their attempts to infiltrate agents into Britain. On 3 September 1943, Norwegian coalminer Nicolay Hansen was parachuted in near Fraserburgh, Scotland, with two wireless sets. Having hidden one, he met two lorry drivers carrying Aberdeen kippers from Fraserburgh and told them he was a German agent.

Arrested by the police he was taken to Camp 020 for interrogation. His heavily redacted file revealed that he claimed to have been blackmailed by the Abwehr to undertake the mission. He provided details of his recruitment and intention, once released, to get a job in a Scottish coal mine, retrieve his hidden set and report to the Germans in Oslo on the movement of British convoys.

There was no hint that he had to make contact with MUTT and JEFF or engage in sabotage. However, when a capsule containing crystals of secret ink was found in a cavity in one of his rotten teeth, his story was doubted. It was presumed that he intended to communicate in writing to the Germans. Considered unsuitable for use as a double agent, it was thought to be awkward to prosecute him for fear of revealing details of Camp 020 officers to the media, so he was interned for the rest of the war.[7]

According to Kronberger, a 35-year-old German from Upper Silesia named Gussner, aliases Gold and Gerhard, who had been trained by Amt VI F in Ottoladen Camp near Berlin was sent on a sabotage mission to London in February or March 1943 by Hauptsturmführer Manuel. There he was to find sabotage material himself and also perform destructive acts such as putting sand into machinery. KRONBERGER believes that GUSSNER was later to find his way back to GERMANY. Using a genuine Polish passport, he travelled by Spain to Portugal where he was instructed to sign on as a sailor and use any ship to get to England. He was described as 1.73m in height, black hair, brown eyes, strong with an oval face 'like a Pole', dark skinned, his chin stuck out and up towards his lower lip. Having a cheerful nature, he was fond of drinking, had an average education, had been imprisoned in Germany for forgery and fought with the Republicans in the Spanish Civil War.

As Kronberger had left for Athens in September 1943, he was unable to comment on the outcome of Gussner's mission. A note beside the entry indicated he was Antoni Guzner. A subsequent note stated that 'A German named GOLDIGUSHNER went to England through Spain in 1943. (It seems probable that this is Anton GOLD, alias GUZNER alias GERHARD.)'[8]

In July 1940, the British Consul in Oporto, Portugal, was informed that Antoni Guzner, Polish seaman and suspected German agent, had disembarked from a ship at the request of the German Consul. Was he the same person?

The British Security Service made detailed inquiries with consular officials, Immigration Control, shipping offices, police officers, seamen and others he had contact with. Piecing together their reports, they learned that he was born on 26 June 1908 in Reichenstein, Silesia, and claimed to have worked on Greek vessels in the Mediterranean, fought for the Republicans during the Spanish Civil War and for the Polish Army in France during the German invasion. He spoke German, Spanish and French but little English.[9]

With the evacuation of Allied personnel from France, the Polish Consulate in Marseilles gave him a passport. Sailing on the SS *Higny*, he arrived in Cardiff on 21 June 1940. Reporting to the British police, he was told to find work on another ship. There was no evidence that he undertook any sabotage work at that time; fellow seamen reported him enjoying the social life in Swansea pubs. He found another seaman's job and left from Swansea in July on the SS *Falvik* to Leixoes, Portugal. As he refused to work, the captain had him arrested but a request for his release by the German Consul promising that he would take full responsibility, led to him being put ashore where he spent 19 days in a police hostel in Oporto.

Pinkus Holender, a Polish businessman who stayed in the same hostel, reported Guzner telling him that the ship's master had complained to the Portuguese police authorities about him. In fact, the Captain reported Guzner to the British Consul as deserting his ship, suspecting him as a German agent and that certain Portuguese police officers were in the pay of the German Consul or the Gestapo.

Whilst at the hostel, Holender noticed him being visited by German consular officials. Afterwards, Holender plied Guzner with drink, who claimed to have given information about British merchant convoys to the Germans. He then offered to buy Holender's car as it would be useful for business he wanted to do in Spain, claiming he could get hold of 10,000 escudos and more if he needed. As Guzner painted a gloomy picture of Britain, complaining about food shortages, Holender determined him to be anti-British and, if not a German agent, he was thoroughly pro-German. Accordingly, he reported him to the British Consul.

The Captain reported requesting Guzner's release so he could have him interned in Gibraltar. The police refused, claiming he was a German citizen and requested he be given his pay. As the captain needed crew, Holender was given his job and Guzner got work on the SS *Thysuille*, a Belgian steamer going to

Gibraltar. During the voyage, he and three others, Chyla, Osiecki and Bakaisz, whom he claimed never to have met before, complained to the captain about the poor food and bed bugs. As they refused to do any work unless conditions were improved, the captain had them taken off the ship in Gibraltar, and transferred under armed guard onto the French SS *Pasteur*. A fortnight later, they were taken to Greenock, Scotland.

During the voyage, there was an altercation with a civilian who requested they undertake some cleaning jobs. They thought he was a captain in the Polish Intelligence Service. The Officer in charge of the Polish troops on board also reported Guzner attempting to cause disaffection amongst them. All four were imprisoned at Gateside Prison in Greenock for causing trouble on the high seas. The statement he made to the Scottish Police differed significantly from the above but, as they were all released in January 1941, MI5 failed to question him about it. What he did over the following weeks is unknown.

Enquiries were made determining that he then worked on SS *Porjus*, a Swedish ship bound for Takaradi, Ghana, where he was laid off in Melilla, Spain, in February. His name was added to the 'Black List', names of wanted personnel and on 13 May, instructions were issued to Security Control Officers at all British reports that Guzner, alias Gesner, was to be arrested. He was described as about 5' 9", broad built, dark hair, tanned complexion, scars on arm and abdomen and strongly suspected of being a German agent. Once apprehended he was to be sent under escort to the Royal Victoria Patriotic School with his belongings, which he was not to have access to, and MI5 informed.

A fortnight later, Petrie wrote to Commissioner Wood, the Head of the Royal Canadian Mounted Police in Ottowa, asking him to arrest Guzner if he arrived in a Canadian port, send him back to Britain and interrogate the other three men, Chyla, Osiecki and Bakaisz, to determine whether they were in any way involved with 'most probably a most dangerous German agent'.[10]

Whilst Most Secret Sources picked up references to him travelling between Spain, Portugal, France and Germany, he was not apprehended until 1945 in Lisbon. During his interrogation, he admitted that he had been working for the Abwehr from 1940. A captured SD officer named Swedkowicz identified a man called Gold undergoing a course in sabotage and small arms training in December 1942 at the *Poliseipraesidium* at Alexanderplatz 264, Berlin. They both did a lock-picking course in the Kriminal Museum and Skedowicz thought he would also have been trained in ciphers, geography and motor transport driving.

Although the Germans had planned to send him on a sabotage mission to London, the evidence suggests he spent the rest of the war involved in black market activities, supplying the Abwehr and Gestapo with Spanish and Portuguese goods, infiltrating a Polish escape organisation in Madrid, acting as a passeur, a guide over the Pyrenees, and denouncing Poles.[11]

In May 1943, Belgian Johannes Huysmann and his wife arrived in England having been arrested by the Portuguese police in Lisbon. Their intention had been to get a visa for the Congo via the United Kingdom but MI6 had refused one. Most Secret Sources had identified as early as September 1942 that the Abwehr intended him to come to England on a visa.

One imagines that Huysmann's wife was detained whilst he was sent to Camp 020. When his original claim that it was a case of mistaken identity was disproved, he eventually admitted working for the Abwehr in early 1941 to escape trouble with the Gestapo in Brussels. Having been given various questionnaires, he was sent to Barcelona where he was unsuccessful in obtaining visas for the UK, the United States, Mexico and Brazil. There was no indication he was sent on a sabotage mission.

After he provided valuable intelligence about the Abwehr in Belgium, it was decided that trying him under the Treachery Act would be difficult due to the circumstances of his deportation from Portugal, so MI5 used him as a 'stool pigeon', to report on conversations he had with other interned inmates. He helped MI5 until the end of the war; the Belgian authorities sentenced him to life imprisonment for offences he had committed before coming to England.[12]

On 16 July 1943, Pierre Neukermans arrived in England from Lisbon claiming that he had escaped the Nazis and wanted to help the Allied cause. Unfit for military service, he worked for the Free Belgian government-in-exile. Six months later, he was interrogated by MI5 when they found out that the person who had helped him escape from Belgium was working for the SS. He admitted that he had sent messages about convoy movements to the Germans to addresses in neutral countries. Whether his mission also included sabotage is unknown. Tried under the Treachery Act, he was hanged at Pentonville Prison on 23 June 1944.[13]

In November 1943, 58-year-old Oswald Job arrived in Poole from Lisbon and told Immigration Control that he had been born in Stepney, London, of German parents and moved to Paris in 1911. Having a British passport, he was sent to St Denis internment camp following the outbreak of war. Whilst on parole in June 1943, he escaped to Spain. MI5 knew of his imminent arrival from the Abwehr's response to Dragonfly's requests for money. Dragonfly was MI5's code-name for Hans George, a German born in Britain who had been recruited by the Abwehr in Holland in 1939. On informing MI5 of their approach, George was given a room in Bayswater, London and paid as a double agent to send wireless messages to the Germans until November 1944. As he needed funds, they told him that a reliable person would bring him some jewellery which he could sell. The Security Officers in Poole had been alerted and found the jewellery on Job. Rather than interning him, he was released and placed under strict surveillance to check who he made contact with.

When he made no move to contact Dragonfly, he was apprehended after the postal censorship noticed him writing a lot of letters to his family and fellow inmates at St Denis internment camp. When MI5 interviewed his family and were told that they had not written any letters to him, he was interrogated again and found to have a large set of keys for a small flat. Inside the keys was found secret ink. When the handle of his razor was examined, further secret writing equipment was found.

He admitted to having been friendly with German guards in the internment camp and being recruited by the Abwehr and taught secret writing. The code he had to use was to be passed to him in German broadcasts from Paris. He claimed to have agreed to the mission to report on bomb damage and the morale of the British public as a means of escaping France but made no mention of a sabotage mission. His insistence that the jewellery was his was disproved when he was shown the address to which Dragonfly had asked for it to be delivered.

A further message from the Germans in November confirmed Job as a spy but MI5 doubted his story that he was to report on bomb damage and public morale. Whether they suspected a sabotage mission was not mentioned but he was hanged at Pentonville prison on 16 March 1944, the oldest person executed under the Treachery Act.[14]

On 11 February 1944, Josef van Hove arrived from Stockholm claiming that he was a Belgian wanting to join his country's armed forces in Britain. At the London Reception Centre, he stated that he had been in trouble with the Belgian police for black market activities. Most Secret sources confirmed that he had a reputation as an unpleasant hanger-on around Antwerp night clubs and worked for the Abwehr.

He was detained until April and, following interrogation, admitted that to avoid arrest, he had agreed to work for the Germans informing them about French and Belgian workmen at airfields in Northern France. In 1942, a plan to send him to Britain with another agent via Switzerland failed. They then arranged for him to work as a steward on a ship going to Stettin, north-west Poland. He had to pretend to jump ship in Gothenburg and visit the British Consul with a request to go to Britain. As they had been informed of his past, they sent him to the Belgian authorities who arranged his trip to England.

He admitted that, needing money, he had agreed to a mission in England to provide the Germans with military intelligence using secret writing. Whilst in Sweden he had already written fifteen letters to the same addresses given to Pierre Neukermans. There was no indication that he had to contact German agents in England or undertake sabotage. Having confessed to working for the enemy, he was hanged on 12 July 1944, the last spy to be executed in England during the war.[15]

20

ZIGZAG's return and Sabotage before D-Day – 1944

After fifteen months behind enemy lines carefully observing and listening to the Germans' plans, Eddie Chapman was prepared for a mission back to England. Most Secret Sources and his subsequent interrogation produced the following file.

In March, 1944 CHAPMAN left Oslo with GRAUMANN and STUBE for Berlin, final destination to be England.

On 20 March, CHAPMAN left Berlin for Paris with: GRAUMANN, STUBE, von FLOETNER, Hans KLAUSUS and MUENICH.

On 19 April CHAPMAN left for Brussels, the party included:- GRAUMANN, von FLOETNER, KLAUSUS and MOENICH; the trip to England was abandoned owing to the danger of night-fighters. CHAPMAN, GRAUMANN and KLAUSUS returned to Paris, von FLOETNER to BERLIN, and STUBE to Oslo.

26 June CHAPMAN was told that he would leave Brussels for England on 27 June. CHAPMAN left for Brussels with GRAUMANN and MOENICH. On the morning of the 27th they entrained for an aerodrome at Huisterheide, near Den Holden. After discussion of plans CHAPMAN was given a camera and £1,000 for another agent in this country, whose name CHAPMAN would receive by wireless. CHAPMAN did not know whether the agent was already in England or if he was to follow him. (This agent was in fact BRUTUS [Roman Czerniawski, a Polish double agent]) Two Junkers 88 planes were in readiness and took off at 2345 hours.[1]

MI5 expected the second Junker to be dropping another agent, code-named LEHAR, but Chapman later claimed its purpose was to distract attention from his plane.

On 29 June 1944, he landed by parachute near Six Mile Bottom, Cambridgeshire, with two wireless sets, £6,000 and a new mission. When he told his story to the local police, he was told, 'Don't be so silly. Go to bed.' He told them to ring up the officer at Littleport who arrested him in 1942, as he would remember him.

When eventually he got to talk to MI5, he told them he did not have a sabotage mission this time, but he had been asked to report on the Asdic gear for spotting submarines, the radio location system fitted to night fighters to detect plane direction, the damage caused by Germany's flying bombs and the location of American air force bases. He also had to collect information about a new wireless frequency the Germans believed Britain was using to interfere with their V-2 weapon.

Set up with a flat in Kensington, his major success was reporting to the Germans that their flying bombs were overshooting Central London, which led them to redirect the bombs to sparsely populated areas further south; and he grossly exaggerated the casualty figures.

One imagines that he met Rothschild and discussed his experiences with him but there was no record of such a meeting, nor whether he supplied the answers to the questions: target, other chemicals, camouflage, steady supply. Although he was allowed to return to Norway towards the end of the war with MI5-inspired intelligence, his high life style and lack of security led Masterman to terminate his case.[2]

In recognition of his contribution to the Intelligence Services, MI5 arranged for him to be pardoned for his earlier crimes, gave him £6,000 to start a new life and allowed him to keep £1,000 of the money the Germans had given him.

Returning to life in the criminal underworld in London, he bragged about his wartime adventures in Germany. In a post-war article in the *Etoile du Soir*, Chapman admitted that in a moment of confidence, Vosch had told him that 'he had been responsible for the Hammersmith Bridge explosion, and that a considerable amount of the explosions believed to have been committed by the I.R.A. were the work of the German espionage service'.

MI5 attempted to find evidence of Vosch's pre-war activities. Their file included the transcript of Chapman's conversation with Rothschild in which he had mentioned Vosch's confession but it appears it had not been acted upon at the time.

According to Macintyre, Chapman was a walking compendium on explosives. TAR reported cross-examining him about Vosch and being told that

> He was a man who had done a little work in England and Paris and was supposed to have been responsible for some of the cloakroom explosions, and that he had some idea that he had something to do with sabotage of bridges. CHAPMAN also said that he thought VOSCH had probably worked with the I.R.A., having been sent here by the Germans before the war for that purpose.[3]

He was reported to have arrived in England in March 1939 and worked as a waiter at the Carlton Hotel, W.1, living at 1 Neal Street, Hammersmith, using the name Karl Barton. As Chapman claimed Vosch had an Irish girlfriend who worked in the Hyde Park Hotel, MI5 suspected that she might have been involved in his sabotage activities but found no trace of her.[4]

Booth described him as 'one of the more remarkable characters at the Stelle, a man who, it transpired, was better paid that anyone there. [He] drove a car plastered with Breton separatist stickers, had been in Paris in the early days of the war when he had apparently killed a number of Allied officers by planting a bomb in a hotel. In recognition of this attack, he was awarded an Iron Cross.'[5]

Although Booth claimed Chapman was not on friendly terms with Vosch, he told him that before the war started, he had been sent to England by Germany to help the IRA stir up trouble in London.

> My opinion is that many of the bomb outrages in 1939 were really the work of this man. If you ask me for conclusive proof, I don't have it. I can only report the facts.
>
> The two simplest methods of sabotage can be carried out either with a watch attached to batteries or with acid. An ordinary ink bottle is filled with sulphuric acid. The lid is pierced, and a piece of cardboard is placed between the lid and the hole, it takes two hours for the acid to eat through the cardboard. This flows on to some specially prepared burning mixture which explodes the detonator and charge. Now, Herbert Vosch was certainly in London during the time of the IRA outrages, and in my opinion it would have been difficult for Irish Irregulars to have acquired the training essential for such hazardous work.
>
> I sincerely believe that some of the unfortunate Irishmen who served long sentences for these offences were not so guilty as people were led to believe at the time. Nor was this expert saboteur, Vosch, the only German agent who was in England during this period. Franz Schmidt, now also a member of my unit, A.S.T. was then working as a waiter at Frascati's, the well-known London restaurant. Was it an accident that a skilled saboteur and a radio man were in London at the same time?[6]

MI5 investigated Schmidt but there was nothing in Vosch's file that suggested he had also been involved in the sabotage campaign.

With Vosch claiming responsibility for the Hammersmith Bridge and cloakroom bombings, Irish investigative journalist John Ryan, wrote to Mr Skeffington-Lodge, MP for Bedford, expressing his concerns about the way IRA activists had been treated before and during the war, and that some had been wrongly imprisoned.

> I know that it would be both futile and pointless to suggest that the I.R.A. were innocent of all bombing outrages etc. in 1939 nor do I wish to convey any such thing but in view of the fact that an English secret service agent has placed information in the hands of the English authorities proving that unknown to the I.R.A. German agents were carrying out acts of terror at the same time and under their names. The fact that none of the Irishmen would plead guilty or not guilty nor would they conduct any defence, in fact, played into the hands of the Germans. The information that CHAPMAN has disclosed throws a shadow of doubt over the entire prosecution during the 1939 trials. Who can say, in fact, which men were guilty and which weren't? It certainly would seem to call for a re-trial of all concerned or at least of some. In my opinion, the fact that this information has been in the hands of the government for some time and has not been acted upon speaks poorly for the sincerity of the Home Secretary. However,

I do not propose to level criticism at the Labour Party in view of the fine courage they have shown in taking up the cause of these wretched men.[7]

Whether Skeffington-Lodge raised the issue with the Home-Secretary and cases were re-opened is unknown.

In 1953, MI5 attempted to block Chapman from publishing his wartime exploits in England but Owen's *The Eddie Chapman Story* (1953); *Free Agent: The Further Adventures of Eddie Chapman* (1955) and *The Real Eddie Chapman Story* (1966) gave redacted versions.

Following his death in 1997, the National Archives released his personal file in 2001 which led to the works of Nicholas Booth and Ben Macintyre. As mentioned earlier, a 1966 film, *Triple Cross*, some TV interviews and a 2011 BBC Timewatch documentary told the story of the only Englishman to have been awarded the Iron Cross; his role in helping Britain successfully defend itself against enemy sabotage has now been given greater coverage.

While there had been successful sabotage of Allied merchant navy ships in Gibraltar and other overseas ports, the main method had been the use of frogmen, using diving suits, flippers and a respiratory system to swim underwater and attach magnetic bombs to the ships' hulls. Another method used was the planting of sabotage material in the cargos loaded in foreign ports. How extensive this method was, was not mentioned in the counter-sabotage files, but there was a report of one case.

In February 1944, a bomb was discovered at a village near Kettering, Northamptonshire, in a wooden crate of onions. This crate of onions has been identified as part of the cargo of the S.S. EMPIRE HEYWOOD. This ship left Valencia for Gibraltar on 21.12.43, from where it proceeded in convoy to the U.K. while bound for the U.K. on 31.12.43, an explosion occurred in her cargo, which included crates of oranges and onions.

This explosion, and similar ones on another ship in the convoy, received wide publicity in the press.

The bomb discovered in the crate of onions near Kettering failed to explode through mechanical faults in the time clocks which were included.

The bomb was dismantled by a member of the Security Service, and photographs of it will be sent to you in due course. It consisted of ten cast rectangular blocks, each about the size of a brick, of high explosive, and two blocks of plastic explosive of about the same volume as the cast blocks, in each of which was buried a German Mark II delay (which will be familiar to Security Service representatives) with primer.

There is no reason to think that any other crates of onions or oranges contain time bombs, and the Security Service is of the opinion that no special searches of such crates should be undertaken; nor need they be segregated in any way.

In the event of there being a reason to expect further bombs, the Security Service will, as usual, inform their representatives in the various regions or at ports, who in turn will pass the information to the appropriate authorities, including the Police.

At the present time, no such information exists and there is, therefore, no action to be taken in regard to searching for bombs.[8]

The member of the Security Service who dismantled the bomb was Rothschild. When Churchill was informed of his 'dangerous work in hazardous circumstances' he arranged for him to be awarded the George Medal in April 1944.[9]

Whilst Rothschild was instrumental in reducing the threat of enemy sabotage, he admitted that there were still cases being reported in 1944. What has not come to light is whether these were carried out by undetected Nazi agents, the IRA, or pro-German British citizens.

As regards sabotage, the recent examples of outbreaks of fires at Glasgow, Liverpool and Birkenhead illustrates the necessity of having trained investigators at M.I.5, who can carry out investigations in different parts of the country, which the local Police cannot do.

B.5 have good contacts with almost every important Police Force in England, Scotland and Northern Ireland, and we have found that these Police Forces willingly cooperate with members of B.5.

About a week ago, every member of B.5 was out of this office investigating sabotage cases, and you will remember that when B.5 originally came, we undertook to carry out any investigation into suspected cases of sabotage which the D.N.I. (Division of Naval Intelligence) might require, when H.M. ships were concerned.[10]

In March 1944, two men were charged with sabotaging telephone boxes in Bristol and the case was reported by a Canadian newspaper:

Bristol. Eng. March 1 – Described by police as 'definitely anti-British and pro-German' Robin Pinckard, 29, Bristol, former member of the British Union of Fascists, was sentenced to five years in prison. He pleaded guilty to conspiring to damage telephone apparatus and to 15 cases of damaging telephones.

18-year-old Raymond Dale, Bristol, who admitted damaging 65 telephones, was sentenced to 12 months' imprisonment. The prosecutor said the men entered telephone kiosks and tore or cut away receivers. On one occasion Pinckard first rang the operators and said: 'We are former member of the Fascist party and are going to damage the telephone.'

Police said Dale told them he caused the damage because Pinckard asked him to do so and that he termed Pinckard 'a former Fascist' who 'wants to hold up the war effort'.

Police testified that Pinckard was discharged from both the British navy and army when it found he was pro-German. He had been interned for six months but released when he swore he was no longer in sympathy with Axis views.[11]

Wichmann reported another agent, code-named WHISKY, who was infiltrated into Britain before D-Day and supposedly evaded detection having travelled through France and Spain. 'He was an agent of Hamburg VI T/Wi/T who started in the second half of 1944. Wireless traffic was not extensive and he supplied information on new construction and inventions in the air industry.[12] Whether WHISKY was also engaged in sabotage was not mentioned but, even as late as December 1944, there were still reports of attacks. Len Burt informed Petrie, head of MI5:

> We are still dealing with allegations of sabotage in various parts of the U.K. on behalf of the Admiralty, M.A.P. [Ministry of Aircraft Production] and other Government Services and Departments. The incidence of these cases obviously fluctuates a good deal, but only a few weeks ago, four officers were engaged simultaneously in carrying out investigations at Scapa Flow, Portsmouth and the Clyde on independent matters. There have been other occasions when the whole of the section has been engaged on this work. In recent months, this work has eased off considerably, and at the moment there are only two cases of alleged sabotage under investigation, one at Southampton and one at Bristol. ...
>
> The security of Public Utility Undertakings is at the moment of little concern to this Department, but in the past we have spent a good deal of time in visiting these establishments and advising and making certain recommendations involving matters of security.[13]

The measures taken by the 'water undertakers' were in place until six months after VE Day, when the War Office notified the Security Officers:

> It can be accepted that the risk of armed sabotage and secret sabotage organised by Germany within the U.K. is so small as to be negligible. On general grounds of freedom from enemy interference of this kind, military (including Home Guard) and police protection have been withdrawn from many vulnerable points.
>
> In case this action would have the effect of persuading Management that all forms of control can now be abandoned (an unlikely contingency), it may be necessary to point out that public utilities are still vital to the war effort and reasonable measures must still be continued to meet the possible danger of interference by subversive individuals, malicious damage, arson and larceny.
> Such measures should, it is felt, take the following forms:-
> (a) Control of entry to be exercised and the Pass and permit systems enforced.
> (b) Material safeguards which have been erected should not be dismantled without reference.
> (c) Employees to be acquainted with present circumstances and be asked to remain on the alert and to report unusual occurrences as heretofore.
> As the responsibility for local security precautions now devolves upon respective managements, the services of the Vulnerable Points Adviser and this department are available should any security of de-restriction problem arise.[14]

Throughout the war, Rothschild had amassed a large collection of German sabotage material. In order to disseminate illustrations of these devices to Security Officers in Britain and the Colonies, he commissioned Laurence Fish, a freelance artist, to sketch twenty-five drawings of camouflaged German explosive devices that had been collected during MI5's counter-sabotage operations. The drawings were found in Rushbrooke Hall, the family's Suffolk estate.

They included bombs or incendiaries hidden in shoes, hair brushes, shaving brushes, match boxes, bars of chocolate, thermos flasks, mess tins, throat pastilles, cans of motor oil, tins of plums, tins of cassoulet, French stew and exploding pea detonators. Whilst they show German ingenuity, the only one thought to have been used in Britain was the exploding peas.

On 4 May 1943, Rothschild asked Fish if he could do a drawing of an explosive slab of chocolate.

> We have received information that the enemy are using pound slabs of chocolate which are made of steel with a very thin covering of real chocolate. Inside there is high explosive and some form of delay mechanism, but we do not know what, so it could not be put in the drawing. When you break off a piece of chocolate at one end in the normal way, instead of it falling away, a piece of canvas is revealed stuck in the middle of the piece which has been broken off and sticking into the middle of the remainder of the slab. When the piece of chocolate is pulled sharply, the canvas is also pulled and this initiates the mechanism. I enclose a very poor sketch done by somebody who has seen one of these. It is wrapped in the usual sort of black paper with gold lettering, the variety being PETERS. Would it be possible for you to do a drawing of this, one possibly with the paper half taken off revealing one end and another with the piece broken off showing the canvas? The text should indicate that this piece together with the attached canvas is pulled out sharply and that after a delay of seven seconds the bomb goes off.

There were concerns that German agents were plotting to smuggle explosive chocolate into the War Cabinet and into the hands of Prime Minister Winston Churchill, who was known to have a sweet tooth.[15]

These explosive devices were not limited to the German arsenal. The boffins at Aston House developed a range of similar, if not identical, items for Allied agents to use in the field. The War Office compiled and issued a 'Descriptive Catalogue of Special Devices and Supplies', rather like a shopping catalogue, with illustrations and details and reference numbers. They included exploding wooden logs, rusty bolts and nuts, soap, cigarettes, bicycle pumps, torches, briefcases, attaché cases, suitcases, books, shaving brushes, razor handles, Balinese wood carvings, Chinese stone lanterns, oil cans, wooden road blocks, bottles of chianti, tins of food, tins of fruit, sugar beet, lumps of coal and dead rats. Camouflaged drums of oil and paint, flagons, fish barrels, hollowed-out driftwood and logs, cement bags, fish boxes, packing cases, plaster and papier-mache fruit and vegetables were used to hide grenades, rifles, Sten guns and explosives.

There were also cleverly constructed everyday items in which agents could hide codes and messages, often printed on silk. They included collar studs, matchboxes, sponges, toothpaste tubes, shaving brushes, hair and clothes brushes. Itching powder, cream that frosted glass, deodorant that threw dogs off the scent and a range of pills were available, including the L pill which could be hidden in a tooth cavity. Potassium cyanide contained in a rubber capsule once chewed would kill the agent in seconds.

Conclusion

There were many reasons why the IRA's S-Plan and the German sabotage operations against Britain failed. A series of failed bomb attacks, lack of funds and the crackdowns against the IRA in London and Dublin were part of the reason. The British and Irish Governments, the War Office, the Intelligence Services, the XX Committee, the Police, the Home Guard and the British public all played important roles. There were also failures in the IRA, the German Intelligence Service and the quality of the saboteurs they selected and trained for their operations.

The British government's response to the S-Plan was to implement a number of measures to counter the IRA offensive. In January 1939, to improve the security of England's infrastructure, all power stations, gas works, telephone exchanges, and the Droitwich transmitting station were put under police protection. Police patrols around the government buildings at Whitehall were strongly reinforced and all ships from Ireland arriving at Holyhead, Fishguard and Liverpool were closely inspected.

On 8 February 1939, two bills were introduced in the *Dáil*. The 'Treason Act' imposed the death penalty on perpetrators found guilty of acts of sabotage as defined in Article XXXIX of the Irish Constitution. This penalty was to apply whether the act was committed within or outside the boundaries of the state. Its aim was curtailing IRA activity both within the Irish state and the United Kingdom. The 'Offences against the State Act' gave the police greater powers of search, arrest and detention without trial. It also declared seditious any suggestion in a newspaper or magazine that the elected Government of Ireland was not the lawful government.

On 30 June, the 'Prevention of Violence (Temporary Provisions) Bill' was passed giving the government comprehensive powers to prevent the immigration of foreigners, for their deportation and extending the requirement for Irish people to be registered with the British police. Special Branch had the powers to tap suspects' telephone communications, open their mail. The use of Home Office Warrants, signed by the Home Secretary, allowed the Security Services to intercept all incoming and outgoing correspondence of suspected individuals and enter their house and place microphones so as to listen in on conversations. Identified leaders of IRA groups in each English district were arrested and interned. When other known IRA members were sent to make attacks in neighbouring districts, they were followed by the police to identify their contacts and further arrests were made. As a result, 119 people were expelled from Britain.

Following the outbreak of war in September 1939, the 'Special Powers Act' in Ireland allowed the government to make precautionary arrests of forty-six IRA members. This led to increased liaison between MI5, Special Branch, the Royal Ulster Constabulary, the Irish Intelligence Service, and the Gardai, the Irish Police.

The 'Emergency Powers (Defence) Act', introduced on 24 August 1939, provided the police with even greater powers of search, arrest and detention for seditious acts and permitted trial by military tribunals which could order executions. Amendments made in January 1940 allowed to police to intern and deport suspected IRA activists. MI5 used their network of paid informers to gather intelligence on the perpetrators of acts of sabotage as well as obtain permission from the Home Office to open mail and tap telephones. The two IRA members who were found guilty of the Coventry attack, despite protests, were hanged in February 1940.

In July 1940, when Most Secret Sources indicated the imminent arrival of twenty-eight enemy agents, the Admiralty issued a warning to all coastguards and coast watching authorities, the immigration and customs authorities, chief security officers at the ports and the police in coastal areas to be on the look-out for small boat landings.[1]

Wardens were appointed in every community. The black-out, introduced two days before the war started, was strictly enforced and tighter security was introduced. Posters, advertisements, radio and television broadcasts encouraged the general public to report anyone behaving suspiciously to the police, especially if they had a foreign accent. While there was an increased police presence on the streets, especially at night, there were also undercover operations.

Under the Explosive Substances Act of 1883, chemists had stricter regulations about the sale of chemicals which could be used for manufacturing home-made explosives. Investigations had to be made on purchasers of large quantities of charcoal, potassium chlorate, iron oxide, powdered aluminium and sulphuric acid. Contact details of the purchasers were to be forwarded to the police. Increased security was introduced at explosives stores of dynamite and gelignite, detonators and fuses at mines and quarries to prevent theft.

When the Abwehr started infiltrating German espionage agents and saboteurs into Ireland to support IRA activities against Britain, only individuals or small groups arrived. The vast majority of these agents were captured, partly because of increased vigilance amongst the Irish population but also because the Abwehr was ignorant of conditions in Ireland and their agents made elementary mistakes. The interrogation of captured agents increased MI5's knowledge and understanding of German methods.

Exactly how many suspected Irish and German saboteurs were arrested, interned or deported is unknown but with reduced numbers and instructions from the Abwehr to halt their attacks prior to Operation SEALION, the IRA's S-Plan failed to achieve its objectives.

Following the German surrender in 1945, General Lahousen, who had been chief of Abwehr II between 1939 and 1943, was arrested and the report written up after his interrogation in Nuremberg included his overview of the Abwehr's relationship with the IRA.

Sabotage work against England was sharply curtailed by CANARIS. In so far as I can remember, with a fair degree of accuracy, only three or four II-agents were sent to England and Ireland from the beginning of the war to the middle of 1943, despite the activity which was naturally ordered, especially after the attempted invasion had been given up, and the air offensive against England had been stopped. Furthermore, all actions concerning Ireland – I believe from 1940–41 on – the military Abwehr Abt II was referred to the Foreign Office Specialist on Ireland, Dr VEESENMAYER, and was told in writing that the Foreign Office itself would carry out and be responsible for this diversion activity, and that Abw. Abt II should only act at the instigation of the Foreign Office (Dr VEESENMAYER), by giving technical help in the transport of people (dropping and landing of agents).

CANARIS completely agreed with this policy, because through the rule, it meant that he would always (at least, for a certain period) know the far-fetched plans of the Foreign

Office for Ireland, without, at the same time, being himself directly under the orders of HITLER and KEITEL (i.e. the Wehrmachtfuehrungstab) which would have put him in a difficult position from which to carry out either his policy of passive activity or active sabotage.

Dr VEESENMAYER's Irish Bureau was becoming very active at that time (1940–41), but the military and political-military aims I can no longer remember very clearly. It must have had to do with the instigation of a civil war in Ireland, with the assistance of the IRA (Irish Republican Army), which would have served as the opening step to the possibility of a military invasion.

For this purpose, JIM RUSSEL [sic], a leader of the IRA, was to be brought to Ireland from America, via Italy and through Germany.

JIM RUSSEL saw RIBBENTROP, in order to receive from him the general political directives for his Diversion action. All further instructions RUSSEL received from Dr VEESENMAYER,

A U-boat was to have brought him to Ireland, but a few hours after its departure RUSSEL died – in my opinion under somewhat unclear circumstances.

I heard later, that certain circles of the Foreign Office accused CANARIS, by implication, of having liquidated him. That is absolutely untrue.

However, I think it is possible that he may have been poisoned by his very radical associate, Frank Ryan, who accompanied him until the U-boats departure. Internal difficulties and political rivalries within the IRA probably played a part in this matter.[2]

The SIS's D Section officers amassed a great deal of intelligence of IRA tactics and the explosives and sabotage devices they used. Although they failed to prevent small-scale attacks, the establishment of B.1.C, MI5's sabotage and explosives section, helped disseminate knowledge of the saboteurs' equipment and methods and ensured security officers were appointed across the country to raise awareness and implement counter-sabotage measures. Research and development to improve SOE's explosives was carried out at Aston House.

When the SOE was formed, it used D Section's knowledge about the IRA's and communist cells' tactics in the demolitions courses they gave their agents. Specialist industrial sabotage courses were provided at Brickendonbury.

By 1941, MI5 and MI6 had received increased funding and manpower Their Counter-Espionage and Security Sections played a major role in minimising the threat of sabotage across the country.

The allocation of police inspectors to B5, MI5's Counter-Espionage Section, to investigate incidents of suspected sabotage was helpful but how many cases were brought to court is unknown. The fact that there were still alleged sabotage cases being investigated in December 1944 suggests these measures had not acted as a deterrent to the more determined saboteur but tighter security at potential targets reduced incidents of serious damage.

MI5 identified potential sabotage targets and took measures to protect them. Stricter security was enforced. Night watchmen with guard dogs were introduced. Police patrols were increased. High walls with glass embedded in cement on the top surrounded important sites. Removal of trees by site boundaries, gravel approaches, barbed wire fences, electric signalling fences, lethal electrified fences, trip wires and floodlights gave added protection. Fire watchers were put in place and fire stations and crews were put on alert. Security passes and stricter checks on people and vehicles entering and leaving sites were introduced. Vulnerable Points Advisers were appointed whose responsibilities included the regular checking of all vital machinery for any unusual attachments.

Sensitive coastal areas, particularly those considered to have potential German invasion beaches, were identified and made into exclusion zones with military guard posts set up to deter trespassers.

On 8 October 1939, Churchill called for a Home Guard to be set up of 500,000 men aged over 40. By 14 May 1940, the Local Defence Volunteers was created which increased awareness in the British public's mind of the possibility of invasion and the importance of security.

In expectation of a German invasion following the evacuation from Dunkirk, another secret organisation was established, the Auxiliary Units. Under the control of Colin Gubbins, an SOE officer, men were selected and trained as stay-behind saboteurs and wireless operators. Provided with food, weapons and sabotage equipment, they were to hide in secret shelters and, in wireless contact with their headquarters, only emerge once the enemy had advanced inland on missions to destroy their supply lines and communications.[3]

Not only were Auxiliary Units given a life expectancy of 12 days, but they were also under orders not to be captured. If surrounded, they would need to shoot each other or blow themselves up with their own explosives.[4]

The appointment of Regional and District Security Officers and the training they were given, notably in the recognition of camouflaged explosive devices, reduced the prospects of saboteurs bringing such devices into the country.

The British public played their part. Spy hysteria before the war intensified during the IRA's sabotage campaign, which led to a heightened awareness of the threat of saboteurs and enemy agents. The government's propaganda programme of posters and radio broadcasts made people more vigilant.

From 1940, Stephens' team at Camp 020 interrogated suspected Fifth Columnists, collaborators and captured enemy agents. Most of the saboteurs were questioned there and those who refused to cooperate were executed under the Treachery Act. Seventeen spies were hanged, including four British citizens. Some were turned into double agents and those who talked, once all valuable intelligence had been extracted, were interned for the duration of the war.

The Arrival from Enemy Territory Act allowed all refugees to be interrogated at the ports and airports. Few enemy agents were claimed to have passed through this process. The provision of X-Ray equipment allowed careful examination of passengers' luggage, the Security Officers having been given photographs by B.1.C of camouflaged sabotage devices. The creation of the London Reception Centre in June 1941, allowed in-depth interrogation of all refugees arriving in Britain and those suspected of being an enemy agent were passed on to Camp 001 and Camp 020.

Masterman's XX Committee used turned saboteurs and wireless operators to feed MI5-inspired misinformation to the Abwehr and arrange the arrival of new saboteurs and sabotage material, often straight into the hands of the police. He reckoned that of the 115 or so agents targeted against Britain during the war, apart from a few who committed suicide, all were caught with several successfully turned to become double agents. His Double Cross System played a major role in deceiving the Germans into believing the D-Day landing would be in Pas de Calais.

The breaking of Enigma Code allowed intercepted enemy communications to be decoded and translated. These Most Secret Sources gave the Security Section advance details of the arrival of enemy saboteurs and the opportunity to not only apprehend potential saboteurs but also to acquire German sabotage material and money. This money was used to cover the expenses of maintaining the double agents throughout the war.

Following the post-war arrest of Colonel Otto Skorzeny, the SS head of sabotage, espionage and paramilitary training, MI5 contacted his American captors and requested they ask him

to write a memorandum on the views held by the German Intelligence Service on security measures in the United Kingdom with particular reference to the following points:

a. Did he get reports or stray information to the effect that security was good at industrial concerns which might be the subject of sabotage attack or espionage?
b. Dis he consider, on the contrary, that such security was not good?
c. Did he consider security at ports was good and that entry into the country would be difficult?

d.   Did he receive any benefit from peacetime espionage about British industry?

e.   If so, what details does he know now about how and by whom such information was collected; who collated it in Germany; through what channels it was received?[5]

Skorzeny's response arrived three weeks later, claiming to have had no reports about security measures taken in England.

> It was generally known that in England it was possible to execute such measures in a thorough and strict manner due to its 'splendid isolation'. I never tried to obtain such reports as I was convinced that such attacks on the British Isles could hardly be carried out, and because sabotage attempts of individual agents would have had little effect in view of the decentralisation of British industry. It was common knowledge that the British Intelligence due to its long existence is well organised and difficult to overcome.[6]

As regards the security not being good enough, he claimed not to have had experience on that point and so felt unable to answer the question. In response to the question about port security he again claimed to have had little experience but mentioned that,

> In my opinion the entrance of even neutrals was so strictly supervised that access into England in this way was practically impossible. It must have been somewhat easier through the resistance movements conducted by England in France, Belgium, Holland, Denmark and Norway. If we had succeeded in establishing one of our own people in the resistance movement, we could have smuggled them into the country along the channels actually employed therefore.[7]

He thought that during his time in office there was no use in taking any active measure against British industry but one of the old Amt Abwehr/Ausland officers would provide more information on the peacetime espionage as their job was to receive and collate it. In conclusion, he commented, 'In my opinion, the west coast ports were the only vulnerable points (locks, etc.) An attack with special combat weapons from the sea was not expected but if sufficiently prepared might yield success.'[8]

When Lahousen was captured after the German surrender, a similar request was made for him to answer the same questions as he had been involved with infiltrating agents into Britain. His translated response provided some general information about his work but significantly played down the importance of his agents and their effectiveness.

> The answers to questions a. to e. comprise the period from the beginning of the War until the middle of 1943, the period during which I had left Amt Abwehr Ausland in order to take command of troops on the Eastern Front [for which he was promoted to General].

General.

1. The technical difficulties in the execution of sabotage attempts against were essential industrial and armament objectives in England and were due to the insular geographical location of the country.

2. Before the War not a single II-agent was employed in England, and thus there had been no preparation of any kind for the execution of sabotage attempts against industry in case of war. (This is clearly stated in the War Diary of Abwehr Abteilung II).

3. After the outbreak of war even the transportation of agents to England caused the greatest difficulties. They could only be brought to England by air, by U-boat and sailing boat.

4. Of the few agents who were brought to Ireland and England between September 1939 and July 1943 (maybe five or six in all), not a single one was able to prove that he had executed sabotage tasks of any size. The majority of these people were caught and made harmless immediately after their parachute landing. (This is evident from the War Diary of the Amt Abwehr Abt. II)

5. Apart from the above mentioned factual and technical difficulties this passive attitude towards England of Amt II was in accordance with secret orders from Canaris and Oster to the Chief of II, the then Colonel Lahousen.

Particular points

To a. No reports or direct information were received regarding the degree of security of industrial plants, as there probably was not a single size-able sabotage attempt made during that period. (See War Diary of Abw. Abt. II)

To b. According to information received from agents of Abw. I both general security measures against espionage (system of identification and supervision of the coast) as well as in particular measures for the security of industrial objects were very thorough and difficult to get around.

To c. The security of the ports was in every respect complete.
To me (Lahousen) no case is known in which even a single agent of Abw. II reached a British port. A few sabotage attempts were undertaken in 1940 from Dutch, Bulgarian, Greek and later from Spanish ports against British ships. They yielded if any only very moderate results. Ordinarily natural accidents or losses caused by mines were used to put down as proof of the seeming activity of the Abwehr. (Equally to be proved by the War Diary of Abt. II)

To d. Not known to me as it comes under the subjects treated by Abwehr I (then under Col. Pieckenbrock [head of Abwehr III – espionage].

To e. Dealt with in the section of Abwehr I by I-wi (economics) by group leader Major Dr Bloch.[9]

His suggestion that Canaris had secretly ordered Abwehr II to adopt a passive attitude towards sabotaging England must have surprised many MI5 officers but the post-war release of Abwehr documents, particularly the copying and translation of their War Diary and other statements made during interrogation, led historians to believe that Canaris did in fact order sabotage operations against Ireland and Britain to cease. This was part of his aim to undermine Himmler and achieve peace with the Allies. In a subsequent report, Lahousen listed the secret instructions he received from Canaris:

1. Formation of a secret organisation within Abwehr II and the Brandenburg Regiment, with the purpose of embodying the anti-Nazi forces and preparing them for all illegal acts that might be possible to fight in the future against the system.
2. Gradual but systematic removal of the fanatical Nazis or SD [Sicherheitdienst – the Nazi's Secret Police] from the section
3. Passive conduct of Abwehr II work, with external show of apparent very great activity.
4. Failure to carry out enterprises whose execution can be avoided in any way.[10]

He admitted preventing or failing to follow orders for kidnapping, assassination, poisoning, or similar actions related to the methods of the SD and to cooperate with Canaris's 'confidential mission' in sabotaging a German victory. He admitted reporting to High Command 'daring' exaggerations and falsifications. 'But in a system built on lies, self-deception and over-waning self-confidence, this part of the counter-activity cost the least effort of all.'[11]

Haller's reasons for the Abwehr's failure did not mention passive sabotage. His interrogators commented that, in Haller's opinion, the German Foreign Office tried to exploit Irish nationalism, in particular the IRA, for their own ends. They deliberately penetrated and sponsored the IRA in the hope of finding an experienced and willing sabotage organisation that would attack military targets in Britain. A second, more dangerous plan was to foment unrest throughout Ireland and use the IRA as the spearhead of an Irish Fifth Column which would strike a blow at Britain at the same time as the German invasion. Once the Germans had occupied England, the IRA would be used to build up an effective resistance in Eire in case the British tried to occupy the country. Haller was later involved in a third undertaking, recruiting Irish prisoners-of-war in Germany for sabotage work in Britain and America. All three missions he described as 'very resounding failures'.[12]

On the military side one high-grade agent and organiser was at least sent over and enjoyed a brief period of liberty, but had no success. On the political side the results, according to prisoner, were nil, and he claims that not a single one of the agents recruited for political purposes by his department ever set foot in EIRE. The sorry crew of Irish renegades, though willing to betray GREAT BRITAIN and each other, were judged to be too unreliable to be sent. Fundamentally, prisoner states, the course of the war was to blame for the lack of success. The invasion of ENGLAND would have made a decisive difference to all political and military activities in or from EIRE. Partly, too, the Germans were unlucky; a storm wrecked an operation, a duty officer bungled a vital message, their key man, Seán RUSSELL, died at a most inconvenient moment. Then again, they took the fantastic daydreams of the IRA at face value and greatly overrated the strength and ability of this organisation. To some extent, also, the Germans, by playing a double game – supporting the IRA on the one hand and wooing the Irish government on the other side – made both policies half-hearted in execution.

It is unpleasant to think of what might have been. The Germans gambled boldly, and though they lost, they nevertheless came uncomfortably near to achievement.; as near, it may be, as did their invasion of England. There was much ability and imagination in their planning; the fatal flaw lay outside the control of the men behind Irish affairs, men who had taken the trouble to think in terms of Irish – not German – history and tradition.[13]

During the Allies' interrogation of Hans Scharf, a German agent who admitted knowing Haller, he claimed that he knew nothing of any pre-war German activities for the penetration of the Welsh or Scottish Nationalist movements. However, he was aware that during the war, potential Welsh and Scottish Nationalist separatists were segregated from other British prisoners of war. Given Haller's work recruiting Irish and Breton separatists as agents to help in the invasion of England, it may have been that he had plans to form Welsh and Scottish Brigades.

Scharf admitted that in 1940, his first two missions for Haller in Abwehr II were to interrogate all Bretons, Corsicans, Flemings and Basque prisoners of war in the Lille and Berlin-Lichtenfeld camps. Although it was not stated, it is quite possible that, like Codd and Springer, volunteers would have been trained at Quentzgut and sent on sabotage operations in their own countries.[14]

Inga Haag, Canaris's secretary, admitted after the war that 'unlike the British, the Germans never took spies seriously. We had to have agents and reports, but as real spies they were very inefficient. Anyway, the best spies always worked for both sides.' Nicknamed by Canaris 'The Painted Doll', she joined the Abwehr on leaving school and was described as a beauty and a fervent anti-Nazi. She described the Abwehr as an amateur, snobbish organisation and, in the early stages of the war, a refuge for aristocrats, people with Jewish blood and old-school officers who opposed Hitler. She believed that many of the spies they sent to Britain were determined to defect as soon as they landed and that most of their reports were little more than gossip.

The last word should go to MI5 historian Professor Christopher Andrew: 'German espionage and sabotage of the UK achieved the coveted title of 100 per cent incompetence.'[15]

Appendix

Diary of Mainland Attacks

On 16 January 1939, a bomb exploded outside the control room of a large power station in London, which created a large crater in the forecourt of the building. There were no casualties, and the control station was reportedly undamaged. A second explosion damaged an overhead power cable running over the Grand Union Canal beside Willesden Power Station. Explosions were reported at Alnwick, Northumberland and Coleshill. Bombs placed in electrical manholes at Whitworth Street, Hilton Street and Mosley Street in Manchester killed one man and an electricity pylon was damaged near the Leeds to Liverpool Canal in Crosby, Liverpool.[1]

The following day an attempt was made to bomb an electricity pylon stretching across the Manchester Ship Canal in Barton-upon-Irwell. A faulty timer meant the bag of dynamite and gelignite failed to explode. In Great Barr, South Staffordshire, a bomb exploded at an electricity pylon, but it remained standing on one strut. In Coleshill, two bombs targeted the principal water mains supplying Hams Hall Power Station, the main source of Birmingham's electricity supply. A bomb exploded at Williams Deacons Bank in London which damaged the gas mains.

The Government sought to improve the security of infrastructure in England. All power stations, gas works, telephone exchanges, and the Droitwich transmitting station were put under police protection. Police patrols around the government buildings at Whitehall were strongly reinforced and all ships from Ireland arriving at Holyhead, Fishguard and Liverpool were closely inspected.

On 18 January, *The Times* reported a total of nine explosions in two days designed to 'cripple electricity services'. 14 arrests were made in connection with the attacks, seven in Manchester and seven in London. Each of the men was charged under Section 4 of the Explosive Substances Act 1883. Eight barrels of potassium chlorate each containing 1cwt, a large quantity of powdered charcoal, and 40 sticks of gelignite were uncovered.

The following day, a small bomb concealed in a tobacco tin exploded in the yard of Hawneys Hotel, Tralee, County Kerry. Francis Chamberlain, the British Prime Minister's only son, had been staying there during a shooting holiday.

On 20 January Seán Russell had a notice printed in the Dublin newspapers in which he dissociated himself from the Hawneys Hotel attack stating that the 'IRA Headquarters had no knowledge of this attack, nor would it order or countenance such an action.' This unsanctioned action is assumed to have been carried out by a local non S-Plan-involved IRA unit.

In Lancashire, an unexploded package of gelignite and a stopped alarm clock timer were found attached to an electricity pylon. Arrests were made, with a London man charged with possession of two tons of potassium chlorate and a ton of iron oxide between 1 October and 5 November 1938. Two days later, an arrest was made in Vauxhall, London, in connection with the Southwark explosion.

On 23 January, two women in Manchester were arrested on possession of explosives. Items seized included a barrel of potassium chlorate, two Mills bombs, 49 sticks of gelignite, and 10 electric detonators. Sir Dawson Bates, then Northern Ireland Minister of Home Affairs, revealed to the British press the existence of an 'execution list of NI officials' that had been seized in Belfast.

On 4 February, two bombs exploded in the London Underground – one at Tottenham Court Road station and one at Leicester Square station – forcing the closure of the Houses of Parliament. They were timed suitcase bombs stored in the left-luggage rooms overnight. There were no fatalities, although two people were seriously injured and severe damage was done to the station facilities. This attack generated a good deal of alarm amongst the population.

Questions were asked in the British Parliament about the IRA's 12 January ultimatum to the British government. The ultimatum had previously been publicised in the British newspapers following the 17 January attack. Sir Samuel Hoare, then British Home Secretary, informed the House of Commons that the police had already arrested 33 people in connection with the attacks up to that point and that the security authorities were doing everything within their power to find the perpetrators.

In Liverpool, there was an attempt to blow up one wall of Walton Gaol to allow prisoners to escape, but the wall did not collapse. In London, fires broke out within half an hour of each other in shops in one of the suburbs. The British police established that in each case the fire was due to a chemical mixture which ignited when exposed to the air.

Plans to blow up Buckingham Palace were reported by *The Times* to have been found in Belfast. As a result, night and day guards were placed around the grounds of Royal Lodge and Windsor Great Park. All visitors to the state apartments at Windsor Castle and St. George's Chapel were stopped and searched before being allowed entry.

On 5 February, fires started in Marks & Spencer, Owen & Owen Ltd, the packing department of Montague Burton Ltd, and Woolworths in Coventry attributed to incendiary devices, balloon bombs being suspected.

In Bristol, guns were issued to police after the discovery of a note in a petrol storage depot reading 'BEWARE. These tanks are the next to be blown up'. Watches were put on Avonmouth Docks and Bristol Airport. Arrests were made, and seven hand-grenades, gelignite, ammunition, and the S-Plan itself were seized. The S-Plan was found on a detained IRA volunteer.

Threats were received that Bow Street Police Station in London and the offices of the *South Wales Echo* in Cardiff were to be blown up. A man claiming to be the 'Chief of Staff of the IRA in Cardiff' demanded the release of volunteers held there.

The following day, two Bills were introduced in the Dáil giving extraordinary powers to the Government of Ireland, the territory formerly known as the Irish Free State. The Treason Act imposed the death penalty for persons guilty of treason. The IRA had been declared an illegal organisation under the Declaration of Unlawful Organization Order passed 18 June 1936, but the Irish Free State Government used it on only a few IRA volunteers. Éamon de Valera spoke about the IRA and S-Plan in the Dáil for two hours stating that the IRA had no right to assume the title 'Irish Republican Government'.

On 9 February, *The Times* continued in its efforts to calm British public opinion when it stated that 'the signatories of the ridiculous ultimatum to Great Britain are men of no account. Nobody in this country would have taken them seriously, but for the recent outrages in Great Britain. As a political force in Éire, the IRA simply does not count.'

Two bombs exploded at Kings Cross railway station, and bomb threats were made to the National History Museum.

On 13 February, an incendiary balloon device set fire to the steam ship *St. David*. On 2 March, a bomb exploded on an aqueduct ofr the Grand Union Canal near Stonebridge Park, London. A bomb exploded on an aqueduct for the Birmingham Canal Navigations in Wednesbury, Staffordshire. Both devices only damaged the concrete walls of the beds of the canals. Had the dynamite been placed 18 inches lower, they would have caused considerable flooding over the lower lying adjoining fields.[2] The following day, Henry West prevented a bomb attack on a Willesden railway bridge during the night.

On 23 March, five bombs exploded in London in the vicinity of the large wholesale food markets, telephone, gas installations and the advertisement department of the *News Chronicle* in Fleet Street. There were also bomb attacks in Birmingham, Liverpool, and Coventry.

On 29 March, the *Daily Sketch* reported:

Two mystery explosions occurred at Hammersmith Bridge soon after 1 a.m. today. The centre of the bridge was damaged. One of the suspension chains was snapped. Special squad cars were immediately rushed to the scene and a cordon was thrown round nearby streets. Two men were later detained by the Police for questioning, one after a Flying Squad chase of a lorry. Streets near the bridge were littered with broken glass. All traffic across the bridge was stopped. Windows of surrounding houses were smashed. People ran into the streets in terror. People in the districts round the bridge were brought from their beds by the sound of the explosions. A late worker on his way home, told how he saw two flashes light the darkness of the sky, followed by two 'terrific bangs.' A car passing over the bridge was smashed by one of the links of the broken suspension chain. The driver was un-hurt. 'I did not actually see the explosion,' he told the 'Daily Sketch.' 'But I had to swerve to avoid hitting the bridge.' It is understood that the explosions were caused by bombs detonated by a car passing over a wire on the roadway approaching the bridge.

In Farago's *The Game of the Foxes*, he intimated the bombing was the work of the IRA, claiming they snapped the suspension chains and dropped the whole span almost a foot. Eddie Chapman claimed that Vosch/Wojch, a German agent, admitted that he had been involved in this and other cloakroom attacks in London.

Bombs exploded in Birmingham, Liverpool, and Coventry on 30 March and the following day, seven bombs exploded in different parts of London. On 5 April, two bombs exploded at a railway station and council buildings in Liverpool and one exploded in Coventry.

Five days later, at a Republican demonstration commemorating the Easter Rising at the Glasnevin Cemetery in Dublin, a communiqué from the IRA Army Council was read out announcing that the 'operation groups' of the IRA in Britain carried out their tasks in accordance with orders without causing casualties, the avoidance of which had been expressly ordered. The communiqué also stated that the order to avoid casualties could be countermanded if Britain had recourse to extreme measures.

On 12 April, a threat was made to blow up Catford Bridge, Lewisham. The following day, eleven bombs exploded in London and Birmingham. These had the appearance of being no more than trial explosions as all occurred in public lavatories. According to the announcement by public officials, the bombs contained new chemical mixtures which were mainly composed of carbide.

On 4 May, men and women appeared in a Birmingham courtroom charged under the Explosive Substances Act 1883 with belonging to an IRA team working from 'the headquarters in the Midlands for manufacturing incendiary and explosive bombs'. The following day, tear gas bombs exploded in two Liverpool cinemas, causing 15 injuries. Four bombs exploded in Coventry and two in London.

On 16 May, the police made arrests and seized eight pounds of potassium chlorate, two powder fuses, twelve 26½-inch sticks of gelignite, two sticks of saxonite (high explosive, presumably stolen from a mine or a quarry where it was used for blasting rock), fuses, a revolver and ammunition, twenty-nine balloons, and street maps of Salford, Manchester and Liverpool. An unexploded bomb, found abandoned on a bus, was identified with this material when the arrests were made.

Two days later, two men were sentenced to 10 and 15 years' imprisonment for possession of 10 bundles of gelignite, a 5-pound pack of gelignite, 103 detonators, and 4 balloons. On 19 May, eight timed incendiary bombs caused fires in eight British hotels and eight arrests were made in Birmingham in connection with an explosion at a house in Manchester.

On 29 May, four magnesium charges exploded in the Paramount Cinema, Birmingham. The following day, the IRA issued a 'General Call to Arms' with hundreds of IRA members running from house to house collecting gas masks and burning around 1,000 in heaps in 15 streets.[3]

On 30 May, magnesium and tear gas bombs exploded during the evening show in cinemas in Liverpool and Birmingham. Twenty-five people were taken to hospital, but no material damage was done. The following day, Seanad Éireann, the Irish Senate, introduced the Offences against the State Act, and it was put into effect, after having been signed by President Douglas Hyde.[4]

On 31 May, London cinemas were attacked with incendiaries, prompting the police to search every single London cinema.

On 9 June, letter-bombs exploded in twenty post-boxes. One went off in a London sorting office and also in a Birmingham mail lorry. Every post-box in London was searched for further IRA devices.

The following day, seventeen explosions occurred in a space of only two hours in thirty post offices and post-boxes in London, Birmingham and Manchester.

On 24 June, several bombs exploded in London when there was a demonstration, under police protection, to honour Wolfe Tone, the father of Irish Republicanism. The marchers' banners demanded the release of IRA members who had been arrested by the British police.[5]

London branches of the Midland Bank, Westminster Bank and Lloyds Bank were targeted with a series of massive explosions. London police carried out mass arrests. Members of the Irish community in Britain were interrogated with the majority being released soon after.

Sir Samuel Hoare introduced the Prevention of Violence Bill (Temporary Provisions) which provided comprehensive powers for the British government to prevent the immigration of foreigners, for their deportation, and for extending to the Irish the requirement to register with the British police. Hoare referred to the S-Plan of the IRA when presenting the bill to the British Parliament and stated that a total of 127 terrorist outrages had been perpetrated since January 1939, 57 in London and 70 in the provinces. In the course of these attacks, one person had been killed and 55 injured. 66 persons had been convicted of terrorist activity. In all, Hoare stated the British police had seized: 55 sticks of gelignite, 1,000 detonators, 2 tons of potassium chlorate and iron oxide, seven gallons of sulphuric acid and four hundredweight of powdered aluminium. He stated that the IRA campaign 'was being closely watched and actively stimulated by foreign organisations', a reference to German Intelligence. He claimed that the IRA had come close to blowing up Hammersmith Bridge, Southwark Power Station, and an aqueduct in North London. They had collected detailed information about important bridges, railway lines, munition dumps, war factories and airfields and had a plan to blow up the Houses of Parliament.[6]

On 3 July, a bomb exploded in the left-luggage area of London Midland railway station on London Road, Birmingham, causing extensive damage to the station concourse.[7] On 26 July, two incendiary bombs exploded in the left-luggage area of King's Cross Station and Victoria Station, London. In the King's Cross attack, the checkroom was destroyed and a young Edinburgh University lecturer was killed, and his wife, two counter attendants and 12 others wounded. One died later in hospital. Extensive damage was done to the stations. In the Victoria Station attack, five people were severely wounded with a similar amount of damage to the station.

On 27 July, there were three explosions in Liverpool. The first bomb in a suburb blew up a swing bridge spanning the Manchester-Liverpool canal.

The wreckage of the bridge halted all barge traffic. The second bomb completely wrecked the front and large sections of the inside of the central post office. The third bomb went off in a park and no injuries were reported.

On 3 August, the IRA announced that it would continue its campaign against Britain for another two-and-a-half years. From August onwards, deportations of Irish from Britain increased under the Prevention of Violence Act 1939 (Temporary Provisions).[8]

On 25 August, there was an explosion in Broadgate, Coventry. The bomb was in the carrier basket of a bicycle outside Astley's store in the busy shopping district. Five people were killed and over fifty wounded causing widespread revulsion across Britain. Four days later, the wires of a dozen telephone kiosks were cut, assumed to be IRA activity.

On 11 December, the trial opened in Birmingham of three men and two women indicted for murder as a result of the bombing of Coventry. The accused were 29-year-old labourer Joseph Hewitt, 29-year-old labourer James Richards, 22-year-old Mary Hewitt, 49-year-old Brigid O'Hara and 32-year-old clerk Peter Barnes. The Hewitts were a married couple, and Bridgid O'Hara was Mrs Hewitt's mother. All pleaded not guilty to the charge of murdering 21-year-old Elsie Ansell. The prosecution had limited the charge to one victim. Three days later, the verdict of guilty was returned and James Richards and Peter Barnes were sentenced to death. The sentencing triggered a series of IRA attacks on British post offices, post-boxes and mail trains.

On 3 January 1940, the Emergency Powers Act was passed in Ireland. Fifteen days later, there were three violent explosions at various parts of the Royal Gunpowder Factory at Waltham Abbey, which almost completely wrecked the plant. Five people were killed and thirty injured. Although the Government denied it was enemy action, the Abwehr included it in their list of attacks.[10].

An entry in the Abwehr II War Diary for 27 January reported an explosion in electricity works in Irlam, which blocked the Manchester Ship Canal. The German radio assumed it was sabotage. Abwehr II concluded it to have been the work of the IRA. A note alongside suggested that it was pure guesswork. There was no evidence that the IRA were responsible, but it looked well in the Abwher's report to *Oberkommando der Wehrmacht*, the German Army's High Command.[11]

On 5 February, there were demonstrations and resolutions of protest against the executions of the Coventry bombers all over Ireland. De Valera appealed for a reprieve. The *New York Times* analysis of Irish public opinion was that: 'Opinion here is either that two innocent men will hang, or that it is the partition of Ireland by the British who forced these young Irishmen to perpetrate such outrages. Anglo-Irish relations could markedly deteriorate through the hanging of these men.'

The following day, three explosions occurred in mailbags, two in Euston Station, London, and one in the General Post Office on Hill Street, Birmingham. This attack was regarded by *The Times* as a reprisal for the failure to reprieve Barnes and Richards.

On 7 February, Brendan Behan was sent to Borstal for three years for possessing potassium chlorate which he was going to use to blow up ships in Liverpool docks.[12]

When news was released that Richards and Barnes had been hanged at Winston Green Prison, Birmingham Prison on the same day, many protests followed.[13] Former IRA leader, Simon Donnelly, made a speech in Dublin in which he proclaimed to jubilant crowds:

We know very well what outcome we want to this war. We want the enemy, who has kept our people in bondage for 700 years and who continues to pour insults on us, to be pitilessly vanquished. Until such time as the Irish Republic is established, Ireland's youth will continue to sacrifice itself. If the government does not bring foreign overlordship to an end, others must be entrusted with the task.[14]

On Valentine's Day, 14 February 1940, five bombs exploded in Birmingham. Nine days later, two explosions occurred in the West End of London injuring thirteen people. The devices had been placed in rubbish bins. *The Times* reported that since the enactment of the Temporary Provisions legislation, 119 people had been deported.

Whether it was an IRA attack is unknown but on 18 March, a bomb exploded on a rubbish dump in London. On 27 April, the Abwehr II War Diary reported a Reuter message of a fire in an aircraft works in Denham, Buckinghamshire which they assumed to have been work of Welsh Nationalists. A note alongside read 'Sheer guesswork again'.[15]

Notes

Prologue

1 (http://h2g2.com/edited_entry/A87786102
2 TNA INF 1/264–8

1 The 'S-Plan'

1 (http://www.historyireland.com/20th-century-contemporary-history/new-evidence-on-iranazi-link/; http://sonsofmalcolm.blogspot.co.uk/201 National Library of Ireland, Manuscripts Department, 'Demolition of bridges without explosives – instructions', James L. O'Donovan
2 http://i.ebayimg.com/images/g/yA0AAOSwnQhXpIlv/s-l1600.jpg
3 Bryce, Evans, 'Fear and Loathing in Liverpool: The IRA's 1939 Bombing Campaign on Merseyside', *Transactions of the Lancashire and Cheshire Historical Society*, Vol. 162, 2013
4 http://www.historiccoventry.co.uk/articles/s-shaw.php5
6 *Liverpool Echo*, 7 February 1939
7 Evans, op.cit. *The Times*, 14 February 1939. *Liverpool Echo*, 20 January 1939
8 *Liverpool Echo*, 3 May 1939
9 Ibid, 30 May 1939
10 Evans, op.cit.
11 Evans, op.cit; Coogan, T. *The IRA*, Harper Collins, 2000, p. 124; O'Connor, Ulick, *Brendan Behan*, Harper Collins, 1993, p. 38
12 *Liverpool Echo*, 26, 27, 29 August 1939
13 Evans, op.cit.
14 *Liverpool Echo*, 19 September 1939
15 Behan, Brendan, *The Borstal Boy*, Hutchinson, 1958
16 http://mylesdungan.com/2014/02/11/on-this-day-drivetime-7-february-1940-brendan-behan-jailed-for-ira-activity/
17 (Jonason, Tommy & Olsson, Simon, *Agent Tate: The True Wartime Story of Harry Williamson*, Amberley, 2012, p.59; *The Sun*, 5 September 2005; Seosamh Ó Duibhginn, *Ag Scaoileadh Sceoil*, Dublin, 1962)
18 (Stephan, Enno, *Spies in Ireland*, Four Square Books, 1963)
19 TNA KV 6/79
20 TNA KV 3/120, 11 April 1943
21 (TNA KV3/120, 30 March 1939)

2 The British Intelligence Services' response

1 https://www.sis.gov.uk/our-history.html

2 Morrison, Kathryn, *A Maudlin and Monstrous Pile: The Mansion at Bletchley Park*, Buckinghamshire, English Heritage, 2012, pp.102-3; https://www.sis.gov.uk/our-history/sisor-mi6.html; http://www.spartacus-educational.com/ SScumming.htm

3 TNA HS 7/27 SOE Research and Development section 1938-1945

4 TNA HS 7/27

5 Ibid.

6 Turner, op.cit. p.18

7 www.spartacus-educational.com/////GCCS.htm; http://www.ww2warstories.tripod.com/id18.htm

8 TNA KV 4/170

9 TNA KV 4/170

10 TNA KV4/60

11 Ibid, 16 March 1940

3 The Royal Victoria Patriotic Schools

1 (http://www.helen-fry.com/books/the-london-cage/; Scotland, Alexander, *The London Cage*, Evans Brothers, 1957)

2 Footitt, Hilary and Kelly, Michael (eds), *Languages and the Military: Alliances, Occupation and Peace Building*, Palgrave Macmillan, 2012; Andrew, op.cit. p.251

3 TNA KV4/60

4 TNA KV 4/170; Hoare, Oliver, (2000), *Camp 020: MI5 and the Nazi Spies*, Public Record Office

5 Cobain, Ian, *Cruel Britannia*, Portobello Books, 2012

6 https://www.mi5.gov.uk/home/mi5-history/world-war-ii.html

7 Hastedt, G. *Spies, Wiretaps and Secret Operations: An Encyclopaedia of American Espionage*, Vol. 1, ABC-CLIO.LLC, 2011, p.253; Bryden, John, *Fighting to Lose: How the German Secret Intelligence Helped the Allies Win the Second World War*, Dundurn Press, 2014, p.154

8 Masterman, J.C. *The Double-Cross System: The Incredible True Story of How Nazi Spies Were Turned into Double Agents*, Vintage, 2013, pp.87-88

9 Ibid., p.58

10 O'Donoghue, Dave, *The Devil's Deal: The IRA, Nazi Germany and the Double Life of Jim O'Donovan*, New Island Books, 2010; Johnson, op.cit. p.10)

11 TNA KV3/120

12 Miller, Joan. *One Girl's War: Personal Exploits in MI5's Most Secret Station*, Brandon/Mount Eagle Publications Ltd. 1986

13 West, Nigel, *The Guy Liddell Diaries*, 19 September 1939

14 Ibid, 30 September 1939

15 Johnson, op.cit. p.9

16 Email communication with Phil Tomaselli, 15 November 2015

17 TNA KV3/76; Hull, op.cit. p. 698; Wighton, Charles and Peis, Günther, *Hitler's Spies and Saboteurs*, Henry Holt, New York, 1958, pp. 9, 25, 123

18 TNA KV3/120; Curry, op.cit. p 135.

19 Ibid.

20 Ibid.

21 Ibid. 11 July 1939

21 Ibid, 13 July 1939

23 TNA KV2/769; KV2/3410

24 TNA KV2/3410, p.13

25 TNA KV2/769

26 TNA KV2/3410; KV2/301; http://www.Historyireland.com/20th-century-contemporary-history/new-evidence-on-iranazi-links/)

27 Farago, Ladislas, *The Game of Foxes*, Hodder and Stoughton, 1972, pp.193-4

28 TNA KV2/769; Stephan, op.cit.; http://alphahistory.com/northernireland/ira-mainland-campaign/

29 Liddell, op.cit. 30 September 1939

30 Stephan, op.cit; Bradford, Andrew, *Dotty Dorothy: The Perfect Spy*, private publication, 2012, pp.2-3

31 *The Daily Telegraph*, 19 January 1940

32 Farago, op.cit. pp.192-3

33 Bulloch, John, *M.I.5: The Origin and History of the British Counter-Espionage Service*, Arthur Barker, London, 1963, p.171

34 Thomas, Robert, *The Explosions at the Royal Gunpowder Mills*, 2013, pp.61-71

35 Johnson, op.cit. p.13; Archer, op.cit. p. 237; Bulloch, op.cit. p.172; https://www.mi5.gov.uk/world-war-ii; http://www.bbc.co.uk/essex/content/articles/2009/07/08/ gunpowder_mills_feature.shtml

36 Quoted in Walton, Calder, *Empire of Secrets: British Intelligence, the Cold War, and the Twilight of the Empire*, Overlook Press, 2013, Curry, John, *History of the Service 1908-1945*, TNA KV4/1- 3

37 3 February 1940

38 Stephan, op.cit. p.87

39 Liddell, 25 November 1941

40 McMahon, Paul, *British Spies and Irish Rebels: British Intelligence and Ireland, 1916-45*, Boydell Press, 2008, p.408

41 Liddell, op.cit. 8 May 1940

42 TNA HS 7/53 SOE Group B Sabotage Training Handbook

43 Andrew, Christopher, *The Defence of the Realm: The Authorised History of MI5*, Penguin, 2010, p.231

44 TNA KV 2/1296, 2 August 1940; TNA KV 4/60; Liddell, 11 September 1940

45 TNA KV 4/170

46 Macintyre, Ben. *Agent Zigzag*, Bloomsbury, 2007, pp.172-4; Rose, Kenneth, 'Rothschild (Nathaniel Mayer) Victor, third Baron Rothschild (1910 – 1990)', *Oxford Dictionary of National Biography*, Oxford University Press, 2004

47 TNA KV2/3800 Marita Perigoe; KV6/118 Hans Kohout; KV6/119 Hilda Leech; KV2/3799 Edgar and Sophia Bray; https://www.mi5.gov.uk/eric-roberts-undercover-work-in-world-war-ii

48 TNA KV2/4022, 1 November 1943

49 TNA KV2/4022, February 1944

50 TNA KV2/4021-3

51 TNA KV4/60

52 West, Nigel, and Tsarev, Oleg, *Crown Jewels: The British Secrets at the Heart of the KGB Archives*, Harper Collins, 1998, pp.138–9

53 Liddell's diary, 7 March 1940

54 Ibid, 13 March 1940

55 Ibid, 27 March, April 4–18 1940

4 Arthur Owens, Gwilym Williams and the Welsh Nationalist Party

1 Wighton and Peis, op.cit. p.156

2 Davies, John, *A History of Wales*, Penguin, 1994, p.592; Humphries, John, *Spying for Hitler*, University of Wales Press, 2012, p.1

3 Humphries, op.cit. p.3

4 http://irishecho.com/2014/10/forgotten-hero/

5 Farago, op.cit. p.159

6 TNA KV 2/446

7 Farago, op.cit. p.197

8 Andrew, C. op.cit. p.249

9 Ibid, p.253

10 TNA KV 2/446; Hennessy, Thomas and Thomas, Claire, *Spooks: The Unofficial History of MI5 From Agent ZIGZAG to the D-Day Deception 1939–45*, Amberley, 2010, pp.6–13; Crowdy, Terry, *Deceiving Hitler: Double Cross and Deception in World War II*, Osprey Publishing, 2013, pp.20–22

11 TNA KV2/446, 14 September 1939

12 Ibid. 21 September 1939

13 Ibid. 27 September 1939
14 Ibid.
15 TNA KV 2/446; Liddell, 31 October 1939; Humphries, op.cit. p.9; Farago, op.cit. p.80
16 TNA KV 2/446; 27 September 1939; Farago, pp.17,20
17 Ibid. 29 September 1939
18 www.foia.cia.gov, German Intelligence Service, Vol.3, 0001.pdf
19 TNA KV 2/468
20 Ibid. 17 October 1939
21 Ibid, 19 October 1939
22 Farago, op.cit.
23 TNA KV 2/468
24 Farago, op.cit. pp.179–80
25 Liddell, 31 October 1939
26 Hennessey and Thomas, op.cit. p.26.
27 TNA KV 2/468, 23 October 1939
28 Ibid.
29 Ibid, 22 October 1939
30 TNA KV4/170
31 Farago, op.cit. p.286.
32 Liddell, 3 December 1939
33 TNA KV 2/468, 22 December 1939
34 Ibid.27 December 1939
35 Ibid. February 1940
36 TNA KV2/173, p.7
37 Masterman, op.cit. p.43; Liddell, op.cit. 7 April 1940
38 Liddell, 19 May 1940
39 TNA KV2/1333
40 Wighton and Peis, op.cit. p.172
41 Liddell, op.cit. 13 July 1940
42 TNA KV 2/468, 17 July 1940

5 The Nazis' pre-invasion saboteurs in Eire

1 Mallmann Showell, J. P. *U-boats at War – Landings on Hostile Shores*, Ian Allan Publishing Ltd., Shepperton: 2000, p.14
2 Johnson, op.cit. pp.11,14
3 TNA KV2/301; KV2/1296; TNA KV3/118, Mil Amt D Sabotage and Subversion, p.4
4 (http://fas.org/irp/ops/ci/docs/ci2/2ch1_d.htm; O'Reilly, Terence, *Hitler's Irishmen*, Mercier Press, Cork, 2008, p.88)
5 TNA KV2/303
6 TNA KV2/301; http://ronangearoid.blogspot.co.uk/2010/04/ irishmen-in-german-army.html
7 TNA KV2/769. Appendix A, 7 August 1946; KV2/1950
8 TNA KV2/173
9 Ibid
10 TNA KV2/769
11 TNA KV2/103
12 Thomas, Geoffrey & Ketley, Barry, *Luftwaffe KG 200: The German Air Force's Most Secret Unit of World War II*, p.34
13 Ernst Weber-Drohl's U-Boat landing in Sligo Bay – Summary,' *Heritage Connects Communities* Peace III project 50785, July 2014, pp.24–26
14 Ibid; http://www.dubm.de/lang1/u-boats-and-Eire; Moore, Sam & Robinson, Auriel, 'German strong man and spy: Hull, op.cit. pp.72–73
15 TNA KV2/1137, 16 July 1942
16 Liddell, 10 May 1940
17 Liddell, 26 May 1940
18 Liddell, 15 May 1940

6 Operations MAINAU and SEAGULL

1 TNA KV2/769; KV2/301 20 September 1944; O'Reilly, op.cit. pp.46–7
2 TNA KV2/301, 26 September 1944
3 TNA KV2/769; Stephan, op.cit; Hull, op.cit; Bowyer, Bell, op.cit;
4 Liddell, op.cit. 25 – 26 May 1940
5 TNA KV 2/3120, 15 September 1943
6 TNA KV 2/1319–1322 Herman Goertz; KV 2/3119–3120 Joseph Andrews; Dwyer, T. Ryle, *Strained Relations: Ireland at Peace and the USA at War, 1941 – 1945,* Gill and Macmillan, 1988, pp.90–9;
7 TNA KV 2/3120
8 TNA KV 3/120, 20 June 1942
9 TNA KV2/103, 10, 22 August 1945; KV2/170 Praetorius; Mallmann Showell, op.cit. p.16;
10 http://www.dubm.de/lang1/u-boats-and-Eire
11 Liddell, op.cit 9 June 1940
12 Liddell, 17 June 1940
13 Liddell, op.cit. 17 June, 14 July 1940
14 Liddell, op.cit. 18 July 1940
15 Ibid, 18, 27 July 1940

7 Operations SEALION, GREEN, LOBSTER, SEAGULL and WHALE I and II

1 Wighton and Peis, op.cit. p.124
2 TNA KV2/769
3 TNA KV 2/1451
4 TNA KV 2/1451, 17 March 1943
5 TNA KV 2/1296
6 TNA KV 2/1451, 4 April 1942
7 TNA KV 2/1451
8 TNA KV 2/1451
9 TNA KV2/3304
10 TNA KV2/546
11 TNA KV 2/1451
12 TNA KV 2/1296, 17 July 1940
13 TNA KV2/173, p.8
14 TNA KV 2/1296, 20 June 1947
15 TNA KV 2/1296
16 Ibid. 29 July 1940
17 Irish Military Archives, G2/X/0305 September 1945; National Archives of Ireland, S/12013, Criminal charge and disposition sheet; Hull, Mark, The Irish Interlude: German Intelligence in Ireland, 1939–43, *The Journal of Military History*, Vol.66, No. 3, 2002, p.706–7; TNA KV 2/1296 Dieter Gartner; KV 2/1451 Herbert Tributh
18 Liddell, 23, 28 August 1940

8 Operations DOVE/PIGEON and SEA EAGLE

1 TNA KV2/769; Hull, op.cit. 699; Johnson, op.cit. p.14
2 TNA KV2/301
3 Coogan, Tim Pat. *The IRA*, Palgrave, 2002, pp.208–9; http://www.historyireland.com/20th-century-contemporary-history/new-evidence-on-iranazi-links/
4 Bowyer-Bell, J. *The Secret Army: The IRA*, Transaction Publishers, New Jersey, 2008, p.189
5 Hull, op.cit)
6 Bowyer-Bell, op.cit. p.190; TNA KV2/3410
7 TNA KV2/3410, 5 March 1945
8 TNA KV2/301, 26 September 1944

9 TNA KV2/3410l; Bowyer-Bell, op.cit. pp.190–191; Coogan, op.cit. pp.211–212; O'Reilly, op.cit. pp. 133, 196

10 *Irish Times*, 14 March 1941

11 TNA KV2/170

12 TNA KV2/161

13 TNA KV2/173, p.9

14 Adams, Jefferson, *German Intelligence, Historical Dictionaries of Intelligence and Counterintelligence*, Scarecrow Press, 2009, p.414; Stephan, op.cit; Hull, op.cit; Bowyer Bell, op.cit

15 Hoare, op.cit. pp. 167–7

16 TNA HO45/23803 (closed); O'Haplin, Eunan, *Spying on Ireland: British Intelligence and Irish Neutrality During the Second World War*, Oxford University Press, 2010

9 Operations OSPREY (FISCHADLER), PASTORIUS and SEAGULL II

1 Stephan, op.cit; Hull, op.cit

2 www.foia.cia.gov, German Intelligence Service, WWII, Vol.3, 0002

3 Wighton and Peis, op.cit. pp.19–41

4 TNA KV3/413, pp.51–4

5 TNA KV3/413; http://www.paperlessarchives.com /FreeTitles/GermanSaboteursMI5Files.pdf

6 TNA KV 3/413; Wighton and Peis, op.cit. pp.42–82; Johnson, David, *Germany's Spies and Saboteurs*, MBI, 1998; MacDonnell Francis, *Insidious Foes: The Axis Fifth Column and the American Home Front*, Oxford University Press, 1995. p. 131; Dobbs, Michael, *Saboteurs: The Nazi Raid on America*. Knopf. 2004

7 TNA KV3/413, 12 January 1946

8 TNA KV3/413, p.1

9 Hull, op.cit; Stephan, op.cit; Bowyer Bell, J. *The Secret Army – The IRA*, Transaction Publishers, 1997

10 TNA KV2/769, O'Reilly, op.cit. p.91

11 TNA KV2/769

12 Email communication with Martin Briscoe, 24 October 2016

13 TNA KV2/769

14 Ibid.

15 O'Reilly, op.cit. p. 97–8

16 O'Reilly, op.cit. p. 103

17 TNA KV2/769

18 Ibid, Operation Seagull I; TNA KV2/173, 16 May, 22 June 1943; Hull, Mark M. *Irish Secrets. German Espionage in Wartime Ireland 1939–1945*, Irish Academic Press, Dublin, 2003

19 KV2/1950, Thomas Strogan's testimony

20 TNA KV2/1950

21 Ibid.

22 TNA KV2/769; KV2/1950

23 Barton, Brian, *Northern Ireland and the Second World War*, Ulster Historical Foundation, 1995, p.37

24 O'Reilly, op.cit. p.106

25 O'Haplin, op.cit. p.184

26 IMA G2/4174

27 Liddel diary, 7 and 17 December 1942, TNA KV4/191, O'Reilly, op.cit.

28 TNA KV2/170

29 TNA KV2/170

30 Ibid.

31 TNA KV2/170

32 Wighton and Peis, op.cit. p.127

33 Ibid. p.132

34 bid. p.135

36 Ibid. p.147

37 TNA KV2/521
38 Ibid. pp.153–4
39 Ibid.
40 Albertelli, Sébastien, (2016), *Histoire de Sabotage*, Perrin

10 Operation LENA

1 Crowdy, op.cit. p.16
2 Crowdy, op.cit. pp.37–8; http://www.dover-kent.com/2014-project/Rising-Sun-Lydd.html;
3 Booth, Nicholas, *Lucifer Rising*, The History Press, 2016, p.174
4 Booth, 2016, op.cit.
5 TNA KV3/76
6 https://levinehistory.wordpress.com/2014/06/02/the-unlikely-story-of-the-german-invasion-spies/
7 Liddell, 6 September 1940
8 Ibid; TNA CRIM 1/1243; HO 144/21471–2; Hennessey and Thomas, op.cit. pp.54–56; http://sussexhistoryforum.co.uk/index.php?topic=3351.0; https://levinehistory.wordpress.com/2014/06/02/the-unlikely-story-of-the-german-invasion-spies/
9 Booth, 2016, p.117
10 Quoted in Cobain, Ian, *The History Thieves*, Portobello Books, 2016
11 Ibid.
12 TNA KV 4/170
13 Crowdy, op.cit. pp.44–5; Thomas & Ketley, op.cit. p.34; http://homepage. ntlworld.com/andrew.etherington/1940/09/06.htm; https://sites.google.comsite/denton history/ wartime-1/the-spy-from-the-sky; http://www.historiassegundaguerramundial.com/anecdotario/espias-en-accion-gosta-caroli-y-wulf-schmidt/?lang=en
14 Liddell, op.cit. 7 September 1940
15 Crowdy, op.cit. pp.44–5
16 TNA KV2/1333
17 Ibid. pp.46–7; Masterman, op.cit. p.257; West, Nigel, (1982), *MI5: British Security Service Operations 1909–1945*, Stein & Day, New York
18 TNA KV3/76
19 http://www.josefjakobs.info/2016/06/tales-of-spies-mysterious-and-beautiful.html; TNA KV2/171. More details of Schmidt's story can be read in Tommy Jonason and Simon Olsson's '*Agent TATE: The Wartime Story of Harry Williamson*', Amberley Publishing, 2011.
20 Ibid. p.37
21 TNA KV2/114, 3 September 1946
22 TNA KV2/163
23 TNA KV2/1333
24 TNA KV2/114
25 https://cockburndj.wordpress.com/2014/12/03/inspirations-who-put-bella-in-the-wych-elm/
26 TNA KV2/32; Hoare, op.cit. p.165
27 Ibid.
28 Ibid.
29 Ibid, 1 July 1941
30 Ibid, 28 June 1941
31 TNA KV2/30–31; West, Nigel, (1981), *MI5 – the True Story of the Most Secret Counterespionage Organisation in the World*, Briarcliff Manor, New York, p.259
32 TNA KV3/76
33 Hoare, op.cit. p.153; Hinsley, F.H. & Simkins, C.A.G., *British Intelligence in the Second World War: Security and counter-intelligence*, Vol. 4, Cambridge University Press, 1990, p.323; Liddell, p.101
34 TNA KV3/76
35 Ibid)
36 Hinsley, F.H. & Simkins, op.cit. pp.323–5
37 Ibid; Wighton and Peis, op.cit. pp.182–3; http://alchetron.com/Vera-von-Schalburg-1351738-W
38 Searle, Adrian, *The Spy Beside the Sea;The Extraordinary Wartime Story of Dorothy O'Grady*, History Press, 2012

39 Wighton and Peis, op.cit. p.186
40 http://www.veraschalburg.co.uk/html/the_beautiful_spy.html
41 Hinsley, F.H. & Simkins, op.cit. pp.323–5; Guy Liddell, 30 September, 1 October 1940; Hennessey, op.cit. p.57
42 TNA KV2/171
43 Wighton and Peis, op.cit. pp. 204–5; Searle, op.cit.; http://www.heraldscotland.com/sport/spl/ aberdeen/nazi-spy-s-love-child-linked-to-reprieve-1.212503; Email communication with Phil Coldham, 9 March 2015;
44 TNA KV2/20, 27 October 1940
45 TNA KV3/76
46 TNA KV 2/20–23
47 TNA KV 2/21
48 Ibid. 28 October 1940
49 Ibid.
50 TNA KV 2/23, 2 July 1945
51 Ibid, 28 October 1940
52 TNA KV 2/22
53 www.foia.cia.gov, German Intelligence Service, Vol.2, p.8
54 TNA KV2/162
55 Ibid.
56 TNA KV2/162
57 TNA KV3/76; Crowdy, op.cit. pp.49–50
58 TNA KV2/769; KV2/303
59 Hinsley, F.H. & Simkins, op.cit. p.326
60 TNA KV2/114
61 Ibid.
62 Thomas & Ketley, op.cit. p. 35
63 TNA KV3/76
64 Andrew, C. (Ed.) *The Security Service 1908 – 1945*, PRO, 1999, p.229
65 Crowdy, op.cit. p.46
66 Siedentopf, Monika, *Unternehmen Seelöwe Widerstand im Deutschen Geheimdienst*, DTV Premium, 2014
67 TNA KV2/103
68 www.foia.cia.gov, German Intelligence Service, WWII Vol. 3 0013, 25 June 1946

11 Mrs O'Grady

1 http://h2g2.com/edited_entry/A87786102
2 Ibid
3 Ibid.
4 Ibid.
5 Ibid.
6 Liddell, op.cit. 17 September 1940
7 http://h2g2.com/edited_entry/A87786102
8 Liddell, 17 December 1940
9 http://h2g2.com/edited_entry/A87786102
10 Bradford, op.cit. p.15
11 Stephens, David, *Action Stations: Military Airfields of Scotland*
12 Bird, Andrew, *A Separate Little War*, Grub Street, 2003, p.113
13 http://forum.keypublishing.com/showthread.php?100530 -Allied-aircraft-sabotage
14 Smithies, Edward, op.cit. Cassell Military Paperbacks, 2002, p.182
15 Moffat, John, op.cit. Corgi, 2010, p.124
16 Gardiner, Juliet, op.cit. Headline, 2004, p. 590
17 Calder, op.cit. Jonathan Cape, 1969, p. 155

12 Arthur Owens, Gwilym Williams and the Welsh Nationalist Party Part 2

1 Ibid; West, Nigel, *The Guy Liddell Diaries*, Vol. 1, Routledge, 2005, p.103
2 Liddell, 10 October 1940
3 TNA KV 2/446, 11 October 1940
4 Ibid, 17 October 1940
5 TNA KV 2/468
6 Ibid.
7 Ibid. 9 November 1940
8 Ibid.
9 Ibid. 19 November 1940
10 Ibid.
11 Ibid. October 1940
12 Ibid. 1 December 194
13 TNA KV2/173, p.9
14 Ibid. 9 January 1941
15 Ibid. 23 January 1941
16 TNA KV 2/468 January 1941
17 Ibid, 16 February 1941
18 Ibid. 27 February, 13 March 1941
19 Lancashire Archives, WBF 33/55, 22 April 1942
20 Andrew, op.cit. p.260
21 TNA KV 2/468, 17 April 1941
22 Brooman-White's obituary, *The Times*, 27 January 1965; West, op.cit. p.84
23 Masterman, op.cit. p.83
24 TNA KV 2/468, 24 June 1941
25 Ibid. 24 June 1941
26 Ibid. 24 July 1941
27 Ibid. 26 July 1941
28 Author's email communication with Lee Richards, 20 February 2015
27 http://www.psywar.org/caledonia19400826.php
28 TNA KV 2/3535
29 TNA KV 2/468, 6 August 1941
30 Ibid. 6 August 1941
31 Ibid. 8 August 1941
32 Ibid.
33 Ibid. 6 August 1941
34 Ibid. August 1941
35 Ibid.
36 Ibid.
37 Ibid. 7 August 1941
38 Ibid.
39 Ibid, 29 October 1941; TNA KV 4/283 pp.27–33
40 TNA KV2/1333
41 Humphries, op.cit. pp.216–7
42 TNA KV 2/468, 29 October 1941
43 Ibid, 2 June 1942
44 Masterman, op.cit. p.87
45 Ibid p.113
46 Humphries, op.cit. pp.218–9
47 Thomas & Ketley, op.cit. pp.34–5
48 Farago, op.cit; Breuer, William, *The secret war with Germany: deception, espionage, and dirty tricks, 1939–1945*, Airlife Publishing, 1988; Crowdy, op.cit. p.77
49 TNA KV2/1333
50 TNA KV2/546, 27 November 1945
51 Ibid.

52 TNA KV2/1333, 2 February 1946
53 Masterman, op.cit.

13 Three Cuban saboteurs land in Fishguard

1 TNA KV 2/546
2 Ibid.
3 TNA KV2/3304
4 TNA KV3/76
5 TNA KV 2/546
6 TNA KV 4/283
7 TNA KV3/76
8 Ibid 27 November 1945
9 Ibid.
10 Jonason and Olsson, op.cit. pp.29–30
11 TNA KV2/3304, 26 October 1944
12 TNA KV 4/161, 17 September 1941

14 MUTT and JEFF

1 TNA KV 2/1067; KV3/76
2 TNA KV 2/1067
3 TNA KV2/1067
4 Ibid.
5 Ibid.
6 Wighton and Peis, op.cit. pp.245–6
7 Ibid. p.252
8 TNA KV 2/1067
9 Ibid.
10 Wighton and Peis, op.cit. p.261
11 Ibid, pp.253–260
12 TNA KV 4/211; Andrew, op.cit. p.259
13 TNA KV3/76, 20 July 1941
14 Wighton and Peis, op.cit. pp.265–7
15 TNA KV 2/1067
16 Wighton and Peis, op.cit. pp.268–9
17 Ibid.
18 TNA KV 2/1068
19 TNA KV 2/1067
20 Ibid.
21 Wighton and Peis, op.cit. p.269
22 TNA KV 2/1068, 24 October 1941
23 TNA KV 2/1068
24 TNA KV 2/1067, 9 August 1941
25 Hinsley and Simkins, op.cit.
26 Ibid.
27 Ibid.
28 Ibid.
29 Ibid. 9 November 1941
30 Masterman, op.cit. p.88
31 TNA KV 2/1067
32 Ibid. 21 February 1942
33 TNA KV2/1137, 29 May 1942
34 TNA KV3/413, pp.67, 77
35 Ibid. pp.67, 78
36 Liddell, 13 August 1942
37 Telephone communication with Charlie Peachey, 23 April 2015

15 Plan BROCK

1 Liddell, 9 October 1942
2 Turner, op.cit. pp.77–8
3 Liddell, 11 October 1942
4 TNA KV2/1067
5 Masterman, op.cit. p.126; Talty, Stephan, *Agent Garbo: The Brilliant Eccentric Secret Agent who Tricked Hitler and Saved D-Day*, Houghton Mifflin and Harcourt Publishing, 2012, p.75; Montagu, Ewen, *Beyond Top Secret U*, Corgi, 1979, pp.109–110
6 West, Nigel, *The Guy Liddell Diaries, Vol. II: 1942–1945*, Routledge, 2005, pp.18–19
7 Farago, op.cit. p.281

16 Plan BUNBURY and Operations HAGGIS and PORRIDGE

1 TNA KV 2/1067, 29 September 1942
2 Ibid, 2 October 1942
3 Wighton and Peis, op.cit. pp.269–71
4 Liddell, 9 August 1943
5 Wighton and Peis, op.cit. 272
6 TNA KV 2/1067
7 Ibid.
8 Wighton and Peis, op.cit. p. 272
9 TNA KV 2/1067, 23 February 1943
10 Wighton and Peis, op.cit. p. 273
11 Ibid.
12 TNA KV 2/1068, 18 April 1943
13 TNA KV 2/1067
14 TNA KV4/161
15 TNA KV 2/1067, 5 June 1943
16 TNA KV 2/1067
17 Email communication with Andrew Jose, 8 June 201
18 TNA KV2/4022, 27 June 1943
19 Ibid.
20 TNA KV 2/1067
21 Liddell, 7 August 1943
22 TNA KV4/161
23 TNA KV4/161
24 TNA KV 2/1067
25 Liddell, 22 October 1943
26 Quoted by Tom Seeker in http://www.spyculture.com/disinfowars-15-false-flag-ops-in-ww2/
27 Ibid.
28 Levine, Joshua, *Operation Fortitude: The True Story of the Key Spy Operation of WWII that Saved D-Day*, Collins, 2011
29 TNA KV 2/1067; Berbier, Mary, *D-day Deception: Operation Fortitude and the Normandy Invasion*, Stackpole, 2009
30 Farago, op.cit. p.287
31 Ibid. 28 November 1943
32 Ibid. 14 January 1944
33 Wighton and Peis, op.cit. p.276
34 Ibid. 21 April 1944
35 Ibid, 26 September 1945
36 TNA KV 2/1068
37 Ibid. 8 May 1943
38 Ibid. 15 September 1943
39 Communication with Steven Kippax, 10 October 2015

17 Agent ZIGZAG and Operation THOMAS

1   Hoare, op.cit.218
2   Owen, Frank, *Double Agent: The Eddie Chapman Story*, Lightning Source UK, 2014, p.38
3   Crowdy, op.cit. p.43
4   Ibid. pp.42, 44–5
5   TNA KV2/2461
6   Booth, Nicholas, *Zigzag: The Incredible Wartime Exploits of Double Agent Eddie Chapman*, Arcade Publishing, 2007, pp.94–5
7   TNA KV 2/458; https://www.mi5.gov.uk/files/Global/About%20Us/chapman _ statement_1_1200px.jpg
8   Owen, op.cit. pp.56–7
9   Booth, 2007, p.95
10 https://www.mi5.gov.uk/files/Global/About%20Us/chapman_statement_2_1200px.jpg
11 Owen, op.cit. p.61
12 Macintyre, op.cit. pp.84–5
13 Owen, op.cit. p.58
14 TNA KV 2/458
15 Crowdy, op.cit. pp.105, 190
16 Liddell, 1 October 1942
17 Masterman, op.cit. p.122
18 Macintyre, op.cit. prologue
19 Farago, op.cit. p.282
20 https://www.mi5.gov.uk/files/Global/About%20Us/chap man_manifesto_1200px.jpg
21 Masterman, op.cit. pp.122–3
22 TNA KV 4/284, 21 January 1943
23 Owens, op.cit. p.87
24 Macintyre, op.cit. p.133
25 Owen, op.cit. p.71
26 KV 2/458, 8 February 1943
27 Ibid.
28 Owen, op.cit. p.109
29 TNA KV 2/458, 2 February 1943
30 Macintyre, op.cit. pp.172–3
31 TNA KV2/2461, 2 January 1943
32 Ibid. 26 January 1943
33 Ibid. 27 January 1943
34 Ibid.
35 Owen, op.cit. p.92
36 TNA KV 2/458, 28 January 1943
37 Ibid, 27 January 1943
38 Ibid. 28 January 1943
39 Maskelyne, Jasper, (1949) *Magic: Top Secret*, Stanley Paul, London; Stroud, Rick, (2012), *The Phantom Army of Alamein: How the Camouflage Unit and Operation Bertram Hoodwinked Rommel*, Bloomsbury Publishing
40 O'Connor, Bernard, *Churchill's Most Secret Airfield*, Amberley Publishing, 2013
41 Fraser-Smith, Charles, *The Secret War of Charles Fraser-Smith*, Paternoster Press, 1981
42 Macintyre, op.cit. p.165
43 Farago, op.cit. p.288
44 Macintyre, op.cit.165
45 Ibid. 28 January 1943
46 Ibid. 29 January 1943
47 Ibid. 30 December 1942
48 TNA MF 1/61, 2 Feb 1943
49 Ibid. 29 January 1943
50 Ibid.
51 Ibid. 31 January 1943

52 Owen, op.cit. p.93
53 TNA KV 2/458, 1 February 1943
54 Ibid.
55 Ibid. 9 February 1943
56 Ibid. 13 February 1943
57 Ibid.17 February 1943
58 Ibid, 12 February 1943
59 Ibid. 15 February 1943
60 Ibid, 4 March 1943
61 Owen, op.cit. p.102
62 TNA KV2/3001
63 Masterman, op.cit. pp.131–2
64 Macintyre, op.cit. p.223

18 Agent PRINS, Potential Dutch saboteur

1 TNA KV2/125, 24 December 1942
2 Ibid, 7 January 1943
3 Ibid, 12 February 1943
4 Ibid. 1 March 1943
5 O'Connor, Bernard, *Sabotage in Belgium*, www.lulu.com (2013)
6 TNA KV2/125
7 Ibid.
8 Ibid.
9 Ibid, 22 February 1943
10 Ibid.
11 Ibid. 9 March 1943
12 Ibid.
13 Ibid. 28 May 1943
14 Ibid. 13 July 1943
15 Ibid, 27 June 1943

19 More potential saboteurs

1 TNA KV2/202
2 Ibid.
3 TNA KV2/302
4 Ibid.
5 Ibid.
6 TNA KV2/1942
7 TNA KV2/1936
8 TNA KV2/162
9 TNA KV2/2840
10 Ibid, 29 May 1941
11 TNA KV2/2841
12 Hinsley and Simkins, op.cit. p.344
13 http://www.stephen-stratford.co.uk/treachery.htm#PIERRERICHARDC. NEUKERMANS
14 http://www.stephen-stratford.co.uk/treachery.htm#OSWALD JOHN JOB; Hinsley and Simkins, op.cit. p.344–5
15 http://www.stephen-stratford.co.uk/treachery.htm#JOSEPH JAN VANHOVE; Hinsley and Simkins, op.cit. p.345

20 ZIGZAG's return and Sabotage before D-Day

1 TNA KV2/565, 15 October 1945
2 Masterman, (1979), pp.171–3
3 TNA KV2/2461, 31 May 1948

4 TNA KV2/2461

5 Booth, 2007, p.93

6 Owen, op.cit. p.48

7 TNA KV2/2461

8 TNA KV4/161

9 The London Gazette, No 36452, p.1548, 4 April 1944; Rose, Kenneth, *Elusive Rothschild*, Orion, 2003, p.70

10 TNA KV4/165, 17 February 1944

11 British Fascists Sent to Prison for Sabotage, *The Gazette*, Montreal, Thursday, 2 March 1944

12 TNA KV2/103, 8 August 1945

13 Ibid, 19 December 1944

14 Lancashire Archives WBF 33/55, 31 December 1944

15 http://www.history.com/news/sketches-reveal-nazi-chocolate-bombs

Conclusion

1 TNA KV 2/1296, 17 July 1940

2 TNA KV3/120, 9 January 1946

3 Atkin, Malcolm (2015).*Fighting Nazi Occupation: British Resistance 1939–1945*. Barnsley: Pen and Sword; Sykes, Tom, British Resistance Archive. Coleshill Auxiliary Research Team, 28 March 2016

4 Hardman, Robert 'The British Resistance: The true story of the secret guerrilla army of shopkeepers and farmworkers trained to defy the Nazis in a suicidal last stand', *Daily Mail*. 25 November 2015

5 TNA KV2/173, 14 November 1945

6 TNA KV2/403, 7 December 1945

7 Ibid.

8 Ibid.

9 Ibid. 7 December 1945

10 TNA KV2/173

11 Ibid.

12 TNA KV2/769

13 Ibid, 7 August 1946

14 TNA KV2/769, 8 September 1944

15 Andrew, Christopher, *The Defence of the Realm: The Authorized History of MI5*, Penguin, 2012

Appendix

1 TNA HO 144/21357;

2 Enno, Stephan, *Spies in Ireland*, Four Square Books, 1963, p.15

3 Farago, op.cit. p.41

4 Encarta entry

5 Stephan, op.cit. 42

6 Frago, p.43

7 Beazley, Ben, *Wartime Leicester*, Sutton Publishing, 2004, p.13

8 Stephan, op.cit. p.44

9 Smith, M.L.R: *Fighting for Ireland? The military strategy of the Irish Republican Movement*, Routledge, 1995, p.64

10 Farago, op.cit. p.192–3

11 TNA KV2/173, p.5

12 http://mylesdungan.com/2014/02/11/on-this-day-drivetime-7-february-1940-brendan-behan-jailed-for-ira-activity/

13 English & Welsh executions 1932–1964, Capital Punishment U.K.

14 Stephan, op.cit. p.87

15 TNA KV2/173, p.7

Bibliography

Websites

http://alchetron.com/Vera-von-Schalburg-1351738-W
http://alphahistory.com/northernireland/ira-mainland-campaign/;
http://brian-haughton.com/ancient-mysteries-articles/bella_in_the _wych-elm/
http://fas.org/irp/ops/ci/docs/ci2/2ch1_d.htm
http://forum.12oclockhigh.net/archive/index.php?t-19602.html Michael Glesson
http://forum.keypublishing.com/showthread.php?100530 -Allied-aircraft-sabotage
http://h2g2.com/edited_entry/A87786102
http://homepage.ntlworld.com/andrew.etherington/1940/09/06.htm; https://sites.google.
    comsite/dentonhistory/wartime-1/the-spy-from-the-sky
http://i.dailymail.co.uk/i/pix/2015/09/30/10/2CED362C00000578-3254580-
    image-a-37_1443606381684.jpg
http://i.ebayimg.com/images/g/yA0AAOSwnQhXpIlv/s-l1600.jpg
http://irishecho.com/2014/10/forgotten-hero/
http://mylesdungan.com/2014/02/11/on-this-day-drivetime-7-february-1940-brendan-
    behan-jailed-for-ira-activity
http://rgu-sim.rgu.ac.uk/history/ German%20 Spies.htm;
http://ronangearoid.blogspot.co.uk/ 2010/04/irishmen-in-german-army.html
http://sonsofmalcolm.blogspot.co.uk/2010/11/analysing-iras-armed-campaign-against.
    html
http://sussexhistoryforum.co.uk/index.php?topic=3351.0;   https://levinehistory.
    wordpress.com/2014/06/02/the-unlikely-story-of-the-german-invasion-spies/
http://vipprotection.de/english/Course_Germany/Courses_Contents/Anti-Sabotage/
    anti-sabotage.html
http://www.andrewbradfordauthor.com/apps/blog/categories/show/
    1307864-dorothy-o-grady
http://www.bbc.co.uk/ news/uk-26365085
http://www.bbc.co.uk/essex/content/articles/2009/07/08/gunpowder_mills_feature.
    shtml
http://www.britishpathe.com/video/hammersmith-bridge-bombed
http://www.dailymail.co.uk/femail/article-2065714/Captain-Mainwaring-ramshackle-
    lot-Home-Guard-based-worse.html
http://www.dover-kent.com/2014-project/Rising-Sun-Lydd.html
http://www.dubm.de/lang1/u-boats-and-Eire
http://www.geocaching.com/geochache/GC1TT00_spies-lies-and-cache-containers
http://www.greystonesahs.org/gahs/index.php/ component/content/article/233
http://www.helen-fry.com/books/the-london-cage/

http://www.heraldscotland.com/news/13214353.Declassified_
MI5_files_reveal_why_Operation_Seagull_failed_to_take_flight/
http://www.heraldscotland.com/sport/spl/aberdeen/nazi-
spy-s-love-child-linked-to-reprieve-1.212503
http://www.historiassegundaguerramundial.com/anecdotario/
espias-en-accion-gosta-caroli-y-wulf-schmidt/?lang=en
http://www.historiccoventry.co.uk/articles/s-shaw.php)
http://www.history.com/news/sketches-reveal-nazi-chocolate-bombs
http://www.historyireland.com/20th-century-contemporary-history/
new-evidence-on-iranazi-link/
http://www.independent.co.uk/news/uk/home-news/enemy-within-the-network-of-
britons-who-spied-for-hitler-during-second-world-war-9158455.html
http://www.independent.co.uk/news/uk/home-news/is-this-the-bella-in-the-wych-elm-
unravelling-the-mystery-of-the-skull-found-in-a-tree-trunk-8546497.html, 22 March
2013
http://www.independent.co.uk/news/uk/this-britain/pathetic-fantasist-or-nazi-spy-the-
mysterious-mrs-ogrady-7768836.html
http://www.irishnews.com/lifestyle/2015/02/28/news/irish-pows-role-in-nazi-plan-to-
target-scotland-1169 89/
http://www.irishtimes.com/ blogs/politics/2010/12/16/double-life-in-emergency-ireland)
http://www.irishtimes.com/ newspaper/property/2011/0505/1224296137093.
html?via=mr
http://www.irishtimes.com/blogs/politics/2010/12/16/double-life-in-emergency-ireland
http://www.irishtimes.com/letters/index.html#1224296372163
http://www.josefjakobs.info/2016/06/tales-of-spies-mysterious-and-beautiful.html; TNA
http://www.mirror.co.uk/news/uk-news/chocs-away-556224
http://www.paperlessarchives.com /FreeTitles/GermanSaboteursMI5Files.pdf
http://www.psywar.org/caledonia19400826.php
http://www.radiotimes.com/news/2012-04-16/a-bloody-tale-from-the-tower-of-london
http://www.rottentomatoes.com/m/saboteur
http://www.spartacus-educational.com/ SScumming.htm
http://www.spartacus-educational.com////GCCS.htm
http://www.spyculture.com/disinfowars-15-false-flag-ops-in-ww2
http://www.stedmundsburychronicle.co.uk/electricity/elechistory.htm
http://www.stephen-stratford.co.uk/josef_jakobs.htm
http://www.stephen-stratford.co.uk/treachery.htm#JOSEPH JAN VANHOVE
http://www.stephen-stratford.co.uk/treachery.htm#KARL THEO DRUCKE
http://www.stephen-stratford.co.uk/treachery.htm#OSWALD JOHN JOB
http://www.stephen-stratford.co.uk/treachery.htm#PIERRE RICHARD C.
NEUKERMANS
http://www.veraschalburg.co.uk/html/the_beautiful_spy.html
https://cockburndj.wordpress.com/2014/12/03/inspirations-who-put-bella-in-the-
wych-elm/
https://levinehistory.wordpress.com/2014/06/02/the-unlikely-story-of-the-german-
invasion-spies/
https://vnnforum.com/showthread.php?t=143453
https://vnnforum.com/showthread.php?t=143453 Tom Brennan
https://www.mi5.gov.uk/eric-roberts-undercover-work-in-world-war-ii
https://www.mi5.gov.uk/files/Global/About%20Us/chapman_statement_1_1200px.jpg
https://www.mi5.gov.uk/home/mi5-history/world-war-ii.html
https://www.mi5.gov.uk/world-war-ii
https://www.sis.gov.uk/our-history.html
https://www.sis.gov.uk/our-history/sisor-mi6.html
https://www.theguardian.com/uk/2001/jun/03/theobserver. uknews1
https://www.theguardian.com/world/2016/aug/28/britain-nazi-spies-mi5-second-world-
war-german-executed?CMP=Share_iOSApp_Other)
www.foia.cia.gov, German Intelligence Service, Vol.2

www.foia.cia.gov, German Intelligence Service, Vol.3, 0001.pdf
www.foia.cia.gov, German Intelligence Service, WWII, Vol.3, 0002
www.foia.cia.gov, German Intelligence Service, WWII Vol. 3 0013, 25 June 1946
www.josefjakobs.info

Books and Journals

Abela, A. and Gordon, S. *Shadow Enemies*, Lyons Press, Connecticut, 2002

Adams, Jefferson, *German Intelligence, Historical Dictionaries of Intelligence and Counterintelligence*, Scarecrow Press, 2009

Albertelli, Sébastien, *Histoire de Sabotage*, Perrin, 2016

Andrew, Christopher, (Ed.) *The Security Service 1908–1945*, PRO, 1999

Andrew, Christopher, *The Defence of the Realm: The Authorised History of MI5*, Penguin, 2010

Atkin, Malcolm, *Fighting Nazi Occupation: British Resistance 1939–1945*. Barnsley: Pen and Sword, 2015

Aziz, Philippe, *Le Livre Noir de la Trahison*, Histoires de la Gestapo en France, Paris Editions Ramsa, 1984

Barton, Brian, *Northern Ireland and the Second World War*, Ulster Historical Foundation, 1995

Beazley, Ben, *Wartime Leicester*, Sutton Publishing, 2004

Behan, Brendan, *The Borstal Boy*, Hutchinson, 1958

Berbier, Mary, *D-day Deception: Operation Fortitude and the Normandy Invasion*, Stackpole, 2009

Bird, Andrew, *A Separate Little War*, Grub Street, 2003

Booth, Nicholas, *Zigzag: The Incredible Wartime Exploits of Double Agent Eddie Chapman*, Arcade Publishing, 2007

Booth, Nicholas, *Lucifer Rising*, The History Press, 2016

Bowyer Bell, J. *The Secret Army – The IRA*, Transaction Publishers, New Jersey, 1997, 2008

Bradford, Andrew, *Dotty Dorothy: The Perfect Spy*, private publication, 2012

Breuer, William, *The secret war with Germany: deception, espionage, and dirty tricks, 1939–1945*, Airlife Publishing, 1988

Bryce, Evans, 'Fear and Loathing in Liverpool: The IRA's 1939 Bombing Campaign on Merseyside', *Transactions of the Lancashire and Cheshire Historical Society*, Vol. 162, 2013

Bryden, John, *Fighting to Lose: How the German Secret Intelligence Helped the Allies Win the Second World War*, Dundurn Press, 2014

Calder, Angus, *People's War Britain 1939–1945*, Jonathan Cape, 1969

Chapman, Eddie & Owen, Frank *The Eddie Chapman Story*, Messner, New York, 1953

Chapman, Eddie & Owen, Frank, *Free Agent: The Further Adventures of Eddie Chapman*, London, 1955

Chapman, Eddie & Owen, Frank *The Real Eddie Chapman Story*, London, 1966

Cobain, Ian, *Cruel Britannia*, Portobello Books, 2012

Cobain, Ian, *The History Thieves*, Portobello Books, 2016

Coogan, Tim, *The IRA*, Pall Mall, 1970; Harper Collins, 2000; Palgrave, 2002

Crowdy, Terry, *Deceiving Hitler: Double Cross and Deception in World War II*, Osprey Publishing, 2013

Davies, John, *A History of Wales*, Penguin, 1994

Dobbs, Michael, *Saboteurs: The Nazi Raid on America*. Knopf. 2004

Dwyer, T. Ryle, *Strained Relations: Ireland at Peace and the USA at War, 1941–1945*, Gill and Macmillan, 1988

Enno, Stephan, *Spies in Ireland*, Four Square Books, 1963

Ernst Weber-Drohl's U-Boat landing in Sligo Bay – Summary,' *Heritage Connects Communities* Peace III project 50785, July 2014

Farago, Ladislas, *The Game of Foxes*, Hodder and Stoughton, 1972

Footitt, Hilary and Kelly, Michael, (Eds.) (2012), Languages and the Military: Alliances, Occupation and Peace Building, Palgrave Macmillan

Gardiner, Juliet, *Wartime Britain 1939–1945*, Headline, 2004

Hastedt, G. *Spies, Wiretaps and Secret Operations: An Encyclopaedia of American Espionage*, Vol. 1, ABC-CLIO.LLC, 2011

Hennessy, Thomas and Thomas, Claire, *Spooks: The Unofficial History of MI5 From Agent ZIGZAG to the D-Day Deception 1939–45*, Amberley, 2010

Hinsley, F.H. & Simkins, C.A.G., *British Intelligence in the Second World War: Security and counter-intelligence*, Vol. 4, Cambridge University Press, 1990

Hoare, Oliver, (2000), *Camp 020: MI5 and the Nazi Spies*, Public Record Office

Hull, Mark, The Irish Interlude: German Intelligence in Ireland, 1939–43, *The Journal of Military History*, Vol.66, No. 3, 2002

Hull, Mark M. *Irish Secrets. German Espionage in Wartime Ireland 1939–1945*, Irish Academic Press, Dublin, 2003

Hinsley and Simkins, *British Intelligence in the Second World War*, Vol. 4, 1990

Humphries, John, *Spying for Hitler*, University of Wales Press, 2012

Johnson, David Alan, *Germany's Spies and Saboteurs*, MBI Publishing, 1998

Jonason. Tommy and Olsson, Simon 'Agent TATE: The Wartime Story of Harry Williamson', Amberley Publishing, 2011, 2012

Levine, Joshua, *Operation Fortitude: The Story of the Spy Operation that Saved D-Day*. HarperCollins, 2011

MacDonnell, Francis, *Insidious Foes: The Axis Fifth Column and the American Home Front*, Oxford University Press, 1995

Macintyre, Ben. *Agent Zigzag*, Bloomsbury, 2007

Mallmann Showell, J. P. *U-boats at War – Landings on Hostile Shores*, Ian Allan Publishing Ltd., Shepperton: 2000

Maskelyne, Jasper, (1949) *Magic: Top Secret*, Stanley Paul, London

Masterman, J. *The Double-Cross System*, Lyons Press, 2000

Masterman, J.C. *The Double-Cross System: The Incredible True Story of How Nazi Spies Were Turned into Double Agents*, Vintage, 2013

McMahon, Paul, *British Spies and Irish Rebels: British Intelligence and Ireland, 1916–45*, Boydell Press, 2008

Miller, Joan. *One Girl's War: Personal Exploits in MI5's Most Secret Station*, Brandon/Mount Eagle Publications Ltd. 1986

Moffat, John, *I Sank the Tirpitz*, Corgi, 2010

Montagu, Ewen, *Beyond Top Secret U*, Corgi, 1979

Morrison, Kathryn, *A Maudlin and Monstrous Pile: The Mansion at Bletchley Park*, Buckinghamshire, English Heritage, 2012

O'Connor, Bernard, *Churchill's Most Secret Airfield*, Amberley Publishing, 2013

O'Connor, Bernard, *Sabotage in Belgium*, www.lulu.com, 2013

O'Connor, Ulick, *Brendan Behan*, Harper Collins, 1993

O'Donoghue, Dave, *The Devil's Deal: The IRA, Nazi Germany and the Double Life of Jim O'Donovan*, New Island Books, 2010

Ó Duibhginn, Seosamh, *Ag Scaoileadh Sceoil*, Dublin, 1962

O'Haplin, Eunan, *Spying on Ireland: British Intelligence and Irish Neutrality During the Second World War*, Oxford University Press, 2010

O'Reilly, Terence, *Hitler's Irishmen*, Mercier Press, Cork, 2008

Owen, Frank, *Double Agent: The Eddie Chapman Story*, Lightning Source UK, 2014

Rose, Kenneth, *Elusive Rothschild*, Orion, 2003

Rose, Kenneth, 'Rothschild (Nathaniel Mayer) Victor, third Baron Rothschild (1910 – 1990)', Oxford Dictionary of National Biography, Oxford University Press, 2004

Scotland, Alexander, *The London Cage*, Evans Brothers, 1957

Searle, Adrian, *The Spy Beside the Sea; The Extraordinary Wartime Story of Dorothy O'Grady*, History Press, 2012

Siedentopf, Monika, *Unternehmen Seelöwe Widerstand im Deutschen Geheimdienst*, DTV Premium, 2014

Smith M.L.R: *Fighting for Ireland? The military strategy of the Irish Republican Movement*, Routledge, 1995

Smithies, Edward, *Aces, Erks and Backroom Boys*, Cassell Military Paperbacks, 2002

Stephan, Enno, *Spies in Ireland*, Four Square Books, 1963

Stephens, David, *Action Stations: Military Airfields of Scotland*

Stroud, Rick, (2012), *The Phantom Army of Alamein: How the Camouflage Unit and Operation Bertram Hoodwinked Rommel*, Bloomsbury Publishing

Sykes, Tom, *British Resistance Archive*. Coleshill Auxiliary Research Team, 28 March 2016

Talty, Stephan, *Agent Garbo: The Brilliant Eccentric Secret Agent who Tricked Hitler and Saved D-Day*, Houghton Mifflin and Harcourt Publishing, 2012

Thomas, Geoffrey & Ketley, Barry, *Luftwaffe KG 200: The German Air Force's Most Secret Unit of World War II*

Thomas, Robert, *The Explosions at the Royal Gunpowder Mills*, 2013

Turner, Des, *SOE's Secret Weapon Centre: Station 12*, The History Press, 2011

Walton, Calder, *Empire of Secrets: British Intelligence, the Cold War, and the Twilight of the Empire*, Overlook Press, 2013

West, Nigel, *MI5 – the True Story of the Most Secret Counterespionage Organisation in the World*, Briarcliff Manor, New York, 1981

West, Nigel, *MI5: British Security Service Operations 1909–1945*, Stein & Day, New York, 1982

West, Nigel, and Tsarev, Oleg, *Crown Jewels: The British Secrets at the Heart of the KGB Archives*, Harper Collins, 1998

West, Nigel, *The Guy Liddell Diaries, 1939–42*, Vol. 1, Routledge, 2005

West, Nigel, *The Guy Liddell Diaries, 1942–45*, Vol. 2, Routledge, 2009

Wighton, Charles, *They spied on England: Based on the German secret service war diary of General von Lahousen*, Odham's Press, 1958

Wighton, Charles and Peis, Günther, *Hitler's Spies and Saboteurs*, Henry Holt, New York, 1958

Newspapers

Aberdeen Evening Express, 20 February 1943,

Daily Mail. 25 November 2015

Daily Sketch, 29 March 1939

Etoile du Soir, 23 April 1948

The *Indian Express*, Woman Sentenced to Death For Treachery, December 18, 1940

The Irish Times, 14 March 1941

The Daily Telegraph, 19 January 1940, 25 August 2010

Etoile du Soir, 23 April 194

Evening Standard 12 February 1942

The Gazette, Montreal, British Fascists Sent to Prison for Sabotage, Thursday, 2 March 1944

Herald Scotland, Ted Ramsay, 'The Real Hess had no wounds, 5 September 1997

The Independent, Eddi Chapman's Obituary, 6 January 1998

The Independent, Pathetic fantasist or Nazi spy? The mysterious Mrs O'Grady, 20 May 2012

The Independent, Wartime smoke and mirrors. 21 October 2012

Liverpool Echo, 17 January 1939, 20 January 1939, 7 February 1939, 3 May 1939, 30 May 1939, 26, 27, 29 August 1939, 19 September 1939

The London Gazette, No 36452, p.1548, 4 April 1944

The New York Times, 3 February 1940

Portsmouth Evening News, Death Sentence Quashed, 11 February 1941

Press and Journal, 22 February 1943

Saskatoon Star Phoenix, Spy Story 'Huge Joke;' Death Sentence Thrilling, 6 March 1950

The Scotsman, 17 November 2005

The Sunday Express 30 July 1939

Sunday Express, Woman says she had herself sentenced to death as a 'huge joke, [undated article c.1950

The Sun, 5 September 2005
The Telegraph, 'Alex Salmond, the SNP and 'fascist Scotland'; 17 January 2014
The Times, 18 January 1939
The Times, 14 February 1939
The Times, Brooman-White's obituary, 27 January 1965
The Times, 2 October 1999

National Archives, Kew

ADM 1/13124 Admiralty and Ministry of Defence, Nay Dpt correspondence
ADM 1/15294 Admiralty and Ministry of Defence, Nay Dpt correspondence
ADM 116/5293 Admiralty and Ministry of Defence, Nay Dpt correspondence
AIR 20/248 R.A.F. Stations: anti-sabotage measures and alarm systems
CAB 127/198 Lord Cherwell's correspondence with Lord Rothschild on sabotage devices
CRIM 1/1243 Defendents MEIER, WALDBERG, VAN DEN KIEEBOOM, PONS, Treachery
FO 371/24051/13540 Anti-sabotage precautions
FO 371/29250 Anti-sabotage measures
FO 371/32702-6 Anti-sabotage measures and security of shipping
HO 45/23803 Joseph LENIHAN
HO 144/21357 Disturbances known or believed to have been caused by IRA
HO 144/21471-2 Criminal cases: Defendents MEIER, WALDBERG, VAN DEN KIEEBOOM, PONS
HO 45/25408 TREASON: O'GRADY, Dorothy Pamela, alias SQUIRES, Dorothy Pamela: convicted at Winchester ['This record is missing and is unavailable']
HS 7/27 SOE Research and Development section 1938–1945
HS 7/28 Descriptive Catalogue of Special Devices and Supplies
HS 7/53 SOE Group B training syllabus: sabotage handbook (illustrated) part I
HS 8/854 The Use of Pigeons
HS 10/1/10 Explosives Camouflage
HW 14 Government Code and Cypher School Directorate
KV 2/14-16 Vera ERIKSEN 30 September 1940–4 September 1948
KV 2/20 Sigwald LUND 27 October 1940–26 June 1945
KV 2/21-22 Gunnar EDVARDSEN 27 October 1940–31 December 1948
KV 2/23 Otto JOOST 18 January 1941–6 November 1947
KV 2/27 Josef JAKOBS
KV 2/32 Karel RICHTER
KV 2/103 Herbert WICHMANN
KV 2/114 Engelbertus FUKKEN
KV 2/161 Peter SCHAGEN
KV 2/162-3 George KRONBERGER
KV 2/170-171 Friedrich PRAETORIUS
KV 2/173 ERWIN LAHOUSEN
KV 2/301-3 Guy Vissault
KV 2/403 Otto SKORZENY
KV 2/444 – 453 SNOW case 10 September 1936–28 May 1946
KV 2/458 Edward CHAPMAN, codenamed ZIGZAG 22 January 1943 – 4 March 1943
KV 2/468 GW case (Gwilym Williams) 11 October 1939 – 5 August 1942
KV 2/521 Friedrich OBLADEN
KV 2/546 Cornelius EVERTSEN (MV " Josephine"):
KV 2/558 Armand DE CORTE
KV 2/565 Harley MILLER, aka Harry Schulz
KV 2/712 Luis CALVO 24 May 1941 – 7 March 1942
KV 2/713 Luis CALVO 9 March 1942 – 10 April 1943
KV 2/714 Luis CALVO 23 July 1943 – 14 February 1946
KV 2/769 Dr K HALLER, alias VOGEL
KV 2/1067 Helge John Neal MOE, alias 'MUTT', 7 April 1941 – 20 November 1947

KV 2/1068 Tor GLAD, alias 'JEFF', 7 April 1941 – 20 November 1947
KV 2/1137 COBWEB case
KV 2/1152 Pierre MORAL
KV 2/1296 Otto DIETER GAERTNER 1 January 1940 – 31 December 1948
KV 2/1319-1322 Herman GOERTZ
KV 2/1333 Julius BOECKEL
KV 2/1451 Herbert TRIBUTH 1 January 1940 – 31 December 1948
KV 2/1950, Thomas Strogan's testimony
KV 2/3001 Eleuterio SANCHEZ RUBIO
KV 2/3119-3120 Joseph ANDREWS
KV 2/3304 Gottfried TREUTLEIN
KV 2/3410 Olivier MORDRELLEe
KV 2/3535–3541 Angel ALCAZAR de VALSCO
KV 2/3799 Edgar and Sophia BRAY
KV 2/3800 Marita PERIGOE
KV 2/4021–3 Ronald CREASEY
KV 3/76 German espionage from 1939
KV 3/118, Mil Amt D Sabotage and Subversion
KV 3/120 IRA and Germany
KV 3/413 German saboteurs landed in the USA from U-boats in 1942: report of operation 18/01/1943 – 04/02/1946
KV 4/1– 3 History of the Security Service
KV 4/23 report on B1c in connection with the threat of sabotage. A booklet is contained in this file.
KV 4/60 Organisation and functions of B1c in connection with counter-sabotage
KV 4/161 Organisation and functions of B Division.
KV 4/165 Functions of B5 to March 1946
KV 4/170 Guy Liddell's correspondence about counter-espionage
KV 4/191 Liddell diaries
KV 4/283–5 Camouflage for sabotage equipment used by German Sabotage Services
KV 6/79 Jupp HOVEN
KV 6/118 Hans KOHOUT
KV 6/119 Hilda LEACH
MEPO 2/3676 Police cooperation in anti-sabotage at Avon Wharf, Bow
MF 1/61 Plan of de Haviland Aircraft Factory
MT 9/32/3212 Ministry of Transport
WO 71/149 BRADY, CALLEY, STROGEN, JOHNSTON, LEE
WO 71/1132 Frank STRINGER
WO 204/12362 Security of Material: Sabotage
WO 219/1554–5 Counter sabotage measures

Lancashire Archives

WBF 33/1–65 Fylde Water Board: correspondence on ARP and anti-sabotage precautions for reservoirs

Irish Military Archives

G2/X/1263 (KENNY)
G2/X/0305 September 1945;
G2/3824 (O'Reilly)
G2/4174 Hayes Report
G2/4949 (Codd)
MS 21,155, O'Donovan, James L. 'Demolition of bridges without explosives – instructions'

National Archives of Ireland

S/12013, Criminal charge and disposition sheet

National Library of Ireland, Manuscripts Department

MS 21,155, Folder 5'Demolition of bridges without explosives – instructions',
James L. O'Donovan, Papers related to the IRA, 1930s and 40s,
Papers related to the IRA, 1930s and 40s, Folder 5,

Documentaries

Triple Cross, Anglo-French production, 1967
BBC Timewatch, *The Spies Who Fooled Hitler: MI5 at War*, 2 October 1999
Shamrock and Swastika, Akajava Films, 2001
Agent Zigzag: The Eddie Chapman Story, Timewatch, 2012

Index

Allnoch 97
Andrews, Joseph 69, 79, 314
Ansell, Elsie 34, 292
Archer, Liam 67, 237
Arnold, Squadron Leader 141, 145
Ashton-Gwatkin, Frank 30
Aston House 40, 91

Barnes, Peter 34, 36, 292-3
Barnes, Tom 15
Barrington-Ward, Robert 238
Barry, Tom 15-16
Barton, Karl 'Karl Barton', 'Herbert
    Vosch', Herman Vosch', Hermann
    Vojch, 'Herbert Vosh', 'Anton' 227-9,
    236, 272-3, 290
Barton Mills 197
Basingstoke electricity generating station
    203, 207, 213
BASKET, see Lenihan
Bauerle, Clara 114
Beaulieu, New Forest 40
Behan, Brendan 15, 292
BISCUIT, see McCarthy, Sam
Björnson. Jorgen 100
Bletchley Park 18, 20, 228
Boeckel, Major Julius, aliases Karl
    Bruhns, Beyer and Ernesto Werner 60,
    111, 113, 115, 118, 129, 168, 171
Bonneau 261-2, 266
Bossart 262

Brady, Frank, alias 'Metzger', 'Thomas
    Dunphy' 93-4, 95
Brasser, Major 53
Brickendonbury Manor 8, 20-21, 37, 41,
    91, 159, 180, 254, 281
BROCK, Operation 198-200
Broomam-White, Richard 153-4, 157-9,
    161-2, 166
BRUTUS, see Czerniawski
Buckingham Palace 15, 78, 112, 288
BUNBURY, Operation 202-3, 217-9, 224
Burgess, Guy 21,41
Burt, Len 198, 200-1, 218, 231, 276
Bury St Edmunds electricity generating
    station 213-6, 219

Cadogan, Sir Alexander 40
Calvo, Otto 153-6, 158-60, 162-3,
    167-9, 170, 313
Camp 020, Latchmere House 26, 108,
    110-11, 114-5, 117-8, 122, 171-2,
    175, 187, 195, 232-3, 246, 253, 216,
    269, 282
Camp 020R, Huntercombe 175
Canaris, Admiral Wilhelm 29-31, 64, 68,
    73, 79-80, 83-4, 98, 101, 104-6, 121,
    131, 221, 280, 284-6
Campbell, Robert 69-70
Caroli, Gösta 110-13, 116
Chamberlain, Neville 35, 58

Chapman, Edward ('FRITZCHEN', ZIGZAG) 53, 226-242, 245-50, 271-4, 290, 313
Cholmondley, Lt. 236-8
Christiansen, Arthur 238
Churchill, Winston 40-42, 58, 155-6, 158, 239, 250, 275, 277, 281
Clay, Theresa 41
Clissman, Helmut (Harvey Goff) 30, 32-3, 64, 80, 83-5, 87, 127
Clauwers, Rene 263
COBWEB, see Riis
Codd, John, 'Jean Louis' 64, 93, 286, 314
Collins, Michael 10
Cottenham, Lord (Mark Peyps) 52-3
Coventry bomb attacks 15, 34, 36, 170, 279, 288-90, 292,
Cray reservoir 149-50
Creasey, Ronald 42, 213-4, 314
Curry, John 22, 35
Cushing 93, 95
Czerniawski, Roman BRUTUS 271

Dale, Raymond 275
Dalton, Hugh 40
Dasch, George 91, 197
Daufeldt, Christian 'Dresscher' 125-6
Dearden, Harold 26
De Bakker/Backe/Backer 261
De Bray/Debray, Louis 252, 262
De Deeker, Francoise see Drükke
Deegan, Joe 11,15
De Gaulle, General Charles 40, 148
De Graaf, Johannes 251-60, 263
De Havilland Aircraft Factory 41, 230, 234-41,243, 245, 314
Del Pozo, Miguel Piernavieja (POGO) 139-141, 144-5, 147-8, 150, 152, 155, 158, 167-8
De Smidt, Andre, 'Smal, Antoine' 262
De Valera, Eamon 36, 79, 83, 85, 87, 289, 292
De Valasco, Angel Alcazar 158
De Ridder, Mrs 56, 58
Dierks, Hans see Mueller
Dierks. Major Hilmar 65, 71, 97, 119
Dietergartner/Dieter Gaertner, Otto 74-80, 314
Donaldson, Arthur 157
Donnelly, Simon 36, 293
DOVE/PIGEON (TAUBE), Operation 82-5, 114
DRAGONFLY, see Hans George
Drew, John 159, 161
Drükke/Drücke/Druegge, Karl 'Francoise de Deeker/Dekker' 118, 120-22

Edvardsen, Gunnar 122-5, 313
Eibner 98
Eriksen/Eriksson, 'Vera Schalburg' 112, 118-9, 121-2, 124, 137, 313
Evertsen, Cornelius 172-4, 313

Faramus, Anthony 226
Fish, Donald 41
Fish, Laurence 276
Ford, Mr 147
Fort William Hydro-electric power station 8, 93
Franz, Eduard 67
Fraser-Grant, Donald 156
Fraserburgh 204-5, 220, 266
Friesack Camp 64, 87, 83, 95, 97
FRITZCHEN, see Chapman
Fromme, Franz 30
Fukken, Engelbertus 129, 313

GANDER see Graf
Gartenfeld-Staffel 65, 86, 115, 170-1
George, Hans DRAGONFLY 269-70
Gibb, Andrew 157
GIRAFFE see Goose
Glad, Tor 'Olav Klausen' (JEFF/TEGE/TG) 117, 159, 163, 176, 178-80, 184, 314
Godfrey, Captain 21
Goering/Göring, Hermann 65, 155, 230
Goertz/Görtz, Herman 'Kruse, Heinz' 70, 314
Goesta 98
Goose/Gross, Kurt 'GIRAFFE' 104, 126
Graf, George 'GANDER' 104
Graff, Dr 119, 121-2
Grand, Lawrence 18-9
Green, Chief Inspector 196
GREEN (GRUN), Operation 73, 77
Grothe, Oberleutnant 181
Gussner/Guzner, Antoni 'Gold', 'Gerhard' 266-7
GUY FAWKES, Operation 187-91

HAGGIS, Operation 207
Haller, Kurt (VOGE) 32-33, 64, 73, 84. 93-5, 127, 197, 285-6, 313
Halifax, Lord 12
Hammersmith Bridge 272-3, 289, 291
Hansen, Nicolay 266
Harker, Oswald 'Jasper' 35
Harmer, Christopher 184-5, 187, 191-2, 194-5, 202, 204-8, 213-4, 220-3, 225
Hayes, Stephen 66, 68, 70-1, 314
Hecheverria, Pedro 172, 174-5
Held, Michael 69
Hempel, Eduard 64-5, 80, 158

Hess, Rudolf 127, 155-6, 167
Hewitt, Joseph 34, 292
Hewitt, Mary 34, 292
Heydrich, Reinhard 30, 47
Hill, George 21
Himmler, Heinrich 30, 47, 126, 285
Hinchley-Cooke, William 48, 111, 118-9
Holland, Joe 40
Hollevoet, Georges 'Gustave Holvoet', Georges Hullin' 262
Hoover, J Edgar 91, 250
Hoven, Jupp 'Rheinhorst' 16, 30, 32-3, 63-4, 68, 82-3, 93, 97, 127, 197, 314

INNKEEPER (GASTWIRT/GASTWICH), Operation 93
Irish Republican Army (IRA) 7-8, 10-16, 19, 24, 26, 28-39, 47, 49. 54-5, 57, 62-66, 68-72, 74-5, 78-85, 87, 94-7,127, 135-7, 157, 197, 225, 272-3, 275, 278-82, 285-6, 288-93
Irish Brigade 64, 83

Janowski, Werner 93, 127
Jebb, Gladwyn 31
JEFF, see Glad
Job, Oswald 269
Johnson, Tom 158
Joost, Otto 122-5, 313
Joyce, William 'Lord Haw-Haw' 29

KATHLEEN, Operation 68-9
Kelly, Thomas 12-4
Kell, Vernon 17, 29, 35
Koller, see Colepaugh
Knowles, Dorie 56-7
Koblischke 181
Konig, Dr 94
Krafft, Mrs M. 56
Kronberger, George 126, 266-7, 313
KROPF 171
Kruse, Heinz, see Görtz
Kuntsel/Kunze 254

La Bretonnière-la-Claye 227
Lahousen, Erwin von 30, 32, 63-5, 73, 83, 100-1, 103-5, 118,121-2, 127, 131, 184-6, 197, 203-4, 213, 221, 280, 283-5, 313
Langenbach 'Schneider' 126
Langley, Lt. Col. John 19-20
Lassudry, Henri 'Joseph Waldberg' 106-7, 109-10, 116, 313
LEHAR see Harley Miller/Schulz
Lejeune, Robert 261-6
LENA, Operation 98, 106, 111-3, 128-9, 171

Lenihan, 'Leniham', Joseph (BASKET) 85, 313
Lepage, see Stringer
Lewis, Saunders 47, 142-3
Liddell, Cecil 80
Liddell, Guy 16, 27, 29, 33, 36-7, 41, 46, 53, 56, 60, 67, 69-72, 80, 97, 109-12, 133, 135-6, 139, 192, 197-200, 217-8, 314
Linge, Martin 185
Lips 97
LOBSTER (HUMMER), Operation 74, 80, 83
Louis, Jean see Codd
Lund, Sigwald 122-5, 313

MAINAU, Operation 68
Marriott, John 139, 162, 168, 186-7, 195, 219, 224
Marten/Maerten 266
Martin, Superintendent 192-3
Marwede, Freidrich 'Pfalzgraf', 'Neumeister', Meserschmidt 32-3, 63
Maskelyne, Jasper 239-40
Mason-MacFarlane, Lt.Col. 30
Masterman, John 27-8, 59, 104, 112, 139, 153, 157-9, 161-2, 168, 169, 171, 174, 187, 193, 198, 200, 206, 226, 232-3, 239, 246, 249, 272, 282
Maude, John 46
McCarthy, Sam (BISCUIT) 59, 61
McDermott, Joseph 79
McGarrity, Joseph 10, 82
Meek, Colin 18, 19
Meier, Karl 106-7, 109-10, 116, 313
Menzies, 133-5Sir Stewart 20, 27, 40
Messerschmidt see Marwede
Meyer, Werner 181-2
MI5 16-17, 20-22, 24-37, 41-2, 45-6, 49-52, 55-57, 59, 61, 65-6, 72, 78-80, 82-83, 86,, 95, 97, 99, 102, 108-115, 117, 119, 121-2, 126, 128-130, 133-5, 137, 139-42, 145, 147, 149-50, 152-3, 155, 157, 159, 168-9, 171, 173-5, 179-80, 182, 184-5, 187, 191, 193-4, 196, 198-9, 202-5, 214, 220-23, 225, 228, 234-5, 237, 245-6, 248, 250, 252-4, 260, 262-3, 268-74, 276-7, 279-82, 284, 286
MI6 17, 19-20, 24,27-8, 68-9, 137, 139, 176, 180, 198, 259, 268, 281
Miller, Harley see Harley Schulz LEHAR
Miller, Henry see Morel
Miller, Joan 29
Mills, Cyril 182
Milmo, Helenus 79-80, 260, 263
Mitchell, Paddy see Preetz

Moe, Helge 'Jack Berg' (MUTT/JACK) 117, 176-80, 182, 184, 122, 219, 222-5, 233-5, 266, 313
Mooy, C.H. 78
Mordrelle, Olivier 83, 314
Moreels, Lucien 251-2, 259
Mosley, Oswald 29
Mueller, Herman 'Hans Dierks' 98, 100, 120-2, 179-80, 196, 201, 205
Murphy, Jim 13
Murphy, William 64, 93
MUTT, see Moe

Nelson, Frank 40
Neukermanns, Pierre, 269-70
Nissen, Christian, 'Hein Mucck' 74, 80-1, 84

Obed, Henry 74, 76-80
Obladen, Friedrich 104, 132, 313
O'Grady. Dorothy 133-8
O'Hara, Brigid 34, 292
OMNIBUS, Plan 186-7, 193
Opdebeek/Opdebeeck 'Damaert' 262
OSPREY (FISCHADLER), Operation 85, 87
Owens, Arthur (SNOW) 47-57, 59-61, 72, 74, 80, 90-1, 102, 104-5, 108, 110, 113-4, 118, 128, 139, 157, 168, 234
Oxwich Bay 50, 52-5, 61, 167

Palsson, Jens (SPIDER) 194-6
Park, Rosalind 66
PASTORIUS, Operation 92-3
Paulton, Ted 184, 186, 204-5, 207, 220
Pazos-Dias/Diaz, Nicholas 172, 174-5
Perfect, Major Peter 118, 122, 176, 204
Perigoe, Marita 41, 314
Peters, Frederic 21
Petersen, Carl 30, 125
Petrie, David 35, 182, 209, 268, 276
Pfaus, Oscar 82
Philby, Kim 21
Pieckenbrock, Colonel Hans 73, 284
Pierce (RAINBOW) 65-6
PIGEON, Operation see DOVE
Pinckard, Robin 275
Pinto, Colonel 24
POGO, see Del Pozo
Pons 107-9, 313
PORRIDGE, Operation 204, 214
Praetorius, Friedrich 'Walter Thomas' 65, 84, 97-100, 106, 115-6, 122, 132, 231, 313
Preetz, Willy 'Paddy Mitchell' 71
PYRAMID, Plan 118, 185, 187, 193

Quentzgut 63, 76, 92-4, 286

RAINBOW, see Pierce
Rantzau, see Ritter
Reed, Ronnie 195-6, 233-7, 241, 243-50
Reiger, Bruno 81, 85
Rheam, George 159, 254
Rheinhorst, see Hove
Ribbentrop, Joseph, von 16, 83, 87, 155, 280
Richards, James 34, 36, 292-3
Richter, Karel 115-7, 129, 313
Riis, Ib (COBWEB) 194, 196, 314
Ritter, Nikolaus ('Dr Rantzau') 48-9, 71, 98, 106, 112, 129, 132, 170, 174
Roberts, Eric 41-2
Robertson, Thomas Argyll 27, 61, 129, 154, 195, 224, 240, 245
Rowehl, Theodor 65, 170
Rose 60
Roosevelt, Franklin D 92
Rothschild, Victor 41-2, 45-6, 75, 88, 91-2, 122, 151-2, 154, 158-9, 161-2, 168-9, 184, 192, 194, 196-9, 209, 211, 213, 217-8, 223, 234, 236, 246-7, 254, 260-1, 263, 272, 275-7, 313
Royal Gunpowder Mills, Waltham Abbey 34, 292
Royal Victoria Patriotic School 24-5, 182, 268
Rudolfs, Dr 60
Ruis Robles, Silvio 172
Russell, Seán 'Jim Russel' 10-12, 14, 16, 65, 71, 82-4, 280, 286, 288
Ryan, Frank 83-5, 280

Scotland, Alexander 24
Scottish Nationalist Party (SNP) 24, 62, 84, 156-7, 286
Schagen, Peter 84, 313
Schalburg, see Eriksen, VeraScharf, Hans
Scharf, Hans
Schellenburg, Water 221
Schmidt, Franz 273
Schmidt, Hans/Wulf TATE, 'Henry Williamson' 60, 100-5, 110-2, 115-7, 126, 171
Schmitt, Jean 262
Schneider see Langenbach
Schroeder, Major 76
Schulz, Harley 'Harley Miller', LEHAR 116, 313
Schutz/Schuetz, Gunther 65-6, 84
SEAEAGLE (SEEADLER), Operation 85
SEAGULL (MOWE), Operation 80, 93
SEALION (SEELÖWE), Operation 73, 81, 101, 128, 131, 134, 184

Segundo 140, 144, 148, 153
Senter, John 240
Silver, Arnold 79
Simon, Walter 'Simonsen', 'Andersen' 71
Sinclair, Hugh 'Quex' 17-19, 27
Skorzeny, Otto 'Dr Wolff' 95, 221,
    282-3, 313
Smal, Antoine see de Smidt
Smith-Cumming, Mansfield 17
SNOW, see Owens
SOE (Special Operations Executive) 6,
    25, 29, 37, 40, 45, 65, 133, 193, 197,
    199, 200, 204-6, 214, 218, 262, 281
Stanford, Col. 196, 231, 237-8
Stephens, Robert 'Tin Eye' 26, 108-9,
    112, 124-5, 130, 176, 179, 233, 246,
    282
Stopford, Major 195-6
Stringer, Frank 'Willi Lepage' 64, 95-6,
    314
Strogan, Thomas 95, 314
Stuart, Henry 83
Sullivan, James 159, 168-9

TATE, see Wulf Schmid
THOMAS, Operation 237
Thomas, Walter see Praetorius
TINDALL, Operation 219
Tornow, Kapt. 60, 171
Treutlein, Gottfried 173, 175, 314
Tributh, Herbert 74, 76-80, 314
Twenty (XX) Committee 27-8

Unland, Werner 71, 84, 97

Valentine, Lewis 47, 142
Van den Kieeboom 106, 116, 133, 313
Van Loon 84
Van Vleussem 87

Veesenmayer, Edmund 32, 65, 74, 79,
    82-5, 280
Vissault de Coetlogon, Guy 68, 83, 127,
    313
Vogel see Haller
Vogt/Voigt, Otto 117
Von Gröning/Groening/Grunen, Stefan
    227-9, 231, 234
Von Juechem, Hartmann 97
Von Meyenburg 76
Vosch, Herbert see Barton

Waldberg, Joseph see Lassudry
Walti, Werner 118-122, 124
Wealdstone 187-9, 191-4
Weber-Drohl, Ernst 64, 66
Walsh, Andrew 'Vickers' 64, 94-5, 171
Welsh Nationalist Party 71, 103, 142-6,
    152, 154-5, 164-7, 170, 293
WHALE (WALFISCH), Operations I and
    II, 73, 84-5
WHISKY 275-6
White, Dick 20, 24
Wichmann, Herbert 30, 65, 71, 98-9,
    104, 113, 115, 131-2, 275, 313
Williams, D.J. 47
Williams, Gwilym 'GW' 139-43, 145-50,
    152-9, 161-2, 167-75, 313
Williamson, Harry (TATE) see Caroli
Witzke, Lohar 53, 79, 173, 175
Wojch, see Barton
Wood, Leslie 198
'WW' 50-2

XX (Double Cross) see Twenty
    Committee

ZIGZAG, see Chapman